VALUES
IN
EDUCATION
AND
SOCIETY

VALUES
IN
EDUCATION
AND
SOCIETY

Norman T. Feather

THE FREE PRESS
A Division of Macmillan Publishing Co., Inc.
NEW YORK

Collier Macmillan Publishers
LONDON

The Free Press
A Division of Macmillan Publishing Co., Inc.
866 Third Avenue, New York, N.Y. 10022

Collier Macmillan Canada, Ltd.

Library of Congress Catalog Card Number: 75–2812

Printed in the United States of America

Printing number

1 2 3 4 5 6 7 8 9 10

Library of Congress Cataloging in Publication Data
Feather, Norman T
    Values in education and society.

    Bibliography: p.
    Includes index.
    1. Social values. 2. Worth. 3. Educational socio-
logy. I. Title.
HM73.F42   301.2'1   75-2812
ISBN 0-02-910200-6

Copyright Acknowledgments

To the memory of my parents,

Tom and Lilian Feather

Contents

Preface

THIS BOOK IS CONCERNED with values—with how they are conceptualized, how they are measured, how they influence educational choice and adjustment, how they change over time, how they vary across generations and across different segments of society, how they are related to social attitudes, how they are manifested in groups of student activists and juvenile offenders, how they vary across cultures, how they are involved in the subjective assimilation of immigrant groups, and how they relate to action.

The book describes a program of studies in which these issues are examined. In each case the emphasis is not only upon the relative importance of single values across different groups but also upon the way in which values are organized into hierarchies of importance—value systems. One question of major interest is the extent to which the value systems reported by individuals as their own fit those they attribute to defined social environments or to other persons or groups. The consequences of a lack of fit are explored, as are possible methods of checking upon the accuracy of reported value systems. In the attention it gives to the mapping of values and to the effects of disjunctions between personal and actual or perceived environmental value systems, the program of studies may be seen, in a general sense, as taking an ecological stance—indeed, as probing an area that we might christen *cognitive ecology*. We had intended to call the book *The Ecology of Values,* but felt that the title may be too esoteric.

The research has a wide sweep. In presenting it we first discuss the nature of human values and then describe the measuring instrument—the Rokeach Value Survey—that was used throughout the program. Related studies are also cited. The focus then shifts to educational contexts and to the role of value systems in educational choice and adjustment. This analysis is followed by an examination of the impact of educational institutions on value systems. The latter part of the book shifts to the wider societal and cross-cultural context. Successive chapters describe studies concerned with intergenerational similarities and differences in value systems; the relationship of values to conservatism and to how people explain poverty; the value systems of special groups in society (student activists and juvenile offenders); the value systems in different cultures (the United States, Australia, and the developing country of Papua New Guinea); and the value systems of Ukrainians and Latvians who immigrated to Australia and developed a new life. In the final chapter, all of these studies are briefly summarized, some further theoretical issues are examined, and we conclude by discussing what is perhaps the most important question of all: how values influence action.

The sequence of studies described in this book is by no means a haphazard ordering of topics. There is a progression from specific issues to more general considerations. And the entire program is unified in terms of certain theoretical ideas that fertilized the research and that we see as an important contribution of the book. The author has developed these ideas over many years in the course of his interest and research into two main areas: first, the analysis of cognitive structures and the cognitive and behavioral effects that occur when structures are discrepant; second, the development of expectancy-value, models for the analysis of motivated, instrumental action in various areas of psychological interest, such as achievement behavior and information-seeking behavior. Throughout this work the author has been committed to an interactionist analysis of thought and behavior that systematically takes both personal and environmental variables into account, and to the necessity of developing theoretical ideas that guide the flow of research and that are themselves at the mercy of well-established empirical findings.

Why study values at all? We were impressed by the multidisciplinary generality of the concept of value. Social psychologists, sociologists, educational theorists, anthropologists, philosophers, historians, political scientists, economists, and others concerned with the individual and society have all found it necessary in various ways to introduce the concept of value in order to deal with basic topics in their discipline. The concept of value enables the social scientist to bridge the gap between the analysis of the individual and the analysis of the society in which that individual lives. It has a central, integrative role in contemporary social science.

The research program began in 1968 when the author was appointed to the Foundation Chair of Psychology at Flinders University, a new state university in Adelaide, South Australia, that has been in existence for about eight years. The studies could not have been completed without the assistance of a lot of people. I owe a special debt of gratitude to my colleagues and students, especially to members of the psychology discipline at Flinders University; to George Wasyluk, Darryl Cross, and Arnold Rudzitis, who worked with me as honors students; to Andrew Ellerman, who completed a master's degree with me and who served as an extremely effective research assistant on the project for some years; to Christine Heitmann, who followed Ellerman as a research assistant and who gave strong support; to my latest research assistant, Eileen Entin, who read proofs and performed further data analyses; to Max Collins, who was associated with me in the study at the Mitchell College of Advanced Education; to Ed Peay, who took major responsibility for the multidimensional and clustering analyses; and to Malcolm Hutton, who collaborated with me in the Papua New Guinea study. I wish to thank Milton Rokeach for his permission both to use Form E and Form D of his Value Survey, a test that is under copyright to him, and to include some material from his book, *The Nature of Human Values*. I am also indebted to the many people of all ages who served as subjects in the various investigations reported in this volume and to the principals and teachers of the colleges and schools that were involved.

I am grateful to the Flinders University Research Committee and the Australian

Research Grants Committee for providing funds to support studies in the research program. Without their assistance the investigations could never have been carried out.

I wish to thank the American Psychological Association and editors associated with the following journals for permission to reproduce material previously published: *Australian Journal of Psychology, Australian and New Zealand Journal of Sociology, Australian Psychologist, British Journal of Educational Psychology, British Journal of Social and Clinical Psychology, International Journal of Psychology, International Migration,* and the *Journal of Educational Psychology.* In many cases I have included tables from these publications and followed parts of the text rather closely. I also thank my coauthors for permission to use some of this material, and Andrew Ellerman for permission to include certain results from his master's thesis.

The major part of this book was written in 1974 while the author was a Visiting Professor and an Honorary Research Associate at Harvard University. I wish to thank the Department of Psychology and Social Psychology at Harvard for providing me with space, library facilities, and a stimulating environment in which to work.

A number of people read parts of the manuscript and provided me with their comments, which in all cases were helpful. I owe special debts of gratitude to John W. Atkinson, Martin G. Gold, Reid Hastie, Seymour Martin Lipset, Thomas F. Pettigrew, Milton Rokeach, and John W. M. Whiting. Any errors I have made in substance or interpretation are mine and not theirs.

The assistance rendered by Free Press editor Tita Gillespie throughout all phases of this book's production has been invaluable and is deeply appreciated.

The typing of the manuscript was a cross-national activity. At Harvard, Peggy Burlet, Barbara DeWolfe, Sylvia Douglin, and Arlene Pippin lent valuable assistance. At Flinders, Debora Brown, Anne Gabb, Joan Marshall, and Mary Sanders came to my aid—especially Mary Sanders, who has been a key helper in the psychology discipline for some time now. I wish to thank them all heartily for their international cooperation and for their helpful attitudes in enabling me to meet a tight schedule.

Finally to my wife, Daryl, and to my son, Mark, I owe a special debt of thanks, which I cannot adequately express in words, for their love and patience during the many months of my preoccupation with this book. No person is ever entirely responsible for his own creation. There are so many others on whom he depends who help to make it possible.

Harvard University, 1974
Flinders University, 1975

1. Values, Value Systems, and Cognitive Structures

MANY of the important advances in social science in the future will depend upon the social scientist's readiness to go beyond his own discipline so as to learn about the appropriateness of new forms of conceptual analysis and methods of inquiry that have been developed elsewhere. For the social scientist who ventures into multidisciplinary pursuits there are rich rewards as similarities and differences across the various disciplines are encountered and as the theories and methods developed in one or more disciplines are seen as appropriate to others. But the multidisciplinary explorer requires a high degree of faith in the possibility of a final constructive synthesis as well as a thorough grounding in social science if he is to discover patterns in the vast amount of information that social scientists are producing today. Unless he has the support of people from other disciplines, working with them as a team on problems of mutual interest, he may be overwhelmed by the sheer scope and complexity of the flow of information that he encounters. Given the difficulties of multidisciplinary research, it is not surprising that so many social psychologists, sociologists, economists, and others interested in social man and social process elect to work in their own academic gardens, carefully fostering their own specialized products, and comfortable in situations where well-defined limits of inquiry have been set. It is so easy to become threatened by novelty and flooded by diversity if one departs from the secure ground of one's own familiar territory.

We certainly do not mean to condemn specialization of interest for it is an essential part of the strategy of scientific research, enabling the investigation of problems in depth. But occasionally it is also important to take a wider perspective. Interdisciplinary boundaries are somewhat arbitrary and a bird's-eye view of the more extensive territory can reveal advances that are of benefit to all.

One way of becoming involved in interdisciplinary research is to look for concepts that are common to different disciplines and then to explore these concepts both analytically and empirically in a variety of settings. One such concept that spans the social sciences is that of *value*. It appears as a basic concept in theories that have emerged from sociology, political science, education, social psychology, and anthropology, and it also has a secure place in

1

historical analysis, philosophy, and religion. It has been subjected to close conceptual scrutiny and has been the focus of a great deal of empirical research. Its ubiquitous nature indicates that it is an important concept, one that many disciplines have found necessary to invent when coming to grips with the cognitive life of man, with man as a social actor, with the ways in which man is molded by his culture and its social institutions, and, more widely, with the distinctive characteristics of societies or cultures and the process of social change that occurs within them.

The research program that is the basis of this book centers upon the concept of value and the related concept of value system. The program that has been conducted since it began in 1968* by the author and his associates at Flinders University has been especially concerned with the mapping of values and value systems both within and across societies, and with investigating the consequences that occur when value systems are in discrepant relationship. The chapters that follow will report on the studies that were developed within the Flinders program—moving from research concerned with the measuring instrument to studies of educational choice, adjustment, and college impact in relation to values and value systems; to the investigation of similarities and differences in values and value systems for different segments of society (for example, in relation to different generations, sexes, income groups, and so on); to studies concerned with special groups (student activists and delinquents); to studies looking at the dominant values of different societies; and, finally, to research concerned with the subjective assimilation of immigrant groups in regard to their values and value systems. It is a wide canvas—one that spans psychology, sociology, education, and anthropology in an attempt to develop some degree of interdisciplinary synthesis.

Our approach to the psychology of values owes much to recent contributions by Milton Rokeach (1973)—especially in regard to the method of assessment that it employs. The present chapter will describe Rokeach's theoretical approach and then outline some of our own concepts and theoretical assumptions, thereby providing a general framework to which the entire program can be related.

ROKEACH'S CONCEPT OF VALUE

DEFINITION OF VALUE

Because the concept of value has been used so widely, one would expect to find many detailed theoretical discussions in which it is analyzed and

* The research program began when the author was appointed to the foundation Chair of Psychology at Flinders University, a new state university in Adelaide, South Australia. The university is organized into schools rather than departments in an attempt to encourage interdisciplinary collaboration. It offers a wide range of courses within each school and accepts both undergraduate and graduate students. Throughout the book we refer to the program of research as the Flinders program because most people involved in it have been associated with Flinders.

defined, differentiated from other concepts, and related to the broad context of social science, in much the same way that both Allport (1935), some forty years ago, and Rokeach (1968d), more recently, have dealt with the concept of attitude. The sociological and social psychological literature does indeed contain careful and useful analytic discussions on the nature of values and value systems (for example, Albert, 1968; Kluckhohn, 1951; Kohlberg, 1969; Morris, 1956; Parsons, 1968; Rokeach, 1968a, 1968c, 1973; Scheibe, 1970; Scott, 1965; Smith, 1969; Williams, 1971). We do not intend to cover the same ground. It is important, however, to indicate the conceptual background to the present research program and the general theoretical context within which the studies were developed.

The starting point of our research is Rokeach's inquiry into the nature of human values (Rokeach, 1968a, 1968c, 1973), an important theoretical and empirical contribution to the literature that deserves wide attention. Rokeach indicates that the value concept has been used in two distinctively different ways. One might say that a person has a value—that he values honesty or equality or salvation. And one might also say that an object possesses value—that it is worth a certain amount of money or is preferred to other objects according to some index of utility. These two uses of the value concept have often been recognized in the literature (for example, by Morris, 1956; Smith, 1969; and Williams, 1971). According to Rokeach, it is important from the outset to decide whether the systematic study of values will proceed more heuristically if it focuses upon the values that persons are said to have or upon the values that objects are said to have.

This distinction may be too sharply drawn, however, inasmuch as values relate both to persons and to objects. Values involve both the person who is engaged in valuing and the object that is being valued. Thus, values do not exist independently of persons; nor do they exist independently of objects. They are influenced both by the properties of the person engaged in valuing—properties that relate especially to his background of experience—and by the characteristics of the object being valued. This object may be tangible, or it may vary in its degree of abstractness. For instance, one may value a particular work of art that one possesses, or one may value a general concept such as family security. In the one case the object is concrete and easily specified; in the other case the object is an abstraction based upon experience and perhaps more difficult to define. Granted the interactionist character of the valuing process, however, it is possible to weight one's research interest more to the study of values that persons are said to have than to the study of values that objects are said to possess. In other words, one may be more concerned with comparing persons in the values they assign to a standard, delimited set of abstract concepts than with comparing a wide variety of objects in regard to the values assigned to them by a standard set of persons.

Rokeach believes that the bias in research toward persons will in the end turn out to be more fruitful. Following Williams (1968), he argues that there are compelling theoretical reasons for slanting the study of values more to the person pole than to the object pole. In particular, he suggests that the number of values-as-criteria that a person uses to make evaluations is likely to be fairly small. It should be possible to identify these basic human values, to develop methods of assessing their importance for the individual, and to employ them as a common yardstick in comparisons both within and between cultures. Moreover, he believes that the concept of value has a special place in cognitive theory because values are central, dynamic, and economical units influencing a person's attitudes and behavior. Increased interest in the concept of value should help to promote interdisciplinary collaboration and to focus attention upon problems of education and reeducation, which have received less consideration from social psychologists than the questions of persuasion and attitude change (Rokeach, 1968a, 1968c).

How then are the concepts of *value* and *value system* to be defined? Rokeach (1973) provides the following definition:

> A *value* is an enduring belief that a specific mode of conduct or end-state of existence is personally or socially preferable to an opposite or converse mode of conduct or end-state of existence. A *value system* is an enduring organization of beliefs concerning preferable modes of conduct or end-states of existence along a continuum of relative importance. (p. 5)

In discussing this definition Rokeach emphasizes a number of points. A value is assumed to be *enduring;* it is not completely stable, because values may change throughout life, but it is sufficiently stable to provide continuity to personal and social existence. The relatively stable characteristic of values also applies to the way in which they are organized into hierarchies of importance, that is, into value systems. The concept of value system recognizes that some values are more important to a person than are other values. How a person orders his values is not, however, unchanging throughout his life, like a birthmark. Values do change in their relative importance over the life-span, but they do not fluctuate in importance in any erratic sense, depending upon the whim of the moment. Rokeach, therefore, conceives of value systems as fairly stable structures providing continuity amidst changing circumstances.

Values are defined by Rokeach as beliefs—an unusual equating of terms because beliefs commonly are considered to be affectively neutral whereas one's values are not neutral but are held with some degree of feeling. Indeed at times they are the basis of heated controversy, especially when they are being defended. But Rokeach's analysis of different types of belief allows him to subsume values into the framework he provides. More specifically, he argues that values may be classified as prescriptive or proscriptive beliefs rather than as descriptive or evaluative beliefs (Rokeach, 1968a, 1968c). Descriptive beliefs are beliefs that can be tested in terms of their truth or falsity ("I believe that it is snowing"). Evaluative beliefs are those that evaluate an object as good or bad ("I believe that exercise is good for the health"). Prescriptive or proscriptive beliefs are those wherein some means or end of action is judged to be desirable or undesirable ("I believe that it is desirable to behave honestly"). It may be noted in passing that the distinction between evaluative and prescriptive or proscriptive beliefs is not a sharp one. One would expect a person's judgments about what is good or bad to be highly correlated with his views about what is desirable or undesirable. Indeed, it may be very difficult to disentangle the two.

✓ Values, then, are defined in terms of one's beliefs about the desirable (cf., Kluckhohn, 1951). These beliefs, like all other types of belief, are assumed to have cognitive, affective, and behavioral components. Here Rokeach departs from tradition since these components are usually related to attitudes or sentiments rather than to beliefs (see, for example, Katz & Stotland, 1959; Krech & Crutchfield, 1948; McDougall, 1926). But, as indicated already, Rokeach's concept of belief is a broad one and in earlier publications (Rokeach, 1968a, 1968c) he has defended his point of view. A value (or belief about the desirable), therefore, involves some *knowledge* about the means or ends considered to be desirable; it involves some degree of *affect* or feeling, because values are not neutral but are held with personal feeling and generate affect when challenged; and it involves a *behavioral component,* because a value that is activated may lead to action.

✓ A further important point about Rokeach's definition is that the beliefs defining values may refer either to modes of conduct or to end-states of existence—to means or to ends. The values referring to modes of conduct are called *instrumental* values and they encompass such concepts as honesty, love, responsibility, and courage. The values referring to end-states of existence are called *terminal* values and they include such concepts as freedom, equality, a world at peace, and inner harmony. Rokeach suggests that there are two kinds of terminal values, those having a *personal* focus (such as salvation and inner harmony), and those having a *social* focus (such as world peace and true friendship among people). Similarly, he distinguishes between two kinds of instrumental values, those that have a *moral* focus in the sense that not behaving according to the valued mode of conduct may activate pangs of conscience and feelings of guilt, and those concerned with *competence* or *self-actualization.* Moral values are assumed to have an interpersonal focus and would include such modes of conduct as behaving honestly and responsibly toward others. Competence values, on the other hand, are assumed to have a personal focus. They would include such modes of conduct as behaving logically and intellectually. When they are violated, the outcome is likely to be feelings of shame or disappointment about one's personal inadequacy rather than pangs of conscience. Moral values and competence values may conflict. Thus a person may experience conflict between being honest and being polite, or between being ambitious and being helpful, and so on.

The "ought" character of values to which many writers have pointed (Heider, 1958; Kohler, 1938) is assumed by Rokeach to be more typical of instrumental values than of terminal values, and especially characteristic of those instrumental values that concern morality and that involve obligations in the way one behaves toward others—obligations that are rooted in the demands that society places upon us.

Finally, in explicating his definition of value, Rokeach emphasizes that a value is a *preference* as well as a conception of the desirable. Operationally, one can define a belief about what is desirable in terms of the preferences or choices that people make when confronted by a set of alternatives, where the alternatives involve a particular mode of conduct or end-state of existence and its opposite, or where the alternatives consist of other values within a value system. And what the person conceives to be desirable may apply either to himself or to others or to both himself and others. Thus, values have an extensive range of application, as will become evident in some of the studies to be described in subsequent chapters.

THE NUMBER OF VALUES

As we have indicated, a basic feature of Rokeach's analysis of values involves the assumption that they are arranged in relative importance. Values are assumed to become organized into hierarchies of importance, that is, into value systems that may vary from individual to individual at any given time and also in the degree to which they are stable across time when comparisons are made among individuals. Value systems therefore may be conceived as relatively stable structures,

> stable enough to reflect the fact of sameness and continuity of a unique personality socialized within a given culture and society, yet unstable enough to permit rearrangements of value priorities as a result of changes in culture, society, and personal experience. (Rokeach, 1973, p. 11)

How extensive might one expect these value systems to be? How many terminal and instrumental values might one expect human beings to possess? Rokeach argues that there are probably few distinctive human values. He conceives of a small set of terminal values—perhaps a dozen and a half—and a larger set of instrumental values—perhaps five or six dozen. Why so few? Rokeach answers this question in both theoretical and empirical terms. He believes that the total number of values is limited by man's social and biological makeup, especially by his basic needs. Moreover, the empirical procedures used to devise a method of assessment indicate that one can keep the number of values fairly restricted.

THE CENTRALITY OF VALUES

Both terminal and instrumental values are seen by Rokeach as important constituents of a person's total system of attitudes and beliefs (Rokeach, 1968a, 1968c). The terminal values, however, are regarded as more centrally located within this total system than are the instrumental values; and both are more fundamental than the many beliefs and attitudes about specific objects and situations that a person possesses.

Evidence for the greater centrality of values is seen in the widespread ramifications that may occur within the total cognitive system when a change occurs in one or more values (especially terminal values). For example, if for some reason or other equality became a lot more important within a person's terminal value system, one would expect that many changes would occur in related beliefs, attitudes, and behavior. The person might change his political allegiance; he might actively promote egalitarian structures within his work situation; attitudes and beliefs that he has held for many years might alter. In contrast, when attitudes or beliefs about specific objects or situations are modified rather than central values, the effects of this change would typically be much more limited. If a teenager changed his attitude toward a popular singer, for example, and no longer bought his hit records, one would not expect this change to have widespread effects on other attitudes, beliefs, and values that he held. Such a change is like removing or altering an isolated brick in a building whereas changing a person's values is like interfering with the very foundations of the structure.

One can therefore conceive not only of a hierarchy of importance within the sets of terminal and instrumental values but also of a hierarchy of importance within the total value-attitude-belief system, where importance is defined in terms of the amount of change produced when an element of the system is modified. One is reminded of similar system concepts in personality theory that involve the idea of varying degrees of centrality (for example, Lewin, 1935).

THE DISTINCTION BETWEEN TERMINAL
AND INSTRUMENTAL VALUES

Why distinguish two sets of values? Rokeach argues that one can conceive of terminal and instrumental value systems as separate but functionally connected, the values concerning means or modes of conduct being instrumental to the attainment of the values concerning goals or end-states of existence. Thus, behaving honestly may be instrumental to achieving a state of inner harmony. It is fair to comment that any distinction between means and ends is always somewhat arbitrary. Means can be defined as ends in themselves, and ends as means toward some ultimate end (see also, Gorsuch, 1970). Thus, behaving honestly may itself become a goal, and inner harmony may be seen as a halfway stage toward some higher good. But the means-goal distinction, the emphasis upon the structured instrumentality of thought and action, has been a popular one in psychology (and in sociology), especially for those theorists with a leaning toward concepts involving cognitive organization and purpose (for example, Tolman, 1932). Rokeach notes that the instrumentality may not be consciously perceived. Moreover, he indicates that more than one mode of behavior may be instrumental to attaining any one terminal value; and one mode of behavior may be relevant to the attainment of more than one terminal value.

Nevertheless, despite the conceptual difficulty of making a sharp distinction between means and ends, Rokeach (1973) believes that there is

> a conceptual advantage to defining all terminal values as referring only to idealized end-states of existence and to defining all instrumental values as referring only to idealized modes of behavior. . . . the best strategy at an early stage of conceptualization is to conceive all instrumental values as modes of behavior that are instrumental to the attainment of all values concerning end-states of existence. (p. 12)

Moreover, he states that his research program has justified the usefulness of making the distinction between the two sets of values.

THE FUNCTIONS OF VALUES AND VALUE SYSTEMS

According to Rokeach, an important function that values serve is to provide *standards* that guide behavior in various ways. For instance, values may influence our attitudes and our commitment to particular ideologies, religious or political. Values may also be used as standards to guide the way in which we present ourselves to other people (Goffman, 1959), and as a basis for judging our own conduct and the behavior of others. They are central to the study of the social comparison processes (Festinger, 1954; Jones & Gerard, 1967) because comparison of self with others in regard to competence and morality presupposes some standards on which comparisons can be based. Moreover, values serve as standards in the persuasion process and in social influence generally since they provide a basis for determining what is worth arguing about or whether it is worth trying to influence others in order to effect a change in their opinions. Finally, values serve an important function in the way one rationalizes thoughts and actions that would otherwise be personally and socially unacceptable, so that one's feelings of competence and morality can be unaffected and one's self-esteem maintained or even enhanced. In these various ways, then, values provide a basic set of standards that guide thought and action. For Rokeach (1973), the use of values as standards is a distinctively human invention providing

> an Aesopian language of self-justification on the one hand and of self-deception on the other . . . that enables us to maintain and enhance our self-esteem no matter how socially desirable or undesirable our motives, feelings, or actions may be. (p. 13)

Value systems are also assumed to function as *general plans* that can be used to resolve conflicts and as a basis for decision-making. Any given situation may activate a number of different values, some of them in conflict with others. One's organized hierarchy of values enables one to resolve these conflicts—for example, between behaving politely or behaving independently in a given situation, or between acting to promote a comfortable life or fostering a world of beauty. Rokeach (1973) remarks that not all values in a person's value system are simultaneously activated at any one time. Rather, a person's value system is a generalized plan

> that can perhaps best be likened to a map or architect's blueprint. Only that part of the map or blueprint that is immediately relevant is consulted, and the rest is ignored for the moment. Different subsets of the map or blueprint are activated in different social situations. (p. 14)

Finally, following the sort of approach developed by Smith, Bruner, & White (1956), Katz & Stotland (1959), and Katz (1960) in the analysis of attitudes, one can attempt to specify the different *motivational functions* that values satisfy. Rokeach (1973) argues that, in a broad sense, values may be assumed to express basic human needs and, in the final analysis, they are "the conceptual tools and weapons that we all employ in order to maintain and enhance self-esteem" (p. 14). They serve adjustment, ego-defensive, and knowledge functions. For example, for some people being obedient may be seen as a highly desirable mode of conduct for utilitarian reasons. In other cases, a high value placed upon cleanliness may express ego-defensive strivings. Some people may value wisdom highly because it satisfies their need to structure reality in a clear and consistent manner. Values may serve more than one function, but a fundamental striving underlying their emergence is assumed by Rokeach to be the need to maintain and enhance the master sentiment of self-regard (McDougall, 1926). Ultimately, therefore, all values are in the service of the self. In summary, therefore:

> all of a person's attitudes can be conceived as being value-expressive, and all of a person's values are conceived to maintain and enhance the master sentiment of self-regard—by helping a person adjust to his society, defend his ego against threat, and test reality. (Rokeach, 1973, p. 15)

VALUES AND OTHER CONCEPTS

Rokeach (1973, pp. 17–23) distinguishes values from other concepts including attitudes, social norms, needs, traits, interests, and value-orientations. Of particular interest is his discussion of the differences between values and attitudes and values and needs.

He indicates that attitudes have had much more attention from social psychologists than have values, one possible reason being the variety of methods that have been developed to measure attitudes compared with the limited number of procedures available for assessing the importance of different values.

The two concepts have also been confused by psychologists and sociologists, in some cases being used synonymously. According to Rokeach, however, attitudes and values can be distinguished rather easily. An attitude involves an organization of beliefs focused upon a single object or situation (Rokeach, 1968a, 1968c). One's attitude toward religion, for example, involves a number of beliefs concerning that specific object. Some methods of attitude measurement (for instance, Likert scaling) do in fact present statements concerning beliefs assumed to be relevant to the overall attitude, which respondents are asked to endorse with respect to degree of agreement or disagreement. In contrast, a value refers to a single belief about a desirable mode of conduct or a desirable end-state of existence (for example, "I believe that being honest is preferable to being dishonest"). Further, values transcend specific objects and situations serving as important criteria or standards used by persons to guide and evaluate thought and action. Attitudes do not have this transcendental quality about them. They relate to specific objects or situations. Moreover, attitudes do not function as standards or criteria. Rather, the relatively small number of values assumed to underlie attitudes have this function. Attitudes are far more numerous than values, numbering in the thousands according to Rokeach. They do not occupy the central position that values do within one's personality makeup and cognitive system. Values are at the "core"; they are closely bound up with self-conceptions whereas attitudes are less directly connected to the self. Moreover, values are assumed to be more dynamic concepts than attitudes, having a closer link to motivation. Finally, the substantive content of a value is assumed to concern adjustive, ego-defensive, and knowledge or self-actualizing functions more directly than does the content of a particular attitude. These several differences enable one to distinguish values from attitudes within the total belief system.

Values and needs have also been confused. For Rokeach (1973), values may be seen as the cognitive representations and transformations of needs, but they also represent societal and institutional demands. Thus, values

> are the joint results of sociological as well as psychological forces acting upon the individual—sociological because society and its institutions socialize the individual for the common good to internalize shared conceptions of the desirable; psychological because individual motivations require cognitive expression, justification, and indeed exhortation in socially desirable terms. The cognitive representation of needs as values serves societal demands no less than individual needs. . . . Needs may or may not be denied, depending on whether they can stand conscious personal and social scrutiny, but values need never be denied. Thus, when a person tells us about his values he is surely also telling us about his needs. (p. 20)

A person's important values may therefore indicate which needs are the compelling ones as far as he is concerned, but the relationship between values and needs is not isomorphic. Hence one must be cautious in trying to infer needs from values. The transformation of needs into values takes account of social desirability so that, for example, aggressive needs may be transformed into values concerning ambition, an exciting life, national security, and so on, and sex needs into values concerning love, friendship, intimacy, and so on. As Rokeach (1973) puts it: "Needs are cognitively transformed into values so that a person can end up smelling himself, and being smelled by others, like a rose" (p. 20).

ANTECEDENTS AND CONSEQUENCES OF VALUES

Values may be treated as both dependent and independent variables. One can investigate the conditions that determine the development of different values and value systems. And one can study the many effects of values and value systems on individual thought and action and throughout society.

Values may be seen as the products of cultural, institutional, and personal forces acting upon the individual. At the most general level, one's culture provides value priorities that are transmitted to individuals in the course of development. The various social institutions to which one is exposed throughout life within a given culture are the agents of transmission. According to Rokeach (1973, p. 25), the maintenance, enhancement, and transmission of values within a culture tends to become institutionalized so that different social institutions (for example, the family, the church, one's political organization, and so forth) have the task of maintaining, enhancing, and transmitting selected subsets of values from generation to generation. These social institutions may reinforce one another in the values they promote. But they may also compete in the priorities they assign to particular values. Rokeach (1973) believes that "an identification of the major institutions of a society should provide us with a reasonable point of departure for a comprehensive compilation and classification of human values" (p. 25). Society does not act upon a passive organism, however, free from needs and conflicts. In understanding how values develop, one must also allow for the biological makeup of the person and the basic needs involved, and for the unique life experiences to which he has been exposed— experiences that set problems of adjustment that he must resolve in his own way. Hence, the antecedents of values and value systems range from the general to the particular as one moves from cultural, to institutional, to personal factors (see also Kluckhohn & Strodtbeck, 1961, p. 10).

The consequences of values and value systems have already been discussed. Their effects are assumed to be far-reaching, influencing beliefs, attitudes, and behavior in many different ways.

SUMMARY

By way of summary Rokeach (1973) provides the following extended definitions of a value and a value system:

To say that a person has a value is to say that he has an enduring prescriptive or proscriptive belief that a specific mode of behavior or end-state of existence is preferred to an oppositive mode of behavior or end-state. This belief transcends attitudes toward objects and toward situations; it is a standard that guides and determines action, attitudes toward objects and situations, ideology, presentations of self to others, evaluations, judgments, justifications, comparisons of self with others, and attempts to influence others. Values serve adjustive, ego-defensive, knowledge, and self-actualizing functions. Instrumental and terminal values are related yet are separately organized into relatively enduring hierarchical organizations along a continuum of importance. (p. 25)

SOME THEORETICAL UNDERPINNINGS

The conceptual basis for Rokeach's program of research has been described in some detail because his procedure for obtaining terminal and instrumental value systems from respondents, the *Value Survey,* has been consistently employed in the Flinders program. It is therefore important to understand the background of this procedure, especially the theoretical distinctions that have been made.

The program of research to be described in subsequent chapters has not involved a specific commitment to Rokeach's theoretical approach, although we consider his analysis to be a valuable contribution to the literature on beliefs, attitudes, and values. We decided to initiate the research program because we were interested in the conceptual distinctions made by Rokeach, persuaded about the interdisciplinary importance of the concept of value, and convinced that, while the Value Survey was open to criticism on some grounds, it was nevertheless the most appropriate procedure that we could find for investigating the questions we set out to answer. There were some rather general theoretical underpinnings to our research program that should now be made explicit, underpinnings that have characterized much of our previous research.

EXPECTANCY-VALUE THEORY

In the past we have consistently argued for an *interactionist* approach to the analysis of behavior (Feather, 1962), for an approach that is neither situation-specific nor person-specific but that attempts to account for a person's behavior in terms of both the particular situation to which he is exposed and the relatively stable personality characteristics that he brings with him to the situation. Of particular interest is a class of interactionist approaches that are called "expectancy-value theories" (Feather, 1959a); they conceive of motivated behavior in terms of the situationally elicited *expectations* that a person has concerning the implications of his actions and the subjective values or *valences* (positive or negative) that he assigns to the possible outcomes of alternative actions. The general approach owes much to the classic contributions of Tolman and Lewin (Atkinson, 1964; Feather, 1959).

This type of theory has proved to be especially fruitful in the analysis of the sorts of tendencies that are elicited in achievement situations where a person is confronted with the possibility of success or failure as he works at a task or makes choices between different alternatives (Atkinson & Feather, 1966). In this 1966 analysis of choice, performance, and persistence in achievement situations, the positive and negative tendencies elicited were assumed to be determined by relatively stable and general personality dispositions (or *motives*) and by *expectations* and *incentive values* that are more closely tied to the actual situation in which action takes place. Despite the fact that more recent treatments of achievement-oriented activity have introduced new concepts and have adopted new terminology (Atkinson & Birch, 1974; Atkinson & Raynor, 1974), the approach has continued to involve an emphasis upon the interaction of personal and situational variables. In other developments we have moved outside of the achievement domain to apply an expectancy-value model to the analysis of information-seeking behavior, again using the concepts of motive, expectation, and incentive (Feather, 1967a).

We have not explicitly used the expectancy-value theory in the Flinders program of research on values, but it should be possible to map Rokeach's concept of value into this framework—especially if one views values as the cognitive representations and transformations of underlying motives. One could then consider the important question of how values relate to action within an interactionist, expectancy-value context, taking both person and situation into account. This possibility will be explored in the final chapter.

COGNITIVE STRUCTURES

To our commitment to an interactionist approach as it applies to the analysis of *action* must be added a general interest on our part in the psychology of *cognition,* particularly in the concept of cognitive structure. We have been concerned with such questions as whether one can distinguish different types of cognitive structure, how cognitive structures may be organized, what dimensions of cognitive structures can be specified, and under what conditions cognitive and behavioral adjustments may follow from discrepancies in cognitive structures.

In a recent article (Feather, 1971a) we argued that in the course of development a person lays down general *abstract* structures that are residues or summaries of past experience. These abstract structures are formed as he copes with the influx of information from both the social and physical environments. It was assumed that abstract structures are a necessary part of adaptation because they provide continuity and meaning under changing environmental circumstances. Abstract structures are organized and they are relatively stable.

But they are also susceptible to change as the person encounters new and discrepant information that cannot readily be interpreted in terms of existing abstract structures. Abstract structures are general schemata carried by the person with him from situation to situation. In a sense they function like theories about what *ought* to be the case in the physical and social environments— reference standards against which new information can be tested. For example, on the basis of one's experience in communication situations one might formulate the general rule that the people one likes usually have attitudes toward issues similar to one's own and that their communications tend to be consistent with these attitudes. Or, on the basis of one's experience in the physical world, one might formulate the general rule that pictures on walls usually hang straight. These theories are abstractions from many different past encounters in the social and physical world and they tend to be *normative*. What has been perceived on many occasions to be the modal or usual occurrence takes on an *ought* character, so that, for example, one believes that communications should be consistent in the way indicated or that pictures on walls ought to hang straight.

What occurs in any particular situation may, however, be at odds with the relevant underlying abstract structure formed on the basis of past experience. A person one likes may present a communication completely at variance with one's own point of view, or a picture may be seen hanging crookedly on a wall. One needs, therefore, to consider how information from the present situation is perceived and organized. Hence, it is necessary to consider the *perceived* structure as well as the underlying abstract structure.

It should be apparent that perceived and abstract structures can either correspond or be discrepant. When differences exist between perceived and abstract structures it is assumed that there will be pressure to resolve the discrepancy. This resolution can occur in different ways, some of which involve modifications of the manner in which the current information is organized, that is, they involve changes in the perceived structure (the content of the communication may be misperceived); some of which may involve behavior (the crooked picture is straightened or new communication occurs between individuals in an attempt to resolve discrepancy); and some of which may involve changes in the underlying abstract structure itself if the discrepancy persists and is salient over time. These different adjustments have been discussed in relation to social communication, attitude-relevant recall, and causal attribution (Feather, 1971*a*).

This type of analysis that focuses upon the development of cognitive structures in the course of information-processing and that concerns itself with the cognitive and behavioral effects of structural discrepancies may be seen as presenting a general paradigm to which many similar ideas from psychology can be related. Some of these related approaches were discussed in the original article (Feather, 1971*a*, pp. 375–376). They include Hebb's analysis of the fear of the strange (Hebb, 1949), Berlyne's discussion of curiosity (Berlyne, 1960, 1966), Hunt's account of the match between environmental circumstances and existing schemata (Hunt, 1961), and the general approach of those theories that assume that man prefers consistent states of affairs (Abelson, Aronson, McGuire, Newcomb, Rosenberg, & Tannenbaum, 1965)—in particular, the work of Festinger on social comparison processes and (later) cognitive dissonance (Festinger, 1950, 1954, 1957), Heider's analysis of cognitive balance (Heider, 1946, 1958), and Newcomb's discussion of strain toward symmetry as a function of perceived discrepancy (Newcomb, 1961, 1968). To these approaches we can add the following: the emphasis upon general schemata that are built up over time and tested against reality (Bartlett, 1932; Piaget, 1966); spontaneous changes in recall in terms of underlying ideal structures (Koffka, 1935); generalized expectancies or "cognitive maps" that can be confirmed or disconfirmed by experience (Tolman, 1958); neural organizations that become progressively refined as learning occurs (Hebb, 1949); discrepancies between perception and adaptation levels assumed to be associated with affect and the development of motives (Helson, 1964; McClelland, Atkinson, Clark, & Lowell, 1953, chap. 2); disparities in psychological events that define motives (Peak, 1968); images and plans (analogous to computer programs) that guide the form that behavior takes (Miller, Galanter, & Pribram, 1960); categories or concepts that are refined by experience and to which information input is matched in some sense so as to achieve stability in perception and thought (Bruner, 1973; Brunswik, 1939; Harvey, Hunt, & Schroder, 1961); and personal constructs in terms of which a person construes his world (Kelly, 1955). And we can add some more recent contributions to the list—for example, the cognitive approach to social psychology presented by Stotland and Canon (1972) and the emphasis on structures by Foa and Foa (1974). These various approaches involve structural concepts and each is concerned in some way with how new or discrepant information is processed and responded to by individuals.

In our 1971 article the concepts of abstract and perceived structures and the question of how structural discrepancies may be resolved were discussed in terms of models that we had developed previously, models that were concerned with the effects of communication (Feather, 1964, 1967b), attitude-relevant recall (Feather, 1969a, 1970a), and causal attribution (Feather, 1969b; Feather & Simon, 1971)—each of which involved structural balance as the dynamic principle of organization (Heider, 1958). It was recognized, however, that the underlying abstract structures could be organized in ways other than those conforming to the balance principle. Indeed it was emphasized that an important task for structural psychology would be to explore different forms of structural organization, to develop valid indexes of structural discrepancy, and to seek answers to other questions concerned with the further expansion of structural models (Feather, 1971a, pp. 366–375).

What significance does the distinction between abstract and perceived structures have for the study of values? In the first place, if one follows Rokeach and assumes that the sorts of values that are useful analytic tools are those that apply to modes of conduct and end-states of existence, then what is being valued involves some general concept—for example, behaving honestly (a mode of conduct) or freedom (an end-state of existence). This general concept may itself be conceived of as a structure and analyzed in terms of its structural organization and in relation to the effects of discrepancies between the concept and new inputs. It should be clear that individuals may differ in the structural characteristics of their concepts along various dimensions, such as degree of differentiation, integration, isolation, centrality—to mention just a few of the dimensions suggested by various authors (see Zajonc, 1968, pp. 320–338 for a review). Indeed, some of Rokeach's earlier work is concerned with the dimensions of beliefs and belief systems (Rokeach, 1960, 1968a, 1968c). Concepts may therefore differ structurally between individuals yet have the same verbal labels attached to them. For example, two people may each place a very high value on freedom but on close inspection it may become apparent that their concepts of freedom are quite different. One may have a complex and finely differentiated concept of freedom, one that is centrally involved in a sophisticated and well-articulated social theory; the other may see freedom in very simple terms, terms that are not elaborated in any detailed way but nevertheless are very important. Such differences between individuals in the meaning of the general concepts that are being valued are likely to have implications for thought and action. One may be under some pressure to resolve structural discrepancy, for example, if one's own concept of freedom is far removed from the concept of freedom possessed by most others or by key individuals in one's immediate social environment.

Thus, one can conceive of a value as an abstract structure involving an associative network which may take different forms for different individuals. We would make the further assumption that this structure also involves feeling or *affect*—some of the associations involved are affective associations. As Rokeach (1973, p. 7) points out, people can feel emotional about a value, be affectively for or against it, approve of those who support the value and disapprove of those who oppose it. This concept of *value structure* will be explored in more detail in the final chapter.

In addition to investigating the structural characteristics of a particular value, however, and the effects of possible discrepancies between abstract and perceived structures at this level of discrete values, one can also conceive of a person's value system as an abstract structure that may be discrepant with the value system perceived to be dominant in particular social environments. It is this type of variance that receives most attention in the research program to be described in this book. The order of importance that a person assigns to his values can be seen as a summary of his own priorities, an abstraction from past experience, relatively stable over time, giving meaning and continuity to existence, but like other abstract structures, amenable to rearrangement as new, persistent, and discrepant information is encountered. Some of the studies to be described in subsequent chapters will explore the implications of discrepancies between the order of values that individuals assign to themselves and the order of values that they attribute to the various social environments to which they are exposed. The child's value priorities, for example, may be quite different from the order of values that he sees his school or his family promoting. One would expect such differences between abstract and perceived structures to have significant implications for cognitive and behavioral adjustments.

The study of the relationship of a person's own value system (or systems) to the order of values promoted (or perceived to be promoted) by various social environments, and the investigation of the effects of discrepancies in these two types of value systems, involves one in the analysis of an aspect of what might be termed *cognitive ecology*. Such a study attempts to identify important characteristics of the person and of the actual or perceived environment—important in the sense that successful adaptation depends upon a reasonably close match between these personal and environmental characteristics. More will be said about cognitive ecology in subsequent chapters. It should be evident, however, that a focus upon the value match does imply an interactionist analysis of both person and environment. The interaction is at a very complex level, however, because it involves ordered sets of values as the basic units, one set relating to self and the other set (or sets) relating to selected environments that the person is experiencing.

PLAN OF SUBSEQUENT CHAPTERS

This general theoretical framework that treats discrepancies in value systems as particular instances of disjunctions between abstract and perceived structures is the basis for some of the studies to be reported in subsequent chapters and it will be elaborated as the occasion demands. In other studies the emphasis is less upon the consequences of a mismatch in value systems than upon the need to obtain information about how value systems vary for different populations both within societies and across societies. In presenting the entire program of studies we will be concerned not only with theoretical issues but also with methodological problems and directions for future research.

The studies that will be described demonstrate a continual interplay between theory and observation, the theoretical assumptions for the most part being at a very general level. The research strategy demonstrates a firm commitment to *programmatic* study where each investigation allows the possibility for some replication of previous findings and takes us a little farther ahead.

The succeeding chapters are organized as follows:

Chapter 2 describes the measuring instrument developed by Rokeach (the Value Survey), and reports studies from the Flinders program that are concerned with it.

Chapter 3 reports studies from the program dealing with the role of values in educational choice—as when a student has to choose between different faculties or schools at a college or university. The theoretical emphasis in Chapter 3 is on person-environment fit, especially on the assumed tendency for persons to choose congruent environments, in this case minimizing discrepancies between their own value systems and those they attribute to the environment under consideration.

Chapter 4 discusses adjustment within educational institutions and reviews studies concerning the relationship between measures of student adjustment at school and the degree to which the students' own value systems match those they attribute to their school—a positive relationship being expected.

Chapter 5 examines the impact of educational institutions on the values of the students attending them and describes relevant studies from the Flinders program. It also looks at such questions as the effects of coeducation on value systems, the differences in the value systems of children attending state and independent schools, and the effects of university experience on the value systems of students over a 2½-year time period. In particular, the question involving the university experience confronts us with the issue of stability and change in value systems over time.

Chapter 6 moves away from the educational context to society at large and reports studies from the program in which value systems and social attitudes are compared in relation to intergenerational and age differences, sex differences, and income differences. These studies provide some clues about the conditions influencing the development of value systems.

Chapter 7 analyzes studies from the program that investigate the value systems of two "special" groups, namely student activists and male delinquents, and compares results from both.

Chapter 8 takes another step and moves from within-society research to studies from the program that enable cross-cultural comparisons in value systems to be made, as between Australia and the United States and Australia and Papua New Guinea.

Chapter 9 also has a cross-cultural emphasis but here the studies from the program pertain to the degree to which different migrant groups (Ukrainians and Latvians) have become assimilated to Australian society in regard to their value systems and social attitudes.

Chapter 10 offers a recapitulation and raises some further theoretical issues about the concept of value climate, value systems and stereotyping, determinants of value rankings, and the relationship of values to action.

In these chapters, therefore, we move from the educational to the societal to the cross-cultural context, noting as we go along some of the major theoretical and methodological issues relevant to each topic but centering throughout on the study of value systems from a cognitive viewpoint. The scope of our program is wide and interdisciplinary and by its very nature runs the risk of superficiality. We hope that we have avoided this pitfall in the many discussions of different topics throughout this book. We have tried hard to look at problems in some depth and to achieve a certain degree of meaningful integration.

2. The Value Survey

THE VALUE SURVEY used by Rokeach throughout his research program, and also throughout the program of studies to be reported in the present book, was developed by him after several years of research. The Value Survey presents respondents with two lists of values, one a list of terminal values and the other a list of instrumental values. The two lists were designed to be a reasonably comprehensive sample of terminal and instrumental values but they were kept as short as possible. Each list has to be ranked in order of importance from the most important value to the least important value. Hence the procedure provides two hierarchies of value importance (or value systems) for each respondent—a terminal value system and an instrumental value system. These value systems can be the subject of further analytic inquiry. It can be seen that the final procedure developed by Rokeach is consistent with his conceptual analysis of the nature of human values.

In arriving at the final procedure, Rokeach rejected two other possible approaches. One would have been to observe behavior in specially structured situations and to make inferences about an individual's values from the responses he provided. Such an approach, however, would be time-consuming, costly, limited to small groups, not easy to interpret and quantify, and possibly influenced by the observer's own values. The second approach would have been to ask a person to report his own values without providing him with a structure to guide him. Rokeach rejected this procedure because he believed that a person might not be willing or able to report his own values, or he might be highly selective in what he reports. Instead of these two procedures, Rokeach decided to ask respondents to rank-order terminal and instrumental values on specially constructed lists.

THE TWO LISTS OF VALUES

Table 2.1 shows the two lists of values in the Value Survey. Each consists of 18 values, each value accompanied by a short descriptive phrase or definition in parentheses. The values in each list are arranged in alphabetical order and,

TABLE 2–1. Test-Retest Reliabilities for Terminal and Instrumental Values (Form E of the Rokeach Value Survey) after a Five-Week and after a 2½-Year Interval

Terminal Values	r		Instrumental Values	r	
	5 weeks	2½ years		5 weeks	2½ years
A comfortable life (a prosperous life)	.63	.39	Ambitious (hard working, aspiring)	.59	.33
An exciting life (a stimulating, active life)	.60	.35	Broad-minded (open-minded)	.54	.29
A sense of accomplishment (lasting contribution)	.65	.24	Capable (competent, effective)	.37	.29
A world at peace (free of war and conflict)	.71	.36	Cheerful (lighthearted, joyful)	.44	.32
A world of beauty (beauty of nature and the arts)	.77	.39	Clean (neat, tidy)	.71	.38
Equality (brotherhood, equal opportunity for all)	.64	.40	Courageous (standing up for your beliefs)	.60	.32
Family security (taking care of loved ones)	.68	.41	Forgiving (willing to pardon others)	.57	.34
Freedom (independence, free choice)	.60	.35	Helpful (working for the welfare of others)	.53	.35
Happiness (contentedness)	.56	.47	Honest (sincere, truthful)	.52	.26
Inner harmony (freedom from inner conflict)	.46	.29	Imaginative (daring, creative)	.76	.42
Mature love (sexual and spiritual intimacy)	.56	.39	Independent (self-reliant, self-sufficient)	.53	.32
National security (protection from attack)	.63	.30	Intellectual (intelligent, reflective)	.62	.26
Pleasure (an enjoyable, leisurely life)	.53	.37	Logical (consistent, rational)	.43	.34
Salvation (saved, eternal life)	.87	.67	Loving (affectionate, tender)	.58	.44
Self-respect (self-esteem)	.75	.42	Obedient (dutiful, respectful)	.60	.42
Social recognition (respect, admiration)	.68	.38	Polite (courteous, well mannered)	.47	.32
True friendship (close companionship)	.51	.37	Responsible (dependable, reliable)	.37	.36
Wisdom (a mature understanding of life)	.40	.42	Self-controlled (restrained, self-disciplined)	.58	.31
Median =	.63	.39		.56	.33

Source: Data adapted from Feather, 1971c; Feather, 1973d.

in the usual form of administration, the terminal values are presented before the instrumental values. (The headings and the figures shown in the table will be explained later in the chapter.)

Despite Rokeach's assumption that instrumental values outnumber terminal values both lists contain the same number of values. The decision to limit the size of both lists to 18 values was probably an outcome of a wish to sample as widely as possible, modified by a belief that respondents would find larger sets of values increasingly more difficult to rank. Equalizing the two lists (given the assumed difference in the number of terminal and instrumental values) implies, however, that the sample of terminal values would be more complete than the sample of instrumental values.

The usual instruction to the respondent in the Value Survey is to arrange the values ". . . in order of importance to YOU, as guiding principles in YOUR life." The respondent then provides a rank order of values, from the most important to the least important. Data are thus obtained about ordinal relationships between stimuli; information is provided concerning the relative importance of different values when compared to a standard set of other values. That a particular value may be ranked low on the list does not mean that it is unimportant to the individual, only that it is less important than the other values on the list. It should be evident that the procedure is *ipsative;* that is, the importance of each value is expressed, not in absolute terms, but in relation to the importance of the other values on the list. Once 17 values are ranked the position of the final value is automatically fixed. And the mean and variance of the data set (1 to 18) for each list of values are both constant across individuals.

There are two main ways in which the ranking can be achieved. In Form E of the Value Survey the two sets of values are presented on mimeographed forms with a line beside each value. Respondents are instructed to study the list carefully and then to use numbers from 1 to 18 in ranking the values in each set, placing a 1 next to the value they deem to be the most important for them, a 2 next to the value that is second in importance, and so forth. Respondents are encouraged to check back over their lists when they have completed their rankings, taking all the time they need so that the end result is a true representation of the relative importance of their values. In Form D of the Value Survey the values and their short definitions are printed on removable gummed labels which are presented in alphabetical order (see Rokeach, 1973, Appendix A). The respondent rearranges the gummed labels so as to obtain the final order of importance, the most important value being placed in Box 1 to the left of the set of values, the next important value in Box 2, down to the least important value in Box 18. Here, too, respondents are encouraged to take their time and to think carefully. They are told that they are free to change their answers should they want to—by simply moving around the labels, which are designed to peel off easily. Finally they are told that the end result should show how *they* really feel. In neither Form E or Form D is any attempt made to disguise the test. No deception is involved. The test is labeled "Value Survey" and respondents are told from the outset that they will see lists of 18 values arranged in alphabetical order and that they have to put the values in an order of importance to them.

Rokeach argues that the Value Survey has a projective quality about it even though the stimulus material is far more structured than an ambiguous inkblot or a Thematic Apperception Test (TAT) picture. He maintains that, like projective tests, the stimulus material does not suggest a set of "correct" responses. The values on the list are virtually all positive ones and cover a wide spectrum. It is not surprising that most respondents find the task of ranking each set of values in order of importance a very difficult one. They have to collapse a set of what are presumably multidimensional concepts into a linear order and there are no strong cues from the stimulus material about what the socially desirable orders are when they rank the values in regard to self— although, as we will see later, respondents' beliefs about how their answers will be used may make some orders more likely than others. The ranking task is probably more difficult for Form E where the respondent writes down numbers on the lines beside each set of values. If he subsequently wants to change his mind and rank a particular value or values differently, he then has to go back and alter the numbers, and mistakes are easily made. The gummed-label procedure of Form D has something of a game-like quality to it and can be used more generally than Form E, particularly with children, elderly people, and respondents who have had limited education. Moreover, with the gummed-label procedure the respondent's task becomes progressively easier as he ranks each value because he has a smaller set to search through in deciding which of the remaining values he will move to the next box on the lefthand side of the page. According to Rokeach, most respondents take from 10 to 20 minutes to complete Form D of the Value Survey; in our experience, Form E usually takes longer to complete (from 15 to 30 minutes). Generally, Form D is to be preferred as a research tool.

THE SELECTION OF TERMINAL
AND INSTRUMENTAL VALUES

How were the sets of 18 terminal and 18 instrumental values chosen? The terminal values were distilled from a list of several hundred values obtained from various sources: a review of the literature on values in American society and in other societies; Rokeach's analysis of his own terminal values; the values reported by a small group of 30 graduate students in psychology; and the values reported by a representative sample of about 100 adults in Lansing, Michigan, who had the notion of terminal values explained to them. After values were excluded that were synonymous or overlapping, too specific, or not really concerned with end-states of existence, it was possible to reduce the list to 18.

The instrumental values were obtained in a different way—from an analysis of Anderson's (1968) list of 555 personality-trait words (see Rokeach, 1973, p. 29). This list was reduced to less than half by excluding negative values and then other criteria were applied so as to shorten the list further. Retained were values judged as maximally different or minimally intercorrelated with one another; values deemed to provide maximal discrimination across social status, sex, race, age, religion, politics, and so forth; values judged to be meaningful in all cultures; and values that could be admitted to without appearing boastful. Only one value from a group of synonyms or near-synonyms was used. The large initial list of instrumental values was thereby cut down to a set of 18 concerned with modes of conduct. Keeping the two value lists short was an important consideration because the ranking procedure places more and more of a load on the respondent as the number of stimuli to be ranked increases.

When one looks at the two sets of values in Table 2.1 it is possible to think of other values not on the list that might have been included—justice and loyalty, among others. The comment has also been made that the two sets of values are weighted toward those that one might expect to find in middle-class America and may not be sufficiently comprehensive to be useful in other cultures, particularly in non-Western developing nations. And we have been told that lists of "negative" values might also be useful. Yet there is usually a degree of arbitrariness and intuition in the way in which one arrives at final lists, even when one sets up general guidelines. It is important, however, to indicate clearly the criteria that one employs in determining test choices and this Rokeach has done in describing how he made his final selection of the sets of terminal and instrumental values. He also acknowledges that other investigators might end up with different sets. It is likely though that these sets would include many of the values that appear on the lists provided by Rokeach. His two sets of values are sufficiently general to make the Value Survey an appealing instrument for social research.

ANALYSIS OF VALUE DATA

In this section we will describe some of the main procedures used in analyzing the value data obtained from the Flinders program.

TRANSFORMATION OF RANKINGS

In most of the studies in the Flinders program, the raw data were transformed before being subjected to statistical analysis. More specifically, the

ranks from 1 to 18 were transformed to standard scores (z scores) corresponding to a division into 18 equal areas under the normal curve (Hays, 1967,
pp. 35–39). This transformation was made on the assumption that differences
between ranks at the extremes would be more discriminable than differences
between ranks in the middle of the scale—a fairly common assumption in discussions of the process of ranking.

In regard to the Value Survey this assumption implies that respondents
should have less difficulty deciding between values to be ranked in the high
or low ranges of importance than between values to be ranked in the intermediate range. Some evidence for this assumption comes from a study by
Hollen (1967), who found that values initially ranked as most or least important changed the least in their rankings from test to retest, whereas values
ranked in the middle changed the most. Rokeach (1973) argues that these
results suggest that "respondents rank values at the high and low ends of the
scale with considerably more confidence than those they rank in the middle"
(p. 39).

One might argue for other forms of transformation. For example, it might
be assumed that values ranked most important and presumably "closer" to the
self would be better discriminated than values ranked further down the list.
But the evidence just noted supports the assumption of better discriminability
at the high and low ends of the scale than in the middle. This assumption was
the basis of the normal-curve transformation used throughout the present research program.

ANALYSIS OF VARIANCE

Following this transformation, the statistical procedure has usually involved
some form of the analysis of variance. Rokeach (1973, pp. 56–57), who does
not make the normal-curve transformation, in most cases uses nonparametric
statistical procedures in analyzing his ranked data. He does so because he is
dealing with ordinal data and because he has found that the frequency distributions of rankings for each of the 18 terminal and 18 instrumental values de-
viate markedly from normality and from one another (as we also have found).
Hence, he uses the median as his measure of central tendency and the Median
Test (Siegel, 1956) as the main test of statistical significance.

One might object to the use of analysis of variance in the Flinders program,
given the departures from normality noted above. In defense, however, it should
be noted that all of the studies in our program have involved fairly large Ns;
that the analysis of variance is known to be a very *robust* procedure, useful
even when there are quite marked departures from the underlying assumptions
(Scheffé, 1959); and that when other tests of significance, such as the Median
Test and the Kruskal-Wallis Test (Siegel, 1956), have been employed on the
same data by way of comparison, results obtained have been highly consistent

with one another, both in our own studies and in those of Rokeach (for a comment see Rokeach, 1973, p. 57). The analysis of variance does have the advantage of enabling more complex types of comparison than the procedures used by Rokeach. For example, when used in multifactor form, one can investigate whether various interaction effects that may be of interest are significant.

Throughout the research program we have used different forms of the analysis of variance. In some cases data from independent groups have been subjected to a simple one-way analysis. In other cases the design has involved more than one factor and either measures from independent groups or repeated measures on the same group or a mixture of both. In most cases studies have involved unequal Ns and this has been allowed for in the treatment of data by using an unweighted means analysis (Winer, 1962).

In employing the analysis of variance we have typically set a conservative *alpha* level of $p < .01$ in view of the large number of comparisons usually made in studies involving the Value Survey and also in view of the ipsative nature of the measuring instrument, which introduces a lack of independence between statistical tests on the separate values. With 18 values, however, the degree to which the independence assumption is violated is relatively small, though it should be taken into account when interpreting statistical findings.

In addition, the research strategy has emphasized findings that are replicated from study to study even though in some cases differences might not be significant at the alpha level just noted. Thus, we also report differences that are significant at $p < .05$ where replication is involved. The thrust of the inquiry has been to move forward in a programmatic way, developing new studies on the basis of questions raised by previous ones, spreading into different areas to investigate the generality of concepts and procedures, and all the time looking for similar patterns and common threads that link the program of studies in a meaningful way.

AVERAGE VALUE SYSTEMS

In all studies we have represented the average value systems of different groups by using the *medians* of the rank orders assigned by respondents to the different terminal and instrumental values. Medians have been used rather than means because the basic data (rankings) are clearly ordinal and the distributions of ranks for particular values were often skewed. The rank order of these medians is also noted in parentheses beside each median. This rank order corresponds to what Rokeach (1973) calls the Composite Rank Order (p. 56). When groups are being compared the medians for a particular value will usually differ although in some cases the composite rank orders may be the same. The medians are much more sensitive indicators of differences in the relative importance of particular values between groups than are the composite rank orders. They provide a measure of the central tendency (or average) of the distribution of the rank orders obtained from respondents for each value in each condition. It should be remembered that the tests that we conducted to assess the statistical significance of differences did not involve the medians but were based upon analyses of variance of the ranks after these ranks had been transformed by using the normal curve tables. The medians and composite rank orders are therefore employed only for convenience of description, although they reflect the statistically significant differences uncovered by the analysis of variance procedures (more so when the medians are compared across groups or conditions than when the comparisons involve the composite rank orders).

As would be expected, in each study some respondents made errors in ranking (for example, they used the same rank more than once or omitted a rank altogether). These errors were far less likely with Form D (the gummed-label form) than with Form E. In describing each study we have noted the total number of respondents who participated and, when reporting median rankings for different groups, the actual Ns on which the medians were based after the data from those respondents who made errors had been excluded. A comparison of the reported Ns for respondents who participated with the Ns involved in calculating the medians enables one to determine error rates.

COMPARISON OF AVERAGE VALUE SYSTEMS AND INDIVIDUAL VALUE SYSTEMS

In some studies the average value systems for different groups or conditions as represented by the set of median rankings for the terminal values or for the instrumental values have been compared for similarity by using the Spearman rank-order correlation statistic (*rho*) or the Kendall *tau* statistic or both (Siegel, 1956), on the assumption that higher positive values of rho or tau indicate increasing degrees of similarity between average value systems.

These correlations between sets of medians (average value systems) correspond to what have been called ecological correlations based upon aggregate data. The issues involved in interpreting these correlations have received a lot of attention, particularly in the sociological literature (Alker, 1969; Blalock, 1961; Dogan & Rokkan, 1969; Hannan, 1971; Robinson, 1950). From our point of view the main thing to note is that the unit of comparison in these correlations is the group or aggregate because the "scores" that are correlated are averages. The unit of comparison is *not* the person. It would be quite wrong to assume that these ecological correlations can be taken as valid estimates of what the correlations would be if they were calculated for separate individuals and then averaged. When scores are averaged information about individual differences is lost. The correlations involving these averages therefore cannot take account of these individual differences. An important source of variation related to a variety of causal factors is therefore no longer available for analysis. Yet these ecological correlations can indicate meaningful patterns of relationships at the group or aggregate level. In the present context, as we will see later, these correlations involving average value systems tend to be considerably higher than the corresponding correlations calculated at the individual level, with the person as the unit of analysis.

We have also made comparisons of value systems at the individual level, again using Spearman rho and Kendall tau to provide indexes of degree of similarity. For example, these two statistics have been used to compare a respondent's own value system (or systems) with the corresponding value system (or systems) he attributes to a particular social institution such as his school—again with a view to exploring degree of similarity.

It would be possible to use or develop other forms of similarity coefficient. One might argue, for instance, that similarity between units is functionally more significant for thought and action when the similarity occurs between the values ranked high in importance on each list and that dissimilarity in the value rankings for "lower" values may have little significance. If two respondents each assigned highest priority among the terminal values to *freedom, wisdom, equality,* and *family security* in that order, it might be argued that this correspondence has most significance and that the extent of correspondence between their remaining rankings is not particularly informative. On this argument, one might attempt to develop a similarity index that assigned special weight to similarity between the most important values. We have not done this, though it may be a useful avenue to explore in the future. The two similarity indexes that we have employed (rho and tau) have the advantage of using all of the information available and of being suitable for ranked data.

With this general description of analytic procedures in mind, we will now turn to studies from the Flinders program that have been specifically concerned with aspects of the Value Survey itself.

STUDIES OF TEST-RETEST RELIABILITY

It is possible to investigate test-retest reliability both at the level of the value system and in regard to single values. In the first case the test-retest reliability coefficient shows how stable the value system tends to be over time. The test-retest reliability coefficient for a single value provides information about the stability of the ranks assigned to that value over a defined time interval. Both kinds of information have been obtained in the Flinders program.

In a study carried out in 1969 (Feather, 1971c), complete data were available from 77 students (27 male, 50 female) who were enrolled in the introductory psychology course at Flinders University in South Australia. These students had taken Form E of the Value Survey on two occasions: first as one of a series of tests administered to incoming first-year (freshman) students as part of their orientation program (see Feather, 1970b, p. 130) and then again five weeks later in the psychology classroom as a class exercise. For each terminal and each instrumental value, Pearson *r* was calculated between the transformed rankings obtained on the two occasions from the 77 respondents with complete data. This analysis resulted in 36 test-retest reliability coefficients, one for each of the terminal and instrumental values. For each respondent the set of 18 transformed rankings obtained for the terminal values on the first occasion was correlated with the corresponding set obtained on the second, again using Pearson *r*. The same analysis was applied to the two sets of transformed rankings of the instrumental values for each respondent. This type of analysis resulted in 77 test-retest reliability coefficients concerned with the stability of terminal value systems from one occasion to another, and another set of 77 reliability coefficients concerned with the stability of instrumental value systems from one occasion to another.

The same procedure was employed in a second study (Feather, 1973*d*) in which data were available from 392 respondents (232 male, 160 female) from all schools at Flinders University who took Form E of the Value Survey on two occasions separated by a 2½-year interval. Most of these respondents were first tested in 1969 during the enrollment period and as part of the orientation program. A very small group of respondents took the test for the first time five weeks after enrollment in the psychology class session referred to previously. These 392 respondents again completed the test in July 1971 in a postal survey in which Form E was mailed to them. Details of the sample, response rate, and so forth can be found in Feather (1973*d*).

TEST-RETEST RELIABILITY FOR SINGLE VALUES

The test-retest reliability coefficients for *single values* obtained from these two studies are presented in Table 2.1 for the five-week interval and for the 2½-year interval. For the five-week interval the reliabilities ranged from .40 for *wisdom* to .87 for *salvation* in regard to the terminal values, with a median of .63. For the instrumental values the reliability coefficients ranged from .37 for *capable* and *responsible* to .76 for *imaginative* with a median of .56. These reliability coefficients for the five-week interval are very similar to the reliabilities of single values reported by Rokeach (1973, p. 28) using Form D with test-retest intervals ranging from three to seven weeks. The reliabilities obtained with Form D were on the whole somewhat higher than those obtained with Form E.

As one would expect, test-retest reliability coefficients were much lower for the 2½-year interval. Table 2.1 shows that for the terminal values the reliability coefficients ranged from .24 for *a sense of accomplishment* to .67 for *salvation* with a median of .39. For the instrumental values the reliability coefficients ranged from .26 for *honest* and *intellectual* to .44 for *loving* with a median of .33. With the longer time interval between test and retest there is obviously a much greater possibility that intervening events can modify the relative importance of particular values among individuals, resulting in lower test-retest reliability coefficients.

TEST-RETEST RELIABILITY FOR VALUE SYSTEMS

The frequency distributions (f) of the test-retest reliability coefficients for terminal and instrumental *value systems* for the five-week and the 2½-year intervals are presented in Table 2.2. It can be seen that the distributions were highly skewed. For the five-week interval the reliabilities ranged from the .30s to the .90s for the terminal value systems and from the .00s to the .90s for the instrumental value systems. The median reliability was .74 for the terminal and .70 for the instrumental. Rokeach (1973, p. 32) has reported similar results with Form E of the Value Survey for short test-retest intervals. He indicates that reliabilities of value systems were somewhat higher when Form D was employed. Once again, however, reliability coefficients were lower when the time interval increased to 2½ years. The distributions were highly skewed (see Table 2.2) and the reliabilities ranged from less than .00 to the .90s for the terminal value systems and from less than .00 to the .80s for the instrumental value systems. The median reliability was .60 for the terminal value systems and .51 for the instrumental value systems. These lower reliabilities when compared to those based on a five-week test-retest interval indicate that greater restructuring of the order of importance of values in each set occurred for respondents over the longer time interval.

Reliabilities for terminal values and for terminal value systems were generally slightly higher than those for instrumental values and for instrumental value systems (compare the medians in Tables 2.1 and 2.2). The evidence summarized by Rokeach shows a similar difference. Why might this be so? Rokeach (1973, p. 34) suggests a number of possible reasons. Terminal values may be learned earlier than instrumental values and thus become stabilized at an earlier age. The list of terminal values may involve a more complete list of values than the list of instrumental values and the respondent may therefore be more certain of his rankings. Possibly, also, the values on the terminal list pertain to concepts that are more distinctively different than are those on the instrumental list. There may, of course, be other reasons too.

DISPERSION OF RANKS FOR SINGLE VALUES

Table 2.3 presents the standard deviations of the ranks for each terminal and instrumental value based upon data from all respondents who were tested in two surveys conducted in metropolitan Adelaide in 1972 and 1973. Details about the

TABLE 2-2. Flinders Frequency Distributions of Test-Retest Reliabilities for Terminal and Instrumental Value Systems (Form E) after a Five-Week and after a 2½-Year Interval

Reliability	Five-week Interval		2½-year Interval	
	Terminal *f*	Instrumental *f*	Terminal *f*	Instrumental *f*
.90–.99	8	1	3	0
.80–.89	20	12	42	27
.70–.79	23	28	55	42
.60–.69	13	10	80	55
.50–.59	6	9	59	59
.40–.49	6	10	47	51
.30–.39	1	2	20	35
.20–.29	0	3	14	22
.10–.19	0	0	21	27
.00–.09	0	2	11	10
Less	0	0	4	19
N =	77	77	356	347
Median =	.74	.70	.60	.51

Note. Because respondents had to give error-free rankings on both occasions before reliability coefficients could be calculated, *N*s are less than the total *N* tested since some errors in ranking did occur.
Source: Data adapted from Feather, 1971c; Feather, 1973d.

samples are reported in Chapter 6. It is sufficient to note here that the samples were based upon a multistage cluster sampling frame used to generate a random sample of dwellings and that respondents were 14 years of age and above.

Table 2.3 shows that the standard deviations were very similar for both the 1972 and the 1973 survey data. In each case the rankings of *a comfortable life* and *salvation* had the highest variance among the terminal values and the rankings of *social recognition* and *true friendship* the lowest variance. Also in each case the rankings of *ambitious* and *clean* had the highest variance among the instrumental values and the rankings of *honest* and *responsible* the lowest variance. More information is conveyed by the actual frequency distributions for each value; these are not presented here but the relevant information for United States samples is reported by Rokeach (1973, Appendix B). Table 2.3 merely provides an overall comparison for relatively large, heterogeneous samples.

EFFECTS OF DIFFERENT ASSESSMENT PROCEDURES

In evaluating the results of studies in which a particular measurement procedure is used, it is always important to consider to what extent the *method* of assessment influences the results obtained. One would like to be confident that the results are not specific to the method employed but are stable enough to emerge when other procedures are used (Campbell & Fiske, 1959). In regard to the Value Survey, it can be asked: To what extent are the results obtained influenced by the particular method of assessment, namely ranking, that it involves? Might the average value system for a group be different if one used a rating procedure or, alternatively, a pair-comparison procedure? These three methods of data collection require different types of judgment. Respondents who rate values along a scale of importance respond to each value separately and presumably the absolute importance of the value is more salient than its relative importance. Ranking and pair-comparison procedures, on the other hand, are concerned with order relationships between values, with relative importance rather than with absolute importance, comparisons between values being integral to these procedures. One might therefore expect ranking and pair-comparison procedures to yield rather similar results inasmuch as both involve relative judgments, whereas results might be less similar when either the ranking or pair-comparison procedure is compared with a rating procedure.

Our study (1973c) is relevant to these issues. In this study mode of presentation of the values was varied in three ways: ranking, rating, and pair-comparison. In addition, the order of presentation of the value sets was varied so that either the set of terminal values preceded the set of instrumental values (the usual order) or vice versa. Since the terminal—and instrumental—values could be presented in three different ways, as just noted, and since there were two dif-

TABLE 2-3. Standard Deviations of Rankings for Terminal and Instrumental Values Based Upon Data from All Respondents to the 1972 and 1973 Adelaide Surveys (Form D)
(Total Ns = 587 and 667 Respectively)

Terminal Value	SDs		Instrumental Value	SDs	
	1972	1973		1972	1973
A comfortable life	5.19	5.22	Ambitious	5.37	5.47
An exciting life	4.93	4.64	Broad-minded	5.01	5.01
A sense of accomplishment	4.61	4.42	Capable	4.55	4.45
A world at peace	4.30	4.84	Cheerful	4.72	4.57
A world of beauty	4.44	4.42	Clean	5.23	5.24
Equality	5.19	5.05	Courageous	5.07	4.90
Family security	4.20	3.90	Forgiving	4.61	4.60
Freedom	4.21	4.28	Helpful	4.63	4.71
Happiness	3.87	3.76	Honest	3.86	3.67
Inner harmony	4.48	4.40	Imaginative	4.48	4.49
Mature love	4.85	4.81	Independent	5.14	4.94
National security	4.63	4.69	Intellectual	4.37	4.63
Pleasure	4.10	4.01	Logical	4.66	4.66
Salvation	5.84	5.83	Loving	4.73	4.85
Self-respect	4.56	4.31	Obedient	4.52	4.31
Social recognition	3.69	3.96	Polite	4.44	4.47
True friendship	3.76	3.75	Responsible	4.17	4.15
Wisdom	4.41	4.30	Self-controlled	4.80	4.78

ferent orders of presentation of the value sets (terminal-instrumental or instrumental-terminal), there were altogether 18 different ways of presenting the two value sets. For example, the usual Rokeach procedure would correspond to terminal (ranking) followed by instrumental (ranking). But there were 17 other possible modes of presentation of the value sets in addition to the Rokeach procedure. For example, instrumental (pair-comparison) could be followed by terminal (rating), or terminal (ranking) could be followed by instrumental (rating). The study was therefore designed to vary modes of presentation in all the various ways possible. The 18 different forms of the Value Survey were randomly distributed in approximately equal numbers to 382 respondents (214 male, 168 female) who were students at Flinders University, enrolled in undergraduate courses in introductory psychology in 1970 and 1971. Respondents completed the tests anonymously.

The *ranking* procedure was the same as that used in Form E of the Rokeach Value Survey, as described above. In the *rating* procedure, respondents used a scale divided into eight equal parts numbered 1 to 8 with two labels at the extremes—"Not important at all" at the low end and "Very important" at the high end. As in the ranking procedure, the values were presented in alphabetical order with the usual descriptive phrases. Respondents were asked to "put a cross on the rating scale to indicate how important each value is to you. Do not hesitate to use the extremes. The labels are for your guidance." In the *pair-comparison* procedure a random order of the 153 possible pairs of values from each set of 18 values was determined. Each value was accompanied by the usual short descriptive phrase. We advised the respondents that we were "interested in finding out the relative importance of these values for you. For each pair of values put a circle around the value which is more important to you."

The results were analyzed in the following way: To obtain average value systems, mean and median rankings, ratings, and "vote counts" were calculated corresponding to ranking, rating, and pair-comparison procedures. The vote count for each value for any respondent was defined as the number of times that value was chosen as more important in the 17 pairs in which it was paired with another value. Both means and medians were calculated so as to discover whether there was much variation in the average value systems depending upon the type of average (mean or median) that was employed. The average value systems based upon the three different assessment procedures and involving the two kinds of average were compared for similarity using Spearman rho and Kendall tau.

Tables 2.4 and 2.5 show the average value systems for the terminal and instrumental values respectively, and Table 2.6 presents the similarity indexes. These results indicate quite clearly that the average value systems were very similar across the three different assessment procedures. It made little difference whether respondents ranked the values from 1 to 18 in order of importance, rated the values from 1 to 8 for degree of importance, or chose the more important value from all possible pairs. The final average order of importance

TABLE 2-4. Average Value Systems for Terminal Values in Relation to Three Different Flinders Assessment Procedures

Terminal Value	Medians			Means		
	Ranking	Rating	Vote Count	Ranking	Rating	Vote Count
N	122	129	107	122	129	107
A comfortable life	14.48	5.56	3.88	13.93	5.17	4.46
An exciting life	10.22	6.74	7.55	10.02	6.58	7.68
A sense of accomplishment	8.21	6.66	7.86	8.66	6.29	8.29
A world at peace	6.17	7.48	13.25	6.85	6.79	12.13
A world of beauty	12.05	6.41	6.96	11.47	6.15	7.12
Equality	7.20	7.02	11.36	8.23	6.73	10.86
Family security	10.00	6.84	8.89	10.02	6.67	8.95
Freedom	4.79	7.24	12.77	5.92	7.01	12.17
Happiness	6.17	7.24	8.29	7.11	7.02	8.72
Inner harmony	5.89	7.28	11.08	7.39	6.91	10.58
Mature love	4.90	7.51	11.94	6.32	7.18	11.50
National security	15.11	5.75	2.56	14.65	5.40	4.07
Pleasure	14.11	5.36	4.77	13.48	5.21	5.21
Salvation	16.07	3.96	1.47	12.78	4.24	5.10
Self-respect	7.21	6.62	9.58	7.66	6.53	9.64
Social recognition	14.47	5.09	2.68	13.92	4.77	3.81
True friendship	5.21	7.55	12.13	5.94	7.19	11.64
Wisdom	5.80	6.99	11.33	6.66	6.78	11.06

Note. For rankings, lower numbers denote higher relative importance. For ratings and vote counts, higher numbers denote higher relative importance.
*N*s are for error-free rankings.
Source: Data from Feather, 1973c.

TABLE 2-5. Average Value Systems for Instrumental Values in Relation to Three Different Flinders Assessment Procedures

Instrumental Value	Medians			Means		
	Ranking	Rating	Vote Count	Ranking	Rating	Vote Count
	N 124	129	115	124	129	115
Ambitious	9.80	6.18	5.53	10.03	5.91	5.84
Broad-minded	5.73	7.24	11.15	6.97	7.02	10.45
Capable	8.88	6.36	8.36	9.18	6.33	8.39
Cheerful	8.93	6.40	9.31	9.52	6.32	8.82
Clean	15.00	5.31	2.64	14.17	5.20	3.71
Courageous	7.83	6.92	10.54	8.72	6.73	10.17
Forgiving	7.59	7.17	12.00	8.52	6.94	11.22
Helpful	7.50	6.61	11.22	8.36	6.46	10.53
Honest	3.33	7.31	13.67	5.27	7.17	12.79
Imaginative	10.78	5.82	8.73	10.46	5.59	8.17
Independent	8.89	6.64	9.00	8.99	6.32	8.93
Intellectual	9.43	6.00	6.57	9.36	5.86	7.46
Logical	10.43	6.12	7.45	10.27	5.95	7.48
Loving	6.25	6.90	13.44	7.48	6.71	12.66
Obedient	15.33	4.98	1.54	14.62	4.80	2.99
Polite	14.00	5.65	4.20	13.26	5.39	5.07
Responsible	4.83	6.89	11.35	6.17	6.72	10.99
Self-controlled	9.27	6.19	7.29	9.65	5.92	7.31

Note. For rankings, lower numbers denote higher relative importance. For ratings and vote counts, higher numbers denote higher relative importance. *N*s are for error-free rankings.
Source: Data from Feather, 1973c.

across respondents turned out to be much the same. And this was also so regardless of whether the averages were means or medians or whether the similarity coefficients were rhos or taus.

Table 2.6 also shows that for the terminal values the average value systems based upon ranking and pair-comparison procedures were more similar to each other than those based upon either of these procedures and the rating procedure, when type of average (median or mean) was held constant. (Compare the similarity coefficients in the small triangular matrices above the diagonal.) This greater similarity for procedures involving relative judgments did not occur, however, in relation to average value systems for the set of instrumental values. (Compare the similarity coefficients in the small triangular matrices below the diagonal.)

TABLE 2-6. Similarity Indexes Comparing Average Value Systems across Three Different Flinders Assessment Conditions

Average Value System	Medians			Means		
	Ranking	Rating	Vote Count	Ranking	Rating	Vote Count
Medians						
Ranking		.90 (.72)	.93 (.83)	.97 (.88)	.93 (.79)	.93 (.80)
Rating	.94 (.83)		.89 (.74)	.87 (.67)	.98 (.90)	.87 (.69)
Vote Count	.92 (.78)	.91 (.76)		.91 (.77)	.87 (.71)	.98 (.92)
Means						
Ranking	.99 (.96)	.93 (.82)	.91 (.76)		.91 (.72)	.95 (.83)
Rating	.95 (.85)	.98 (.91)	.91 (.77)	.93 (.81)		.87 (.71)
Vote Count	.93 (.79)	.91 (.78)	.99 (.96)	.93 (.80)	.92 (.77)	

Note. Similarity indexes for average terminal value systems are above the diagonal; similarity indexes for average instrumental value systems are below the diagonal. Similarity indexes not in parentheses are Spearman rhos; similarity indexes in parentheses are Kendall taus. Higher similarity indexes indicate greater similarity between the average value systems involved in the comparison.
Source: Data are from Feather, 1973c.

When one examines the cross-correlations in the small rectangular matrices in Table 2.6 it is apparent that the similarity coefficients were highest in the diagonal cells of these matrices, that is, where (for each cell) the assessment procedure was constant but the type of average (median or mean) varied. Apparently, use of either type of average determined very similar average value systems when the same assessment procedure was employed. Moreover, even when different types of average and different assessment procedures were involved, the average value systems were still quite similar. (Compare the similarity coefficients not in the diagonal cells in the small rectangular matrices in Table 2.6.)

It is still useful, however, to compare the three procedures in regard to their relative advantages and disadvantages (see Feather, 1973c, pp. 228–230). Most of the arguments in favor of the ranking procedure (especially the gummed-label form of the Value Survey) have already been given. Its main disadvantages are that it is ipsative (and this poses some problems of statistical analysis because of lack of independence), and that it can only be used with fairly small sets of values, the ranking procedure becoming far too demanding with large sets. Furthermore, the fact that ties are not allowed—respondents are instructed to discriminate between all values—makes the task difficult and may foster resentment in those cases where a respondent considers two or more values to be equally important.

The rating procedure avoids these difficulties and can be used quickly. But it has disadvantages too. Ratings are probably more subject to response sets than are rankings. It is apparent in Tables 2.4 and 2.5, for example, that respondents used the top half of the scale in making their ratings, thereby narrowing the degree of discrimination. They may also have been providing easy solutions because ties were fairly common. Finally, the rating procedure, where each value is treated on its own, would be less likely to confront the respondent with the task of searching through his priorities to establish his own value system.

Of the three procedures pair-comparison is least attractive. Although it gets into the fine grain of the comparison process and provides the basis for determining several other indexes (for example, an index of degree of transitivity), it is extremely time-consuming and fatiguing to respondents. It shares with the ranking procedure the disadvantages of being ipsative and of involving forced discriminations because no ties are allowed—one of the two alternatives has to be selected on each occasion.

For practical purposes, therefore, the choice of assessment procedure really lies between the ranking and rating methods. We lean toward Form D of the Value Survey (the gummed-label version) because it is simple to administer and has a wide range of application, it appears better able to capture the concept of a hierarchy of values based upon an individual's own comparisons, and it provides results that can be compared with those obtained in the mainstream of research in this area.

ORDER EFFECTS

Does it make any difference to the relative importance of values if the terminal values are presented before the instrumental values (the usual order) or vice versa? Does the ranking assigned to a value depend upon whether the set in which it is contained is responded to first or second? The study just described involved order of presentation as one of the manipulated variables (Feather, 1973c). The results showed an absence of any general order effects, that is, of effects that occurred for all three assessment procedures. What order effects did emerge were specific to a particular procedure and they were difficult to interpret. They may not be replicable. At the present time, therefore, the evidence suggests that order of presentation of the terminal and instrumental value sets makes little difference to how particular values are ranked in their order of importance.

Other types of order effects that can be investigated relate to the order of presentation of the values within each set. As we have seen, the standard method of presentation is to present the values alphabetically. There is a possibility, therefore, that values met first (those higher up in the alphabetical order) will have some advantage in being ranked higher in importance than those lower down in the list. This type of possible order effect has been discussed by Rokeach (1973, pp. 39–42), drawing upon evidence obtained by Cochrane and Rokeach (1970). They found no order effect for the 18 terminal values but an order effect for the 18 instrumental values, median rankings for the first nine values in alphabetical order being higher than the median rankings for the last nine values. However, Rokeach believes that this effect is not due to some response set but rather happens because, by chance, there are some values in the top half of the instrumental list that are generally regarded as more important than values in the second half.

It would obviously be worthwhile in future research, however, to study the effects of randomizing the order of presentation of the values within each set in comparison to the standard, alphabetical method of presentation. A recent study by Greenstein and Bennett (1974) did in fact use a unique and randomized presentation order of values for each respondent, the orders being generated by a computer program. On the basis of their analysis they concluded that, for all practical purposes, the Value Survey is free of presentation order effects.

RESPONSE ANONYMITY

Rokeach (1973) has reported a study by Kelly, Silverman, and Cochrane (1972), the results of which suggested that the ranking of terminal values cannot be explained as the outcome of a general social desirability response set. No such evidence was available in regard to the instrumental values, however. The whole question of the extent to which the rankings assigned to values can be distorted by respondents so as to make a good impression remains an important one to investigate. Some relevant evidence has been provided in a study of the effects of response anonymity on the assessment of value systems and students' satisfaction with school (Feather, 1973b).

In this investigation, which was part of a very extensive survey involving schools in metropolitan Adelaide (Feather, 1972*a*, 1972*b*, 1972*c*—also Chapters 4 and 5), it was possible to test one group of respondents from a boys' school and another group of respondents from a girls' school under name and anonymous conditions. Both schools were fee-charging, single-sex colleges associated with a particular church. The boys were in their last two years of secondary school education at an Anglican college. Of the 263 boys involved in the study, 127 completed the test under the name condition (writing their names at the top of the first page) and 136 under the anonymous condition (no names required). The girls were in their last two years of secondary school education at a Catholic convent. Of the 155 girls involved in the study, 77 completed the test under the name condition and 78 under the anonymous condition.

Because there was not sufficient time available to permit respondents to rank both sets of terminal and instrumental values, the questionnaires were randomly distributed so that approximately half of the respondents ranked the terminal values only while the remaining respondents ranked the instrumental values only. Each set of values was ranked in two ways, first in relation to self (the usual instruction), then in relation to school attended, respondents being asked to

> assume that your school is attempting to turn out children with certain kinds of values, some of which the school considers to be more important than others. . . . Think of a student who has these values that the school strives to emphasize and think of the order in which the school would emphasize them. (Feather, 1973*b*, p. 142)

The values were presented as in Form E of the Value Survey, that is, alphabetically with each value accompanied by a short descriptive phrase, and numbers from 1 to 18 were used to rank the values for self and then for school.

When respondents had finished the two sets of rankings, either under name or anonymous conditions, they then completed a modified form of the Cornell Job Description Index (Smith, Kendall, & Hulin, 1969) applied to the school situation. This test will be described more fully in Chapter 4. It required respondents to check lists of 18 items as they applied to *schoolwork, people in my class,* and *the typical teacher* in order that satisfaction scores could be obtained for these three different aspects of the school situation. Finally, respondents rated how much they enjoyed being at school by putting a cross on a 5-inch scale labeled "Very happy at school" at one end, "Don't like school at all" at the other, and "Moderately happy at school" in the middle. Responses were scored from 1 to 9 in the direction of increasing happiness, with the figure 5 spanning the midpoint of the scale.

What were the main results? The detailed tables are presented in the original report (Feather, 1973*b*). When differences in the transformed rankings of single values were investigated between the name and anonymous conditions using the analysis of variance, very few differences were significant at the conservative *alpha* level adopted ($p < .01$): In the boys' school being *independent* was ranked as more important in the name condition than in the anonymous condition, irrespective of whether respondents ranked for self or for school. Also in the boys' school being *clean* and *salvation* were both ranked relatively high in importance in the anonymous condition when rankings were made in regard to the school's priorities. Neither of these effects was significant in the analysis of data from the girls' school.

The following statistically significant differences emerged when the more specific attitudinal measures concerning the school situation were analyzed: In the boys' school respondents in the anonymous condition reported less satisfaction with *people in my class* ($p < .05$), less satisfaction with *the typical teacher* ($p < .05$), and provided lower ratings of happiness with school ($p < .01$) than did respondents in the name condition. In the girls' school, respondents reported more satisfaction with *schoolwork* ($p < .05$) and provided higher ratings of happiness with school ($p < .05$) in the anonymous condition than in the name condition.

In summary, therefore, there was very little evidence that response anonymity had much effect when each value was considered separately. Nor was there evidence of anonymity effects when the average value systems were compared using factor-analytic procedures (for these results see Feather, 1973*b*). What few differences emerged in the value rankings between the name and anonymous conditions occurred for the boys and not for the girls and they have been discussed elsewhere, together with the differences involving the attitudinal measures (Feather, 1973*b*, pp. 147–148).

It would be premature to generalize from these results, however, and conclude that it makes no difference to the value rankings whether respondents identify themselves or answer anonymously. In the first place the study just described involved only two schools. Obviously, if one is interested in educational settings, a much wider sampling is required in future studies. Second, it would be important to explore situations in which a clear connection existed between test responses and positive and negative consequences. Boys and girls in the two schools might have seen their answers in relation to possible benefits and costs in the school situation (for example, social approval or disapproval), but in future studies the contingencies could well be more clearly established. One can easily imagine situations where certain values might be ranked high or low in the interests of attaining rewards or avoiding punishments. If the respondent was an applicant for a job in a highly competitive business organization, for example, he might rank *a sense of accomplishment* and being *ambitious* very high if he thought that the survey was being used for selection purposes. Similarly, an employee who wished to be transferred to another section in his firm might provide low satisfaction scores on the Job Description Index in relation to his present situation. This type of deliberate faking, for which there is plenty of evidence (Anastasi, 1968, pp. 456–458), would be unlikely to occur if responses were anonymous because answers could not then be attributed to the person responsible for them. When a person's responses can be identified (as when names are required at the top of a test), any rewards or punishments consequential upon his answers can then flow to him. Thus, "whether anonymity or lack of anonymity has an effect on our subjects' responses would therefore depend very much upon the goal structure of the test situation, particularly upon the rewards and/or punishments contingent upon the answers given" (Feather, 1973*b,* p. 149). Clearly, there is scope for further studies involving the Value Survey in which the goal structure of the test situation is varied and the degree of distortion of responses is investigated under both name and anonymous conditions. In real-life settings, where rankings of particular values may be seen to influence possible outcomes, respondents who can be identified by name may provide value rankings that do not reflect their own priorities at all but which are seen as maximizing benefits and minimizing costs.

The tendency for respondents to "fake good" would depend not only upon their being motivated to create a favorable impression but also upon their knowing what responses are regarded as favorable (Scott, 1968). Most studies have revealed small or no differences in responses given to self-report inventories by subjects in anonymous and name conditions. When differences have appeared, however, they have usually been consistent with the assumption that subjects would be more likely to "fake good" or to provide socially desirable answers in a condition where they can be singled out by name or some other form of identification (see Elinson & Haines, 1950; Fuller, 1974; Rosen, 1961). As Fuller (1974, p. 295) points out, however, guarantees of anonymity frequently may be ineffective. Those respondents who are more predisposed to social desirability bias may be more likely to be suspicious about assurances of anonymity (see also Becker & Bakal, 1970), thereby diminishing the possibility of finding differences in responses under name and anonymous conditions.

THE STRUCTURE OF VALUES: DIMENSIONS AND CLUSTERS

ROKEACH'S FACTOR-ANALYTIC STUDIES

A study by Feather and Peay (in press) used multidimensional scaling to investigate the structure of the terminal and instrumental values in terms of the dimensions that might be assumed to underlie them. Multidimensional scaling and factor-analytic techniques enable one to discover whether it might be possible to reduce a set of variables (for example, a set of test items) that have been intercorrelated or for which other pair-wise similarity measures have been obtained, to a smaller number of dimensions or factors. For example, a factor analysis of a correlation matrix involving a large number of intelligence test items might reveal that, given certain assumptions, one can "explain" the intercorrelations between the items by reference to a smaller set of abilities (such as verbal ability, numerical ability, mechanical ability, and so forth). In a corresponding way, one might be able to account for the intercorrelations between the rankings assigned by respondents to the values on Rokeach's lists by using dimensions or factors that are smaller in number than the original set of values. These dimensions can be named (at least tentatively) by inspecting the output that emerges from the analysis. For example, in the case of factor analysis, the naming of the factors would follow examination of the matrix of factor weightings or loadings. Some of the more common multivariate analytic procedures have been described by Comrey (1973) and by Coombs, Dawes, and Tversky (1970).

Rokeach (1973) has already provided some relevant evidence about the dimensional structure of the Value Survey by using factor-analytic procedures. He intercorrelated the rankings obtained in 1968 for the 36 values from 1,409 adult Americans over 21 in the National Opinion Research Center (NORC) area probability sample. He found that the resulting 36 × 36 correlation matrix involved relatively low correlations between the values. They ranged from +.35 (between *a comfortable life* and *pleasure*) to −.32 (between *a comfortable life* and *wisdom*). Of the correlations about 58 percent were negative and 42 percent were positive. The average intercorrelation among the 18 terminal values was −.06; it was also −.06 among the 18 instrumental values. According to Rokeach, one would expect these average intercorrelations to be slightly negative because the measures are ipsative within each set of values. The average correlation between the terminal and instrumental values was .01, and very few of these correlations were substantial. On the basis of these results Rokeach concluded that for the most part the 36 values of the Value Survey were negligibly correlated with one another in the adult American population.

When the 36 × 36 correlation matrix was factor-analyzed (principal factor solution with iteration using the varimax rotation technique), seven bipolar factors emerged but none accounted for more than 8 percent of the variance and all factors together accounted for only 41 percent of the variance. The following factors emerged (with the poles of each factor identified by those values having the highest weightings): Immediate vs. delayed gratification (*a comfortable life, pleasure* versus *wisdom, inner harmony*), competence versus religious morality (*logical, imaginative* versus *forgiving, salvation*), self-constriction versus self-expansion (*obedient, polite* versus *broad-minded, capable*), social versus personal orientation (*a world at peace, national security* versus *true friendship, self-respect*), societal versus family security (*a world of beauty, equality* versus *family security, ambitious*), respect versus love (*social recognition, self-respect* versus *mature love, loving*), other-directed versus inner-directed (*polite* versus *courageous, independent*). When various subgroups of the total 1968 sample were investigated, similar factors again emerged. Moreover, Rokeach obtained similar clusterings with Guttman's nonmetric technique (Guttman, 1966). When "smallest space analysis" was applied, however, the values formed a "circumplex" or circular structure, indicating to Rokeach that the values were at the same level of generality. More recently, Rokeach (1974) has provided information about similar analyses of the interrelationships between the rankings of all 36 terminal and instrumental values using a NORC sample of 1,429 adult Americans over 21 tested in 1971. The results were essentially similar to those obtained with the 1968 sample for the first six factors, leading Rokeach to conclude that it was unlikely that the 36 values could be reduced to a smaller number of values.

A recent Australian study by Dwyer (1974) has also reported the results of a factor analysis applied to the intercorrelations of rankings on the 36 values obtained from a sample of farmers. The factors emerging from Dwyer's analysis were very similar to those reported by Rokeach.

MULTIDIMENSIONAL SCALING AND CLUSTERING

The study by Feather and Peay used multidimensional scaling techniques rather than factor-analytic procedures to examine the structure of terminal and instrumental values. It also employed a method recently developed by Peay (1974) to determine how variables cluster. These techniques were thought to have an advantage over factor-analysis because they require only rank-order properties of the data. Moreover, it was considered important to apply the procedures not only to the 36 × 36 correlation matrix involving the combined set of terminal and instrumental values (the correlation matrix investigated by Rokeach), but also to the 18 × 18 correlation matrix for the terminal values alone and the 18 × 18 correlation matrix for the instrumental values alone. Rokeach did not report analyses based upon the separate consideration of terminal and instrumental values. But such analyses are important to conduct because the two sets of values are ranked independently, each value being related to every other value within each set. One is on less secure ground when considering intercorrelations involving the entire set of 36 values for at no time are all of these values ranked together. In calculating correlation coefficients for the entire set of 36 one therefore assumes that the ranks obtained from the separate rankings of the 18 terminal and 18 instrumental values have the same significance—for example, that a terminal value ranked 1 in the terminal set by a respondent must be equivalent in importance to the instrumental value he ranks 1 in the instrumental set, and so forth. This assumption could easily be in error. For example, had the respondent been given the opportunity to consider all 36 values together he might have had no difficulty at all in distinguishing between the importance of terminal and instrumental values that had been assigned the same order in the separate rankings of the two value sets.

Two samples of respondents were involved in the study, one a group of 548 students at Flinders University and the other a group of 530 students at the Mitchell College of Advanced Education, both of whom completed Form E of the Rokeach Value Survey in 1969 and 1971, respectively (Feather, 1970*b;* Feather & Collins, 1974). For each of the two data sets, Spearman rhos were obtained for the complete set of 36 values. The 36 × 36 correlation matrix that resulted contained an 18 × 18 matrix involving the intercorrelations of rankings between the 18 terminal values (T-T), a similar 18 × 18 matrix for the instrumental values (I-I), and an 18 × 18 matrix involving the cross-correlations between the terminal and instrumental values (T-I). Because of missing data and because some students made errors in ranking, the number of cases for Flinders upon which the Terminal-Terminal, the Instrumental-Instrumental, and the Terminal-Instrumental sets of intercorrelations were based were: T-T, 514; I-I, 501; T-I, 479. For Mitchell, they were: T-T, 506; I-I, 509; T-I, 493.

These correlations were taken as measures of the proximity between pairs of values and they were subjected to two kinds of structural analysis: Multidimensional scaling involving the Young and Torgerson TORSCA-9 procedure (Young, 1968) and a clustering procedure developed by Peay (1974). The multidimensional scaling analysis enabled a representation in Euclidean space for the data elements on the basis of merely ordinal information about their interrelationships. A geometric representation was sought in which the order of the interpoint distances maximally reproduced the (inverse) ordering of the data interpoint proximities (higher positive correlations imply shorter interpoint distances). For each set, Flinders and Mitchell, a geometric representation was derived for all 36 values, for the 18 terminal values alone, and for the 18 instrumental values alone. A sufficiently good fit in five dimensions was found for the full set of 36 values, and in four dimensions for the terminal values alone and the instrumental values alone, based upon examination of acceptable "stress" or "goodness of fit" values (Kruskal, 1964). The solution configuration produced by TORSCA-9 was rotated according to a varimax criterion so that successive dimensions accounted for decreasing amounts of variation.

Peay's (1974) clustering procedure was used to derive groupings of values that reflected high proximities. The proximity criterion selected was the correlation level required for significance of relationship ($p < .05$, one-tailed). Hence, all groupings of values were identified for which every pair of values in the same group showed a correlation (interpoint proximity) greater than this criterion level.

We will not report the results of the multidimensional scaling procedure for both groups, Flinders and Mitchell, since the solutions were very similar, supporting the reliability of the dimensions that emerged. Instead, only the solutions for the Flinders data will be presented. The detailed coordinates used to define each dimension are given in Feather and Peay (in press). It will be noted that the same criticism that applied to Rokeach's factor-analysis also applies to the multidimensional scaling of the 36 × 36 value matrix in the present study because the ranks may not be comparable across the terminal and instrumental value sets. But this criticism does not apply to the *separate* analyses of the terminal and instrumental value sets.

Some possible interpretations of the five dimensions that emerged in the analysis of all 36 values are as follows:

DIMENSION 1: Appeared to contrast discipline and virtue with ability and outer-directedness. It paralleled Rokeach's "self-constriction" versus "self-expansion" and contrasted the following values: *obedient, responsible, family security, self-control* versus *imaginative, intellectual, broad-minded, an exciting life.*

DIMENSION 2: Appeared to distinguish between concern for oneself and concern with others and contrasted the following values: *capable, ambitious, a comfortable life, an exciting life* versus *forgiving, helpful, loving, a world of beauty.*

DIMENSION 3: Appeared to distinguish between achievement orientation and a pleasant state of being, between achievement and competence on the one hand and serenity on the other. It contrasted the following values: *wisdom, a sense of accomplishment, logical, self-respect* versus *cheerful, happiness, pleasure, clean, family security, a comfortable life.*

DIMENSION 4: Appeared to correspond to Rokeach's "personal" versus "social" orientation and contrasted the following values: *social recognition, true friendship, mature love, happiness* versus *a world at peace, freedom, national security, equality.*

DIMENSION 5: Paralleled to some extent Rokeach's "immediate" versus "delayed" gratification but was difficult to interpret. It contrasted the following values: *clean, polite, a comfortable life, cheerful, pleasure* versus *inner harmony, courageous, self-respect, self-controlled.*

Some possible interpretations of the four dimensions that emerged when the 18 terminal values were analyzed separately are as follows:

DIMENSION 1: Appeared to distinguish altruistic or "noble" values from hedonistic values and involved the following contrasts: *wisdom, equality, a world of beauty* versus *a comfortable life, pleasure, happiness.*

DIMENSION 2: Appeared to distinguish between serenity or self-realization and initiative and accomplishment. It contrasted the following values: *salvation, inner harmony, family security* versus *a sense of accomplishment, a comfortable life, an exciting life.*

DIMENSION 3: Distinguished between personal and social values and clearly corresponded to Rokeach's "personal" versus "social" orientation. It contrasted the following values: *social recognition, self-respect, a sense of accomplishment* versus *a world at peace, equality, freedom.*

DIMENSION 4: Was more difficult to interpret but appeared to involve a distinction between fulfillment and safety. It contrasted the following values: *mature love, a world of beauty, an exciting life* versus *national security, family security, equality.*

Some possible interpretations of the four dimensions that emerged when the 18 instrumental values were analyzed separately are as follows:

DIMENSION 1: Appeared to distinguish between virtuous or approved values and self-reliance and competence values. The values involved in the contrast were as follows: *honest, obedient, helpful* versus *intellectual, logical, imaginative, independent.*

DIMENSION 2: Appeared to distinguish between a self-assertive and achievement orientation and an altruistic orientation involving concern for others. It contrasted the following values: *ambitious, capable, independent, responsible* versus *loving, forgiving, helpful, polite.*

DIMENSION 3: Paralleled Rokeach's "other-directed" versus "inner-directed" orientation and appeared to distinguish between adherence to social norms and an individual or independent orientation. It contrasted the following values: *clean, polite, obedient, cheerful* versus *courageous, independent, imaginative.*

DIMENSION 4: Appeared to distinguish between an ascetic or self-disciplined orientation and a warm, humane orientation. It resembled Rokeach's "self-constriction" versus "self-expansion" dimension and involved the following contrasting values: *self-controlled, responsible, logical, obedient* versus *cheerful, broad-minded, imaginative, loving.*

It can be seen that the dimensions that emerged from the nonmetric multidimensional scaling analysis partially overlapped those reported by Rokeach (1973, 1974) when the analysis involved all 36 values. But fewer dimensions (four or five) emerged in our investigation than in the Rokeach studies (six or seven). The detailed results (not reported here) showed that the coordinates of the values were spread fairly evenly across each dimension. There was little evidence of distinctive clumping of values along a dimension. Hence, it would be difficult to isolate representative subgroups of values using the multidimensional analysis although, as we have seen, in most cases interpretation of the dimensions was reasonably straightforward.

When the clustering procedure was applied to the similarities (the original correlations) for the Flinders and Mitchell terminal and instrumental values, the results of the analyses showed that the sets of groupings of the terminal values were quite similar for the Flinders and Mitchell data but the groupings of the instrumental values differed. At the arbitrary criterion level selected, there were more identifiable subgroupings of instrumental values for the Flinders data than for the Mitchell data. Very few clusters involving more than three values emerged from the clustering analyses.

These different analyses (multidimensional scaling and clustering), therefore, yielded no firm basis for reducing the sets of values in the Rokeach Value Survey to a smaller number. Moreover, the results of the multidimensional scaling analysis provided quite encouraging evidence that a useful value domain has been captured by Rokeach's value set because the distribution of values was fairly homogeneous throughout the solution space, the dimensions were interpretable, and the value structures for the Flinders and Mitchell data were essentially quite similar.

OTHER STUDIES

In this chapter we have dealt mainly with research issuing from the Flinders program that relates to the Value Survey as an assessment device. In the course of discussion we have also referred to research emanating from Rokeach's program concerned with test-retest reliability, social desirability, and the structure of terminal and instrumental values.

To round out the picture we should note that Rokeach (1973) provides information about some other questions regarding the Value Survey as an assessment procedure. Thus, he reviews the various measures that might be obtained with the rank-ordering procedure and related investigations using these measures; he reports research in which value importance is related to the strength of needs as indexed by projective measures of n Achievement, n Affiliation, and n Power (Rokeach & Berman, 1971); and he discusses the question of the meaning of values (one that we have already raised in the previous chapter and will again take up subsequently).

Rokeach concludes that the Value Survey emerges from these studies as a useful all-purpose instrument for research on human values with many positive advantages. Most of the results reported in the present chapter support that conclusion. Over the short term, test-retest reliabilities are of respectable magnitude; average value systems do not seem to depend upon the particular method (ranking) that the Value Survey employs; it seems to make very little difference whether the terminal values are ranked before the instrumental values or vice versa or whether, when answering the test, respondents give their names or respond anonymously (although there remains the possibility that value rankings could be influenced by the kind of impression the respondent wants to make, especially in settings where the benefits and costs of response are important); and the value domain involved in the Value Survey appears to involve a fairly wide and heterogeneous sample of values, not readily reducible to smaller sets. On these grounds, we were encouraged to use the Value Survey as the basic instrument in our research program. In the next chapter we review those studies from the program relevant to values and educational choice.

3. Values and Educational Choice

LET US NOW consider the studies from the Flinders program that have been concerned with the problem of educational choice. The studies will be presented sequentially in order to underscore the development that occurred in the research program from fairly simple ideas and procedures to rather more sophisticated concepts and research strategies.

EDUCATIONAL CHOICE: EARLY STUDIES

THE 1969 FLINDERS STUDY OF EDUCATIONAL CHOICE

The earliest investigation of this problem (Feather, 1970*b*) dealt with the question of whether a student entering the university for the first time will choose a faculty or school or program of studies related to the values he holds. For example, one might expect that a student who places a high value on being logical would be more likely to gravitate toward science subjects in the curriculum whereas a student who assigns great importance to being intellectual and imaginative would be more likely to enroll for courses in humanities. This is not to say that students' choices among educational alternatives are *dominated* by their values. Indeed, a student's value priorities may be relatively unimportant factors in influencing these choices when compared with other considerations. For instance, his record of accomplishments in the past, his information about his own abilities, the difficulty level of the alternatives with which he is confronted, are among other factors (some of them beyond his control) that might push him in a particular direction. Even so, one might expect educational choice to bear some relationship to value priorities, however small this relationship might be. And there is some evidence to support this expectation. For example, Dukes (1955, p. 28) describes studies involving the Allport-Vernon-Lindzey "Study of Values" in which the educational choices made by students were related to the relative importance of values they held. And theories of vocational choice have assigned an important role to personality variables including needs, interests, attitudes, and values (Holland, 1966, 1973; Rosenberg, 1957).

It was possible to test this general hypothesis early in 1969 when incoming students at Flinders University, in Adelaide, South Australia, were involved in an orientation program in the course of which they completed a number of psychological tests. In these test sessions Form E of the Value Survey was the first test they answered and it was presented in the usual manner, that is, with the values arranged alphabetically together with the short definitions of each value. Students wrote their names at the top of the survey, indicated the school they proposed to work in while at the university, and then ranked each set of values in relation to their own priorities according to the usual instructions. At that time there were four schools at Flinders University—Humanities, Social Sciences, Physical Sciences, and Biological Sciences—and these involved the following disciplines: drama, English, fine arts, French, music, philosophy, Spanish (Humanities); American studies, economics, education, geography, history, politics, psychology, social administration (Social Sciences); applied mathematics, chemistry, earth sciences, mathematics, physics (Physical Sciences); biology (Biological Sciences). Students who enrolled for a bachelor of science degree or who intended to proceed to professional courses in medicine, dentistry, or agricultural science were required to complete a common first-year course organized jointly by the Physical Sciences and Biological Sciences schools. In the results to be presented, these students are classified as enrolling in sciences. No such common first-year requirement existed in the other two schools of the university where students selected three disciplines from among those offered.

The Value Survey was completed by a total of 530 first-year students, the answers of 67 of whom had to be excluded from the data analysis because they made errors in ranking, either omitting to rank-order one or more values or using the same rank more than once. In later studies, respondents were usually specifically instructed not to leave any blanks and not to use the same rank more than once. The error rate with this addition to the usual instructions for Form E then dropped to between 3 to 6 percent. There remained 463 respondents with usable data and their distribution by school and sex was as follows: Humanities (26 male, 77 female); Social Sciences (89 male, 73 female); Sciences (164 male, 34 female).

The median rankings of the terminal and instrumental values by the Flinders students in relation to the school in which they proposed to work are presented in Tables 3.1 and 3.2 respectively. (Results of a similar survey made two years later at Mitchell College of Advanced Education [CAE] are also shown in the tables; they will be discussed in the next subsection.) Differences in the rankings assigned to each value across schools were analyzed in two different ways, both of which yielded essentially similar results: Kruskal-Wallis one-way analysis of variance (Siegel, 1956), and a 3×2 analysis of variance on the

TABLE 3-1. Median Rankings and Composite Rank Orders of Terminal Values for Students at Flinders University and Mitchell CAE

Terminal Value	Flinders University (1969)				Mitchell CAE (1971)			
	Humanities	Social Sciences	Sciences	All Schools Combined	Business Administration	Teacher Education	General Studies	All Programs Combined
N	103	162	198	463	61	420	25	506
A comfortable life	14.44 (17)	13.28 (14)	12.18 (13)	13.10 (14)	4.83 (2)	13.51 (15)	14.17 (16)	13.00 (15)
An exciting life	9.63 (12)	10.75 (12)	9.12 (12)	9.63 (12)	9.83 (13)	12.40 (12)	12.75 (13)	12.17 (12)
A sense of ac-complishment	7.50 (8)	6.85 (6)	5.71 (4)	6.42 (4)	4.58 (1)	7.94 (10)	8.13 (10)	7.63 (10)
A world at peace	7.23 (6)	7.22 (8)	7.77 (8)	7.44 (8)	8.10 (7)	3.93 (1)	5.25 (2)	4.57 (1)
A world of beauty	10.86 (13)	13.00 (13)	12.94 (15)	12.55 (13)	13.50 (17)	12.50 (13)	11.75 (12)	12.55 (13)
Equality	8.17 (9)	9.21 (10)	8.57 (10)	8.65 (10)	9.70 (12)	6.70 (7)	8.17 (11)	7.28 (9)
Family security	9.56 (11)	9.31 (11)	8.62 (11)	9.11 (11)	6.70 (5)	7.12 (9)	4.25 (1)	6.92 (7)
Freedom	5.07 (3)	5.82 (3)	4.87 (2)	5.19 (3)	5.63 (4)	6.03 (4)	6.25 (4)	6.00 (4)
Happiness	8.23 (10)	6.00 (4)	7.86 (9)	7.45 (9)	5.30 (3)	5.51 (3)	5.38 (3)	5.48 (2)
Inner harmony	7.13 (5)	6.73 (5)	7.46 (7)	7.13 (6)	7.50 (6)	6.67 (6)	7.17 (9)	6.78 (6)
Mature love	5.83 (4)	7.00 (7)	6.76 (5)	6.63 (5)	8.83 (8)	6.09 (5)	7.13 (7.5)	6.29 (5)
National security	13.42 (14)	13.71 (16)	14.13 (17)	13.80 (16)	12.75 (16)	12.65 (14)	13.10 (14)	12.67 (14)
Pleasure	14.27 (16)	13.30 (15)	12.89 (14)	13.32 (15)	10.17 (14)	13.62 (16)	14.06 (15)	13.40 (16)
Salvation	15.28 (18)	14.50 (18)	15.80 (18)	15.30 (18)	15.17 (18)	13.69 (17)	15.70 (18)	14.21 (17)
Self-respect	7.39 (7)	7.31 (9)	7.15 (6)	7.27 (7)	9.13 (11)	8.77 (11)	6.50 (5)	8.74 (11)
Social recognition	13.59 (15)	14.32 (17)	13.88 (16)	14.01 (17)	12.58 (15)	15.04 (18)	14.75 (17)	14.74 (18)
True friendship	4.82 (2)	4.95 (1)	4.74 (1)	4.84 (1)	9.08 (10)	5.35 (2)	6.83 (6)	5.67 (3)
Wisdom	4.34 (1)	5.50 (2)	5.07 (3)	4.89 (2)	8.90 (9)	6.85 (8)	7.13 (7.5)	7.15 (8)

Note. The lower the median the higher the importance of that value. Numbers in parentheses are the rank orders of the medians. *N*s are for error-free rankings.

Source: Adapted from Feather, 1970*b*; Feather & Collins, 1974.

TABLE 3-2. Median Rankings and Composite Rank Orders of Instrumental Values for Students at Flinders University and Mitchell CAE

Instrumental Value	Flinders University (1969)				Mitchell CAE (1971)			
	Humanities	Social Sciences	Sciences	All Schools Combined	Business Administration	Teacher Education	General Studies	All Programs Combined
N	103	162	198	463	62	424	23	509
Ambitious	10.75 (14)	7.80 (6)	7.83 (6)	9.02 (11)	4.83 (1)	11.46 (14)	12.83 (16)	10.70 (13)
Broad-minded	4.96 (2)	4.82 (2)	5.33 (3)	4.98 (3)	6.25 (4)	6.74 (5)	8.25 (6)	6.75 (5)
Capable	10.13 (12)	8.67 (11)	7.95 (7)	8.79 (10)	5.67 (3)	9.68 (9)	10.13 (12)	9.33 (9)
Cheerful	8.50 (8)	7.36 (5)	8.73 (10)	8.21 (7)	10.00 (12)	7.78 (7)	9.75 (9.5)	8.10 (7)
Clean	13.83 (17)	13.64 (17)	13.50 (17)	13.65 (17)	10.86 (16)	10.74 (13)	9.50 (8)	10.73 (14)
Courageous	7.21 (5)	8.44 (10)	8.62 (9)	8.09 (5)	9.67 (10.5)	10.11 (10)	8.83 (7)	10.02 (11)
Forgiving	7.83 (6)	8.22 (9)	9.69 (12)	8.64 (9)	9.33 (9)	5.86 (4)	7.50 (5)	6.29 (4)
Helpful	9.59 (11)	10.19 (12)	9.67 (11)	9.84 (12)	10.67 (15)	7.75 (6)	6.50 (4)	7.90 (6)
Honest	2.83 (1)	3.00 (1)	4.00 (1)	3.39 (1)	6.50 (5)	2.37 (1)	2.50 (1)	2.69 (1)
Imaginative	8.44 (7)	12.80 (16)	12.42 (16)	11.67 (15)	13.67 (18)	13.93 (18)	13.25 (17)	13.85 (18)
Independent	8.92 (9)	7.87 (7)	8.00 (8)	8.13 (6)	9.00 (7)	10.17 (12)	9.90 (11)	9.98 (10)
Intellectual	9.06 (10)	11.43 (14)	11.50 (15)	10.87 (13)	10.40 (14)	13.46 (16)	11.25 (14)	13.08 (16)
Logical	12.06 (16)	11.27 (13)	10.22 (13)	11.17 (14)	9.67 (10.5)	11.71 (15)	12.17 (15)	11.50 (15)
Loving	5.13 (3)	7.25 (4)	7.18 (4)	6.94 (4)	9.20 (8)	4.29 (2)	2.90 (2)	4.74 (2)
Obedient	15.86 (18)	15.00 (18)	15.17 (18)	15.23 (18)	13.50 (17)	13.48 (17)	13.50 (18)	13.49 (17)
Polite	11.79 (15)	12.55 (15)	11.45 (14)	11.81 (16)	10.14 (13)	10.13 (11)	10.83 (13)	10.18 (12)
Responsible	5.81 (4)	4.93 (3)	4.42 (2)	4.88 (2)	5.20 (2)	5.41 (3)	5.75 (3)	5.40 (3)
Self-controlled	10.17 (13)	8.13 (8)	7.69 (5)	8.33 (8)	8.00 (6)	8.42 (8)	9.75 (9.5)	8.47 (8)

Note. The lower the median the higher the relative importance of that value. Numbers in parentheses are the rank orders of the medians. *N*s are for error-free rankings.
Source: Adapted from Feather, 1970*b*; Feather & Collins, 1974.

transformed ranks with schools and sex as the separate factors in the analysis, and with an alpha level of .05 for statistical significance. For purposes of comparison with subsequent findings, only the results of the latter analysis will be presented here (the results of the Kruskal-Wallis analysis can be found in the original publication: Feather, 1970*b*).

In regard to those significant differences that occurred across schools irrespective of the sex of the respondent ("main effects" from the analysis of variance), it was found that students in sciences ranked being *ambitious, responsible,* and *self-controlled* as more important in their priorities than did students who intended to work in the other two schools. Students in humanities ranked *a world of beauty* and being *imaginative* and *intellectual* as more important in their priorities than did students in the other schools. Male science students ranked *a comfortable life* as more important than did the other students. These differences suggest that students enrolling in science courses were more interested in materialistic values, in competence and achievement and in controlling impulses, than were students enrolling in the humanities. The latter were relatively more concerned with aesthetic values and with values involving imagination and the world of ideas. Social science students tended to be intermediate. The value differences between the humanities and science students recall Hudson's (1966) distinction between the "contrary imaginations" of arts and science students, the arts students being more divergent and less controlled in their thinking.

In regard to general sex differences that were statistically significant, males assigned more importance to *pleasure, wisdom* and being *imaginative* and *logical* and less importance to *a world of peace, family security* and being *honest* than did females. These differences were also main effects from the analysis of variance since they occurred for all schools.

THE MITCHELL COLLEGE STUDY OF EDUCATIONAL CHOICE

A similar study was conducted in 1971 at the Mitchell CAE in Bathurst, New South Wales (Feather & Collins, 1974). At the time of the investigation, Mitchell enrolled students in three main programs: business administration, teacher education, and general studies. The main differences between these programs can be indicated in terms of the career possibilities of students graduating from them. Thus, graduates of the business administration course were expected to seek careers in business, public administration, and related fields. Students completing courses in teacher education were qualified for employment in either primary or infants schools, and those completing courses in the general studies program were expected to move into such fields as public relations, welfare communications, and journalism.

A questionnaire consisting of a number of attitude items followed by Form E of the Value Survey was administered to incoming students approximately three weeks after they had enrolled and to all continuing students. Form E was presented in the standard manner, and the 530 respondents completed the questionnaire anonymously. Sixty-six were in business administration (58 male, 8 female), 439 in teacher education (102 male, 336 female, one unidentified person), and 25 in general studies (12 male, 13 female). About 64 percent of the students tested were in their first year of studies at the CAE, the remainder being in their second year. It is evident that the predominance of respondents were female and enrolled in teacher education.

The median rankings of the terminal and instrumental values for all students in relation to the program they were taking are also presented in Tables 3.1 and 3.2. Differences in the rankings assigned to each value were analyzed using a 3 × 2 analysis of variance on the transformed ranks with program of study (3 levels) and sex (2 levels) as the two factors in the analysis and with an alpha level of .05 for statistical significance. Detailed results of the survey with significance levels can be found in the original report (Feather & Collins, 1974).

The following significant main effects from the analysis of variance occurred in relation to program of study: Students in business administration ranked a *comfortable life, social recognition* and being *ambitious* as much more important than did those in the other two programs. Teacher education and general studies students assigned more importance to *a world at peace, mature love, true friendship* and being *honest* and *loving* than did students in business administration. These effects occurred irrespective of whether the respondents were male or female. Thus, the evidence suggested that students entering business studies were relatively more concerned with values relating to achievement, competence, and materialistic gain and with being admired by others, whereas students in the other two programs gave greater weight to moral and social values involving relationships with other people.

The following significant main effects of sex occurred: Males in general tended to rank *a comfortable life, pleasure* and being *imaginative* as relatively more important than did females; females ranked *inner harmony, self-respect, wisdom* and being *forgiving* and *loving* as relatively more important than did males. These effects took place irrespective of the respondents' program of study. There were also some significant interaction effects; these have been reported in the original article (Feather & Collins, 1974).

In the two studies just described, it is important to emphasize that there were general similarities in the ordering of terminal and instrumental values among all respondents irrespective of their sex or the School or program in which they had enrolled. Among the Flinders students, for example, the terminal values *true friendship, wisdom* and *freedom* were all ranked uniformly high and *national security, social recognition* and *salvation* were all ranked uniformly low. Among the instrumental values, the Flinders students ranked *honest, responsible* and *broad-minded* uniformly high and *polite, clean* and *obedient* uniformly low. The average value systems of the Flinders and Mitchell students were also quite similar.

THE CONCEPT OF PERSON-ENVIRONMENT FIT

One of the difficulties that arises in interpreting the kind of results just described is the possibility that a student who has selected a particular course of study may attempt to describe his values according to how he thinks he *ought* to describe them, that is, according to the values he believes are held by those in the field of science, business administration, humanities, or whatever. The student may attempt to show that he is *consistent* by reporting value priorities that are in line with the choice he has already made. Furthermore, once a student has made his choice, he probably begins to internalize some of the values, attitudes, and behavioral patterns that he believes are consequences of the choice he has made—which means that a process of anticipatory socialization is likely to occur (see Rosenberg, 1957, p. 125). The value rankings provided by the student would then be influenced by his decision and particularly by his idea and stereotypes about what the decision entails—for example, his stereotypes about the typical scientist, teacher, social worker. How then might one distinguish between a respondent's own value system and his assumptions about the value systems typical of other types of persons or of groups and institutions and what theoretical significance might such a distinction have? The attempt to answer these questions led into the next study of educational choice.

This third study was based upon the idea that, given a range of options (for example, as between faculties, programs, schools), a student will be biased toward choosing those alternatives that, according to his view, best fit his own personal characteristics. Obviously, his choice will depend upon a lot of other considerations as well, such as whether he has the financial means available to enable him to follow a particular course of study, the degree to which he is influenced by pressures from his parents and others, whether other goals compete with the academic ones, and so on. Yet it is obvious that a mismatch between the characteristics that a person sees himself as having and those that he perceives as being demanded by the work situation may have detrimental consequences leading to failure and personal unhappiness.

PERSON-ENVIRONMENT FIT IN VOCATIONAL PSYCHOLOGY AND EDUCATION

The idea that persons tend to choose environments that they perceive best fit their own personal characteristics (given the availability of choice) is not a new one. In psychology and education the person-environment fit has been related to various aspects of behavior and adjustment on the assumption that the better the fit, the more favorable the consequences for the person (see Hunt, 1971; Pervin, 1968). In regard to vocational selection and adjustment, for instance, Holland (1973) argues that "people search for environments that will let them exercise their skills and abilities, express their attitudes and values, and take on agreeable problems and roles" (p. 4). When there is congruence between one's personality and the environment in which one works, then one is more likely to find evidence of vocational satisfaction, stability, and achievement. Holland develops a theory of personality types and model environments, both of which may be described in terms of the following six categories: realistic, investigative, artistic, social, enterprising, and conventional. Thus, realistic types are assumed to be more likely to select realistic environments, artistic types artistic environments, and so on—each environmental model being conceived as one that involves people of a given dominant type. Holland elaborates upon these ideas and presents procedures that can be used to assess personality and environment, together with relevant evidence about people in environments. In the field of organizational psychology there has also been considerable interest in person-environment fit (Fiedler, 1967; Herzberg, Mausner, & Snyderman, 1959; Schutz, 1966). Similar approaches have been applied to the match between person and environment in educational contexts (Astin & Panos, 1969; Brown, 1962; Mitchell, 1969; Stern, 1970; Hunt, 1971) —much of the general orientation being influenced by Murray's analysis of person-environment interaction in terms of needs and environmental press (Murray, 1938).

In an important contribution to the social psychology of education, Getzels (1969) has viewed the school and the classroom as social systems within a wider cultural context and has analyzed the institutional and individual components of these systems, using the concepts of role and expectation at the institutional level and personality and disposition at the individual level. The school as a social system is influenced by the ethos of the culture or community in which it is embedded, as represented by the values that the wider culture holds to be important. Getzels examines the relationship between the various components of his general model, reviews relevant empirical evidence, and identifies different types of discrepancy that can occur within the system, some of which are relevant to the concept of person-environment fit. These discrepancies affect the functioning of the system in adverse ways, and they may involve incongruities between cultural values and institutional expectations; incongruities between personality dispositions and role expectations; incongruities between and within roles; conflicts deriving from personality disorder; and conflicts arising from personality differences, incongruent interpersonal perceptions, and idiosyncratic definitions of expectations. Again, therefore, we find an emphasis upon the importance of maintaining congruent relationships— in this case between system components.

ORGANISM-ENVIRONMENT FIT IN BIOLOGY AND GENERAL PSYCHOLOGY

From a biological point of view, one can relate the emphasis on person-environment fit to current thought on ecology and adaptation, although one needs to tread carefully when extending evolutionary concepts to human concerns (Mead, 1958; Simpson, 1958). In the animal world, a mismatch between the organism and its environment may have fatal consequences, and species are, therefore, usually found to exist in habitats to which they are adapted. According to Klopfer (1969), the association of a particular species with a particular habitat may be the result of extrinsic factors, as would occur, for example, when the more conspicuously colored members of a species are removed by predators. It may also be due to the physical structure of the animal, which sets limits on its ability to adapt to particular habitats. Or it may be a direct consequence of some psychological preference or choice that the animal exercises, the development of such preferences relating to either the reinforcement properties of the environment, the "imprinting" processes involving neonatal exposure, or the establishment of socially imposed traditions. Underlying these various possible explanations is the general evolutionary principle of natural selection, with its emphasis upon species survival, and a closely related concern with the adaptive processes involved in learning as an organism interacts with particular environments and develops coping behaviors on the basis of concrete experience.

Evolutionary and learning principles have also had a long history in general psychology. Campbell (1974) has traced one aspect of this history in regard to evolutionary concepts and in his own writings (Campbell, 1959, 1960, 1974) looks at inductive achievements, at genuine increases in knowledge, and at the fit of system to environment in relation to a "blind-variation-and-selective-retention process" in which there are assumed to be three essentials: mechanisms for introducing variation, a consistent selection process, and mechanisms for preserving and propagating the selected variations. All psychologists recognize the complex interplay between biological givens and learning processes as organisms develop effective ways of coping with their environments. Skinner (1969, 1974), for example, distinguishes between the ontogeny and the phylogeny of behavior, the former being traceable to contingencies of reinforcement and the latter to contingencies of selection (or survival). He argues that

> The process of operant conditioning . . . supplements natural selection. Important consequences of behavior which could not play a role in evolution because they were not sufficiently stable features of the environment are made effective through operant conditioning during the lifetime of the individual, whose power in dealing with his world is thus vastly increased. (p. 46)

And, Seligman and Hager (1972), in a collection of papers from various sources, present some interesting evidence from the areas of classical conditioning, instrumental learning, avoidance learning, ethology and comparative psychology, and human functioning to show that learning has its biological boundaries:

> The animal may be more or less prepared by the evolution of its species to associate a given CS and US or a given response and reinforcer. . . . the very

laws of learning might vary from one class of situations to another with the preparedness of the animal. (p. 4)

One could go on multiplying examples from the past and from the present, from biological science and from behavioral science, but the conclusion is clear: There is now general agreement about the importance of relating behavior to the physical properties of the environment and the biological equipment of each species and of viewing organisms and environments as interdependent systems, any marked change in the habitat having implications for the species that inhabit it and any marked change in species distribution having implications for the environment in which members of the species live. And in this adaptation, both genetic endowment and the learning that comes with organism-environment interaction are assumed to be involved.

The appeal to some principle of organism-environment fit in accounting for choice and adaptation is, therefore, widespread. Our short discussion has merely provided some illustrations of its application in different areas. It should be evident that, if the approach is to be useful, one needs to fill out the principle by specifying those characteristics of the organism and the environment that are important in the match, why these characteristics rather than some other characteristics are important, what the underlying mechanisms might be, what modes of adaptation might be expected to follow in the event of mismatch, and why some modes of adaptation might be more likely to occur than others. In regard to human adaptation therefore, what is required is a detailed mapping of those personal characteristics that relate to particular environmental characteristics, some theory about why these characteristics are related and what makes certain of them more important than others, some means of specifying how closely the personal characteristics fit particular environments, and some account of the different forms that adaptation may take and under what circumstances these forms will appear.

THE CHOICE OF UNITS

Specifying the units (characteristics) of the person and the corresponding properties of the environment is not an easy task, however, especially when the units are of a psychological nature. At a very basic level, one might identify certain fundamental needs that have to be satisfied by the environment if the organism is to survive and grow to maturity, and the resources that the environment must provide to satisfy these needs. One might also specify general skills and abilities that have to exist or be developed through learning and maturation if a person is to cope with environmental problems. But it should be possible to examine person-environment adaptation in terms of higher order structures as well, structures that may themselves be complex products of person-environment interactions. We think here, for example, of a person's learned motives and interests and the degree to which his environment can satisfy them, of his complex abilities and skills and the extent to which they enable him to solve problems and perform effectively in specialized situations, and of his beliefs, attitudes, and values and their degree of similarity to those that he sees his environment as promoting. Some of these higher order variables have had a lot of attention from psychologists concerned with the task of advising people about suitable work situations for which they might be qualified (as in vocational and educational guidance). Indeed, an emphasis on adaptation and person-environment fit is implicit throughout occupational psychology and in other areas of psychology concerned with adjustment. In the present context, our attention will be directed toward the *value fit* and the degree to which it influences educational choice.

CONCEPTUALIZING DIFFERENT ENVIRONMENTS

Before turning to this question, however, one other important issue needs to be mentioned. So far we have been talking about *the* environment as if it can be easily identified. In fact, a person is exposed to a number of different environments involving physical and social objects in his day-to-day life and over longer time spans. These various environments need to be mapped and systematically described in relation to theoretical frameworks. Some work has already been done in this direction. Indeed, in recent years there has been increased interest among psychologists in developing ways of conceptualizing human environments. Before then there were a few lone pioneers like Murray (1938), Lewin (1951), and Barker (1968) who emphasized the importance of achieving some conceptual representation and means of specifying differences in environments as well as the related task of developing ways of conceptualizing and measuring differences in personalities.

Some of the recent approaches to environmental analysis have been summarized by Moos (1973), who describes six ways of *conceptualizing* environments. They may be distinguished in terms of whether they concentrate upon ecological dimensions, dimensions of organizational structure, the personal characteristics of the milieu inhabitants, behavior settings, their functional or reinforcement properties, or their psychosocial characteristics and organizational climate. Subsequently, Insel and Moos (1974) have argued that the *measurement* of human environments needs to consider relationship dimensions (concerning the nature and intensity of personal relationships within the environment), personal development dimensions (concerning the degree to which the environment provides the opportunity for personal growth and the development of self-esteem), and system maintenance and change dimensions (concerning the extent to which the environment is clear in its expectations, maintains control, and is responsive to change). Insel and Moos claim these three dimensions appear to be involved in scales devised by different investigators to describe and measure various human environments (for example, industrial and educational) and so have considerable generality. This burgeoning interest in describing important features of environments fills an important gap in the study of person-environment relationships. Attempts to develop comprehensive taxonomies of environments are part of a growing interest at a cross-disciplinary level with the study of environments and their effects (see Craik, 1970; Ittelson, Proshansky, Rivlin, & Winkel, 1974; Proshansky, Ittelson, & Rivlin, 1970).

OBJECTIVE OR SUBJECTIVE ENVIRONMENTS?

In addition to the types of analysis just noted, one can approach the description of environments from objective or subjective vantage points, depending upon whether it is the objective or actual situation that is to be described or the environment as perceived by the individual. This distinction between the actual and the perceived situation is one that has a long history in psychology (see, for example, Koffka, 1935; Lewin, 1935; Murray, 1938) and in other disciplines mindful of person-environment interactions (Klausner, 1971). Needless to say, one's perceptions might not mirror reality accurately; the objective and the perceived environments might not coincide. The values a child attributes to his school environment might not correspond at all to the values the school is actually trying to foster. Attributed meaning can be at odds with objective reality.

Just how the objective environment comes to be perceived by individuals and represented in cognition is a basic question that has prompted much speculation and research in the past (see Chapter 1), and one that continues to receive attention not only from cognitive psychologists but also from people in other disciplines, such as geography and architecture. A recent collection of papers by Downs and Stea (1973) reports theory and research dealing with this issue. It is interesting to note that the old ideas of schemata, cognitive maps, and related abstractions, as internal representations of external reality are again being used as key concepts in attempts to deal with the way reality is structured (or constructed) in regard to space and time (see Kaplan, 1973; Lee, 1973).

PERSON-ENVIRONMENT FIT AND DISCREPANCY THEORY

As we indicated in Chapter 1, our own approach also focuses upon cognitive structures. In our research program, we have sidestepped the task of developing ways of classifying different aspects of the person and the environment that can be brought together in some kind of relationship because our interest is in a single concept, namely, values. We do, however, opt for an approach that attempts to deal with the person's own cognitions, with the way in which he perceives situations and structures reality. This approach is, therefore, a sort of cognitive ecology, a mapping of the person-environment system from the view-point of the person.

As described in the first chapter, one can conceive of a person developing relatively stable, organized abstract structures as he deals constructively with the flow of information from his environment—organized schemata that give meaning and stability to his social and physical environments. At any given time, perceived information may be discrepant with corresponding underlying abstract structures. It is assumed that the person will attempt to resolve these structural discrepancies inasmuch as he wants to achieve a relatively stable view of his physical and social environments, that he does not want to live in an uninter-pretable world of flux but in one that has continuity and meaning for him.

Structural discrepancies may be resolved in various ways, involving cognitive or behavioral adjustments or both. For instance, one may reinterpret the information received, look for new information, move to a new situation where information is congruent with underlying schemata, and so on. Or, if the perceived structure cannot be modified or if behavioral adjustments are ineffective and the structural discrepancy persists, one may reconstruct the underlying abstract structure in the direction of congruence with present reality as it is perceived. Implicit in this possible sequence of events is the assumption that perceived structures relating to immediate situations are usually more amenable to change than are abstract structures, which are grounded in the individual's past experience.

The approach assumes that both perceived and abstract structures are likely to be more resistant to change if they concern the physical world than the social world, since it is probably less easy to distort physical reality than social reality. And abstract structures may be especially difficult to reconstruct if there is a long history involved in their development and use. These ideas have been elaborated in relation to models of social communication, attitude-related recall, and causal attribution (Feather, 1971*a*). Again, it should be emphasized that they concern the cognitive world of the person not only in terms of the relatively stable, functional structures he has developed to give meaning to physical and social reality, but also in terms of the perceived, organized characteristics of the immediate environment.

In these terms, the general question of person-environment fit can be conceptualized according to the degree to which discrepancies exist in abstract and perceived structures, one set of structures relating to the person and the other set to the environment. In the context of choice, where a person has to decide between different environments (for instance, between alternative work situations), it may be assumed that he will be biased toward those environments that minimize structural discrepancies. The abstract and perceived structures involved in these discrepancies may refer to various characteristics of the person and the environment, and one of the important future tasks of a cognitive ecology is to identify these essential person-environment properties and map the cognitive structures that relate to them. In our research, the focus was upon those structures that involve the person's own values and their relationship to the values he attributes to the different social environments with which he is in contact. Thus, the degree of value-fit was of major concern.

THE DYNAMICS OF
PERSON-ENVIRONMENT FIT

It should be emphasized that the principle that persons, given a range of available choices, will prefer environments that best fit their own personality characteristics states an expected *correlation* between properties of the person and properties of the environment. Where discrepancies exist, we have assumed that the person will attempt to resolve them either by cognitive or behavioral means or by a combination of both. In this way the person-environment correlation would be improved.

The mechanisms underlying this assumed tendency to reduce discrepancies are probably quite complex. We shall mention two of them only. There may be others involving built-in mechanisms or programs based upon natural selection that underlie adjustment to particular types of discrepancy, but these we will not consider.

The first underlying dynamic has already been discussed. We have argued that at the cognitive level the task of coping with varied and complex information inputs involves some sort of abstracting process whereby relatively stable and organized structures develop from diverse encounters giving meaning, continuity, and stability to experience. These abstract structures are then used as reference frames to which new information is related. Thus, at a very general level, one can conceive of the tendency to reduce cognitive discrepancies in terms of an attempt on the part of the organism to achieve consistent views of reality (for a summary of related approaches, see Chapter 1). This bias toward relatively stable and structured internal representations is adaptive in a world of flux. Innate determinants may be involved, as the Gestalt theorists have asserted. Learning undoubtedly plays a role because, from birth, demands are made upon persons to behave consistently (for a discussion of these issues, see Feather, 1967a, 1971a).

The second underlying dynamic concerns the reward or reinforcement implications of a good fit. The matching of personality and environmental properties is more likely to assure the occurrence of desired reinforcements. Hence, the seeking of compatible environments may be determined by the reinforcement properties of situations as well as by a general preference for consistent states of affairs. In the case of choices that lead to a match between needs and environmental resources, the importance of reinforcements that follow these choices is obvious. One chooses environments where there is food and water to satisfy hunger and thirst. The behavior is clearly adaptive to the organism in terms of what it needs and what the environment has to offer. For higher order structures such as values, the reinforcements that come from a good match are also likely to be very important in the selection of environments. A person who values freedom, equality, and wisdom, for example, would be more likely to encounter the reinforcements associated with those values in congruent environments that also assign these values high importance. Selection of congruent environments should therefore have the effect of enabling the organism to move in the direction of maximizing positive reinforcements and minimizing negative costs.

It should be clear, therefore, that we do not assign the consistency principle sovereign status. The situation is analogous to the approach adopted in a previous analysis of information-seeking behavior where not only consistency pressures but also sources of utility were important determinants of the search for new information (Feather, 1967a). Similarly, in the case of preference for compatible environments, one also has to acknowledge the importance of other factors in addition to the assumed tendency in people to prefer relatively stable and organized structures that provide meaning and consistency to life. Among these other factors the reinforcements or rewards that are contingent upon a close fit are likely to be especially important. One may prefer a new and strange environment if it offers a significantly greater range and quantity of reinforcements than are available in the present situation. Indeed, the fact that it is novel may give it a special attraction (see Chapter 5), depending upon how discrepant it is from what one has become used to. Under such conditions one might be quite willing to expose onself to new and perhaps inconsistent information if one has the opportunity to move to this more reinforcing environment. The additional reinforcements achieved outweigh the cost of modifying and perhaps radically reconstructing existing cognitive structures. People are making such choices every day as they change occupations, go to new schools, take marriage partners, visit different countries, and, in other ways, switch from a familiar environment to a more rewarding but less familiar situation.

EDUCATIONAL CHOICE AND THE VALUE MATCH: THE 1970 FLINDERS STUDY

In the study of educational choice now to be described, it was predicted that a person will be biased toward selecting environments whose perceived value systems match his own—a prediction that may be seen as a particular case of a person's general attempt to minimize discrepancies between abstract and perceived structures.

SUBJECTS AND PROCEDURE

How was this prediction tested? The following study (Feather, 1971b) provides the answer. Incoming students at Flinders University in 1970 were administered Form E of the Rokeach Value Survey as part of their orientation-testing program. Two sets of instructions were used. One set asked respondents to rank the terminal and instrumental values according to their own priorities (own values); approximately three-fourths of the Science students and two-thirds of the students from the schools of Humanities and Social Sciences completed this form of the test following the usual instructions for Form E. The second set asked respondents to rank the values in relation to their school (school values). They were asked to assume that

> students who have enrolled in your school at Flinders University end up with certain kinds of values, some of which are more important than others. Think of a student who has enrolled in the same school as you have and the values he might end up with . . . place a 1 next to the value which the student in your school would emphasize as most important, place a 2 next to the value which this student would emphasize as second most important, etc. The value which this student would rank as least important, relative to the others, should be ranked 18. (Feather, 1971*b*, p. 203)

The two forms of the test (Own Values, School Values) were randomly distributed in the ratios previously indicated and respondents wrote their names at the top of the Value Survey and indicated the school in which they had enrolled. After 17 respondents were excluded because they made errors in ranking—a marked improvement when compared to the earlier study (Feather, 1970*b*) due to the fact that respondents were specifically instructed to check their answers to make sure that they had given a ranking to all 18 values in each set and that they had not used the same ranking twice in each set—and after three further respondents had been excluded because it was not possible to determine the school in which they had enrolled, there remained 562 respondents with usable data. Their distribution by school, sex and form of test is presented in Table 3.3.

TABLE 3–3. Number of Subjects Involved in Each Condition of Experiment; Flinders University; 1970

School	Male		Female	
	Own Values	School Values	Own Values	School Values
Humanities	16	9	33	14
Social Sciences	66	35	53	27
Sciences	191	67	42	9

Source: Data are from Feather, 1971*b*.

RESULTS

Tables 3.4 and 3.5 present the median rankings of terminal and instrumental values respectively for students enrolling in each of the three schools and in relation to the form of the test they completed (own values or school values). These average value systems were intercorrelated using Spearman rho and the similarity indexes (rhos) that resulted are presented in Table 3.6.

The main data of interest to the hypothesis of person-environment fit are those in the small rectangular matrices in Table 3.6. Our hypothesis implies that the correlation between own values and attributed school values would be highest for the school selected than for the schools rejected. In regard to the terminal values, the best support for this hypothesis came from the Humanities School (rhos of .88 versus .86 and .77). The difference in correlations was in the predicted direction for Social Sciences and Sciences but was very small indeed (rhos of .87 versus .86 and .82 for Social Sciences, and rhos of .91 versus .89 and .85 for Sciences). In the case of the instrumental values, the best support for the hypothesis also came from Humanities (rhos of .55 versus .21 and .18). Differences were again in the predicted direction for Social Sciences but very small indeed (rhos of .38 versus .36 and .32). But there was no support for the hypothesis from Sciences (rhos of .36 versus .44 and .35). For each of the small rectangular matrices in Table 3.6 it was possible to test the hypothesis that there is no significant difference between the three diagonal correlations (the within-school correlations) and the remaining six correlations (the across-school correlations). In each case, the within-school correlations were significantly higher than the across-school correlations ($p < .05$), in line with our prediction.

It will also be noted in Table 3.6 that the cross-correlations in the small rectangular matrices were much lower for instrumental values than for terminal values. This result implies that the similarity between own values and attributed school values was greater in regard to terminal values than for instrumental values.

A $2 \times 3 \times 2$ analysis of variance was applied to the transformed ranks for each value with sex, schools, and type of ranking (own versus school) as factors in the analysis and with an alpha level of .05 for statistical significance. The detailed results with significance levels are presented in the original report (Feather, 1971b).

The following statistically significant main effects from the analysis of variance occurred in relation to the schools factor: Students enrolling in Sciences ranked *a comfortable life, an exciting life, pleasure,* and being *ambitious, clean,* and *logical* as relatively more important than did students enrolling in Social Sciences or Humanities. In contrast, students who elected to work in Humanities ranked *a world of beauty, mature love, wisdom,* and being *broad-minded, courageous, imaginative,* and *loving* as relatively more important than did students enrolling in Social Sciences or Sciences. These effects occurred irrespective of sex and irrespective of whether values were ranked in relation to self or school. The differences obtained provided some replication of results from the 1969 data (Feather, 1970b) to the 1970 data.

There were significant main effects from the analysis of variance concerned with the type of ranking factor: Students as a whole ranked *a world at peace, mature love, true friendship,* and being *cheerful, clean, forgiving, honest, loving,* and *polite* as relatively more important when rankings referred to self rather

TABLE 3-4. Median Rankings and Composite Rank Orders of Own and School Terminal Values for 1970 Flinders Students Enrolling in Humanities, Social Sciences, and Sciences

Terminal Value	Humanities		Social Sciences		Sciences		All Respondents	
	Own	School	Own	School	Own	School	Own	School
N	49	23	119	62	233	76	404	161
A comfortable life	15.2 (17)	14.5 (16)	13.2 (14)	13.3 (15)	12.0 (14)	11.1 (13)	13.1 (14)	12.4 (14)
An exciting life	9.9 (13)	11.2 (13)	10.3 (12)	11.7 (12.5)	10.4 (12)	7.8 (7)	10.3 (12)	10.3 (12)
A sense of accomplishment	7.7 (9)	5.3 (3.5)	6.1 (6)	4.0 (2)	6.9 (6)	3.3 (1)	6.8 (7)	3.8 (2)
A world at peace	5.9 (6)	9.8 (11)	5.7 (4)	8.3 (9)	7.3 (7)	7.7 (6)	6.7 (6)	8.2 (9.5)
A world of beauty	9.4 (11)	9.5 (10)	13.0 (13)	11.7 (12.5)	11.9 (13)	13.1 (15)	12.0 (13)	12.3 (13)
Equality	5.7 (4)	9.3 (9)	5.6 (3)	6.2 (6)	8.0 (9)	8.2 (9)	7.0 (8)	7.4 (6.5)
Family security	9.6 (12)	10.1 (12)	9.0 (10)	9.0 (10)	8.4 (10)	8.3 (10.5)	8.9 (10.5)	8.8 (11)
Freedom	5.6 (3)	4.3 (2)	5.1 (2)	5.1 (3)	5.6 (3)	5.4 (3)	5.4 (2)	5.1 (3)
Happiness	7.4 (8)	7.1 (7.5)	6.2 (7)	8.0 (8)	5.8 (4)	7.0 (4)	6.1 (4)	7.4 (6.5)
Inner harmony	6.1 (7)	5.5 (5)	6.8 (8)	5.6 (4)	7.5 (8)	8.3 (10.5)	7.1 (9)	6.4 (4)
Mature love	5.8 (5)	7.1 (7.5)	7.4 (9)	9.5 (11)	6.3 (5)	8.1 (8)	6.6 (5)	8.2 (9.5)
National security	13.6 (14)	14.3 (15)	14.0 (16)	13.1 (14)	14.5 (16)	14.5 (17)	14.3 (16)	14.0 (16)
Pleasure	15.0 (16)	13.8 (14)	13.8 (15)	14.3 (17)	12.9 (15)	12.7 (14)	13.5 (15)	13.6 (15)
Salvation	16.5 (18)	15.8 (18)	16.1 (18)	15.6 (18)	16.2 (18)	16.4 (18)	16.2 (18)	16.1 (18)
Self-respect	8.9 (10)	6.8 (6)	9.4 (11)	7.5 (7)	8.8 (11)	8.7 (12)	8.9 (10.5)	8.0 (8)
Social recognition	14.8 (15)	14.8 (17)	14.6 (17)	14.0 (16)	15.2 (17)	14.3 (16)	15.0 (17)	14.2 (17)
True friendship	4.3 (2)	5.3 (3.5)	4.9 (1)	6.0 (5)	4.8 (1)	7.1 (5)	4.7 (1)	6.5 (5)
Wisdom	3.9 (1)	2.5 (1)	5.8 (5)	3.1 (1)	5.6 (2)	5.0 (2)	5.6 (3)	3.7 (1)

Note. The lower the median the higher the relative importance of that value. Numbers in parentheses are the rank orders of the medians. *N*s are for error-free rankings. The School enrolled in could not be identified for three respondents.
Source: Data are from Feather, 1971*b*.

TABLE 3–5. Median Rankings and Composite Rank Orders of Own and School Instrumental Values for 1970 Flinders Students Enrolling In Humanities, Social Sciences, and Sciences

Instrumental Value	Humanities		Social Sciences		Sciences		All Respondents	
	Own	School	Own	School	Own	School	Own	School
N	49	23	119	62	233	76	404	161
Ambitious	12.9 (15)	8.5 (10)	8.9 (10)	6.2 (6.5)	7.0 (4)	5.5 (5)	8.3 (7)	6.1 (7)
Broad-minded	4.4 (2)	2.5 (1)	6.4 (3)	4.2 (1)	5.7 (3)	4.8 (1.5)	5.7 (3)	4.3 (1)
Capable	10.6 (13)	6.8 (7.5)	8.3 (6.5)	5.1 (4)	9.7 (12.5)	5.0 (3)	9.4 (10.5)	5.4 (3.5)
Cheerful	9.2 (11)	11.5 (15)	9.9 (11)	12.3 (13)	9.5 (10)	12.2 (14)	9.5 (12)	12.2 (13)
Clean	14.4 (17)	16.8 (18)	12.6 (16)	15.8 (18)	12.3 (16)	14.6 (18)	12.7 (17)	15.3 (18)
Courageous	6.8 (6)	5.8 (3)	8.8 (9)	8.5 (10)	9.6 (11)	9.3 (11)	8.9 (8)	8.7 (10)
Forgiving	6.4 (4)	10.8 (13.5)	8.1 (5)	12.5 (14)	8.4 (7)	13.4 (15)	7.8 (5)	12.5 (15)
Helpful	8.7 (9.5)	10.8 (13.5)	8.6 (8)	10.0 (11)	9.2 (9)	9.8 (12)	9.0 (9)	10.0 (12)
Honest	2.8 (1)	6.8 (7.5)	3.3 (1)	7.3 (9)	3.2 (1)	8.5 (9)	3.2 (1)	7.7 (9)
Imaginative	7.5 (7)	5.7 (2)	13.6 (17)	11.8 (12)	12.8 (17)	9.1 (10)	12.5 (16)	9.1 (11)
Independent	9.5 (12)	6.3 (4.5)	10.1 (12)	5.2 (5)	9.0 (8)	6.1 (6)	9.4 (10.5)	5.6 (5)
Intellectual	8.3 (8)	6.5 (6)	10.2 (13)	6.2 (6.5)	11.0 (14)	4.8 (1.5)	10.5 (13.5)	5.4 (3.5)
Logical	13.5 (16)	10.5 (11.5)	11.1 (14)	4.6 (2)	9.7 (12.5)	5.4 (4)	10.5 (13.5)	5.3 (2)
Loving	5.1 (3)	10.5 (11.5)	6.9 (4)	13.5 (16)	7.3 (5)	11.9 (13)	6.7 (4)	12.3 (14)
Obedient	15.1 (18)	15.6 (17)	14.8 (18)	14.3 (17)	14.8 (18)	14.0 (17)	14.9 (18)	14.4 (17)
Polite	12.1 (14)	13.6 (16)	11.8 (15)	12.6 (15)	11.4 (15)	13.8 (16)	11.7 (15)	13.3 (16)
Responsible	6.6 (5)	6.3 (4.5)	3.8 (2)	4.9 (3)	4.9 (2)	6.3 (7)	4.9 (2)	5.8 (6)
Self-controlled	8.7 (9.5)	7.9 (9)	8.3 (6.5)	7.0 (8)	8.0 (6)	7.7 (8)	8.2 (6)	7.5 (8)

Note. The lower the median the higher the relative importance of that value. Numbers in parentheses are the rank orders of the medians. Ns are for error-free rankings. The School enrolled in could not be identified for three respondents.
Source: Data are from Feather, 1971b.

TABLE 3–6. Rank-order Correlations of the Median Rankings of Own and School Values for 1970 Flinders Students Enrolling in Humanities, Social Sciences, and Sciences

	Own Values			School Values		
	Humanities	*Social Sciences*	*Sciences*	*Humanities*	*Social Sciences*	*Sciences*
Own Values						
Humanities		.92	.91	.88	.86	.77
Social Sciences	.77		.92	.82	.87	.86
Sciences	.64	.91		.89	.85	.91
School Values						
Humanities	.55	.36	.35		.94	.81
Social Sciences	.18	.38	.44	.70		.83
Sciences	.21	.32	.36	.73	.94	

Note. Correlations of median rankings of terminal values are above the diagonal; correlations of median rankings of instrumental values are below the diagonal. Higher similarity indexes indicate greater similarity between the average value systems involved in the comparison.
Source: Data are from Feather, 1971*b*.

than school. But they ranked *a sense of accomplishment, self-respect, wisdom,* and being *ambitious, broad-minded, capable, independent, intellectual,* and *logical* as relatively higher in importance when the rankings referred to school rather than to self. These differences occurred irrespective of the sex of the respondent or of the school in which the respondent was enrolled. The latter set of values is obviously more concerned with competence and accomplishment than the former, which have more of an interpersonal focus.

The following significant main effects occurred in relation to the sex factor: Males gave more importance to *pleasure* and being *imaginative* and *logical* and less importance to *equality, national security,* and being *honest* than did females. These differences occurred irrespective of the school in which respondents were intending to work and irrespective of whether they ranked the values in relation to self or school. Hence, some of the sex differences obtained from the 1970 sample replicated those from the 1969 Flinders sample.

The analysis also indicated a small number of significant interaction effects, that is, effects that were not general but occurred only for particular levels of a factor. These have been reported in the original article (Feather, 1971*b*).

Finally, it is of interest to note that the average orders of importance for own values (see Tables 3.4 and 3.5) were very similar to those obtained with the 1969 Flinders students. *True friendship, freedom, wisdom* were ranked highest in importance among the terminal values on the average, and *national security, social recognition,* and *salvation* were ranked lowest. Among the instrumental values being *honest, responsible,* and *broad-minded* were ranked highest on the average and being *imaginative, clean,* and *obedient* were ranked lowest.

DISCUSSION OF RESULTS

The main contribution of the study, however, was to lend support to the matching hypothesis in relation to educational choice. There was evidence from the comparisons of median rankings that the students' own value systems more closely resembled the perceived value systems of the school they entered than the perceived value systems of the school they rejected, the results being most clear-cut for Humanities students. But in most cases, the predicted differences in degree of similarity were not very large and, in some cases, they did not occur at all (see Table 3.6).

As we have suggested, there are probably other aspects of personality apart from values and abilities that a person considers in relation to the demands of the work situation when he has to choose between alternatives. Nonetheless, abilities and values would be important considerations, abilities having greater weight in choice of a work situation than values. One would expect to obtain better evidence for the assumption of person-environment fit in the case of abilities than for values. One does not usually select courses of action completely outside of one's perceived competence. Nor does one remain in jobs at which one continually fails due to lack of required abilities.

Sometimes abilities and values may reinforce one another. The choice of an environment may satisfy both one's values and one's abilities. In other cases these two aspects may be in conflict, as when choice of a particular environment would satisfy one's values but would be incompatible with one's abilities. Generally, however, one would expect choice to be as congruent as possible with a person's perceived aspects of self, some of which he may believe are more important than others to match to the work situation.

One should not conclude from the preceding discussion that a person's choices among alternatives will necessarily lead to a situation where there is good adjustment to his environment, nor that the sorts of decisions made are entirely rational, involving a weighing of all crucial factors in an accurate, objective way in order to arrive at the best person-environment match. This position would obviously be far too simple a one to take. In some cases a person might misperceive or be ignorant of important aspects of the environment or self, so that the match that occurs at the subjective level is not, in the objective sense, accurate at all. What might appear to be a sensible decision to the person involved might then be seen by an outside judge as foolish and irrational. There are obvious limits, however, to the degree to which reality can be distorted or ignored if one is to adapt to objective physical and social conditions. In the long run, one has to come to terms with the real world, and inaccurate self-perception and distorted interpretation of the environment are both dysfunctional when one has to cope with social and physical reality.

In considering the quality of adaptive choice, two other factors should be noted. First, a person may be influenced in the choice he makes by other people, such as a student being advised by his parents to select a particular course of studies. The recommended course may be quite unsuitable, yet the student may not be able to resist the pressure. There are many similar examples that one could give where the final choice departs from the best possible person-environment match because of the influence of external agents and their power in directing action. The second factor is that a person usually has only a *limited* number of alternatives from which to choose; he does not have total freedom to select alternatives from a wide range of possibilities. Various matters constrain the range of available choice, social and economic circumstances being particularly important. Many of these factors are outside a person's control. For example, a student from a lower income family suffering economic hardship would have a more restricted range of options at the crossroads of his education than would a student from a wealthy and well-educated family. Without other means of support, options requiring a large financial outlay from his family would be closed to him even though he might be suited to them. Moreover, his social milieu and educational background could also sharply circumscribe the extent to which various alternatives are even considered.

The point is that the "goodness" of a person's choice of work situation or environment is always relative to the range of alternatives open to him. A narrow range of possibilities, which for one or another reason excludes the better options, increases the likelihood of an unsuitable choice. Even so, within the available range, one would expect that a bias toward selecting alternatives that best matched personal characteristics would still operate, despite the fact that the match might not be the one that would eventuate in the best of all possible worlds.

Finally, it would be worthwhile to obtain information about the different environments from among which a person is selecting *in addition to* the information contained in the individual's own reported perceptions. In a university or college context, for example, one could attempt to discover the value priorities of the professional staff in the different faculties or schools and relate these orders of preference to the value systems students attribute both to the academic areas they are entering and to themselves. This three-way comparison, which also has obvious applications in studies of vocational choice, would provide information about the degree to which attributions about the "typical" value systems of defined areas of study and work are accurate reflections of reality as well as information about the degree of discrepancy between a person's own value priorities and the "actual" value priorities as defined in terms of the value systems of professionals in the work situation. We will return to the important question of *accuracy* of judgments in subsequent chapters.

In the next chapter, we extend the present analysis to studies of educational adjustment.

4. Values and Educational Adjustment

IN THE NEXT TWO CHAPTERS, we move from the investigation of educational choice to a consideration of educational adjustment and the impact of the secondary school and university on the students attending them. Again, the organizing principle concerns the cognitive and behavioral consequences of discrepancies between abstract structures and perceived structures. In the last chapter we applied this principle to situations of choice, where the individual could minimize potential discrepancies by selecting relatively congruent alternatives. In this chapter we explore situations in which a person has already committed himself to work in a particular educational environment, the focus being upon his adjustment to it. In Chapter 5 we will deal with the effect the educational environment has upon him.

EDUCATIONAL ADJUSTMENT AND THE VALUE MATCH

In line with our previous arguments, one would expect a person to be more adapted to a particular environment when structural discrepancies are small. Someone who assigned a lot of importance to *equality* in his terminal value system might be very discontented in a hierarchical organization that emphasized elitism. A student who downgraded being *polite* and *obedient* in his instrumental value system might feel quite out of place in a school that stressed these modes of conduct. If, on the other hand, the organization placed considerable emphasis upon equal opportunity and the school deemphasized conventional modes of conduct of a deferential kind, then the employee and the student might be relatively happy in their respective environments.

Level of adjustment can be investigated in terms of behavioral or other types of measure. For example, in a school one can observe children who are problems in the classroom, whose school performance is unsatisfactory, who withdraw or show aggressive behavior, who appear not to be involved in their work, and who display other indications that they are not functioning effectively in that environment. And one can also observe the child whose behavior indicates satisfactory adjustment to school. Similarly, one can develop behavioral indexes relating to level of adjustment in other organizations or social environments, such as the work situation, the family, the peer group, the leisure group, and so on. This type of information might be obtained either from people in a position to observe behavior as it occurs from day to day (teachers, supervisors, parents) and who have been trained to observe reliably, or from outside observers similarly trained in the use of appropriate procedures. The final result would be a set of measures from a number of different observers sampling a range of behaviors over a reasonable time span, these behaviors being coded in terms of certain defined criteria of adjustment.

One can also seek information from the individual himself—by intensive interview, questionnaires, self-ratings, projective techniques, or other procedures. In the study now to be presented, adjustment as indexed by each person's reported satisfaction with the environment was the main dependent variable of interest. Once again, the focus was upon the value-fit within an educational context.

The 1970 Flinders study of educational choice described in the previous chapter used a design in which some groups were required to rank the values in the usual way whereas other independently selected groups ranked them according to the order of priorities they thought a student enrolled in their school might end up with. It can be argued that a more sensitive design would be one in which each respondent was used as his own control, that is, one in which each respondent was required to rank the values *both* for himself and for his school. Such a design has some disadvantages. For example, in the interest of appearing consistent to others, or of gaining their approval, or for some other reason, a respondent might systematically distort his answers so that the value priorities he reports for himself, or those he reports for his school, or indeed both sets of rankings he reports, depart from the real state of affairs. But this second design would have the advantage of controlling other factors (abilities, for instance) that might also influence his choice and subsequent adjustment. The study of educational adjustment now to be described used this second procedure. It was set up to test the hypothesis that adjustment at school improves the more a student's own reported values match those he sees his school as emphasizing.

Our study involved a shift from using university samples to extensive sampling of schoolchildren in a wide range of secondary schools in metropolitan Adelaide. The shift was made for two main reasons—first, on the assumption that one should attempt to deal with different populations when testing general psychological hypotheses, and thereby not restrict samples to the university undergraduate as is so often the case; and, second, on the assumption that if one is to work within the framework of person-environment fit it is necessary to sample not only persons but also environments in order to achieve a genuinely representative design (Brunswik, 1955). Thus, the basic hypothesis was investigated in many different types of school environments involving respondents with a variety of family and social backgrounds.

THE VALUE FIT-ADJUSTMENT STUDY

SUBJECTS AND PROCEDURE

The respondents were boys and girls attending the last two years of secondary school education (leaving and matriculation classes involving the fourth and fifth years of secondary school respectively) in 19 schools in Adelaide. Details of the samples are contained in the original reports (Feather, 1972a, 1972b). Most children were in the 15-to-17 year age range. Schools were selected to cover a variety of institutions. Eight were high schools administered and funded by the state government. Of these, five were offering a fairly general mixture of courses (three coeducational, one boys', and one girls' high school); the remaining three concentrated more upon technical and clerical courses (one coeducational technical, one boys', and one girls' technical high school).

The other 11 were secondary schools not under the control of the state government; each was administered by an independent organization and, in all but one case, associated with a particular church. Of these 11 independent schools only one was coeducational (the Lutheran). The remaining 10 comprised four boys' schools (one Methodist, one Anglican, one Catholic, and one Presbyterian), and six girls' schools (two Catholic convents, one Methodist, one Presbyterian, and one school without a religious association). Most of the independent schools took boarding as well as day students. None of the state schools boarded students.

With the exception of the Lutheran school, respondents from the independent schools had attended the same school for a longer period of time than respondents from the state schools (5.30 years on the average for the independent schools versus an average of 3.81 for the state schools). Respondents from the independent schools also tended to have fathers with higher status occupations (mean = 3.13) than respondents from the state schools (mean = 4.39). The measure of occupational status was based upon each respondent's description of his father's occupation and the scale devised by Congalton (1969) for the prestige ranking of occupations (scored 1–7 in the direction of *decreasing* prestige). Both mean differences were highly significant ($p < .001$).

Altogether, 2,947 respondents took part in the study. They answered a questionnaire in regular class periods during school hours, the questionnaire taking them about 40 minutes to complete. Details on test administration can be found in the original reports (Feather, 1972a, 1972b). It is sufficient to note here the following points: The test program extended from mid-1970 to early 1971. The questionnaire was introduced as an educational survey and in most schools respondents were asked to put their names at the top of it. (In two schools it was possible to examine the effects of response anonymity; see Chapter 2.) After providing background information, respondents completed Form E of the Value Survey. Because of time limitations approximately half of them (1,465) were asked to rank the terminal values only and the remainder (1,482) ranked the instrumental values only. The values were presented in the standard manner, that is, in alphabetical order, each accompanied by a short definition, and with a line beside each value where the rank order was to be written.

The values were first ranked in regard to the respondent's *own* priorities according to the usual instructions, which were as follows:

> Below is a list of 18 values arranged in alphabetical order. We are interested in finding out the relative importance of these values for you.
>
> Study the list carefully. Then place a *1* next to the value which is most important to *you,* place a *2* next to the value which is second most important to you, etc. The value which is least important, relative to the others, should be ranked *18.*
>
> When you have completed ranking all of the values, go back and check over your list. Please take all the time you need to think about this, so that the end result is a true representation of *your* values.
>
> Be careful not to use the same number twice when making your rankings and be careful not to leave any blanks. Work as quickly as possible.

Respondents then ranked the same set of values in regard to their *school's* priorities according to the following instructions:

> Now assume that your School is attempting to turn out children with certain kinds of values, some of which the School considers to be more important than others.
>
> Think of a student who has these values that the School strives to emphasize and think of the order in which the School would emphasize them.
>
> Study the list carefully. Then place a *1* next to the value which the School would emphasize as most important, place a *2* next to the value which the School would emphasize as second most important, etc. The value which the School would emphasize as least important, relative to the others, should be ranked *18.*
>
> When you have completed ranking all the values, go back and check over your list. Please take all the time you need to think about this, so that the end result is a true representation of the values in the order in which your School emphasizes them.
>
> Be careful not to use the same number twice when making your ranking and be careful not to leave any blanks. Work as quickly as possible.

An index of similarity between own and school values was computed for each respondent by correlating the transformed ranks for own values and for school values using Pearson product-moment correlation—the higher positive correlations indicating a greater degree of similarity. Thus, each respondent had a similarity index involving either terminal values or instrumental values (own with school values). These were similarity indexes computed at the individual level—not at the level of averaged or aggregate data as were the correlations presented in the previous chapter. As in other studies, a small number of respondents (from 3 to 4 percent) had to be excluded in each school because they made errors in ranking.

Two kinds of measure of adjustment at school were obtained from respondents. One measure involved satisfaction scores; the other involved happiness ratings. The satisfaction scores were obtained in the following way: When they had completed ranking the set of values (terminal or instrumental) for self and then for their school, the respondents completed the Cornell Job Description Index (JDI) modified by the author to measure students' satisfaction with aspects of the school situation. In the usual form of the JDI as applied to industrial settings, respondents are required to check lists of word-items describing their work, the people with whom they work, their supervisor, their pay, and their promotions (Smith, Kendall, & Hulin, 1969). For example, some of the words describing *work* are as follows: fascinating, routine, satisfying, boring, good, simple, endless, gives a sense of accomplishment; some of the words describing *people* are: stimulating, boring, slow, ambitious, stupid, narrow interests, loyal, hard to meet; and some describing *supervisor* are: hard to please, impolite, praises good work, tactful, influential, leaves me on my own, around when needed, lazy. When respondents answer the JDI, they must indicate whether each word-item in each scale describes what that scale refers to (work, people, supervisor, pay, or promotions), whether it does not, or whether they can't say. Each of the five scales is keyed to provide a measure of satisfaction with that aspect of the work situation. In the present study, the last two aspects of the work situation (pay and promotions) were not included, and respondents checked the JDI items as they applied to *schoolwork, people in my class,* and the *typical teacher.* There were 18 items in each of these scales corresponding to the word-items used by Smith, Kendall, and Hulin (1969). Separate satisfaction scores, which could range from 0 to 18, were obtained for each of these three aspects of the school situation using the scoring procedure described by Smith (1967, pp. 346–349). In addition to securing scores for the three subscales, we also got a total satisfaction score, which was the sum of the separate satisfaction scores. These satisfaction scores (subscale and total) were taken as measures of adjustment.

A further measure of adjustment was obtained by asking respondents to rate how much they enjoyed being at school. They used a 5-inch scale labeled "Very happy at school" at one extreme, "Don't like school at all" at the other, and "Moderately happy at school" in the middle. Responses were scored from 1 to 9 in the direction of increasing happiness, with a score of 5 spanning the midpoint of the scale.

RESULTS

Because it was predicted that adjustment at school would be positively related to the degree to which own values matched perceived school values, the relationships of interest in the present study were those involving the measures of adjustment and the similarity indexes. Tables 4.1 and 4.2 present the relevant correlations of the similarity indexes with total satisfaction scores and happiness ratings for each school. These tables show that there was indeed a tendency for satisfaction scores and happiness ratings to be positively related to the degree of similarity between a student's own values and those he attributed to the school. Nearly all the correlations in Tables 4.1 and 4.2 were positive and many of them were statistically significant.

For all the schools combined, the correlation of the similarity index based upon the terminal values was .28 with total satisfaction scores and .23 with happiness ratings (both highly significant, $p < .001$). Similarly, for all schools combined the correlation of the similarity index based upon the instrumental values was .27 with total satisfaction scores and .23 with happiness ratings (both highly significant, $p < .001$). These correlations were also highly significant when computed separately for boys and girls in the total sample. It should be noted, however, that although the evidence supported the hypothesis of a positive relationship between the value match and school adjustment, the correlations were quite low.

When the satisfaction scores for the separate components of the JDI (*schoolwork, people in my class, typical teacher*) were correlated with the similarity indexes for all schools combined, the correlations were again positive but lower for *people in my class* ($r = .17$ with the terminal similarity index, $r = .11$ with the instrumental similarity index) than for the other two components. The correlations between the similarity indexes and satisfaction with *schoolwork* were .24 and .25 respectively for the terminal and instrumental similarity indexes. The corresponding correlations involving satisfaction with the *typical teacher* were .24 and .23. Thus, there was some evidence that satisfaction with the more job-oriented aspects of the school situation (*schoolwork, typical teacher*) was more closely related to the value match than was satisfaction with the more social, affiliative aspects of school (*people in my class*).

As one would expect, the various measures of school adjustment (namely, the satisfaction scores and happiness ratings) were all positively interrelated. These intercorrelations are presented in Table 4.3 for all respondents. The correlations in Table 4.3 imply that rated happiness at school depended more upon the students' satisfaction with schoolwork and their teachers than upon their satisfaction with other students in their class. Probably, the children were identifying schoolwork as the most important activity in the school situation, indeed the reason for the school's existence, and accordingly it had great-

TABLE 4-1. Correlations of Terminal and Instrumental Similarity Indexes with Satisfaction and Happiness in Adelaide State Schools

State School	Terminal Similarity Index				Instrumental Similarity Index			
With:	Satisfaction	N	Happiness	N	Satisfaction	N	Happiness	N
Coeducational schools								
High School A								
Boys	.53[c]	41	.41[b]	42	.64[c]	45	.37[b]	46
Girls	.29	38	.15	41	.14	35	.10	35
High School B								
Boys	.28[b]	81	−.01	81	.18	73	.15	75
Girls	.27[a]	52	.20	53	.30[a]	65	.42[c]	66
High School C								
Boys	.37[a]	45	.36[a]	45	.17	42	.20	43
Girls	.20	39	−.08	39	.42[b]	41	.43[b]	42
Technical High A								
Boys	.26	35	.21	37	.06	30	−.04	31
Girls	.23	22	.07	22	.12	29	.05	29
Single-sex schools								
Boys								
High School D	.31[a]	63	.27[a]	65	.39[b]	64	.17	65
Technical High B	.31[a]	67	.27[a]	69	.31[b]	71	.17	73
Girls								
High School E	.10	61	.13	61	.30[a]	58	.53[c]	59
Technical High C	.25	47	.25	49	.15	45	.15	46
All state schools	.28[c]		.19[c]		.29[c]		.24[c]	

[a] $p < .05$ [b] $p < .01$ [c] $p < .001$
Source: Data are from Feather, 1972a.

TABLE 4-2. Correlations of Terminal and Instrumental Similarity Indexes with Satisfaction and Happiness in Adelaide Independent Schools

Independent School	With:	Correlations							
		Terminal Similarity Index				Instrumental Similarity Index			
		Satisfaction	N	Happiness	N	Satisfaction	N	Happiness	N
Coeducational schools									
Lutheran									
Boys		.38[a]	28	.42[a]	23	.17	33	.27	35
Girls		.48[b]	35	.11	33	.34	29	.12	29
Single-sex schools									
Boys									
Methodist		.24	49	.20	49	.16	45	.42[b]	47
Anglican		.21[a]	121	.31[c]	120	.29[c]	126	.23[b]	127
Catholic		.42[c]	71	.34[b]	71	.16	81	.26[a]	81
Presbyterian		.38[c]	76	.26[a]	78	.33[b]	85	.29[b]	88
Girls									
Catholic A		.18	72	.25[a]	72	.20	71	.00	74
Catholic B		.22	42	-.04	42	.21	47	.27	47
Methodist		-.06	59	.35[b]	59	.11	58	-.08	59
Presbyterian		.07	75	.16	73	.23[a]	75	.13	76
Anglican		.20	63	.29[a]	63	.28[a]	61	.50[c]	62
Independent		.40[b]	46	.17	47	.22	52	.14	53
All independent schools		.26[c]		.25[c]		.23[c]		.20[c]	

[a] $p < .05$ [b] $p < .01$ [c] $p < .001$
Source: Data are from Feather, 1972a.

TABLE 4–3. Intercorrelations between Satisfaction Scores and Happiness Ratings in Adelaide Survey

Variable	1	2	3	4
1. Schoolwork		.30	.45	.47
2. People in my class			.35	.24
3. Typical teacher				.33
4. Happiness				
Means:	8.22	10.77	10.88	5.40
SDs:	3.25	3.66	3.61	2.18

Note. All correlations are highly significant ($p < .001$). In the columns, 1 = Schoolwork; 2 = People in my class; 3 = Typical teacher; 4 = Happiness.
Source: Data are from Feather, 1972a.

est weight as an influence on their ratings of happiness at school. The means in Table 4.3 also suggest that students were less satisfied with *schoolwork* than they were with *people in my class* and with the *typical teacher* in their school.

The mean adjustment scores for male and female respondents in the different types of schools are presented in Table 4.4. The data were analyzed using a variety of analysis of variance procedures (for details, see Feather, 1972b). Only those results relating to sex differences and differences between

TABLE 4–4. Mean Satisfaction and Happiness Scores for Male and Female Subjects in Adelaide State and Independent Single-sex and Coeducational Schools

Type and Composition of School	Mean Happiness Rating	Mean Satisfaction Scores			
		School-work	People in My Class	Typical Teacher	Total
State schools					
Coeducational					
Boys	5.17	7.93	10.27	11.00	29.24
Girls	5.30	7.57	11.14	10.39	29.15
Single-sex					
Boys	5.03	7.63	9.24	10.58	27.44
Girls	5.31	8.33	10.96	10.93	30.23
Independent schools					
Coeducational					
Boys	5.50	8.98	12.14	12.14	33.17
Girls	6.36	9.35	11.81	13.08	34.29
Single-sex					
Boys	5.37	8.32	10.41	10.84	29.64
Girls	5.66	8.59	11.51	10.88	31.04

Note. Mean total satisfaction scores were not exactly equivalent to the sum of the mean component scores since a small number of *Ss* did not complete all three subscales of the JDI.
Source: Data are from Feather, 1972a.

state and independent schools will be presented here. The reader is referred to the original report for the results of other comparisons including some interaction effects (the effects of coeducation will be considered in the next chapter).

The results showed that girls tended to report more satisfaction with *people in my class* than did the boys and to provide higher ratings of happiness with school than did the boys. In both cases, the differences were highly significant ($p < .001$). There were no sex differences in regard to *schoolwork* and the *typical teacher*. The results also showed that students from the independent schools had higher mean satisfaction scores on all three components of the JDI and higher mean happiness ratings than did students from the state schools. These differences were also highly significant ($p < .001$).

Finally, students who were in their final year of secondary school (the matriculation class) had higher mean satisfaction scores ($p < .001$) for *people in my class* and the *typical teacher* than did students in the immediately preceding year (the leaving class). The matriculation students were also slightly higher in regard to the mean happiness rating ($p < .05$) but they were slightly lower than the leaving students in their evaluation of *schoolwork* ($p < .05$).

DISCUSSION AND CONCLUDING REMARKS

As we have seen, the results of the present study supported the predicted positive relationship between the value match and measures of adjustment at school but the correlations were very low. The correlations might have been higher had we increased the sensitivity of our measures in order to obtain a wider range of scores on the variables being considered, although the respective distributions were fairly well spread (see the SD's in Table 4.3). With this qualification, however, the results showed that very little of the variance in adjustment scores could be accounted for by the extent to which student values were congruent with attributed school values. This result is not surprising because one would expect that the degree to which a student is happy and satisfied at school would be influenced by a great number of factors, the extent of value match being only one of them and perhaps not a particularly important one. As we have indicated, one could also examine discrepancies in other types of variables, some of which may be more crucial for adaptation than others. It would be very important, for example, for a student's *abilities* to fit the abilities demanded by the school situation. If they did not then his performance would be impaired and he would be unhappy and dissatisfied with school. In this regard, we have already noted that satisfaction with schoolwork seems to have special weight as an influence on rated happiness at school. And doubtless there are other characteristics of the student in addition to abilities and values that need to match the requirements of the school environment if satisfactory adjustment is to ensue, the mapping of which is a task for future research.

Does this mean that the happy, satisfied student at school would be one whose personal characteristics fitted fairly closely the demands of the school environment? Such a conclusion would indeed follow if one were to define adjustment in a narrow sense as referring specifically to the school environment to which the student was exposed. General adjustment, however, would relate to a whole spectrum of environments, not only to the situation that confronts the child at school but also to environments outside the school concerned with family, peer groups, and other influences. The degree to which personal characteristics were congruent with the demands of these different and sometimes overlapping environments would influence overall adjustment as reflected in experience and behavior. Indeed, an individual's ratings of satisfaction with a particular environment might be influenced by sources of satisfaction or dissatisfaction elsewhere. Thus, the discontent engendered by one badly fitting environment (the family situation) might spread to other environments (the school situation), and the happiness that comes from one well fitting situation (the work environment) might also spread elsewhere—both *generalization effects* adding to those particular effects of structural discrepancies that are specific to defined environments.

This analysis indicates the need to be able to specify the variety of environments that the person encounters, the demands that these environments make upon the person, and the characteristics of the person that can be considered in relation to these demands. Such an approach would be two-pronged, focusing upon both person and environment within a general ecological framework. It would involve a very detailed analysis of person-environment interaction and would take account of the complexity of both personality and environmental domains and the need to provide appropriate techniques to measure the critical variables and to study their interactive effects in multivariate designs.

In regard to this last point, the *accuracy* with which students can perceive school values should be investigated. The whole thrust of this (Chapter 4) study was directed toward the cognitive world of the person. But it is important also to explore "objective" measures of the person and environment outside of individual perceptions so that one can examine the processes by which perceptions are shaped and the distortions that may occur. In the present case, for instance, it is possible that students unhappy for other reasons, distorted the values of the school situation when they reported their school's priorities, whereas the more satisfied child would be less likely to distort them. The judgments of a generally unhappy child may be serious misrepresentations of reality, inaccurate and sometimes extreme visions that may reflect personal distress and inadequacy far more than objective reality.

We therefore need studies that also obtain measures of the "real state of affairs." One could relate the value systems that a student attributes to his school to those that his classmates report and to those that his teachers claim to be promoting. One could then go on to compare the effects of discrepancies between the student's own value systems, those he attributes to his school, and those reported by his peers and by his teachers. In this way, one might be able to discover significant distortions and examine whether discrepancies have different relationships to school adjustment according to whether school value systems are "perceived" or "actual." In Chapter 9, we will return to the question of accuracy of judgment in another context—the subjective assimilation of immigrant groups.

The differences in adjustment scores obtained in the present study (Table 4.4) are probably due to a variety of factors. The higher satisfaction scores and happiness ratings provided by students in the independent schools could reflect a genuinely better school environment (for example, better teachers and educational facilities), or they could involve a halo effect since children in the independent schools typically came from families materially more prosperous and better educated, or they could be the outcome of a better match in these schools between personal characteristics and the nature of the school environment (similarity indexes were indeed higher in the independent schools than in the state schools, as we will see in the next chapter). The sex differences obtained in the present study deserve further investigation. Girls were more satisfied with their classmates and provided higher happiness ratings than did boys—perhaps reflecting stronger affiliative concerns at the age when they were tested and a readier acceptance of authority. The higher adjustment scores of students in their final year at school (the matriculation class) could reflect a selection process whereby students dissatisfied with school drop out, leaving behind those who are relatively better adjusted to the school environment.

Finally, it is worth noting that the hypothesis tested in the present study was supported across a broad range of conditions involving different types of schools and boys and girls with different family backgrounds. Hence, the results have wide generality. However, we should recognize that the study was at a very molar level. It will be useful for investigators to conduct further studies in a variety of schools at a more detailed level so that the whole process of social influence within the school situation can be examined. In this way it should be possible to discover who are the main purveyors of values and the degree to which they are able to influence changes in students' value systems, given the particular school environment in which they work.

Some of these questions concern the extent to which one might expect educational institutions to have an impact upon the values of the students attending them. The next chapter will be concerned with a general treatment of this topic using findings from the Flinders program.

5. Values and School Impact

BECAUSE of the relatively extensive sampling of schools in the study described in the previous chapter, it was possible to compare different types of schools in regard to similarities and differences in values and value systems. It is not easy to determine the effects that a school may have upon a child's values, however, because basic values develop in a social milieu that includes many influences of which the school is only one. It becomes difficult to isolate just what the school adds after important influences such as the child's family and his peer group have been accounted for and difficult also to specify how the different socializing influences interact. Yet one has to make a start and look for differences in value patterns between children attending different types of schools even though it may be difficult to interpret any differences obtained. In subsequent studies, it may be possible to identify the fine grain of the shaping process and to come to some understanding of how the observed value differences occurred. It may also be possible to discover the conditions under which lasting changes eventuate.

In the next two sections, we present the results of comparisons involving coeducational versus single-sex schools and state versus independent schools, using data obtained from the Adelaide study. Finally, we report the results of a study of value change conducted at Flinders University.

VALUES IN COEDUCATIONAL AND SINGLE-SEX SCHOOLS

SOME PREVIOUS STUDIES

Most educationalists would argue that coeducation at the secondary school level is necessary to prepare children to take their places naturally in the world of men and women. It is contended that the social environment of the co-educational school is less artificial than that of the single-sex school, providing children with the opportunity to learn adaptations that better equip them to adjust to the adult world beyond the school. The coeducational school is seen as a more accurate mirror of the wider social context; the single-sex school as a more unusual and artificial environment when compared with society at large.

Surprisingly, there are very few studies that compare the effects of coeducational and single-sex schools on the children attending them. Some of the evidence has been summarized by Feather (1974*a*) and it is mixed. Thus, in Britain Dale (1969, 1971) found that coeducational schools were generally preferred to single-sex schools by both teachers and students. The school atmosphere was thought to be more congenial in coeducational schools, and students saw their teachers as friendlier and more helpful. Single-sex schools were perceived to involve stricter discipline, and their teachers were viewed as more distant. Dale also noted there was no evidence that the education of the sexes together resulted in a lowering of academic standards. Indeed, the weight of evidence seemed to be on the opposite side as far as boys were concerned.

In a study conducted in New Zealand, however, results were obtained that were less positive toward coeducation (Jones, Shallcrass, & Dennis, 1972). These authors were interested in testing Coleman's suggestion that status in the adolescent society of the coeducational secondary school may depend more upon popularity than upon scholastic achievement, leading to an emphasis upon "rating and dating." Hence, coeducation may have a stultifying effect on intellectual activities and "may be inimical to *both* academic achievement and social adjustment" (Coleman, 1961, p. 51). The results of the Jones et al. study did, in fact, provide some support for Coleman's suggestion. In both the Dale and Jones et al. studies there was a tendency for differences to be more evident among girls than among boys.

GENERAL PREDICTIONS

What predictions might one advance about the possible effects of coeducation on students' values and attitudes toward school as they were assessed in the Adelaide secondary schools study described in the previous chapter? If Coleman and Jones et al. are correct, then one might expect students from coeducational schools to regard values relating to social approval and affiliation (for example, *true friendship, mature love*) as more important for self than would students from single-sex schools, and this difference might be especially pronounced among the girls. If Dale is correct, one might also expect students from single-sex schools to see their schools as placing more emphasis upon values concerned with discipline and control (being *polite* and *obedient*) than would students from coeducational schools. Moreover, if teachers are indeed perceived as friendlier and more helpful in coeducational schools, then one would expect this difference to be evident in students' reported satisfaction with the *typical teacher*. Similarly, if the social environment of the coeducational school is seen as richer and more complete because it involves both sexes, then one would expect students in coeducational schools to report more satisfaction with *people in my class*.

ANALYSIS OF SINGLE VALUES

There was only one coeducational independent school in the sample of secondary schools; the data from the independent schools, therefore, were excluded from the analysis. The analyses to be reported were based upon results from the eight state high schools listed in Table 4.1. These schools were classified as coeducational or single-sex. The median rankings for the terminal and instrumental values for boys and girls in both types of schools for both self (own) and for school are presented in the original report (Feather, 1974a).

The transformed rankings for each value were separately analyzed using 2 × 2 analyses of variance involving the sex composition of the school (coed versus single-sex) and the type of school (general versus technical) as factors. The analyses were run for males and females separately, first for the transformed rankings of own values, then for the transformed rankings of school values. A conservative alpha level ($p < .01$) was adopted to test for significance.

The results of the analysis showed that there were no significant differences between the coeducational and the single-sex schools in the relative importance assigned to particular terminal values by either boys or girls for either self or school rankings. In regard to particular instrumental values, however, both boys and girls from single-sex schools ranked being *clean* as higher in relative importance than did students from coeducational schools. This was true for both self and school rankings. Girls in single-sex schools also saw their schools as placing more emphasis upon being *helpful* and *polite* than did girls in co-educational schools. They also saw their schools as assigning less importance to being *intellectual* and *logical*. In summary, therefore, the main effects of the sex composition of a school (coed versus single-sex) that emerged from the analysis were found only in regard to the instrumental values and then, with the exception of being *clean,* only for the girls and only for the perceived school values. Some of the differences supported Dale's suggestion that single-sex schools might assign more importance to rules of conduct, but there were other values related to control and conduct (for example, being *obedient*) that showed no significant differences at all. Nor was there any support for Coleman's suggestion that coed students might set greater store upon being popular and accepted by their peers than would students in the single-sex secondary schools.

There were some main effects of the type of school (general versus technical) on value rankings. In particular, for both boys and girls, *inner harmony* was ranked as relatively less important and *a comfortable life* as relatively more important in the technical high schools than in the general high schools when rankings were for self. These results may reflect the greater vocational emphasis characteristic of the technical high schools.

There was an almost complete lack of significant interaction effects. The original article (Feather, 1974*a*, p. 13) contains the relevant details.

ANALYSIS OF ADJUSTMENT SCORES

Table 5.1 presents the mean satisfaction scores and the mean happiness ratings for boys and girls in relation to schools attended. Once again 2 × 2 analyses of variance were conducted on the separate data for boys and then for girls. These analyses, when applied to the data for the boys, showed that the boys in the coeducational high schools reported more satisfaction with both *people in my class* and with the *typical teacher* than did boys in the single-sex high schools ($p < .001$ and $p < .05$ respectively). These differences, which were main effects in the analyses for boys, did not occur for the girls; there

TABLE 5-1. Mean Satisfaction and Happiness Scores for Adelaide Boys and Girls in Relation to School Attended

		Mean Satisfaction Scores		
Type and Composition of School	Mean Happiness Rating	School-work	People in My Class	Typical Teacher
Coeducational				
General				
Boys	5.08	7.81	10.22	10.90
Girls	5.22	7.40	11.36	10.19
Technical				
Boys	5.64	8.56	10.57	11.55
Girls	5.73	8.48	10.04	11.43
Single-sex				
General				
Boys	4.84	6.32	8.92	10.53
Girls	5.34	8.24	10.58	10.06
Technical				
Boys	5.23	8.86	9.55	10.63
Girls	5.29	8.45	11.43	11.99

Source: Data are from Feather, 1974*a*.

were no significant main effects of the sex composition of school for the girls when the various adjustment scores were analyzed.

There were some significant main effects of type of school (general versus technical). Both boys and girls in the technical high schools expressed greater satisfaction with *schoolwork* than did boys and girls in the general high schools ($p < .001$ for boys, $p < .05$ for girls). Girls in the technical high schools reported greater satisfaction with the *typical teacher* than did girls in the general high schools ($p < .001$), and boys in the technical high schools expressed greater happiness with school than did boys in the general high schools ($p < .05$). In the technical high schools children may see their schoolwork as more relevant to future careers than do children in the general high schools, where the vocational emphasis tends to be much less apparent and where the curriculum is rather more academic and general.

There were also some significant interaction effects which are presented in detail in the original report (Feather, 1974a). We would feel more confident about interpreting some of these interaction effects had we been able to take a wider sample of schools than was possible.

CONCLUSIONS

The general conclusion that one can draw in regard to the effects of co-education on values is one that emphasizes similarity rather than difference. Very few differences occurred between coeducational and single-sex schools in the relative importance assigned to particular values. Indeed the average order of importance of values was very similar in coeducational and single-sex high schools both when the students' own values were compared and when the schools' values were compared. Furthermore, separate factor analyses of the intercorrelations of the average terminal value systems (medians) and of the intercorrelations of the average instrumental value systems (medians)—similar to the procedure used in the study of the effects of response anonymity described in Chapter 2 and in a study to be described in the next section—showed that the major distinction that children made was between the value systems they assigned to themselves and the order of values they believed their schools were trying to promote (see Feather, 1974a, for details). Neither factor analysis provided evidence for a factor contrasting coeducational high schools with single-sex high schools in regard to average value systems.

The evidence that coeducation was having an effect was somewhat stronger when attitudes toward aspects of the school situation were compared between coeducational and single-sex schools. Boys in particular were more positive toward their classmates and their teachers when they were in coeducational schools than when they were in single-sex schools (see Tables 4.4 and 5.1).

In future investigations, one might employ more refined measures in the hope that they would be more responsive to the effects of coeducation and, if possible, take an even wider sample of schools than was involved in our study. This latter suggestion may be difficult to meet, however, because the move toward coeducation is fairly widespread in western societies and single-sex schools that are not privately funded are becoming increasingly difficult to find.

Moreover, one should consider the implications of differences in the sex of the teachers in each kind of school. In the present study teachers in the single-sex schools were usually of the same sex as the students whereas in the co-educational schools both male and female teachers were involved. Compared to the respective all-male or all-female single-sex schools, therefore, coeducational schools would be more "feminine" for boys and more "masculine" for girls.

The reactions of children to their school might depend upon the extent to which each sex perceives the climate of the school to be masculine, feminine, or "androgynous" and how this perceived school characteristic interacts with the level of masculinity or femininity of the students themselves and the sex-role stereotypes they hold. There is evidence from some North American studies, for example, that highly masculine boys may be at a disadvantage relative to their less masculine counterparts in some high school environments. Thus, in a preliminary study, Abrash and Schneider (1973) found that the highly masculine student, when compared to the less masculine student, experienced a disadvantage in a coeducational school environment and that he adjusted more favorably to the environment of an all-male school. Finally, it is important to remember that any effects obtained in studies comparing coeducational and single-sex schools may be relative to the culture involved in the study. There may be some general differences spanning different cultures, but one would expect distinctive results to occur for particular societies inasmuch as schools are influenced by the ethos of the culture and community of which they are a part.

VALUES IN STATE AND INDEPENDENT SCHOOLS

AN EARLY STUDY

An early study in the Flinders program explored value differences between boys in a large state coeducational high school in metropolitan Adelaide and boys attending a private (independent) secondary school associated with the Methodist Church (Feather, 1970c). It was this study that first used the procedure of asking one group of respondents to rank the values in regard to self and another group to rank them in regard to how they thought their school would emphasize them. The results of this study showed that students apparently shared similar value systems despite the fact that they were attending different schools. And they also tended to see their schools as stressing similar values. To be sure, there were some differences when the value rankings were compared between the two schools, and many of these differences were in the direction one would predict. For example, students in the church school saw their school as assigning relatively greater importance to religious values such as *salvation* and being *forgiving*. But the "between-schools" differences were not as striking as were the differences between the way in which students ranked their own values and the way in which they ranked them for their school, a result that (as previously noted) also occurred in the 1970 Flinders study and in the co-education study just described.

This early study, while interesting both in its development of new procedures and in the results it produced, suffered from the disadvantage of involving only two schools and of testing only one sex (boys), with the consequence that results were quite specific and not easily generalizable. The extensive survey of secondary schools involved in the Adelaide study enabled us to overcome this difficulty to a considerable extent and to explore possible differences in values and value systems between students of both sexes from state and independent schools.

ENVIRONMENTAL DIFFERENCES BETWEEN STATE AND INDEPENDENT SCHOOLS

As we have seen, a basic variable of interest in the Adelaide study was the degree to which a student's own value priorities matched the perceived value priorities of his school. One might expect the value match to increase the more a school provides an environment in which the important influencing agents are associated with the school over long periods, the more a school accents particular values and sees this emphasis as part of its educational function, and the more this emphasis is reinforced in different ways within the school.

It can be argued that the independent schools are more likely to provide relatively constant environments involving mutually reinforcing channels of influence than are the state schools. They better approximate what Goffman (1961) calls a "total institution." Children attending independent schools are likely to have been there longer (at least in the Adelaide independent schools— Chapter 4 and Feather, 1972a) and there is probably less turnover in staff than at the state schools. In addition, many of the independent schools have been in existence for a considerable time and have developed traditions and a history, both of which are passed on to the students by teachers and by parents who send their children to the same school they themselves have attended, as many do. In addition, most independent schools stress that an important part of their function is to influence character and to impart Christian values. These ideals are usually communicated to students at school assemblies and end-of-year "speech day" ceremonies, and they are reflected in the attention given by many independent schools to chapel attendance and team sports. Finally, in addition to enrolling day students, most of the independent schools take boarders who are, apart from vacations, more or less continuously in contact with the school environment. With very few exceptions (such as some agricultural colleges) the state schools take day students only, usually from the immediate neighborhood.

It would be wrong to infer from this description that the state schools have no concern with communicating basic human values. They certainly have. And it would also be wrong to infer that attempts to influence character are systematically contrived within the schools. They are not in the majority of cases.

Influence within the schools is probably most often generated in the day-to-day contacts between staff and students, and between students and their peers, in formal and informal ways, sometimes casually without conscious planning. The important point is that influence attempts are more likely to be effective when the school provides a relatively constant and self-contained environment as opposed to one that involves greater change, and when a declared emphasis on values is reinforced in various ways within the school. On these grounds one would expect that the students' own value priorities would more closely match the perceived value priorities of their school if they attended independent schools than if they attended state schools.

ANALYSIS OF SIMILARITY INDEXES

This prediction was explored by comparing the similarity indexes for students from the two types of school (for a detailed presentation of results see Feather, 1972*b*). It will be remembered that these indexes indicated the degree of similarity between a respondent's ranking of his own values and his ranking of his school's values, and that the similarity index could apply either to the terminal values or to the instrumental values, depending upon which set of values the respondent was asked to rank. The mean similarity indexes for respondents from the state schools and from the independent schools are presented in Table 5.2.

A 2 × 2 analysis of variance was applied to the individual terminal similarity indexes and then to the individual instrumental similarity indexes. In each analysis sex was the first factor and type of school (state versus independent) the second factor. As predicted, it was found in both analyses that the similarity indexes tended to be higher for students in the independent schools than for those in the state schools ($p < .001$ in each case). These differences were general ones, occurring for both boys and girls. The analysis of the terminal similarity indexes also showed that girls tended to have higher similarity indexes than boys irrespective of type of school ($p < .01$), but this difference did not occur in the analysis of the instrumental similarity indexes. There were no significant interaction effects.

A further analysis of data from those independent schools that took both day students and boarders showed that mean similarity indexes were higher for boarders than for day students. In the case of the terminal similarity index, the means for boarders and day students were .32 and .27 respectively. In the case of the instrumental similarity index, they were .31 and .20 respectively. Only the latter difference was statistically significant ($p < .01$; see Feather, 1972*b*, for details of the analysis procedure). Thus, some evidence was obtained that the value match was greater for students who lived at the school than for those who attended on a day-to-day basis and who lived at home in most cases. The boarders would have more exposure to the school environment and one

TABLE 5–2. Mean Terminal and Instrumental Similarity Indexes for Adelaide State Schools and Independent Schools

State School	Mean Similarity Index For:			
	Terminal		Instrumental	
	Index	N	Index	N
Coeducational schools				
High School A				
Boys	-.01	42	.05	46
Girls	.15	41	-.09	36
High School B				
Boys	.22	81	.16	75
Girls	.29	54	.18	66
High School C				
Boys	.22	46	.26	44
Girls	.22	39	.05	42
Technical High A				
Boys	.20	37	.03	32
Girls	.25	22	.20	29
Single-sex schools				
Boys				
High School D	.14	65	.10	65
Technical High B	.17	71	.24	73
Girls				
High School E	.22	61	.10	59
Technical High C	.21	50	.14	46
All state schools	.19		.13	

Independent School	Mean Similarity Index For:			
	Terminal		Instrumental	
	Index	N	Index	N
Coeducational schools				
Lutheran				
Boys	.24	28	.22	35
Girls	.44	36	.31	31
Single-sex schools				
Boys				
Methodist	.11	49	.15	47
Anglican	.17	121	.17	127
Catholic	.36	72	.25	82
Presbyterian	.29	79	.30	88
Girls				
Catholic A	.41	72	.30	75
Catholic B	.54	42	.38	47
Methodist	.20	60	.23	59
Presbyterian	.22	77	.09	76
Anglican	.27	66	.32	62
Independent	.21	47	.13	53
All independent schools	.28		.23	

Source: Data are from Feather, 1972*b*.

would therefore expect their values to match more closely those they perceived their school as having.

There was also a tendency for similarity indexes to be higher among those respondents who ranked the terminal values than among those who ranked the instrumental values. This difference, which occurred in both the state and independent schools, might reflect the higher test-retest reliability of terminal value rankings (see Chapter 2). The overall mean similarity indexes were .24 for the terminal values and .19 for the instrumental, and these means were significantly different ($p < .001$).

So the results supported the main prediction. The value match tended to be closer in the independent schools than in the state schools, suggesting that the former were having more impact upon the students' values. The interpretation that this effect might relate to the more controlled and self-contained environments within the independent schools was supported by the fact that boarders, more constantly exposed to the school environment, tended to have higher similarity indexes—the value match was better for them than for day students.

But the results can be interpreted in other ways. Students in the independent schools had on the average been there for a longer time and so had been subject to more influence from their schools. The greater degree of value match might be an outcome of this longer exposure to influence. Yet students in the Lutheran school, who had been in attendance for less than three years on the average, also had relatively high similarity indexes (see Table 5.2), suggesting that it is not just amount of contact with the school that is the important variable but other factors as well, one of which (as we have argued) relates to the distinctive characteristics of the school environment.

Another important factor determining the differences in the similarity indexes could be "subject selection." We have already said that the students in independent schools usually came from families in the higher socioeconomic strata who could afford to pay the school's fees (see Chapter 4). One would expect these children to have undergone different socialization experiences from those who came from lower income families, and that these differences might be reflected in some of their value priorities. Even more relevant, however, is the fact that parents from the higher socioeconomic strata would have had more choice in deciding upon schools for their children, given their financial resources. Thus, the range of alternatives was wider for these parents with higher incomes; they were less limited in the choices they could make, and, therefore, had more opportunity to choose congruent environments for their children (see Chapter 3). It follows that they were more likely than lower income families to send their children to schools whose values matched theirs and the children's; a choice of schools would not be open to a lower income family whose children usually attend a state school in the immediate neighborhood. Such a selective factor would lead to higher similarity indexes among students in the independent schools quite apart from possible molding effects that might occur within them. One would also expect these higher similarity indexes to be accompanied by higher measures of reported satisfaction and happiness in the independent schools, as indeed they were (see Chapter 4, Table 4.4).

Nonetheless, for all schools the similarity indexes obtained were relatively low, implying that some marked differences existed in the way students ranked their own values and the perceived school values. This finding is one with which we are already familiar.

ANALYSIS OF AVERAGE VALUE SYSTEMS

To explore similarities and differences in average value systems, factor-analytic procedures were again employed (as in the anonymity and coeducation studies). For the 24 different groups in Table 5.2 (corresponding to the classification of respondents by sex and school) there were 48 sets of median rankings relating to the terminal values (each group had a set of medians for own values and a set for school values). These 48 sets of medians were inter-correlated, using the Spearman rank-order procedure, and the resulting 48 × 48 correlation matrix with unities in the diagonal cells was factor-analyzed using the principal components method in conjunction with varimax rotation for eigenvalues greater than one. Four factors emerged. The first accounted for 38 percent of the variance and was clearly identifiable as an own values factor indicating a basic similarity between the rankings of own values across all groups. The second factor accounted for 29 percent of the variance and it was clearly identifiable as a school values factor indicating a basic similarity in the median rankings of school values across all groups. The third factor accounted for 20 percent of the variance and could be identified as an independent schools factor applying to school values only—implying that there was a basic similarity in the median rankings of school values in the independent schools over and above the general similarity across all groups implied by the second factor. The fourth factor accounted for only 4 percent of the variance and could tentatively be identified as an independent schools factor applying to the own values of boys.

A similar factor analysis of the 48 × 48 matrix of intercorrelations for the instrumental values also yielded four factors. The first accounted for 45 percent of the variance and was clearly identifiable as a school values factor. The second factor accounted for 24 percent of the variance and was clearly identifiable as an own values factor. The third accounted for 19 percent of the variance and could be identified as an own values sex factor, separating boys from girls. The fourth factor, which accounted for only 2 percent of the variance, will be ignored because it could not be firmly identified.

The relevant median rankings showing the nature of these factors are presented in Tables 5.3, 5.4, and 5.5. There it can be seen that, in regard to the factors that indicated similar orderings of own values across groups, respondents ranked *true friendship, a world at peace, freedom,* and *happiness* as most important for themselves on the average and *pleasure, national security,*

TABLE 5-3. Median Rankings and Composite Rank Orders of Terminal Values for Adelaide Students in Relation to Schools (State versus Independent) and Values (Own versus School)

Terminal Value	State Schools		Independent Schools		All Schools	
	Own	School	Own	School	Own	School
N	632	631	776	777	1408	1408
A comfortable life	11.67 (13)	9.40 (9)	11.58 (13)	12.06 (14)	11.62 (13)	11.11 (13)
An exciting life	8.93 (10)	11.99 (15)	8.74 (10)	13.29 (16)	8.83 (10)	12.69 (16)
A sense of accomplishment	7.84 (9)	2.07 (1)	7.00 (6)	2.79 (1)	7.37 (7)	2.47 (1)
A world of beauty	12.28 (15)	11.09 (14)	12.11 (14)	11.57 (13)	12.19 (14)	11.40 (15)
A world at peace	4.89 (1)	7.99 (7)	5.82 (3)	7.80 (7)	5.42 (2)	7.90 (7)
Equality	6.76 (4)	5.50 (3)	7.89 (9)	5.79 (4)	7.41 (9)	5.68 (3)
Family security	7.48 (8)	9.88 (11)	7.27 (7)	9.08 (10)	7.38 (8)	9.39 (9)
Freedom	5.24 (3)	7.70 (6)	5.59 (2)	9.32 (12)	5.45 (3)	8.62 (8)
Happiness	6.79 (5)	9.71 (10)	5.96 (4)	9.16 (11)	6.30 (4)	9.43 (10)
Inner harmony	9.45 (11)	11.01 (13)	9.28 (11)	8.73 (9)	9.34 (11)	9.73 (11)
Mature love	7.02 (7)	15.67 (18)	7.35 (8)	13.95 (18)	7.21 (6)	14.88 (18)
National security	13.47 (16)	9.89 (12)	13.45 (16)	12.19 (15)	13.45 (16)	11.31 (14)
Pleasure	11.89 (14)	12.61 (16)	12.69 (15)	13.82 (17)	12.36 (15)	13.35 (17)
Salvation	15.72 (18)	14.13 (17)	14.84 (18)	5.72 (3)	15.23 (18)	9.87 (12)
Self-respect	10.41 (12)	5.91 (4)	10.46 (12)	6.23 (5)	10.44 (12)	6.07 (4)
Social recognition	14.09 (17)	6.12 (5)	14.44 (17)	8.67 (8)	14.27 (17)	7.48 (5)
True friendship	5.17 (2)	8.40 (8)	4.84 (1)	6.59 (6)	4.99 (1)	7.50 (6)
Wisdom	6.92 (6)	2.63 (2)	6.56 (5)	2.89 (2)	6.72 (5)	2.78 (2)

Note. Data are for males and females combined. Lower numbers denote higher relative value. In each column the rank order of each median (low to high) is denoted in parentheses after the median. *N*s are for error-free rankings.
Source: Data are from Feather, 1972b.

TABLE 5-4. Median Rankings and Composite Rank Orders of Instrumental Values for Adelaide Students in Relation to Schools (State versus Independent) and Values (Own versus Schools)

Instrumental Value	State Schools		Independent Schools		All Schools	
	Own	School	Own	School	Own	School
N	633	632	805	800	1438	1432
Ambitious	7.80 (4)	2.34 (1)	7.29 (4)	4.10 (2)	7.53 (4)	3.31 (1)
Broad-minded	6.63 (3)	11.18 (13)	7.03 (3)	11.59 (13)	6.84 (3)	11.43 (13)
Capable	8.93 (8)	6.44 (7)	9.17 (9)	7.80 (7)	9.07 (8)	7.19 (7)
Cheerful	8.16 (5)	13.65 (15)	8.31 (6)	12.96 (15)	8.24 (6)	13.28 (15)
Clean	9.44 (10)	7.66 (8)	10.76 (14)	8.02 (8)	10.16 (14)	7.87 (9)
Courageous	9.93 (13)	13.84 (16)	10.18 (13)	13.63 (16)	10.06 (13)	13.74 (17)
Forgiving	9.72 (11)	14.30 (17)	9.61 (12)	12.87 (14)	9.66 (12)	13.62 (16)
Helpful	9.84 (12)	10.17 (11)	8.84 (8)	8.43 (9)	9.27 (10)	9.14 (10)
Honest	3.78 (1)	5.93 (5)	3.52 (1)	4.61 (3)	3.64 (1)	5.17 (5)
Imaginative	13.70 (18)	11.86 (14)	14.04 (18)	14.22 (17)	13.90 (18)	13.27 (14)
Independent	9.98 (14)	10.98 (12)	9.21 (10)	11.18 (12)	9.49 (11)	11.08 (12)
Intellectual	12.60 (17)	5.96 (6)	12.97 (17)	8.72 (10)	12.81 (17)	7.45 (8)
Logical	11.04 (15)	8.41 (10)	11.23 (15)	10.20 (11)	11.14 (15)	9.37 (11)
Loving	9.04 (9)	17.08 (18)	8.75 (7)	15.73 (18)	8.86 (7)	16.44 (18)
Obedient	11.87 (16)	4.72 (3)	11.46 (16)	4.76 (4)	11.63 (16)	4.74 (3)
Polite	8.74 (7)	5.42 (4)	9.39 (11)	4.82 (5)	9.11 (9)	5.05 (4)
Responsible	4.46 (2)	4.52 (2)	4.51 (2)	3.74 (1)	4.49 (2)	4.10 (2)
Self-controlled	8.43 (6)	7.88 (9)	7.65 (5)	6.68 (6)	8.03 (5)	7.17 (6)

Note. Data are for males and females combined. Lower numbers denote higher relative value. In each column the rank order of each median (low to high) is denoted in parentheses after the median. *N*s are for error-free rankings.
Source: Data are from Feather, 1972*b*.

TABLE 5-5. Median Rankings and Composite Rank Orders of Own Values by Adelaide Male and Female Students

Terminal Value	Males	Females	Instrumental Value	Males	Females
N	715	690		734	703
A comfortable life	9.39 (11)	13.58 (16)	Ambitious	6.45 (3)	8.79 (10)
An exciting life	7.33 (8)	9.93 (11)	Broad-minded	7.48 (5)	6.25 (3)
A sense of accomplishment	7.31 (7)	7.44 (8)	Capable	7.88 (6)	9.94 (12)
A world of beauty	12.94 (15)	11.31 (13)	Cheerful	9.02 (8)	7.53 (4)
A world at peace	6.22 (3)	4.54 (1)	Clean	10.18 (12)	10.11 (13)
Equality	8.70 (10)	6.05 (4)	Courageous	10.30 (13)	9.87 (11)
Family security	7.71 (9)	7.07 (7)	Forgiving	10.64 (15)	8.71 (9)
Freedom	5.46 (2)	5.43 (3)	Helpful	10.56 (14)	7.91 (5)
Happiness	6.30 (4)	6.30 (6)	Honest	4.72 (2)	2.54 (1)
Inner harmony	10.38 (12)	8.51 (10)	Imaginative	13.31 (18)	14.45 (18)
Mature love	6.46 (5)	8.11 (9)	Independent	8.47 (7)	10.41 (14)
National security	13.78 (16)	13.15 (14)	Intellectual	11.48 (16)	13.95 (17)
Pleasure	10.76 (14)	13.54 (15)	Logical	9.73 (11)	12.46 (16)
Salvation	15.63 (18)	14.79 (18)	Loving	9.69 (10)	7.96 (6)
Self-respect	10.71 (13)	10.09 (12)	Obedient	11.97 (17)	11.36 (15)
Social recognition	13.84 (17)	14.58 (17)	Polite	9.67 (9)	8.51 (7)
True friendship	5.24 (1)	4.74 (2)	Responsible	4.56 (1)	4.41 (2)
Wisdom	7.30 (6)	6.27 (5)	Self-controlled	7.46 (4)	8.66 (8)

Note. Data are for all schools combined. Lower numbers denote higher relative value. In each column, the rank order of each median (low to high) is denoted in parentheses after the median. *N*s are for error-free rankings.

Source: Data are from Feather, 1972b.

social recognition, and *salvation* as the least important when they considered terminal values. When they considered instrumental values, respondents ranked being *honest, responsible, broad-minded,* and *ambitious* as most important in relation to their own priorities and being *logical, obedient, intellectual,* and *imaginative* as least important.

It can be seen from the similar orderings of school values across groups that respondents perceived their schools as emphasizing *a sense of accomplishment, wisdom, equality,* and *self-respect* as most important on the average among the terminal values and *a world of beauty, an exciting life, pleasure,* and *mature love* as least important. For the instrumental values they saw their schools as accenting being *ambitious, responsible, obedient,* and *polite* as most important and being *cheerful, forgiving, courageous,* and *loving* as least important.

The factor concerned with school values in independent schools with respect to the terminal values was probably due to the fact that respondents in these schools saw their schools as stressing *inner harmony, mature love, salvation,* and *true friendship* as more important and *a comfortable life, an exciting life, a sense of accomplishment, freedom, national security, pleasure,* and *social recognition* as less important than did respondents in the state schools. As in the earlier study (Feather, 1970c), *salvation* was ranked especially high as a school value by respondents in the independent schools—not surprising inasmuch as most of these schools were associated with churches.

The sex factor concerned with own values and applying to the set of instrumental values probably arose because boys saw being *ambitious, capable, independent, intellectual, logical,* and *self-controlled* as more important and being *cheerful, forgiving, helpful, honest, loving,* and *polite* as less important than did the girls.

All differences just noted were highly significant ($p < .001$) when 2×2 analyses of variance involving sex as the first factor and type of school (state versus independent) as the second factor were applied to the transformed rankings for each value. The alpha level of .001 was adopted in view of the large Ns involved in the comparisons. These differences were also highly significant ($p < .001$), based upon the same form of analysis: On their own terminal values boys assigned more importance to *a comfortable life, an exciting life, mature love,* and *pleasure* and less importance to *a world at peace, a world of beauty, equality, inner harmony,* and *wisdom* than did girls. In regard to school instrumental values the results showed that respondents from the independent schools saw their schools as emphasizing being *honest, forgiving, helpful, loving, responsible,* and *self-controlled* as more important, and being *ambitious, capable, imaginative, intellectual,* and *logical* as less important than did respondents from state schools.

No separate factor appeared in the factor analyses just reported separating average own values for the independent schools from average own values for the state schools. And the medians for own values in Tables 5.3 and 5.4 show just how similar these average value systems were between the two types of school. Indeed, when students from the state and independent schools were compared in regard to how they ranked each terminal and instrumental value for themselves, only three values differed significantly in relative importance at the high level of significance adopted ($p < .001$)—using the 2 × 2 form of analysis described above. These values were *a world at peace, equality,* and being *clean,* and each was ranked more important on the average by the students from the state schools. Thus, there were very few differences between the state and independent schools in how students ranked the values in regard to their *own* priorities. Differences were more likely to occur when rankings applied to their *schools.* And, as we have already indicated, respondents from the state and independent schools also differed in their individual similarity indexes and in the various measures of adjustment to the school situation (Chapter 4).

The higher mean similarity indexes obtained in the independent schools should not divert attention from the fact that in all schools these indexes were very low. This fact, together with the emergence of a separate own values factor and a separate school values factor in both factor analyses, underlines the discrepancy between the way in which students ranked their own values and the order of importance of the values they attributed to their schools. Students were basically similar in the way in which they assigned their own priorities (on the average) and in the way in which they ranked their school's priorities (on the average), but these two sets of median rankings showed little correspondence. Moreover, as shown by the relatively low similarity indexes, this discrepancy was also very evident at the individual level. One could certainly not conclude that the schools were having a large impact on the values of the students attending them, if by "large" we mean close congruence to the values the schools were perceived as trying to promote.

STABILITY AND CHANGE IN VALUE PRIORITIES AT COLLEGE

The two studies just described looked at value similarities and differences between schools in a *cross-sectional* way, students having been tested at about the same time and at the same levels of educational advancement (leaving and matriculation classes). The study now to be described was *longitudinal.* It was designed to investigate the extent to which the value priorities of students at Flinders University changed in the course of their undergraduate experience during a 2½-year interval (Feather, 1973*d*).

COLLEGE IMPACT STUDIES

The background literature concerning college or university impact is quite extensive, going back at least to the classic Bennington Study (Newcomb, 1943;

Newcomb, Koenig, Flacks, & Warwick, 1967). Only a small number of studies have been conducted in the Australian context, however (for example, Katz, Katz, & Olphert, 1965; Little, 1970), and some of these suffer from methodological difficulties (Feather, 1973d).

Feldman and Newcomb (1969) have reviewed the American research in an attempt to discover the types of changes that occur in students as a result of their college experience, the conditions associated with these changes, and the degree to which these changes persist after students leave college. Their review showed that freshman-to-senior changes occurred in several characteristics with considerable uniformity across different colleges and universities. There was a tendency for senior students to be less authoritarian, less conservative, less prejudiced, and more sensitive to aesthetic experiences. Senior students also showed evidence of increasing intellectual interests and capacities and a declining commitment to religion, particularly in its orthodox forms. Some of these freshman-to-senior changes took place more consistently than others, but the overall picture was one of increasing openness to new experience and of developing tolerance. Feldman and Newcomb argue that the effect of college may be to accentuate differences between students that were already present when they made their initial selection of college, academic majors, and so on. Jacob (1957), on the other hand, regards college experience as socializing students so they can fit comfortably into the ranks of American college alumni. Feldman and Newcomb also considered some important methodological questions involved in studies of college impact and they stressed the necessity of asking more complex questions that would not only lead to research on different institutional environments, different kinds of students, and different ways of change, but would also allow for possible interactive effects involving these various factors.

THE FLINDERS STUDY

To a large extent the Flinders study was exploratory, though there were certain general predictions based on the previous findings reviewed by Feldman and Newcomb. Thus, we expected aesthetic values such as *a world of beauty* and values concerned with independence and autonomy (for example, being *independent*) to increase in relative importance over the 2½-year interval as students moved from their first year of studies to their third year. And it was expected that religious values of an orthodox kind (for example, *salvation*) would decrease in relative importance.

The students involved in the study were first tested during enrollment at Flinders University in 1969 using Form E of the Rokeach Value Survey (Feather, 1970b; Chapter 3). In July 1971 a postal survey was conducted of all of these students who had completed the Value Survey in 1969, Form E being sent to them with the request that they complete it. They were also asked to provide information about whether or not they were still enrolled at Flinders University and their academic progress. The letter that accompanied the survey explained its purpose and pointed out the importance of getting a good response rate. A reply-paid envelope was enclosed with the survey. In both the 1969 and 1971 test administration Form E was presented in the usual format and with the usual instructions except that in 1971 respondents were asked to check back over their rankings to make sure they had not left any value unranked and that they had not used the same rank more than once. Respondents ranked the values only in terms of their *own* priorities. Information about the sample is presented in Table 5.6.

TABLE 5-6. Sample Characteristics of Value Change Study at Flinders, 1971

Total number of *S*s:	(*N* = 553)
Total number of respondents:	(*N* = 392)
Still at Flinders:	*N* = 257 (136 males, 121 females)
At another tertiary institution:	*N* = 71 (54 males, 17 females)
No longer engaged in tertiary study:	*N* = 64 (42 males, 22 females)
Total number of nonrespondents:	(*N* = 161)
1971 whereabouts unknown:	*N* = 55
Failed to return surveys after	
follow-ups:	*N* = 106

Source: Data from Feather, 1973*d*.

About 79 percent of the surveys were returned after two follow-up letters to those who could be contacted, an excellent response rate since about 10 percent of the original sample could not be contacted because their address was unknown. Of those respondents still enrolled at Flinders University, there were 59 in the School of Humanities, 130 in the School of Social Sciences, and 68 in one or other of the Science Schools. As Table 5.6 shows, it was also possible to identify respondents no longer at Flinders University either as students who had left to complete tertiary studies elsewhere (usually in professional courses at Adelaide University) or as those who had quit tertiary studies altogether. We therefore had *two* control groups whose responses could be compared with those of the group who remained at Flinders. The requirement of a control group has been met in very few other studies in this area (Feldman & Newcomb, 1969, pp. 64–68), although it is obviously necessary.

Tables 5.7 and 5.8 present the median rankings for the terminal and instrumental values for all three groups in 1969 and in 1971. The six sets of median rankings in Table 5.7 were compared for similarity by using Spearman's rho and Kendall's tau. The same procedure was used to compare the six sets of median rankings in Table 5.8. The results of these comparisons are presented in Table 5.9.

When one examines the similarity coefficients in Table 5.9, it is evident that they tended to be high throughout. The Spearman rhos were all above .85 for the terminal values and all above .72 for the instrumental. The average

TABLE 5-7. Median Rankings and Composite Rank Orders of Terminal Values in 1969 and 1971 for Ss Still Enrolled at Flinders and for Ss Who Transferred to Another Tertiary Institution or Who Quit Tertiary Studies

Terminal Value	Still at Flinders		Transferred to Other Tertiary Institution		No Longer Engaged in Tertiary Study	
	1969	1971	1969	1971	1969	1971
N	247	244	67	71	58	60
A comfortable life	13.76 (16)	14.14 (15)	11.70 (13)	13.50 (15)	13.20 (14.5)	13.00 (14.5)
An exciting life	10.25 (12)	9.40 (11)	9.17 (12)	10.30 (13)	9.33 (12)	8.33 (11)
A sense of accomplishment	6.86 (6)	8.56 (10)	4.94 (3)	7.25 (10)	7.00 (5)	7.00 (6.5)
A world at peace	7.39 (9)	6.59 (6)	7.88 (9)	6.17 (5)	9.00 (11)	8.00 (9.5)
A world of beauty	12.36 (13)	9.83 (13)	13.30 (15)	9.79 (12)	12.83 (13)	10.00 (13)
Equality	9.11 (10)	7.53 (9)	8.88 (11)	7.08 (8)	8.00 (10)	9.00 (12)
Family security	9.31 (11)	9.57 (12)	7.81 (8)	9.58 (11)	7.40 (8)	8.00 (9.5)
Freedom	5.64 (3)	4.61 (2)	5.50 (4)	5.36 (4)	6.00 (3)	4.67 (2)
Happiness	5.83 (4)	7.06 (8)	8.75 (10)	6.88 (7)	7.20 (6)	7.00 (6.5)
Inner harmony	6.95 (7)	5.50 (4)	6.50 (7)	6.21 (6)	7.75 (9)	7.20 (8)
Mature love	6.68 (5)	4.21 (1)	5.90 (5)	4.90 (2)	6.25 (4)	4.40 (1)
National security	13.75 (15)	16.00 (17)	14.28 (16)	15.63 (17)	13.20 (14.5)	15.08 (17)
Pleasure	13.71 (14)	13.42 (14)	13.06 (14)	13.06 (14)	14.00 (17)	13.00 (14.5)
Salvation	15.03 (18)	16.61 (18)	15.64 (18)	16.93 (18)	14.50 (18)	17.03 (18)
Self-respect	7.03 (8)	6.96 (7)	6.42 (6)	7.21 (9)	7.25 (7)	6.67 (5)
Social recognition	13.86 (17)	14.33 (16)	14.79 (17)	15.26 (16)	13.33 (16)	14.22 (16)
True friendship	4.77 (1)	6.16 (5)	4.90 (2)	4.50 (1)	4.33 (1)	5.75 (4)
Wisdom	5.27 (2)	5.33 (3)	4.36 (1)	5.30 (3)	4.57 (2)	5.00 (3)

Note. Lower numbers denote higher relative value. In each column the rank order of each median (low to high) is denoted in parentheses after the median. *N*s are for error-free rankings.
Source: Data are from Feather, 1973d.

TABLE 5–8. Median Rankings and Composite Rank Orders of Instrumental Values in 1969 and 1971 for *Ss* Still Enrolled at Flinders and for *Ss* Who Transferred to Another Tertiary Institution or Who Quit Tertiary Studies

Instrumental Value	Still at Flinders		Transferred to Other Tertiary Institution		No Longer Engaged in Tertiary Study	
	1969	1971	1969	1971	1969	1971
N	238	243	67	69	58	63
Ambitious	9.67 (12)	12.43 (15)	7.25 (5)	12.19 (15)	8.50 (7)	12.93 (16)
Broad-minded	5.62 (3)	5.80 (3)	3.95 (2)	6.17 (4)	6.00 (4)	5.58 (4)
Capable	8.73 (10)	9.32 (10)	8.50 (8)	7.90 (7)	10.00 (11)	7.63 (6)
Cheerful	8.00 (7)	8.71 (9)	8.75 (9)	8.10 (8)	9.25 (9)	9.13 (11)
Clean	13.88 (17)	15.25 (17)	14.25 (17)	15.05 (17)	12.67 (16)	13.10 (17)
Courageous	7.18 (4)	6.98 (6)	9.39 (11)	9.50 (13)	9.80 (10)	10.38 (13)
Forgiving	7.38 (5)	6.77 (5)	9.92 (12)	8.17 (9)	9.00 (8)	7.17 (5)
Helpful	9.33 (11)	7.93 (8)	9.17 (10)	9.08 (11)	10.40 (12)	8.75 (7)
Honest	3.06 (1)	2.98 (1)	3.44 (1)	4.08 (1)	2.67 (1)	3.56 (1)
Imaginative	11.92 (16)	10.89 (14)	11.88 (15)	11.88 (14)	12.75 (17)	10.70 (14)
Independent	8.64 (9)	7.13 (7)	7.93 (7)	6.63 (5)	8.00 (6)	8.90 (9)
Intellectual	10.93 (13)	9.59 (11)	12.94 (16)	8.50 (10)	11.00 (14.5)	9.10 (10)
Logical	11.64 (15)	10.61 (13)	11.31 (13)	7.75 (6)	10.43 (13)	9.83 (12)
Loving	7.39 (6)	4.93 (2)	7.10 (4)	5.31 (2)	5.14 (3)	3.75 (3)
Obedient	14.68 (18)	16.21 (18)	15.59 (18)	16.45 (18)	15.00 (18)	15.72 (18)
Polite	11.56 (14)	14.02 (16)	11.58 (14)	13.88 (16)	11.00 (14.5)	12.08 (15)
Responsible	5.00 (2)	5.98 (4)	4.17 (3)	5.50 (3)	5.00 (2)	4.42 (3)
Self-controlled	8.63 (8)	10.46 (12)	7.42 (6)	9.36 (12)	7.50 (5)	8.79 (8)

Note. Lower numbers denote higher relative value. In each column the rank order of each median (low to high) is denoted in parentheses after the median. *N*s are for error-free rankings.
Source: Data are from Feather, 1973*d*.

value systems were more similar when comparisons were made for the same year than across years. But the overriding impression was one of similarity between the groups and of stability rather than change in average value systems from 1969 to 1971.

TABLE 5-9. Similarity Indexes Comparing Median Rankings across Groups

Group	1969			1971		
	1	2	3	1	2	3
1969						
1. Still at Flinders		.92	.96	.90	.93	.94
		(.79)	(.86)	(.75)	(.80)	(.80)
2. At other tertiary institution	.81		.95	.86	.86	.93
	(.65)		(.83)	(.70)	(.70)	(.80)
3. No longer in tertiary study	.88	.95		.86	.88	.95
	(.75)	(.82)		(.66)	(.71)	(.81)
1971						
1. Still at Flinders	.92	.74	.81		.96	.93
	(.76)	(.54)	(.68)		(.87)	(.84)
2. At other tertiary institution	.73	.74	.77	.86		.91
	(.57)	(.58)	(.61)	(.73)		(.76)
3. No longer in tertiary study	.81	.75	.79	.90	.88	
	(.65)	(.58)	(.66)	(.78)	(.76)	

Note. Similarity indexes for average terminal value systems are above the diagonal; similarity indexes for average instrumental value systems are below the diagonal. Similarity indexes not in parentheses are Spearman rhos; similarity indexes in parentheses are Kendall taus. Higher similarity indexes indicate greater similarity between the average value systems involved in the comparison. In the columns, 1 = Still at Flinders, 2 = At other tertiary institution, 3 = No longer in tertiary study.
Source: Data are from Feather, 1973d.

The transformed rankings for each value were analyzed using a two-factor analysis of variance with group (Flinders, Other Tertiary Institution, No Present Tertiary Study) as the first factor in the analysis and year (1969 versus 1971) as the second factor, and with repeated measures on the last factor because the same respondents were involved. In view of the ipsative nature of the ranking procedure and the large number of comparisons to be made, it was decided to adopt a conservative alpha level of .01 for statistical significance.

This analysis revealed that the following values increased significantly in relative importance over the 2½-year interval for all three groups: *a world of beauty, mature love, intellectual, forgiving,* and *loving.* The following values decreased significantly in relative importance for all three groups: *a sense of accomplishment, national security, salvation, ambitious, obedient, polite,* and *self-controlled.* Most of these differences were consistent with the general pattern of change noted by Feldman and Newcomb (1969). Values concerned with affectionate personal relationships, with aesthetic experiences, and with being intellectual increased in relative importance from 1969 to 1971, but values concerned with competitive striving, with national security, with orthodox religion, with rules of conduct related to status and authority, and with control and self-discipline decreased in relative importance. These general changes were not confined to the university group but occurred in all three groups (see Tables 5.7 and 5.8). They emerged as main effects in the analysis of variance.

The only significant change occurring in one group but not in the others was in regard to *happiness*. This value decreased in relative importance from 1969 to 1971 for students still at Flinders but increased in relative importance for respondents in the other two groups. This difference, which emerged as a significant group by year interaction effect in the analysis, is not easy to interpret, however (see Feather, 1973*d*, p. 67).

There was only one significant main effect from the analysis relating to group. Students who transferred to another tertiary institution assigned relatively less importance to *social recognition* than did respondents in the other two groups. Students who remained at Flinders assigned relatively more importance to being *courageous* than did respondents in the other two groups and this difference was nearly significant at $p < .01$. These group differences occurred both in 1969 and 1971.

When the data from students still at Flinders were analyzed separately using a two-factor analysis of variance of the transformed rankings, but this time with school (Humanities, Social Sciences, Sciences) as one factor and year (1969 versus 1971) as the other, the significant changes from 1969 to 1971 that we have just noted were again apparent in all schools. In addition, *true friendship* was assigned less importance in 1971 than in 1969 ($p < .001$) and *equality* and being *independent* were assigned relatively greater importance in 1971 than in 1969 ($p < .01$). Also evident were differences between schools in the relative importance assigned to particular values occurring in both 1969 and 1971, differences that were consistent with those described in Chapter 3. For example, students in the Humanities School ranked *a world of beauty* as higher in importance than did students in the other two schools and students in Sciences ranked being *logical* as higher in importance than did the other students. The tables of medians for students in Humanities, Social Sciences, and Sciences both in 1969 and 1971 are presented elsewhere (Feather, 1972*c*, pp. 145–146).

In these analyses, there were no significant interaction effects involving school and year as factors—in particular, no evidence that the differences between schools noticed in 1969 became *accentuated* by 1971. For example, there was no evidence that the relatively high priority given by Humanities students in 1969 to being *imaginative* (when compared with the other schools) was even more pronounced in 1971. Accentuation of differences would be expected to occur if the different school environments were exerting distinctive molding effects. But the results showed no such "fanning-out" of differences. Those differences between schools that occurred in 1969 (see Chapter 3) also tended to occur in 1971, but without evidence of accentuation.

In a recent, carefully conducted longitudinal study, Thistlethwaite (1973) also failed to find evidence supporting accentuation of attitude and value differences over time between students who differed in their major fields of study, although accentuation was found to occur in regard to measures of college environments (see also, Thistlethwaite, 1969). As in the Flinders study, Thistlethwaite followed students who started and remained within the given curriculum—an important procedural consideration. Most previous studies have failed to do this and usually they have grouped students according to major fields of study at graduation (see Feldman & Newcomb, 1969, Vol. 2, pp. 140–142). When accentuation effects are obtained using this ambiguous procedure, they are difficult to interpret because they may be an outcome of *selective migration,* meaning that students discontented with their original field of study change to another they perceive as more suitable for them.

FURTHER DESIGN CONSIDERATIONS

The design of the Flinders study just described would have been improved had we been able to obtain information from each respondent about the value systems he attributed to his immediate educational environment both in 1969 and 1971. One would then have been able to chart person-environment discrepancies in value systems over time and to relate these to agents of influence within the environment, to selective migration of students to new and more compatible environments, and to subjective and objective measures of their educational adjustment. But this procedure was not possible because we had limited time for testing and wished to keep the questionnaires as short as possible.

In its favor, however, the study did follow up the same subjects over time and it did use control groups, a procedure that has been the exception rather than the rule in most studies in the general area of college impact. Ideally, one would prefer an experiment where groups are randomly assigned to experimental and control conditions, one group attending college and the other group not subjected to college influence. For obvious reasons, this design is impossible to achieve and one has to deal with groups that may systematically differ in important respects, in addition to whether they attended college or not. In our study, the comparison groups could not be set up in advance. All three groups in Tables 5.7 and 5.8 involved students who enrolled at Flinders University in 1969 (a highly selected population already) and the two comparison groups were the outcome of a selective process involving a migration of students who had to leave Flinders University to complete their studies elsewhere or who had decided to quit university work altogether. This selective process could lead to groups that differed in various unmeasured respects. To complicate matters further, those students who left to go to another university would have been exposed to the kinds of influences that one encounters in universities generally, influences that could have strong general effects thereby obscuring or diluting any specific effects that might occur in any one institution.

In future studies, one might seek to obtain different types of control groups, perhaps by using multiple comparison groups consisting of subjects of comparable age, varying from students enrolled at other tertiary institutions (for example, teachers' colleges, colleges of advanced education, institutes), to subjects in institutions that might be quite different (training hospitals, armed services, prisons), to subjects in the population at large who were not involved in training programs or exposed to the effects of a large institution. One would also hope to sample from different social classes. In this way one might begin to isolate the *specific* effects of the institution and to observe systematic changes as the comparison groups diverged more and more from the particular group of interest. Some control over initial subject differences might be achieved by using covariance designs together with multivariate procedures. One also needs to consider more sophisticated approaches than the simple test-retest procedure; the pretest can often have undesirable effects, though these would be minimized with a long time interval (Campbell & Stanley, 1963). Effects of a pretest, particularly when change scores are being used, are often complex and difficult to disentangle (Cronbach & Furby, 1970).

The difficulties of ruling out alternative interpretations in quasi-experimental research are well known. Progress probably lies in the accumulation of reliable pieces of evidence from studies in different settings using different individuals and different assessment procedures. One would hope to proceed to integrated team efforts employing multivariate forms of analysis and a sophisticated approach to the measurement and interpretation of stability and change.

Interpreting Value Change over Time

We have stated that the evidence from the present study pointed to stability rather than to change in the average value systems over the 2½-year interval. On this point Newcomb (personal communication) has commented:

> Altogether, these findings suggest that what the three populations have in common (being of a certain age and drawn from a "common pool" at the same time in 1969) have more influence on their responses than their differences (whatever personal characteristics led them to make different decisions after entering Flinders plus differing subsequent environments).

And we would repeat that perhaps there was not a great deal of difference in these subsequent environments anyway. To detect environmental effects one needs to be sure that the environments differ in important respects.

Most of the changes that did occur in our study were general, not specific to any one of these three groups. Are these changes age-related or ontogenetic, the sorts of changes that usually occur among late adolescents as they grow older and come under normative pressures from their family and peer groups? It is difficult to say. More information is needed about developmental changes in late adolescence and adulthood and the norms that are stressed by important reference groups.

Some of the changes could be the outcome of societal influences having wide currency at a particular time. The widely publicized concerns over environmental pollution, for example, may have led to general increases in the relative importance assigned to *a world of beauty*. It is not easy to separate the effects of developmental factors from those of particular societal influences. One would need to use the same procedures at various points in a society's history to control for social change. Would the same general changes in value importance across the time interval and ages studied still occur 10 years from now if the procedures used in our study were repeated? If they did, then one might be more confident that the changes were age-related and typical of late adolescence rather than due to specific influences at a particular time in history. It is interesting to note that Hoge and Bender (1974) found some rather large changes that occurred in theoretical, aesthetic, and religious values among three groups of Dartmouth College students who were tested with the Study of Values (Allport & Vernon, 1931) between 1931 and 1956 and restudied as alumni between 1952 and 1969. Their data supported a "current experiences" model which stressed the similar impact of historical events on college graduates of all ages and also on students. But they also noted that one needs to consider the appropriateness of other models for interpreting change as well. For discussions of some of these issues, see Buss, 1974; Nunnally, 1973; Riley, 1973; Schaie, 1970; Wohlwill, 1970. We will return to this question in the next chapter.

THE NEED FOR THEORETICALLY BASED RESEARCH ON SCHOOL IMPACT

In addition to meeting some of these complex methodological issues, future research in the area of school or college impact needs to be guided by theory. Throughout this chapter and the preceding ones we have sketched in some theoretical ideas that might guide future inquiry. In particular, psychologists need to make a close analysis of the environment and its inputs, of the discrepancies that may occur between cognitive structures laid down by individuals on the basis of their past experience and the varying demands of new environmental inputs, and of the modes of resolution that individuals may adopt in response to these discrepancies. These modes may themselves vary and cognitive adjustments such as value change are important possible outcomes, though not the only ones.

The detailed analysis of the social environment is especially important.

Within a school, for example, a number of different social environments correspond to the different classes that students attend, the staff with whom they have contact, and the different groups with whom they interact outside of the teaching situation. To refer to *the* school environment may be useful in a very general sense, but it is obviously an oversimplification. Closer analysis, then, is required of the social environments to which the student is exposed within the school and of the main influencing agents within them.

One cannot assume that these environments are all in harmony. Far from it. They are typically associated with demands and priorities that conflict. Teachers in the school, for example, may require a certain degree of politeness and obedience whereas the students may assign these modes of conduct fairly low priorities. An important basis for differentiating social environments within the school would be in terms of the groups that exist either formally in terms of the school's structure and functions, or informally on the basis of less structured social interactions. These various groups are associated with sets of roles, rules, attitudes, and values that are to some degree distinctive for each group but not completely unique because the characteristics of some groups overlap. For instance, one would expect student groups from different classrooms in a school to be more similar in their value systems than students and their teachers. Indeed, one could map the degree to which different social environments are similar in basic characteristics by investigating the matrix of discrepancies (such as in actual and attributed value systems) when all individuals (or, at a more molar level, all groups) are related one to another. In Chapter 10 we will discuss how such a matrix might be useful. For the present, it is sufficient to note that one would expect different groups within a community or large organization (like a school or college) to communicate different value priorities, the discrepancy increasing when people in these groups have different roles within the overall institutional structure and when these groups involve persons with markedly different background characteristics—such as age and education.

Because individuals encounter many social environments and agents of influence, it seems inevitable that discrepancies in value systems will occur as a matter of course. And in a pluralistic world of competing and overlapping influences, one has to accept the fact that many of these discrepancies cannot be resolved and are often ignored or tolerated. One does not usually play the chameleon, changing one's values according to the immediate social context in which one is located.

It is obvious, however, that some discrepancies are more significant than others in the sense that they will be more likely to lead to value change, behavioral adjustments, or both. The results of the Adelaide secondary schools study suggest, for example, that the discrepancy between own values and school values was not an especially important one for the students. Had it been important one might have expected that the pressure to resolve the discrepancy would have led to (as one mode of resolution) closer correspondence between the students' own values and those they attributed to their school. What is the basis for differences in the functional significance of different types of discrepancy? Why are some discrepancies associated with more pressure for resolution than others as far as individuals are concerned?

To answer these questions properly would require a detailed treatment of theories of social influence far beyond the scope of our discussion (see, for example, Abelson, Aronson, McGuire, Newcomb, Rosenberg, & Tannenbaum, 1968; Jones & Gerard, 1967; Katz, 1960; Kelman, 1961, 1974b; McGuire, 1969). The discrepancies between value systems that turn out to be important are those that arise when the discrepant information about values comes from a highly attractive, legitimate, and credible source—especially if this source belongs to a reference group (Hyman & Singer, 1968; Pettigrew, 1967), when that source is seen as acting voluntarily and without coercion, when the receiver of the communication is also exposing himself to the discrepant information of his own free will and accord, when the discrepant information is clear and unequivocal and cannot be distorted, when the extent of the discrepancy is within reasonable bounds and not so great as to evoke outright rejection, and when the discrepant information concerns some issue that is important to the receiver of the communication—especially when it implicates central aspects of the self-concept, such as one's important values (see Rokeach, 1973). Thus a person would be more likely to be influenced by someone he likes and trusts, whose authority he sees as legitimate, who belongs to the same groups as he does, who is similar in other important characteristics, whose interest in trying to influence the person can be taken as genuine and not related to "ulterior" or selfish motives, whose communication is clear and unambiguous but not radically discrepant from the person's own point of view, to whom the person is willing to listen without being forced to, and whose communication is about issues that the person sees as very important and related to his own self-concept. Not all of these conditions will be present at any one time. The evidence shows, however, that these various factors are important if social influence is to be effective. Their conceptual interrelatedness has been discussed previously in terms of a structural balance model of communication effects (Feather, 1964, 1967b, 1971a). There is firm evidence for the validity of the model which provides an integrative summary of the structure of the interpersonal communication situation and the possible outcomes of influence attempts.

In the context of the school environment, the most important source of influence is likely to be a student's own peer group, especially those members who are his close friends and acquaintances and with whom he interacts from day to day. The reliance of the adolescent upon his peer group has been noted by many authors (for a perceptive review of theory and research on adolescent socialization, see Campbell, 1969). In his well-known study of the adolescent society, for example, Coleman (1961) argues that the child of high-school age

is "cut-off" from the rest of society, forced inward toward his own age group, made to carry out his whole social life with others of his own age. With his fellows, he comes to constitute a small society, one that has most of its important interactions *within* itself, and maintains only a few threads of connection with the outside adult society. (p. 3)

In the North American school environment, one effect of such an adolescent society may be for schoolchildren to devalue scholarship relative to other activities such as athletics for boys and club activities for girls (Coleman, 1961). But such an effect would presumably be relative to time and place. It might occur in some other cultures, but that remains to be shown. The values of an adolescent society would be related to a complex set of factors, not the least of which is the culture in which children grow up and the point in historical and developmental time when they are studied. And the same values may be articulated in different ways depending upon the circumstances.

The teachers and staff within the school, having different status and functions and also being older and different from students in other respects, are not as likely to be as influential as the student's own peer group, although occasional gifted and well-liked teachers may exert an important influence. As Campbell (1969, pp. 847–851) points out, however, the different roles to which teachers and students are assigned, the way in which the school is organized and its composition vis-à-vis the personal and background characteristics of its members, all provide students with an example of an organization at work from which they may learn lessons about such matters as the management of time, the nature of organized routines, patterns of authority, the long-term goals of organizations, age-heterogeneous relations, the values of other people, in addition to the knowledge and skills they obtain from their exposure to the school curriculum.

Outside of the school environment and the peer group, the child's family provides an important reference group as well—a source of influence almost too obvious to mention and one that has molded the child from the very beginning. In regard to adolescent socialization, Campbell (1969) argues that

> any scholarly attempt to describe and dramatize the growth of peer group influences, the power of youth culture, the adolescent's struggle for freedom, etc., must eventually come to terms with the fact that family structures endure through the entire period of adolescence—as residential, affectional, and companionship units . . . . (p. 829)

> The research literature is almost entirely compatible with the conclusions that ties between parents and children remain close throughout the adolescent years; that the positive orientation toward parents does not diminish, and may indeed increase, during adolescence; and that parents and the parent-child relationship are both important influences on the adolescent. (p. 831)

In short, the peer group and the parents are the important agents of influence as far as adolescent socialization is concerned and any discrepancies that may arise between abstract and perceived structures when peer or family reference groups provide information about important issues (such as basic values) are likely to be significant discrepancies, leading to cognitive adjustment and possible changes in behavior. Thus, when an adolescent student's peer group challenges his values or when his parents criticize the position he takes, the effect is usually likely to be more dramatic than when the challenge comes from his teacher. And, of course, these two reference groups may be in conflict in regard to some of the values they emphasize but in harmony as far as other values are concerned.

Just how different reference groups exert their effects, whether these effects are more or less specific to particular areas depending upon the reference group involved, why some reference groups are more important than others, and the relationship of this importance to stages in the life cycle are questions that deserve a lot more attention from psychologists and sociologists than they have had in the past. We have suggested that the adolescent probably pays more attention to his parents and peer groups as far as his values are concerned than to other agents of influence, such as his teachers. Perhaps one's important reference groups are more likely to come from people who are perceived as similar to oneself in various basic respects, people who are able to meet one's needs and who provide and control reinforcement, people who are frequently involved in interaction with oneself, people who have acquired legitimate status in matters of values, and people with whom one has established bonds of attraction and belonging. These variables are interdependent and influence one another in a systemic way. For instance, the more one interacts with a person, the more one gets to discover similarities and differences along various dimensions and the more opportunity one has to satisfy one's needs by obtaining the appropriate rewards or reinforcements.

People from these *positive* reference groups are probably more likely to present congruent information than those outside the reference group. Some of these "outsiders" may even constitute a *negative* reference group, being more likely to present information that is markedly discrepant from present value systems. Such highly discrepant communications have a greater chance of being rejected because they have little impact on existing cognitive structures.

In a similar vein, Jones and Gerard (1967) have suggested that the co-orienting peer, by virtue of his similarity in value perspective, may function as "the reference person for evaluating the goodness or badness of the person's present state, S_0, or the state or states, S_1, S_2, . . . , to which he may aspire" (p. 320). They also suggest that the "expert" may function as a reference person

> in informing the person as to how he may move from one state of the world to another. He sheds light on the skills likely to be required, the costs of action, possible dangers and side effects, or other matters on which goal attainment may be contingent. (p. 320)

Jones and Gerard also point out that reference groups have commonly been assumed to have at least two functions: providing rewards and punishments relevant to the enforcement of norms (a *normative* function) and providing information that is important as far as cognitive development and social comparison are concerned (an *information* function).

It should be apparent, therefore, that over time the child's reference groups, functioning both in normative ways and as sources of information, have a significant role in the maintenance and modification of existing cognitive structures, including those cognitive structures that involve values. Reference groups may also influence the initiation or development of completely new cognitive structures in the child or the elaboration of structures already formed (as when new values come to be included in relatively simple value systems already in existence). Thus, reference groups and other important agents of influence may function as transmitters of information that can be new, consonant, or discrepant in relation to existing cognitive structures. They may also function as sources of rewards for conformity to group norms and punishments for deviation from group norms. These different functions affect the maintenance of cognitive structures and their development and elaboration as well as their readjustment. And, of course, they also influence overt action, such as choice.

What are some of the consequences that might occur when there are *important* discrepancies between a person's value systems and those he attributes to a particular social environment? One possible outcome is that the individual might reorganize his own value systems in the direction of congruence. Or he might misperceive or distort the value priorities of the social environment so that they are seen as closer to his own. He might also denigrate the social environment that promotes the discrepant values, seek more information about the value priorities of the social environment, attempt to change the social environment in an active way by influencing the important agents within it, or move to an alternative social environment that is viewed as promoting value priorities more consonant with his own.

For example, a disgruntled student who finds the value priorities of his school discrepant from his own might end up by modifying his own values if he has a great deal of liking and respect for the agents of influence within the institution and if the values being promoted are also shared by important reference groups, like his peers. But he might also retain his own value priorities and adopt other modes of resolution, such as ridiculing the institution, proselytizing his point of view in an attempt to change others, joining groups with similar values who react against the institution, seeking further information in an attempt to discover closer points of contact between himself and the institution, or leaving the institution entirely and moving to a more compatible environment.

Of course, a person might also tolerate the discrepancy, especially if his cognitive structures are complex and differentiated (Feather, 1971*a*, 1973*a*). In some cases also, he might rationalize his relative passivity in the face of dissatisfaction with the institution by viewing the discrepancy as short-term, as something to be experienced for a limited period only in the interests of achieving longer term goals that might be associated with one's life beyond the school. The dissatisfaction arising from value discrepancies might also be counteracted by satisfactions arising from other consonances involved in the person-environment interaction, as would occur if the student found that he was able to meet the performance demands of his situation in regard to the work he was called upon to do despite the discrepancy in values.

There are, then, many ways in which people react to the discrepancies that confront them as they experience social environments. Moreover, the dissatisfactions associated with some discrepancies may be diluted by satisfactions arising elsewhere. In applied research it becomes very difficult, therefore, to specify the concrete outcomes of cognitive discrepancies, particularly when so many avenues of resolution are usually open to individuals. The question of which mode of resolution is likely to be selected is not an easy one to answer. Various theoretical speculations about this question have been proposed (as in Abelson et al., 1968). It seems obvious, however, that the mode of resolution will depend upon both specific situational characteristics—for example, some possible solutions to the discrepancy may be blocked—and upon individual difference characteristics—for example, people may differ in their habitual modes of resolving discrepancies (see Feather, 1967a, 1971a).

How might one proceed to test some of these ideas in a natural setting, such as within a university or college or some other work situation? Clearly, if one were focusing upon the effects of value discrepancy, one would require an extensive mapping of the various social environments and the agents of influence within them, knowledge of the individual's own and attributed value systems and the discrepancies between them, some means of specifying which discrepancies were important and when value change as a mode of resolution would be likely to occur, knowledge about other sources of satisfaction and dissatisfaction with the institution as related to other person-environment characteristics, and so forth. The research would attempt to sample relevant information at various times during the individual's contact with the institution. Obviously, these requirements are difficult ones to meet and it is not surprising that they have not all been met in past research. Theory and research have so far been at a fairly simple level; more sophisticated efforts are required in the future.

The important point, however, is that research should be guided by elaborated theory. There is no substitute for good ideas.

MATCHING OR OPTIMUM DISCREPANCY?

In developing most of the studies concerned with educational choice and adjustment and college impact as reported in the previous two chapters and in the present chapter, it was assumed that people will make the choice on the basis of *matching* personal characteristics to environmental characteristics and that they will be happiest in environments where this match has been achieved. It was recognized that individuals are characteristically exposed to discrepant information from their social environments, corresponding to the different socializing agents they encounter, but that some discrepancies will be more important for them than others. It was also recognized that external pressures and ignorance or misinterpretation of reality by individuals may often cause them to make less than optimum choices and that the range of alternatives from which choice can be made is in any case usually limited, especially by socioeconomic factors. Hence, one would expect the occurrence of discrepancies to be the normal course of events in everyday life.

Indeed, the existence of such discrepancies is an important component of the whole process of development. If one lived in a lotus-land environment where all needs were satisfied, where all problems set by the environment could be easily solved, and where all higher-order cognitive structures such as attitudes and values were completely verified by the social environment, it is hard to see how new structures could even develop. Existing structures would have no reason to accommodate and information would not have to be assimilated (Piaget, 1950, 1966, 1967, 1971) because there would be no discrepancies to resolve.

Yet it would be a world devoid of excitement. Several authors have suggested that a small amount of discrepancy may be optimum in arousing interest and curiosity. They have also noted that large discrepancies may be associated with fear and avoidance (see Berlyne, 1960, 1965, 1966; Hebb, 1949; Hunt, 1961). Thus, Hunt (1961), in an interesting account of accommodative modification and growth in terms of the match between environmental circumstances and existing schemata, suggests that

> any discrepancy between central processes and circumstances beyond the limits of an organism's capacity for accommodation evokes distress and avoidance, while any discrepancy within the limits of an organism's capacity for accommodation is a source of pleasurable interest or curiosity . . . when circumstance and central process match perfectly, the result is stultifying boredom in which development fails. (p. 269)

Similar kinds of assumptions are made in models that relate information input to expectation or adaptation level (Cofer & Appley, 1964) where the adaptation level is seen as the zero or neutral point—although these models vary according to whether or not they take account of the direction as well as the degree of discrepancy (Feather, 1969b; Helson, 1964; McClelland, Atkinson, Clark, & Lowell, 1953; Verinis, Brandsma, & Cofer, 1968).

This line of argument would suggest that previous assumptions should be modified somewhat to take account of the motivational significance of optimum cognitive discrepancies. Thus, individuals may seek and be happier in environments where discrepancies between higher-order cognitive structures and information input are neither too small nor too large but somewhere in between. Ultimately, some of the rewards and satisfactions may come from resolving these optimum cognitive discrepancies so as to achieve new order and organization within the cognitive world of the person—this in addition to the fact that a good fit may imply a maximization of the reinforcements and a minimization of the punishments or threats that the environment may provide (Chapter 3). Such a principle of optimum discrepancy would allow for the individual's pursuit of novelty and change, and would introduce a further basis for the normal occurrence of cognitive discrepancy in everyday life, which we have argued is an important prerequisite for cognitive development.

The question still to be resolved, however, is how to specify what is meant by optimum and how to identify an optimum discrepancy in advance of response. It is easy to specify after the event that some discrepancy was optimum but such post hoc interpretations are of doubtful value unless they can provide new theoretical insights. What one needs is a testable theory of what makes a discrepancy optimum. Tranferring the focus to some optimum level of arousal will not solve the problem, for one then has to be able to identify in advance what is an optimum level of arousal. Perhaps the optimum discrepancy depends upon characteristics of both the cognitive structure and the incoming signal at any given time, both of which affect the likelihood that accommodation or assimilation or both can occur (Beswick, 1971; McReynolds, 1971). As yet we have no clear answer to these questions and theoretical developments are still to be made. The issues are particularly important ones and it is encouraging to see that they are being confronted in current work on intrinsic motivation (Day, Berlyne, & Hunt, 1971; Hunt, 1971).

Prior to these questions is the need to develop adequate conceptualization of cognitive structures and the processes involved in their formation, organization, and readjustment, together with ways of representing and measuring properties of these structures and the discrepancies between them (Feather, 1971*a*). This is no easy task. In the present context we have been able to define value systems in terms of linear orders and to use measures of correlation as estimates of degree of discrepancy. But these are simple assumptions— perhaps too simple. In more complex realizations, forms of mathematics that deal with structures, such as graph theory (Harary, Norman, & Cartwright, 1965) and the mathematics of groups (Piaget, 1950, 1971) will be required for the representation of structural organization and structural discrepancy.

SIMILARITIES ACROSS STUDIES

We will conclude by noting the similarity in average value systems that emerged for the various student groups involved in the studies that we have described in this chapter and the two preceding ones. The samples used in these studies were either from late secondary or early tertiary levels of education, most students falling within the 16-to-20 age range. Table 5.10 summarizes the main similarities in relation to the various samples employed.

TABLE 5-10. Four Highest and Four Lowest Values in Average Importance for Student Samples Answering Form E

Study		Values
Flinders Freshmen (Feather, 1970a)		
Terminal:	Most important:	True friendship, wisdom, freedom, a sense of accomplishment
	Least important:	Pleasure, national security, social recognition, salvation
Instrumental:	Most important:	Honest, responsible, broad-minded, loving
	Least important:	Imaginative, polite, clean, obedient
Flinders Freshmen (Feather, 1971b)		
Terminal:	Most important:	True friendship, freedom, wisdom, happiness
	Least important:	Pleasure, national security, social recognition, salvation
Instrumental:	Most important:	Honest, responsible, broad-minded, loving
	Least important:	Polite, imaginative, clean, obedient
Flinders Freshmen (Feather, 1973c)		
Terminal:	Most important:	Freedom, mature love, true friendship, wisdom
	Least important:	Social recognition, a comfortable life, national security, salvation
Instrumental:	Most important:	Honest, responsible, broad-minded, loving
	Least important:	Imaginative, polite, clean, obedient
Mitchell CAE (Feather & Collins, 1974)		
Terminal:	Most important:	A world at peace, happiness, true friendship, freedom
	Least important:	A comfortable life, pleasure, salvation, social recognition
Instrumental:	Most important:	Honest, loving, responsible, forgiving
	Least important:	Logical, intellectual, obedient, imaginative
Adelaide Secondary Schools (Feather, 1972b)		
Terminal:	Most important:	True friendship, a world at peace, freedom, happiness
	Least important:	Pleasure, national security, social recognition, salvation
Instrumental:	Most important:	Honest, responsible, broad-minded, ambitious
	Least important:	Logical, obedient, intellectual, imaginative

TABLE 5-11. Significant Main Effects of Sex in Analyses of Relative Importance of Individual Terminal and Instrumental Values

Study	Values
Flinders Freshmen (Feather, 1970a)	
More important for males:	Pleasure, wisdom, imaginative, logical
More important for females:	A world at peace, family security, honest
Flinders Freshmen (Feather, 1971b)	
More important for males:	Pleasure, imaginative, logical
More important for females:	Equality, national security, honest
Flinders Freshmen (Feather, 1973c)[a]	
More important for males:	Logical
More important for females:	Honest, loving, cheerful, obedient
Mitchell CAE (Feather & Collins, 1974)	
More important for males:	A comfortable life, pleasure, imaginative
More important for females:	Inner harmony, self-respect, wisdom, forgiving, loving
Adelaide Secondary Schools (Feather, 1972b)	
More important for males:	A comfortable life, an exciting life, mature love, pleasure, ambitious, capable, independent, intellectual, logical, self-controlled
More important for females:	A world at peace, a world of beauty, equality, inner harmony, wisdom, cheerful, forgiving, helpful, honest, loving, polite

[a] These were results that were replicated across at least two different measurement procedures.

No further comment is required. It is sufficient to note the general similarity across samples in regard to the four most important values and the four least important values for each value set—a remarkable consistency across groups.

Similarly, Table 5.11 compares the different samples in regard to significant sex differences in value priorities.

These data suggest that overall the male students gave greater importance to hedonistic values and to values concerned with achievement and competence than did the female students. The female students were more concerned with values relating to security, peace and harmony, honesty, and positive affiliative relationships with other people than were the male students. Rokeach (1973) also found that men in his 1968 NORC sample placed more emphasis upon values concerned with achievement and intellectual pursuits, whereas women in the sample assigned more importance to values concerned with love, affiliation, and the family. These differences are probably the products of differences in socialization practices within society which result in men and women ending up with different perceptions of their sex roles (see Block, 1973; Emmerich, 1973; Maccoby, 1966; Kagan, 1964; Parsons & Bales, 1955, Mischel, 1970). In the chapters to follow, we shall move from the educational environment to society more generally, beginning with descriptive studies and ending with studies that again involved the investigation of discrepancies between own and attributed values. Thus the canvas becomes larger but the basic concepts remain the same. The next two chapters again focus upon youth but not within the context of the school situation. They are concerned especially with the value system of adolescents in relation to those of their parents (generational similarities and differences) and with the value systems of special groups (student activists and juvenile offenders). Subsequent chapters take up the question of cross-cultural similarities and differences in value systems and the subjective assimilation of immigrant groups as far as their values are concerned.

6. Values across Generations

So FAR we have been mainly concerned with the discrepancies in values and value systems that occur within the educational context of the school or college. But, as we have indicated, such discrepancies are normal occurrences in all kinds of social interaction, whether the interaction be in the school, in the family, in the work situation, or in other settings where information about values is transmitted either verbally or in terms of overt behavior. One could develop taxonomies that classify the various sources of information about values and that take account of how these sources vary across different stages of the life-span of individuals. As Rokeach (1973) suggests, one way of classifying general sources of value inputs would be in terms of the important social institutions within society, where an institution is conceived of as "a social organization that has evolved in society and has been 'assigned' the task of specializing in the maintenance and enhancement of selected subsets of values and in their transmission from generation to generation" (pp. 24–25). Thus, one could attempt to discover the degree to which families and educational, religious, legal, economic, and political institutions, as well as the mass media, transmit distinctive sets of values and the degree to which these institutions overlap and reinforce one another in their value priorities.

LEVELS OF ANALYSIS

This form of analysis of sources of value discrepancy and their relationship to social institutions should recognize that there may be a great deal of variation in what is maintained, enhanced, and transmitted by a general class of social institutions. There are many different types of churches, for example, each of which may involve a similar set of value priorities to the church conceived as a total entity, but with some unique aspects. Obviously, it would be useful to classify social institutions into finer subsets so as to explore variation in value priorities across exemplars of a social institution as well as across different

118

classes of social institutions. Moreover, variation may occur over time in the value priorities characteristic of social institutions as new generations succeed old ones and as historical events have their effects.

It should be apparent that the agents of influence within an exemplar of a social institution may not necessarily agree with the institution's ideology, which may have been set by tradition, by higher authority, or by other societal factors. Yet one of the important roles of these agents of influence is to transmit the institution's value priorities. Institutional compliance, however, does not imply private acceptance. Teachers in a school may have value priorities that differ from the values involved in that school's overall educational philosophy. They may promote the school's educational philosophy because to do so is one of the tasks associated with their role as teachers. Privately, however, they may disagree with it. We would expect such instances of value discrepancy to be accompanied by a certain amount of dissatisfaction with the environment. Value conflicts may occur at all levels of a complex organization, and they are exacerbated when persons, as agents of influence, have to promote value priorities widely different from their own, that is, where value-discrepant behavior is involved.

The macrolevel of analysis noted in the preceding discussion is also evident when, instead of looking at social institutions, one explores value priorities that are associated with "social aggregates." For example, one could investigate value systems in the very poor, the aged, the blacks, the males, the females, the affluent, and in other groups that can be clearly defined within society. These forms of macroanalysis are especially typical of sociological inquiries.

Social psychologists, however, would be more concerned with the micro-analysis of the influence process itself, with who presents information about values, how this information gets to the person, what sort of person receives the information, and with the conditions under which communication is effective or ineffective in leading to value formation, elaboration, or modification, and possible behavior change. In this regard a person's reference and member-ship groups, and those individuals within them who are seen as legitimate, attractive, and credible sources of information, become very important as agents of social influence, as we have previously noted. These various groups and sources of influence are not static but may change as a person grows older and takes on new tasks and responsibilities—in particular new roles within social structures that typically evidence some form of stratification, roles such as becoming a husband, parent, supervisor in a work situation, owner of a business, or member of a school committee.

One of the child's crucial reference groups is his family, and within the family one can study the degree of similarity and difference between the value systems of parents and their children. In making these comparisons it becomes possible to identify points of agreement and conflict between different genera-tions, between siblings, and between parents. The comparison of different generations takes one into the area of intergenerational relations—a field of inquiry that has a long history in classical sociology (see, for example,

Mannheim, 1952) and one that has received a lot of attention in recent years in studies of the so-called generation gap. Some have argued that a very wide gap exists in modern society between generations, one that may lead to revolutionary change; others that the generation gap has been overemphasized, that it is an illusion, and that there is much continuity between generations. Still others maintain that there is continuity between generations in important aspects of life (such as values) but differences in less important, peripheral aspects (such as political opinions and sexual attitudes). These different viewpoints, together with the relevance of intergenerational relations to socialization and social change, have been summarized and discussed in excellent reviews by Bengtson (1970), Bengtson and Black (1973), and by Bengtson, Furlong, and Laufer (1974)—the latter paper appearing in the first of two issues of the 1974 *Journal of Social Issues* concerned with the theme of youth, generations, and social change. Sears (1969) has provided a useful summary of findings from the area of political behavior.

Bengtson and Black indicate that the study of intergenerational relations can proceed at a *macrolevel* of analysis where cohorts involving age-based social aggregates are the units, where the dimensions of the generational relationship concern intercohort solidarity, where time is studied in the historical sense, and where the important socialization issues concern the continuity of social institutions and the problems of cohort replacement and succession. Or one can use a *microlevel* of analysis where family members of different generations are the units, where lineage and interpersonal solidarity are examined, where time is studied from the viewpoint of events related to individual development and the life cycle, and where the issues of socialization pertain to the preparation of the individual for maturity and the transmission of attitudes and behavior. These two approaches overlap. The studies to be reported in this chapter (see also Feather, 1974b, 1975a, 1975b) were designed to be closer to the microlevel of analysis where similarities and differences in values and value systems between family members were of major interest.

What types of differences might one anticipate? One would expect values to shift in their importance across the life-span as the individual encounters new demands, new tasks, new problems, and new situations that are not only age-related and relatively universal within his culture, but that involve adaptation both to the biological and psychological changes that are an inevitable product of growth and development and to the new roles that people are generally thought to assume as they mature and grow older. In terms of this approach one might attempt to relate hypotheses about dominant values to theories about development across the life-span (for example, Erikson, 1950, 1959, 1968; Havighurst, 1972, 1973). Using Erikson's approach, one might view the adolescent's key values in the context of his search for "identity," and the adult's key values in relation to the psychosocial tasks of achieving "intimacy," "generativity," and "integrity." These statements could be used to generate broad predictions about values. For instance, it could be expected that, in their search for identity, the young might place high value on affiliation, friendship, and approval from peers because the peer group is a prime source of reflected appraisal (Douvan & Adelson, 1966). It could also be anticipated that adults, taken up with the responsibilities of marriage and raising their children, would attach high importance to the security of the family. And one could make similar intuitive guesses based upon these general theoretical statements, some of them consistent with what we already know from empirical studies.

Such an approach would be premature, however. The various taxonomies of change across the life-span have not been elaborated in detail in regard to values. They tend to be descriptive statements and not tightly organized theories. What we need is more information about values at the family level and at different ages so that theory can be fertilized by reliable information in order to generate new empirical inquiries that in turn can assist further theoretical development—theory moving along with observation, in tandem as it were. The main thrust of the present studies was, therefore, descriptive—to provide information from two social surveys about similarities and differences in value priorities across generations. The studies were cross-sectional rather than longitudinal in nature, each based on data collected at the same point in time from different family members. In addition, the two surveys also provided information about social attitudes across generations, these social attitudes relating to general conservatism in the first survey and to how people explain poverty in the second. It was also possible to relate the attitude information to the value priorities that the different generations provided.

TWO ADELAIDE SOCIAL SURVEYS

SAMPLING PROCEDURE

The two surveys were conducted in the Adelaide metropolitan area—one in 1972, the other in 1973. Both were based upon a multistage cluster sampling frame of the Adelaide Statistical Division maintained by the School of Social Sciences at Flinders University.

In the 1972 survey this frame was used to produce a random sample of 1,074 dwellings or households. It was decided to use only those dwellings that included children of 14 years of age or older. Hence, 790 dwellings with no children or where all children were younger than 14 were excluded from the sample. A further 89 dwellings were excluded because of refusals or language problems or both, leaving a total of 195 usable dwelling samples. An attempt was made to interview all adult members, including children of 14 or older, who lived in each selected dwelling. Out of a total of 659 possible respondents there were 72 refusals. That left questionnaires available from 587 respondents, 147 of them coming from heads of households, 145 from wives, 152 from sons, 126 from daughters, and 17 from other members in the dwelling. Of the respondents who described themselves as heads of households, 117 were males and 30 females.

In the 1973 survey a random sample of 545 dwellings was used. In this case it was decided not to exclude dwellings that did not contain children or where all children were younger than 14. The effect of this decision was that the age distribution of respondents was more evenly spread in this second survey because it involved younger heads of households with either no children at all or with young children, whereas in the 1972 survey the age distribution was bimodal with a bunching of ages for children and a bunching of ages for parents. In the 1973 survey an attempt was made to interview all adults and all children 14 years of age and older, who lived in each selected dwelling. A total of 217 dwellings could not be included in the survey because of refusals, language problems, or both, leaving a total of 328 dwellings which could be included, a slightly lower response rate (60 percent) than in the 1972 survey (69 percent). A total of 667 questionnaires was returned from these dwellings, 241 of them coming from heads of households, 226 from wives, 84 from sons, 77 from daughters, and 39 from other members of the dwelling. Of the respondents who described themselves as heads of households, 201 were males and 40 females.

Information about the ages of heads, wives, sons, and daughters is presented in Table 6.1, and some demographic information about heads of households in the 1972 and 1973 samples is presented in Table 6.2.

TABLE 6-1. Mean Ages and SDs of Heads of Households, Wives, Sons, and Daughters Tested in 1972 and 1973 Adelaide Surveys

	1972 Sample		1973 Sample	
	Mean Age	*SD*	*Mean Age*	*SD*
Heads	49.29	7.93	46.36	14.82
Wives	45.66	7.35	40.43	12.99
Sons	18.58	4.02	18.37	3.25
Daughters	17.31	3.92	18.40	6.68

QUESTIONNAIRES

Interviews were conducted by one experienced interviewer in 1972 and by two experienced interviewers in 1973. In most cases, questionnaires were left at each selected dwelling and collected later, up to three calls being made at each dwelling. A cover letter prefaced the questionnaires explaining that the research was concerned with discovering whether there was or was not a generation gap. The letter stated: "It may happen that parents and children think alike on some things but not on others. This is what we want to find out. We want to obtain accurate information about this question." Respondents were requested not to discuss their answers with other members of the household, to read each part of the survey carefully so that they were quite sure what to do, and to give their own true opinions. Finally, they were assured that their answers would be confidential. Names were not required, but households could be identified by code number.

TABLE 6-2. Income, Educational Attainment, and Religion of Heads of Households Tested in 1972 and 1973 Adelaide Surveys

	Percent of Sample	
Income ($ Per Year)	1972	1973
Under 2,000	16.3	11.6
2,000 − 3,999	23.8	17.0
4,000 − 5,999	25.2	36.1
6,000 − 7,999	12.2	10.8
Above 8,000	12.9	11.6
No response	9.5	12.9
Age	1972	1973
30 or under	0	17.8
31–40	10.2	17.8
41–50	46.3	21.6
51–60	32.0	24.5
Over 60	9.5	16.6
No response	2.0	1.7
Educational Attainment	1972	1973
University or college	16.3	16.6
Secondary or high school	55.7	61.4
Primary or elementary school	25.2	15.8
No response	2.7	6.2
Religion	1972	1973
Church of England	32.7	29.5
Catholic	13.6	18.7
Methodist and Presbyterian	22.4	18.3
Other Protestant	20.4	12.0
Other religions or no religion	9.5	16.6
No response	1.4	5.0

Note. N = 147 for 1972 survey; N = 241 for 1973 survey.
Source: Data are from Feather, 1975b.

The initial items of the questionnaire were designed to obtain information about the respondent's status in household (head, wife, son, daughter, and so forth), age, sex, birthplace, occupational status, job description, marital status, educational attainment, religion, and income. Respondents then completed Form D of the Rokeach Value Survey (the gummed-label version) with the standard format and instructions (Rokeach, 1973).

The questionnaires for the 1972 and 1973 surveys differed in regard to what respondents were asked to do next. Those who were tested in 1972 finished the questionnaire by answering a test designed to provide a measure of conservatism—conceptualized by Wilson (1973b) as "a general factor underlying the entire field of social attitudes" (p. 3)—with the "ideal" conservative being one who tends to be fundamentalist in his religious orientation and whose political leanings are likely to be pro-establishment and supportive of the *status quo;* who tends to insist upon strict rules and punishments; who is likely to favor militarism; who tends to be ethnocentric and intolerant of minority groups; who tends to prefer what is conventional, traditional, and familiar; who is likely to be antihedonistic in outlook and to favor restriction of sexual behavior; who tends to oppose scientific progress and "new-fangled" ideas; and who is likely to be superstitious and fatalistic. These characteristics, which obviously overlap, are sampled in a Conservatism Scale, detailed information about which is provided both in the original report on it (Wilson & Patterson, 1968) and in a recent collection of papers on the psychology of conservatism (Wilson, 1973d). The scale consists of 50 items, each relating to some issue or concept such as the death penalty, striptease shows, divine law, apartheid, disarmament, censorship, student pranks, hippies, and the evolution theory. Respondents are asked, "Which of the following do you favor or believe in?" and they may respond to each item by circling "Yes" or "?" or "No." The scale is balanced for acquiescence response set, that is, it attempts to control for individual differences in the tendency to agree with items despite their content. A total conservatism score which can range from 0–100 is obtained for each respondent—a liberal response to an item being scored 0, an ambiguous response being scored 1, and a conservative response being scored 2.

Respondents in the 1973 survey did not complete the Conservatism Scale. Instead, they responded to 11 items concerning reasons for poverty taken, with minor alterations, from an American survey conducted by Feagin (1972). These reasons were as follows: (1) prejudice and discrimination against poor people; (2) failure of private industry to provide enough jobs; (3) lack of thrift and proper money management by poor people; (4) low wages in some businesses and industries; (5) failure of society to provide good schools for many Australians; (6) just bad luck; (7) lack of effort by the poor themselves; (8) sickness and physical handicaps; (9) being taken advantage of by rich people; (10) lack of ability and talent among poor people; and (11) loose morals and drunkenness. Feagin identified Reasons 3, 7, and 11 as *individualistic* explanations, Reasons 1, 2, 4, 5, and 9 as *structural* explanations, and Reasons 6, 8, and 10 as *fatalistic* explanations of poverty (for some factor-analytic evidence which gave strongest support to the structural classification, see Feather, 1974b). Respondents checked whether they considered each reason to be "Very Important," "Somewhat Important," or "Not Important" as a possible cause of poverty in Australia.

In summary then, both samples completed a questionnaire consisting of three sections, the first containing items designed to obtain background and demographic information, the second containing Form D of the Rokeach Value Survey, and the third containing a measure of social attitudes which, for the 1972 sample, consisted of the Conservatism Scale and which, for the 1973 sample, involved a set of items concerning reasons for poverty. Information obtained from the first section has been summarized in Tables 6.1 and 6.2. We now turn to those results that relate to generational similarities and differences in value priorities.

GENERATIONAL COMPARISONS OF VALUE PRIORITIES

ANALYSIS OF AVERAGE VALUE SYSTEMS

Tables 6.3 and 6.4 present the median rankings of terminal and instrumental values respectively for heads, wives, sons, and daughters in both the 1972 and 1973 surveys. The eight sets of median rankings in Table 6.3 were compared for similarity using Spearman's rho and Kendall's tau. The same procedure was used to compare the eight sets of median rankings in Table 6.4. The results of these comparisons are presented in Table 6.5.

When one looks at the similarity indexes in Table 6.5 it is evident that they were all positive and fairly high throughout, indicating that the average value systems of parents and children were similar in certain respects. The basis for this similarity can be seen in Tables 6.3 and 6.4 where, for example, both parents and children ranked values such as *a world at peace, happiness, honest,* and *responsible* high in importance and values such as *pleasure, social recognition, salvation, obedient,* and *imaginative* low in importance.

At the same time, Table 6.5 shows some interesting differences. The average value systems of heads and wives were similar throughout, both within the same year and across years, as were the average value systems of sons and daughters. The parents, however, tended to be more similar than the children within the same year (note the small triangular matrices).

The similarity indexes across generations tended to be lowest when the average value systems of sons were compared with those of heads and wives. Put another way, the average value systems of daughters were closer to those of heads and wives than were those of sons. These data suggest differences in socialization experiences for boys and girls, girls being socialized in such a way that their value systems become more similar to those of the adults within each family, and boys, perhaps more reactive against parents and more concerned with achieving their own identity, being socialized in such a way that they develop value systems less consonant with those of the adult family members. It should be noted that these findings were based upon correlations between averaged data. In analyses of the data to be conducted in the future, it should

TABLE 6-3. Median Rankings and Composite Rank Orders of Terminal Values by Heads of Households, Wives, Sons, and Daughters Tested in 1972 and 1973 Adelaide Surveys

Terminal Value	1972 Survey				1973 Survey			
	Heads	Wives	Sons	Daughters	Heads	Wives	Sons	Daughters
N	140	139	145	123	226	219	83	75
A comfortable life	11.38 (14)	13.38 (14)	9.95 (11)	13.39 (15)	10.57 (13)	12.09 (14)	9.93 (11)	12.75 (14)
An exciting life	13.07 (15)	13.85 (15)	8.25 (8)	12.06 (13)	12.70 (15)	13.57 (15)	8.50 (7)	11.79 (13)
A sense of accomplishment	9.08 (9)	9.05 (10)	8.91 (10)	10.07 (12)	8.22 (9)	9.77 (11)	9.69 (10)	10.21 (12)
A world at peace	4.33 (2)	2.79 (2)	2.45 (1)	2.35 (1)	5.10 (3)	2.61 (2)	6.06 (4)	2.50 (1)
A world of beauty	11.00 (12.5)	10.59 (12)	10.06 (12)	8.55 (8)	11.94 (14)	11.03 (12)	10.56 (15)	9.90 (10)
Equality	9.22 (11)	9.96 (11)	7.05 (6)	4.21 (2)	9.94 (11)	9.26 (10)	8.88 (8)	6.83 (6)
Family security	2.05 (1)	2.35 (1)	6.42 (5)	4.97 (3)	2.39 (1)	2.10 (1)	8.29 (6)	5.06 (4)
Freedom	6.64 (5)	8.43 (9)	3.72 (2)	5.86 (5)	5.90 (4)	6.68 (4)	5.30 (2)	6.88 (7)
Happiness	5.41 (3)	5.43 (3)	5.81 (3)	6.39 (6)	5.00 (2)	4.13 (3)	4.77 (1)	4.95 (3)
Inner harmony	8.31 (8)	6.81 (5)	10.76 (13)	9.14 (9)	8.00 (8)	8.34 (9)	10.50 (14)	8.19 (8)
Mature love	9.17 (10)	6.95 (7)	8.27 (9)	9.25 (10)	8.57 (10)	8.10 (8)	9.17 (9)	8.93 (9)
National security	11.00 (12.5)	11.27 (13)	12.59 (16)	12.28 (14)	10.25 (12)	11.18 (13)	14.36 (17)	13.50 (15.5)
Pleasure	13.73 (16)	14.72 (17)	11.26 (15)	14.22 (18)	12.84 (16)	13.58 (16)	10.13 (13)	13.50 (15.5)
Salvation	15.42 (18)	14.04 (16)	16.50 (18)	13.72 (16)	15.53 (18)	15.45 (18)	16.13 (18)	16.28 (18)
Self-respect	7.56 (7)	6.82 (6)	11.04 (14)	9.55 (11)	7.71 (6)	7.23 (6)	10.06 (11)	10.06 (11)
Social recognition	15.00 (17)	15.95 (18)	14.82 (17)	13.88 (17)	14.21 (17)	15.37 (17)	13.90 (16)	15.06 (17)
True friendship	7.33 (6)	8.42 (8)	6.34 (4)	5.54 (4)	7.79 (7)	7.28 (7)	5.65 (3)	4.59 (2)
Wisdom	6.50 (4)	6.32 (4)	7.50 (7)	7.15 (7)	7.47 (5)	6.86 (5)	6.13 (5)	6.58 (5)

Note. Lower numbers denote higher relative value. In each column the rank order of each median (low to high) is denoted in parentheses after the median. Ns are for error-free rankings.

TABLE 6-4. Median Rankings and Composite Rank Orders of Instrumental Values by Heads of Households, Wives, Sons, and Daughters Tested in 1972 and 1973 Adelaide Surveys

Instrumental Value	1972 Survey				1973 Survey			
	Heads	Wives	Sons	Daughters	Heads	Wives	Sons	Daughters
N	142	137	142	122	228	219	81	75
Ambitious	9.78 (13)	12.15 (14)	8.10 (8)	11.00 (13)	8.71 (8)	11.56 (14)	8.90 (10)	8.79 (9)
Broad-minded	8.33 (7)	8.50 (10.5)	5.14 (2)	7.64 (6)	6.68 (3)	7.63 (5)	6.58 (4)	6.42 (6)
Capable	8.40 (9)	8.59 (12)	8.11 (9)	11.14 (14)	7.69 (6)	7.68 (6)	9.56 (12)	9.25 (10)
Cheerful	9.27 (10)	8.42 (8)	8.25 (10)	7.58 (5)	9.38 (11)	7.97 (8)	7.75 (5)	7.94 (7)
Clean	8.38 (8)	7.93 (7)	10.17 (13)	10.45 (11)	8.08 (7)	8.63 (10)	11.90 (15)	11.21 (14)
Courageous	8.22 (6)	7.63 (6)	7.38 (6)	8.75 (9)	7.67 (5)	8.53 (9)	8.69 (8)	8.25 (8)
Forgiving	7.22 (3)	5.54 (4)	7.36 (5)	5.29 (3)	8.71 (9)	7.02 (4)	7.92 (6)	6.06 (3)
Helpful	7.55 (4)	6.88 (5)	9.00 (11.5)	7.87 (7)	9.67 (13)	7.91 (7)	9.38 (11)	6.38 (5)
Honest	2.65 (1)	2.60 (1)	4.57 (1)	3.25 (1)	2.88 (1)	2.61 (1)	4.07 (1)	2.79 (1)
Imaginative	15.11 (18)	15.43 (18)	12.50 (17)	14.38 (17)	14.29 (18)	15.11 (18)	12.75 (17)	13.90 (16)
Independent	9.57 (12)	11.36 (13)	9.00 (11.5)	9.67 (10)	9.90 (14)	10.28 (13)	8.70 (9)	9.83 (12)
Intellectual	14.17 (17)	13.09 (16)	12.22 (16)	14.53 (18)	12.94 (16)	14.09 (16)	11.17 (14)	15.06 (18)
Logical	10.33 (15)	12.83 (15)	12.13 (15)	12.10 (15)	11.50 (15)	12.21 (15)	10.69 (13)	12.19 (15)
Loving	7.78 (5)	5.41 (2)	6.60 (4)	4.15 (2)	7.18 (4)	4.79 (3)	6.25 (2)	6.25 (4)
Obedient	12.93 (16)	13.71 (17)	14.85 (18)	12.67 (16)	14.23 (17)	14.74 (17)	13.38 (18)	14.58 (17)
Polite	10.17 (14)	8.50 (10.5)	12.00 (14)	10.88 (12)	9.58 (12)	9.89 (12)	12.64 (16)	10.92 (13)
Responsible	4.87 (2)	5.53 (3)	6.44 (3)	6.53 (4)	5.17 (2)	4.76 (2)	6.50 (3)	5.25 (2)
Self-controlled	9.50 (11)	8.45 (9)	8.00 (7)	8.00 (8)	9.00 (10)	9.03 (11)	7.94 (7)	9.81 (11)

Note. Lower numbers denote higher relative importance. In each column the rank order of each median (low to high) is denoted in parentheses after the median. *N*s are for error-free rankings.

TABLE 6-5. Similarity Indexes Comparing Median Rankings across Heads of Households, Wives, Sons, and Daughters Tested in 1972 and 1973 Adelaide Surveys

Group	1972				1973			
	1	2	3	4	1	2	3	4
1972								
1. Heads		.95 (.85)	.78 (.58)	.83 (.64)	.99 (.94)	.99 (.93)	.76 (.54)	.90 (.74)
2. Wives	.94 (.84)		.67 (.49)	.78 (.63)	.94 (.82)	.95 (.84)	.63 (.42)	.86 (.68)
3. Sons	.84 (.68)	.77 (.63)		.85 (.65)	.76 (.57)	.79 (.62)	.95 (.83)	.89 (.73)
4. Daughters	.89 (.74)	.91 (.79)	.85 (.68)		.78 (.61)	.84 (.66)	.73 (.48)	.94 (.81)
1973								
1. Heads	.82 (.70)	.77 (.64)	.91 (.80)	.73 (.56)		.98 (.92)	.76 (.56)	.85 (.68)
2. Wives	.95 (.84)	.90 (.81)	.87 (.73)	.89 (.76)	.87 (.75)		.76 (.58)	.89 (.73)
3. Sons	.77 (.62)	.76 (.62)	.92 (.79)	.89 (.75)	.77 (.60)	.83 (.67)		.83 (.64)
4. Daughters	.92 (.80)	.87 (.70)	.89 (.75)	.92 (.78)	.79 (.63)	.92 (.78)	.88 (.71)	

Note. Similarity indexes for average terminal value systems are above the diagonal; similarity indexes for average instrumental value systems are below the diagonal. Similarity indexes not in parentheses are Spearman rhos; similarity indexes in parentheses are Kendall taus. Higher similarity indexes indicate greater similarity between the average value systems involved in the comparison. In the columns, 1 = Heads, 2 = Wives, 3 = Sons, 4 = Daughters.

also be possible to look at similarities at the individual level, correlating value systems among family members (for a recent example of such an approach, but one not involving the Value Survey, see Troll, Neugarten, & Kraines, 1969; the authors report considerable similarity between young adults and their parents in the domain of values).

These intriguing findings suggest that future studies of how children are socialized within families might give close attention to the processes involved in the development of value systems in sons and daughters throughout adolescence to early adulthood. Differences obtained could be related to other evidence about sex roles and the development of sex identity (Emmerich, 1973; Kagan, 1964; Kohlberg, 1966; Mischel, 1970). It may be that, in response to role demands, the young male is better able to distance himself from the family when compared with the young female, to see himself as having to make his own way in life, breaking away from dependency on the family and taking on his own responsibilities. The girl, more dependent than the boy and with a vision of nurturant responsibilities in the future, remains closer to her parents in her value priorities.

This interpretation is supported by the results from two national interview studies of adolescent boys and adolescent girls conducted by the Survey Research Center at Ann Arbor in 1955 and 1956 and subsequently reported by Douvan and Adelson (1966). They conclude that

> The key terms in adolescent development for the boy in our culture are the erotic, autonomy (assertiveness, independence, achievement), and identity. For the girl the comparable terms are the erotic, the interpersonal, and identity. . . . What the girl achieves through intimate connection with others, the boy must manage by disconnecting, by separating himself and asserting his right to be distinct. (pp. 347–348)

Moreover, studies in political socialization suggest that women appear to be more susceptible to family influence than men. Sears (1969) summarizes some of the relevant findings as follows:

> Women tend to be oriented toward persons they know, particularly in the family, and less interested in more impersonal stimuli such as mass media or books. Their orientation toward the family prevents them from being fully exposed to the *Zeitgeist,* and they seem to reject innovation, deviation, and conflict. (p. 396)

Perhaps in these changing times such differences are being reduced, but the parallel with Douvan and Adelson's conclusion is apparent.

ANALYSIS OF SINGLE VALUES

The transformed rankings for each value were analyzed using a 2 × 2 analysis of variance. The first factor in the analysis was generation (heads and wives versus sons and daughters) and the second factor was sex (males versus females). These analyses were first applied to the 1972 data and then to the 1973 data with a view to dicovering replicated effects. The results of these analyses are presented in Tables 6.6 and 6.7.

TABLE 6-6. Significant Main Effects of Generation in 2 X 2 Analyses of Variance of Transformed Rankings of Each Terminal and Instrumental Value from 1972 and 1973 Adelaide Surveys

More Important for Parents than Children

1972 Survey

Terminal values:	At $p < .001$: Family security, inner harmony, national security, self-respect; at $p < .05$: a sense of accomplishment, wisdom
Instrumental values:	At $p < .001$: Clean, honest, polite, responsible; at $p < .01$: capable

1973 Survey

Terminal values:	At $p < .001$: Family security, national security, self-respect
Instrumental values:	At $p < .001$: Clean; at $p < .01$: polite; at $p < .05$: capable, responsible

More Important for Children than Parents

1972 Survey

Terminal values:	At $p < .001$: An exciting life, equality, freedom, pleasure, true friendship; at $p < .01$: social recognition; at $p < .05$: a world of beauty
Instrumental values:	At $p < .001$: Broadminded, imaginative; at $p < .01$: loving; at $p < .05$: independent

1973 Survey

Terminal values:	At $p < .001$: An exciting life, true friendship; at $p < .01$: equality, pleasure; at $p < .05$: a world of beauty, freedom
Instrumental values:	At $p < .05$: Broad-minded, forgiving, helpful, imaginative.

As Table 6.6 shows, parents and children differed in the relative importance they assigned to several values, and many of these differences were statistically significant both in 1972 and in 1973. When one examines only the replicated findings, it is clear that parents assigned relatively more importance than their children to values concerning both family and national security, self-respect and responsibility, politeness to others and cleanliness, and competence, that is, being capable. Their children assigned relatively more importance than their parents to such values as excitement and pleasure, equality and freedom, a world of beauty, close companionship with others, and a broad-minded and imaginative stance toward the world. Hence, there was strong evidence of generational differences in the relative importance assigned to the terminal and instrumental values.

These value differences between generations make intuitive sense and some of them can be related to theories about developmental changes across the life-span. Many of the values given greater weight by the children fit one's image of youth, which is often seen as seeking new experiences, as hedonistically oriented, as reacting against authority and rules and constraints that threaten personal freedom, as demanding to be treated as equals, as wanting to be seen as liberal and imaginative and, in their search for identity and expansion of self, as desiring close companionship, especially with others in their peer group (see Campbell, 1969). Their elders gave relatively more weight to values con-

TABLE 6-7. Significant Main Effects of Sex in 2 × 2 Analyses of Variance of Transformed Rankings of Each Terminal and Instrumental Value from 1972 and 1973 Adelaide Surveys

More Important for Males than Females

1972 Survey

Terminal values:	At $p < .001$: A comfortable life, an exciting life, freedom, pleasure; at $p < .05$: a sense of accomplishment
Instrumental values:	At $p < .001$: Ambitious, imaginative, logical; at $p < .05$: broad-minded, capable, independent

1973 Survey

Terminal values:	At $p < .001$: A comfortable life, an exciting life, pleasure; at $p < .01$: social recognition; at $p < .05$: a sense of accomplishment
Instrumental values:	At $p < .01$: Ambitious, imaginative, intellectual; at $p < .05$: logical

More Important for Females than Males

1972 Survey

Terminal values:	At $p < .001$: Inner harmony, salvation; at $p < .05$: a world at peace, self-respect
Instrumental values:	At $p < .001$: Forgiving, loving; at $p < .05$: cheerful, helpful, honest, obedient

1973 Survey

Terminal values:	At $p < .001$: A world at peace; at $p < .01$: equality, inner harmony; at $p < .05$: family security, true friendship
Instrumental values:	At $p < .001$: Forgiving, helpful; at $p < .05$: honest

cerned with security, both at the family and national level; with respect for self; with rules of conduct such as being polite and clean; with responsibility or reliability; and with competence as expressed in being capable. Again, many of these differences fit one's image of middle-age where concerns about the family, about respect and conformity, and about security and competence appear to become more salient (for some relevant discussions about changes after adolescence and the socialization processes involved see Brim & Wheeler, 1966; Bronfenbrenner, 1960; Erikson, 1950, 1959; Gould, 1975; Havighurst, 1972, 1973; Hess & Handel, 1959; Hill, 1970a, 1970b; Hill & Aldous, 1969; Maas & Kuypers, 1974; Neugarten, 1964; Neugarten & Moore, 1965; Neugarten, 1968; Parsons & Bales, 1955; Riley & Foner, 1968; Riley, Foner, Hess, &

Toby, 1969; Riley, Johnson, & Foner, 1972). The high priority given by the adults to *family security* is consistent with the results of an Australian study by Parsler (1971) involving blue-collar, white-collar, and middle-class working males. He found that the great majority in all three groups ranked their life satisfactions in the following order of importance: family relationships, career and occupation, and leisure time activities.

Although it is not easy to compare the studies, some of the age differences that we have described have also been noted by Rokeach (1973) who used data from a national NORC sample of adult Americans over 21, from a college sample at Michigan State University, and from a study of public-school students in New York City (Beech & Schoeppe, 1974). Our results are also consistent with those to be presented in later chapters using more specialized samples (Feather & Wasyluk, 1973*b;* Feather & Cross, 1975).

These various results concerning generational differences should not divert attention from the considerable evidence in the present study of similarity across generations in the relative importance assigned to many of the values. For example, according to the averaged data, all respondents indicated they thought it was important to have peace in the world and to be honest. And all respondents gave much less weight to values relating to social recognition, salvation, and being intellectual. This overall similarity in average value systems has already been noted (Table 6.5). One can conclude, therefore, that there was evidence to suggest both continuity and change in value systems across generations.

The male-female differences summarized in Table 6.7 are similar to those described in Chapter 5 (Table 5.11). They are of interest because they show that many of the differences obtained from the analysis of data from student samples also occurred when the wider community was sampled.

The analyses also indicated a small number of significant generation by sex interactions but, with one exception, none of these effects was replicated from 1972 to 1973 and most were at a low level of significance ($p < .05$). They will, therefore, be disregarded. The exception was in regard to *pleasure* and the interaction occurred because sons were especially likely to give this value higher relative priority (Table 6.3). A similar trend occurred for *an exciting life,* but the interaction was significant in 1972 only ($p < .05$), though it just failed to achieve statistical significance in 1973.

GENERATIONAL COMPARISONS OF SOCIAL ATTITUDES

TOTAL CONSERVATISM SCORES

Table 6.8 presents means of the total conservatism scores for heads, wives, sons, and daughters tested in the 1972 survey.

TABLE 6-8. Mean Total Conservatism Scores and SDs for Parents and Children Tested in 1972 Adelaide Survey

| | Total Conservatism Scores | | | |
| | Male | | Female | |
	Mean	*SD*	*Mean*	*SD*
Parents	50.96	12.72	54.24	10.74
Children	36.46	12.82	43.00	11.74

These scores were also analyzed using the 2 × 2 analysis of variance just described. The analysis revealed highly significant main effects for both the generation and sex factors (both $ps < .001$) but the interaction of generation and sex was not significant. As Table 6.8 shows, parents were more conservative on the average than their children and females more conservative on the average than males. Both of these effects have been found in previous studies (Boshier, 1973; Kish, Netterberg, & Leahy, 1973; Wilson & Patterson, 1968). Table 6.8 also shows that the differences between parents and children were greater than those between males and females—generational differences far exceeded sex differences.

When the total conservatism scores were correlated with age for all subjects the Pearson r was .47 which was highly significant ($p < .001$).

EXPLANATIONS OF POVERTY

Table 6.9 presents the percentage of parents and their children in the 1973 sample who endorsed one of the three possible answers for the 11 reasons for poverty, that is, as being "Very Important," "Somewhat Important," or "Not Important." The final column in Table 6.9 presents the results of x^2 analyses comparing the responses from parents and children in relation to the three categories of importance.

The data in Table 6.9 show that parents and children differed in the way in which they endorsed five of the items. The parents assigned more importance to lack of thrift and proper money management, to lack of effort, to lack of ability and talent, and to loose morals and drunkenness as reasons for poverty than did their children. But they assigned less importance to prejudice and discrimination against poor people as a reason than their children did. The results of more detailed analyses of the poverty data, including a comparison with North American data, a factor analysis of the interitem correlations, and an examination of responses in relation to demographic variables (such as income, educational attainment, and religion), may be found in another publication (Feather, 1974*b*). Three points from these analyses are of special interest: Protestants were more likely than Catholics to appeal to individualistic reasons; heads of households with low occupational status were more likely to appeal to structural reasons than heads of households with high status jobs; and fatalistic reasons for poverty (sickness and bad luck) were more likely to be endorsed as important by the elderly (the over-50 age group).

TABLE 6-9. Percentage of Heads of Households plus Wives and Sons plus Daughters in Adelaide Sample Endorsing Reasons for Poverty in Relation to Degree of Importance

| | Percent Endorsement | | | | | | |
| | By Heads plus Wives | | | By Sons plus Daughters | | | |
Reason	Very Important	Somewhat Important	Not Important	Very Important	Somewhat Important	Not Important	p
1. Prejudice and discrimination against poor people	29	40	31	37	28	35	< .05
2. Failure of private industry to provide enough jobs	27	44	29	25	48	27	N.S.
3. Lack of thrift and proper money management by poor people	56	35	9	33	47	20	< .001
4. Low wages in some businesses and industries	45	42	13	46	40	14	N.S.
5. Failure of society to provide good schools for many Australians	36	38	26	35	39	26	N.S.
6. Just bad luck	9	31	61	6	28	66	N.S.
7. Lack of effort by the poor themselves	45	45	10	35	48	18	< .05
8. Sickness and physical handicaps	62	32	5	56	35	10	N.S.
9. Being taken advantage of by rich people	24	31	45	33	32	35	N.S.
10. Lack of ability or talent among poor people	37	44	19	23	37	40	< .001
11. Loose morals and drunkenness	39	37	25	25	43	32	< .01

Note. Percentages were rounded to the nearest whole percentage. Ns ranged from 433-438 across items for parents, and from 147-148 across items for children. Results of χ^2 analysis per item are presented in final column. N.S. means "not statistically significant."
Source: Data are from Feather, 1974b.

Both the analysis of conservatism scores and of responses to possible reasons for poverty revealed marked generational differences—parents being more conservative than their children on the Conservatism Scale and more likely than their children to explain poverty in terms of individualistic reasons—that is, by blaming the poor for lack of thrift, lack of effort, and so forth—"character" flaws within the poor themselves. When positive, these aspects (thrift, effort) are those that are commonly regarded as part of the so-called Protestant ethic.

VALUES AND CONSERVATISM

It was possible to analyze the 1972 survey data further so as to examine whether differences in conservatism scores were associated with differences in the relative importance assigned to particular values when age differences were controlled. The transformed rankings for each value from all respondents in 1972 were subjected to a 3 × 3 analysis of variance with age (under 30 years, 30-to-50 years, over 50 years) as the first factor in the analysis and conservatism score (below 41, 41-to-55, over 55) as the second factor. There were several main effects of the conservatism factor indicating statistically significant differences in mean value importance across the three levels of conservatism, irrespective of age. The following values increased in relative importance as conservatism increased: *national security, salvation, clean, obedient,* and *polite* (all $ps < .001$), and *a comfortable life* ($p < .05$). The following values decreased in relative importance as conservatism increased: *equality, freedom, broad-minded, imaginative,* and *logical* (all $ps < .001$), *mature love* and *independent* (both $ps < .01$), and *an exciting life* and *intellectual* (both $ps < .05$). There were also several statistically significant main effects of the age factor that were consistent with the generational differences noted in Table 6.6, and a small number of significant interaction effects, but they are not reported in this context because most of them were significant at a low level ($p < .05$) and some were difficult to interpret.

The results relating conservatism to value importance accord rather well with Wilson's description of some of the characteristics of the "ideal" conservative as summarized earlier in this chapter. They indicate that the highly conservative person, when compared with one who is less conservative, has a tendency to place greater stress on values involving national security, orthodox religion, respect for authority, and conventional rules of conduct. Also, he tends to put less emphasis on values having to do with equal opportunity; independence and free choice; a stimulating, active life; open-mindedness; a creative stance toward the world; logic and intelligence; and sexual and spiritual intimacy. This pattern of differences is further supported in some respects by the results of other studies involving the Conservatism Scale—studies covering topics such as religion, racialism, superstitious behavior, aesthetic judgments, response to humor, and stimulus-seeking (Wilson, 1973*d*). These results are interpreted by Wilson (1973*a*) as indicating the importance of a general factor of conservatism in social attitudes. The conservative attitude syndrome is traced ultimately to genetic and environmental factors which determine feelings of insecurity and inferiority. These in turn lead to "a generalized susceptibility to experiencing threat or anxiety in the face of uncertainty" (Wilson, 1973*a*, p. 259) and consequently to a tendency to avoid both stimulus and response uncertainty, an avoidance that is displayed both in conservative attitudes and behavior.

The present results point to the possibility of identifying sets of values that may be more characteristic of conservatives than of liberals. On the assumption that values somehow underlie attitudes, one can argue that the different items on the Conservatism Scale may suggest certain values to the person and that his answers would then reflect the relative importance of these values to him. For example, whether one favors or believes in divine law (item 15 on the scale) might depend upon the relative importance assigned to values such as *salvation,* being *broad-minded,* being *obedient,* and being *clean,* among others. Conservatism may then be conceptualized in terms of the relative importance assigned by the person to certain values that are themselves products of socialization and in the service of basic needs.

The position that conservatism may cohere in patterns of values is consistent with Rokeach's (1973) two-value model of political ideology. For various reasons Rokeach doubts the usefulness of applying general concepts or dimensions such as liberalism-conservatism to the comparison of political ideologies. Instead, he prefers to look for identifiable sets of values that necessarily underlie variations in political ideologies, and the two values he considers to be especially important are the terminal values *equality* and *freedom.* For Rokeach, communist ideologies elevate *equality* but assign *freedom* relatively low priority, socialist ideologies elevate both *equality* and *freedom* in relative importance, capitalist ideologies elevate *freedom* but assign *equality* lower status, and fascist ideologies assign both *equality* and *freedom* relatively low priority.

The kind of conservatism described by Wilson (1973*a,* 1973*b*), however, appears to extend beyond political ideologies because it is also reflected in other attitudes of a nonpolitical nature that are held by the person and in behaviors that are not specifically related to political orientations. Our results show that, as in Rokeach's two-value model of politics, *equality* and *freedom* are involved in this general conservatism syndrome. But the results also show that general conservatism seems to implicate other values as well.

The previous discussion needs to be qualified in two ways, however. First, the evidence for an influential general dimension of conservatism is not particularly strong. When the scores for the 50 items on the Conservatism Scale were intercorrelated for all respondents to the 1972 Adelaide survey and the resulting matrix factor-analyzed, using the principal-factor procedure with iterated communalities followed by varimax rotation for eigenvalues greater than one (the PA2 solution in Nie, Bent, & Hull, 1970), 15 factors emerged with latent roots greater than unity and together they accounted for only 35.3 percent of the total variance. The first *unrotated* factor, which accounted for 35.7 percent of the common variance, could be identified as a general conservatism factor, but clearly it accounted for a very small proportion of the variation in scores (only 12.6 percent of the total variance). After varimax rotation the general factor disappeared and a number of group factors emerged, relating to particular subsets of items (for a detailed account of findings see Feather, 1975*a*). On the basis of this evidence one cannot claim to have found a strong general factor (see also Wilson, 1973*c*).

In the second place, as we noted in Chapter 2, there is no evidence from the multidimensional scaling analysis or from the clustering procedure to suggest extensive subsets of values that cluster together strongly in terms of underlying dimensions.

On both of these grounds we believe that it may be more useful to relate social attitudes and behavior to small sets of values that one would expect to be involved on the basis of some underlying theory rather than to posit general dimensions for which the evidence is at best rather fragile when it relates to the magnitude of their effects.

VALUES AND EXPLANATIONS OF POVERTY

The data from the 1973 survey were also analyzed further so as to examine whether differences in the way subjects answered the items about reasons for poverty were associated with differences in the relative importance assigned to particular values when age differences were controlled. The transformed rankings for each value from all respondents in 1973 were subjected to a 3 × 3 analysis of variance with age (under 30 years, 30-to-50 years, over 50 years) as the first factor in the analysis and importance of reason ("Very important," "Somewhat important," "Not important") as the second factor—the analyses being performed separately for each of the 11 explanations of poverty.

As in the analysis described in the previous section, there were several significant main effects involving the age factor that were consistent with the generational differences noted in Table 6.6 and some significant interaction effects, most of which were significant at a low level ($p < .05$) and some of which were difficult to interpret. These various effects will be disregarded.

Several main effects of the importance of reason factor indicated regular increases or decreases in mean value importance across the three possible levels of response to each explanation of poverty, these effects occurring irrespective

TABLE 6-10. Significant Main Effects of "Importance of Reason" in Regard to Analyses of Variance of Transformed Ranks for Each Value

Reason for Poverty	Increases or Decreases in Mean Value Importance with Increase in Importance Assigned to Reason	
1. Prejudice and discrimination against poor people	Increase in Importance:	A world at peace (.01), equality (.01), clean (.05), helpful (.05)
	Decrease in Importance:	A sense of accomplishment (.01), capable (.01), logical (.05), responsible (.05)
2. Failure of private industry to provide enough jobs	Increase in Importance:	A world at peace (.05), equality (.05), ambitious (.05), clean (.05), obedient (.05)
	Decrease in Importance:	Inner harmony (.05), wisdom (.05), capable (.01)
3. Lack of thrift and proper money management by poor people	Increase in Importance:	National security (.05), capable (.001), responsible (.05)
	Decrease in Importance:	None
4. Low wages in some businesses and industries	Increase in Importance:	A world at peace (.05), equality (.05), family security (.05), salvation (.05)
	Decrease in Importance:	An exciting life (.05)
5. Failure of society to provide good schools for many Australians	Increase in Importance:	Equality (.001), freedom (.05)
	Decrease in Importance:	None
6. Just bad luck	Increase in Importance:	Pleasure (.05)
	Decrease in Importance:	None
7. Lack of effort by the poor themselves	Increase in Importance:	Courageous (.05)
	Decrease in Importance:	Equality (.001)
8. Sickness and physical handicaps	Increase in Importance:	Self-respect (.05)
	Decrease in Importance:	Pleasure (.05)
9. Being taken advantage of by rich people	Increase in Importance:	Equality (.001)
	Decrease in Importance:	Happiness (.05), capable (.01), responsible (.05)
10. Lack of ability and talent among poor people	Increase in Importance:	Courageous (.05)
	Decrease in Importance:	Inner harmony (.05), logical (.05)
11. Loose morals and drunkenness	Increase in Importance:	Family security (.05), national security (.01), ambitious (.05), clean (.001), obedient (.001), polite (.05)
	Decrease in Importance:	Equality (.05), broad-minded (.01), imaginative (.001), intellectual (.01)

Note. Figures in parentheses after each value indicate the level of statistical significance.

of age. The significant effects can be summarized as indicating either *increases* or *decreases* in mean value importance as responses shifted from "Not important" to "Somewhat important" to "Very important" for the explanation of poverty, that is, as that explanation was seen as more and more important. Table 6.10 presents the significant main effects that were found involving these regular increases or decreases (a very small number of curvilinear effects will not be reported).

It is not easy to abstract a general message from Table 6.10, but one consistent finding is worthy of note. On all of the *structural* explanations of poverty (reasons 1, 2, 4, 5, and 9), in which social and structural factors such as prejudice, lack of jobs, low wages, and exploitation were presented as reasons for the plight of the poor, the more such explanations were seen as important by respondents the higher they ranked *equality* in relative importance. Thus this social value, emphasizing brotherhood and equal opportunity for all, was related to endorsement of structural reasons in the direction that one would expect. For three of these structural reasons (1, 2, and 9) the relative importance assigned to being *capable* decreased as importance assigned to the reason increased. Those who gave this competence value lower priority in their rankings were therefore more likely to see prejudice, low wages, and exploitation as important causes of poverty. These results suggest that the degree to which people explain poverty in terms of social, structural factors depends upon the relative importance they assign to those social and competence values that are relevant to the work situation. Thus, where equal opportunity is highly valued and competence devalued (relative to other values) structural reasons become more prominent as important explanations of poverty.

Table 6.10 also shows that typically a number of values were related to how respondents checked each reason for importance. Most of the significant effects obtained make intuitive sense. We will single out one for attention because it has occurred in a similar form in some of our other studies (Feather, 1970*b*, 1971*d*): The higher the relative importance assigned to being *clean,* the greater the endorsement of "Prejudice and discrimination against poor people" as an important explanation of poverty. The degree to which cleanliness was valued was therefore related to the degree to which poverty was attributed to prejudice and discrimination.

No distinctive value or cluster of values emerged for the *individualistic* explanations (3, 7, and 11) or for the *fatalistic* explanations (6, 8, and 10) — using Feagin's (1972) classification — although those respondents who gave being *courageous* higher priority in their value rankings were more likely to endorse lack of effort and lack of ability as important reasons for poverty.

A factor-analysis of the intercorrelations between responses given by the entire 1973 Adelaide sample to the 11 poverty explanations, using the principal-factor procedure with iterated communalities in conjunction with varimax rotation for eigenvalues greater than one (the PA2 solution in Nie, Bent, &

Hull, 1970), provided strongest support for a structural dimension involving reasons 1, 2, 4, 5, and 9. Individualistic and fatalistic dimensions also became evident, but, in contrast with Feagin's classification, lack of ability appeared as an individualistic explanation rather than as a fatalistic explanation (for a discussion of the wider implications of this poverty study and its relevance to attribution theory, see Feather, 1974*b*).

OTHER STUDIES OF ATTITUDES AND VALUES

Rokeach (1973) has summarized other studies that have attempted to relate attitudes and values, including some conducted in the early stages of the Flinders program (Feather, 1970*b*, 1971*d*). He indicates that a given attitude held by different persons might not be in the service of the same value or the same subset of values. But one can usually make a shrewd guess concerning which values would most likely be involved. One would expect that attitudes and values that are within the domain of a particular social institution (for example, the church) would tend to be associated. Thus, one's attitudes toward religion and the church are likely to be related to the degree of importance assigned to such values as *salvation* and being *loving, helpful,* and *forgiving* (Rokeach, 1969*a*). The socializing forces move in the same direction and one's general values formed within a particular context come to underlie the more specific attitudes and behaviors also developed within that context—although to extend the example just given, the values that distinguish the churchgoer from the nonchurchgoer are contradicted by evidence about degree of social compassion in these two groups (Rokeach, 1969*b*).

In the early studies of the Flinders program, values have been related to specific attitudes toward controversial issues, such as American intervention in South Vietnam, the White Australia policy, legalized abortion, and religious instruction in schools (Feather, 1970*b*). They have also been related to more general cognitive styles such as ethnocentrism, dogmatism, and intolerance of ambiguity on the assumption that there might be a core set of values that relate to these styles (Feather, 1970*b*, 1971*d*). The results of these studies are too complicated to summarize and the reader is referred to the detailed reports. There was evidence, however, that respondents with very high dogmatism scores tended to rank *salvation* higher in relative importance than those with very low dogmatism scores. The difference was replicated in successive studies involving university students tested in 1968, 1969, and 1970. Those who had very high intolerance of ambiguity scores ranked *clean* and *obedient* as more important and *imaginative* as less important than those who had very low intolerance of ambiguity scores. These effects were also replicated over the three successive samples. Those respondents with very high ethnocentrism scores ranked *equality* and *a world of beauty* as less important among the terminal values and *a comfortable life* as more important than did those with very low ethnocentrism scores. Since ethnocentrism was tested only in the 1970 sample, no replication check was possible. Yet, as shown in an earlier study (Feather, 1970*b*), respondents who favored a White Australia immigration policy also ranked *equality* as lower in importance than did those who opposed this policy. Among the instrumental values, respondents with very high ethnocentrism scores ranked *clean* as more important and *helpful* and *imaginative* as less important than did those with very low ethnocentrism scores. In the earlier study, there was also evidence that respondents who favored a White Australia tended to rank *clean* as more important and *helpful* as less important than did those who opposed this immigration policy. And we saw in the last section that subjects were more likely to endorse prejudice and discrimination as an important reason for poverty the more they valued being *clean*.

As one sifts through these pieces of information, therefore, patterns come to light, and these patterns do make sense in terms of our notions of what processes might determine relationships between values and attitudes. For example, Bettelheim and Janowitz (1964) also found a relationship between prejudice and concern with cleanliness: war veterans who were outspokenly and *intensely* anti-Negro in their attitudes being much more likely to see Negroes as sloppy, dirty, and filthy than were stereotyped anti-Negro veterans. In a recent study, Epstein, Krupat, and Obudho (1975), using a variation of the Clark and Clark (1947) procedure, presented white and black schoolchildren in elementary schools in the New York City school system with pictures of children differing in both race (white, black) and cleanliness (clean, dirty). They found that cleanliness was a much more salient dimension than race in determining each child's preference for a play partner. Moreover, anecdotal evidence showed that children of both races frequently made derogatory comments about the pictures of the dirty children (of both races).

Cleanliness therefore seems to emerge as one of the values that is relatively salient among those who discriminate against outgroups. As a value, cleanliness is probably inculcated early in childhood as an important aspect of child rearing. It can be used as a basis for justifying negative attitudes both toward various outgroups (ethnocentrism) and toward situations that, because of their novelty, complexity, or contradictoriness, demand to be structured (intolerance of ambiguity). These situations could be perceived as messy and lacking in tidiness.

Similarly, one can understand why the likelihood of holding ethnocentric attitudes would be associated with a tendency to downgrade equality, and why the authoritarian style might relate to the relative importance of equal opportunity and obedience within value systems. And similar results have been shown in other studies also (Rokeach, 1973).

What is slightly disturbing is the on-again, off-again quality of other findings from the earlier Flinders studies where values that related to particular attitudes in one study failed to relate in subsequent studies. None of the results from these earlier studies (Feather, 1970*b*, 1971*d*) has been quite so impressive as some of those reported in the present chapter where, for example, values and general conservatism were shown to be involved in meaningful relationships. Why this difference?

The reasons for the difference are undoubtedly complex. One important factor may be the nature of the populations sampled. The earlier studies all involved first-year university students enrolled in an introductory psychology course, samples that were fairly homogeneous in important respects. Respondents in the 1972 and 1973 Adelaide surveys were sampled from a much wider population and were much more heterogeneous than the university samples. One would expect relationships to be stronger in heterogeneous groups where respondents come from various segments of society and have been subjected to different socialization experiences.

Yet heterogeneity carries its own risks. To be specific, the strong generational effects described in this chapter suggest that studies relating values and attitudes should always attempt to control for *age* differences. Otherwise, relationships between values and attitudes may occur spuriously because one has sampled over a wide age range. The point can be made this way: If one correlated height and mental age for children varying from 5 to 16 years, one would expect to find a positive correlation between these two variables, but one would not want to argue from this finding that height determines mental age or that mental age determines height. In the same way, one would find relationships between conservatism and value priorities over a wide age range simply because conservatism increases with age and because there are also certain predictable changes in value priorities as a person grows older—at least to the extent that these differences are manifested in cross-sectional studies. But it would be simplistic to argue from this evidence that values determined conservatism (or vice-versa). The argument is faulty because sampling over a wide age range would produce spurious correlations. The relationships obtained could be due to other unmeasured factors. In our research relating values and conservatism and values and explanations of poverty, we controlled for age by including it as a factor in each analysis, but this is not always done. As a result, reports of relationships between values and attitudes are not always easy to interpret and may in fact be misleading.

As Rokeach (1973, p. 121) indicates, the study of the relationship between values and attitudes is still at a very early stage where the assembling of descriptive information is important for future progress. One would like to be able to specify in advance which values would be likely to underlie particular attitudes (and behaviors). But this is likely to be a difficult task until we know more about the conditions under which both attitudes and values develop.

INTERPRETATION OF GENERATIONAL EFFECTS

How to interpret the differences seen in value priorities, conservatism, and explanations of poverty between generations? There can be no simple interpretation. Change in the relative importance assigned to particular values over the life-span may have an *ontogenetic* basis, related to the fairly universal adjustments that one has to make at different periods of the life cycle as one copes with biological change, with changing needs, and with those societal expectations that relate to changing roles and responsibilities (Erikson, 1950; Havighurst, 1972). The relatively high priority accorded to *true friendship,* for example, by both boys and girls could reflect the importance of companionship and the peer group for young people coping with the problems of adolescence (Douvan & Adelson, 1966; Rosenberg, 1965) whereas the relatively high priority assigned by their parents to *family security* would relate to their responsibility in raising and caring for their children and in maintaining the family unit. These sorts of problems are universal, rooted in biology, in changing personal needs, and in the different roles and responsibilities that one assumes throughout life.

Additionally, however, value and attitude differences between generations could reflect the impact of *unique* sociocultural trends or events that have been experienced by one generation but not by the other, because generations start at different points in historical time and are shaped in different ways. For example, parents whose childhood overlapped or closely followed the Great Depression and who became embroiled in the Second World War or the Korean War might be expected to be more concerned with *national security* than their children (for a study of children of the Great Depression see Elder, 1974). Younger cohorts would have been exposed to new and (it is to be hoped) improved forms of education when compared with older cohorts, and so on.

Finally, comparisons between generations or different age-cohorts might be influenced by trends or events that are *common* to each, having a similar impact. One might, for instance, expect the recent emphasis on conservation and environmental pollution to be associated with an increase in the relative importance assigned to *a world of beauty* by both parents and children—though such effects might also interact with age.

As we indicated in discussing the question of college impact and value change in the previous chapter, it is not easy to disentangle these factors. One needs longitudinal studies with different groups of age-cohorts—the studies being repeated at different times in history in order to ascertain whether certain age-related differences in attitudes and values occur independently of historical trends or events and more or less universally among people. Such studies, once rare (no doubt because of their complexity and the time and expense involved in their execution) are now becoming more common. They are essential. They may in fact correct mistaken conclusions that have been based either upon cross-sectional studies, in which different samples have been assessed at one point in time, or upon single-cohort longitudinal studies aimed at discovering ontogenetic changes within a single epoch for one age group. For example, Schaie and his associates, using cross-sequential designs involving a combination of cross-sectional and short-term longitudinal studies at different points in time (Schaie, 1973), have provided evidence that challenges the traditional view that advancing age is accompanied by a wide variety of intellectual decrements. Thus, Schaie and Labouvie-Vief (1974), on the basis of analyses of a variety of ability scores, concluded that

> most of the adult life-span is characterized by an absence of decisive intellectual decrements. In times of rapid cultural and technological change it is primarily in relation to younger populations that the aged can be described as deficient and it is erroneous to interpret such cross-sectional age differences as indicating ontogenetic change patterns. (p. 317)

They argue for the application of more rigorous methodologies aimed at differentiating ontogenetic and sociocultural change components and also for consideration of environmental factors as well as biological processes in accounting for continuity and change over the life-cycle and between cohort groups (see also related studies of abilities by Riegel, Riegel, & Meyer, 1967; and by Schaie, Labouvie, & Buech, 1973).

Some other recent studies using these more rigorous designs have dealt with personality variables and with social and political attitudes. Both Baltes and Nesselroade (1972) and Woodruff and Birren (1972) have looked at personality change. And Schaie and Parham (1974) have shown that changes in response to a social responsibility scale depended upon cohort membership as well as upon the specific time period that was monitored. In a recent important contribution based upon surveys of parents and children interviewed first in 1965 and then eight years later, Jennings and Niemi (in press) have looked at the way ontogenetic or life-cycle effects (the kinds of change endemic to the life course), generational effects (differences in the shared community of experiences that different age-cohorts undergo), and period or *Zeitgeist* effects (those influences that reflect important trends and events during a given period of history and that have a roughly common impact on most segments of society), might together interact to influence continuity or discontinuity in political orientations for the two generations over time. On the basis of their evidence they conclude that:

> The flow of the two generations over time has, if anything, worked to bring them closer together now than they were eight years previously. . . . life-cycle effects were working primarily . . . to hold the parents on a plane

while drawing their offspring toward them. . . . Period effects in some instances, most notably regarding political trust and civil rights, prompted parallel shifts in both generations. And there were, indeed, some visible signs of lasting generational effects. . . . On balance the forces acting to establish convergence seem to outweigh those creating divergence. (pp. 31–32 of the mimeographed report; see also Jennings & Niemi, 1974)

In addition to these studies of political orientations, some recent investigations of voting behavior have also gone beyond cross-sectional designs and have employed more rigorous methodologies (for example, Abrahamson, 1974; Glenn, 1973; Glenn & Hefner, 1972). So there is a deepening awareness of the need for more sophisticated approaches to the analysis of continuity and change across time in a number of different areas. We urgently need to apply these improved methodologies to the realm of values. Without them we are confronted by ambiguity. Simple cross-sectional studies or single-cohort longitudinal studies are no longer sufficient. If theoretical advances are to be fertilized by research findings, investigations must employ accurate methodologies that enable at least some disentangling of the complex influences involved in stability and change in value systems over time (Buss, 1974; Schaie & Gribbin, 1975). Indeed, these methodologies are highly relevant to the whole question of continuity and discontinuity in *all* personality characteristics.

This is not to say that the descriptive information that comes from cross-sectional studies is without value. Indeed it may be very important to identify intergenerational similarities and differences in value priorities as measured at the same point in time—especially if one wanted to foster understanding between the generations, or if one was interested in specifying some of the underlying determinants of intergenerational cooperation or conflict at the behavioral level.

Along with more sophisticated methodologies we also need more hard factual information and less speculation about the so-called generation gap; we need to look at differences in a wide variety of characteristics in order to determine the scope of the "gap." Further, we need more evidence on whether the gap is unique to youth and their parents or whether it extends across generations. Some studies are now beginning to appear that compare three generations —the present generation, their parents, and their grandparents (Hill, 1970*a*, 1970*b*; Payne, Summers, & Stewart, 1973). Indeed, the whole area of intergenerational analysis has undergone remarkable development and refinement in recent years (Bengtson, Furlong, & Laufer, 1974).

It is to be hoped that the research findings that issue from these new developments in methodology will stimulate renewed interest in the theoretical analysis of differences in values and attitudes between generations. Many questions can be asked. In the present context, for instance, in comparison with their children, are factors that lead to higher conservatism among parents the same ones that determine the higher relative importance they assign to such values as *family security* and *national security* and the lower relative importance they assign to such values as *an exciting life, equality,* and *freedom?* It is only in recent years that developmental psychologists have begun to address themselves to changes that occur over the entire life-span. Much more needs to be done both in theory and in research to account for stability and change in personal characteristics over the entire life-span, using models that do justice to the complex environmental, biological, and psychological influences involved.

SIMILARITY AS WELL AS DIFFERENCE

But, again, it would be wrong to focus entirely upon *differences* between generations. In the two surveys reported in this chapter, some values did not differ significantly in the relative importance assigned to them by parents and children. In the 1972 survey these values were: *a comfortable life, a world at peace, happiness, mature love, salvation, ambitious, cheerful, courageous, forgiving, helpful, intellectual, logical, obedient,* and *self-controlled.* And in the 1973 survey they were: *a comfortable life, a sense of accomplishment, a world at peace, happiness, inner harmony, mature love, salvation, social recognition, wisdom, ambitious, cheerful, courageous, honest, independent, intellectual, logical, loving, obedient,* and *self-controlled.* So there was value congruence as well as value discrepancy, and the positive similarity coefficients in Table 6.5 also attest to that fact.

The presence of both similarity and difference should not occasion surprise. As we indicated in Chapter 5, the family and the peer group are both important reference groups for the developing adolescent, each having its influence on particular spheres of life. We noted that the evidence is consistent with the view that most teenagers value their families very highly, turning to their parents for advice on important issues and for emotional support. In the Australian home there is also evidence that the mother has emotional ascendancy and that she tends to assume the important tasks of both influencing and maintaining conventional standards of morality in the children and of preparing girls for their futures as wives and mothers—see Dawson (1974) and Encel (1970) for information about the Australian family and the dominant role of the mother in the socialization of the children.

Connell, Stroobant, Sinclair, Connell, and Rogers (1975) have amassed a considerable amount of information about Sydney teenagers from an extensive 1969–1970 survey. Some of their findings are relevant to the understanding of socialization processes in adolescence and to the analysis of intergenerational relations (see also Connell, 1974). For example, their results suggest that the parents appear to determine "a reproduction of their own pattern of sex roles, work, and family life in the next generation" (p. 152); that (according to the teenagers' perceptions) there are points of similarity and difference between children and their parents in the behaviors they approve of and those they disapprove of for young people (some behaviors being seen as unacceptable by both and others as acceptable teenage activities but subject to regulation and control); and that intergenerational conflicts may occur in relation to some behaviors and issues but not others and for a number of different reasons.

We will encounter further evidence for intergenerational similarities and differences in the next chapter. In the meantime it is important to stress that theories that attempt to account for data based upon comparisons between children and their parents should be able to deal with the similarities that occur between generations as well as with the differences. It is likely that many of the similarities relate to the important role of the family as a reference group for the young on all sorts of matters—especially in regard to social and political attitudes and some basic human values.

VALUES AND INCOME LEVEL

With the large amount of data collected from respondents in the two Adelaide surveys, it was possible to make other comparisons of value priorities in addition to those reported. One basis for comparison was income level, a variable usually employed in defining differences in social class (Feather, 1975*b*). Table 6.11 presents the median rankings of terminal values for heads of households from the 1972 and 1973 Adelaide surveys in relation to five income levels (under $2,000 per year; $2,000 to 3,999, $4,000 to 5,999; $6,000 to 7,999; over $8,000 per year). Table 6.12 presents the corresponding median rankings for the instrumental values.

The transformed rankings for each value were compared across the five levels of income, using one-way analyses of variance on the data obtained from heads of households in the 1972 and 1973 surveys separately. The statistically significant effects are also listed in Tables 6.11 and 6.12. If one focuses upon replicated effects from the 1972 sample to the 1973 sample, these results indicate that greater affluence was associated with the assigning of greater importance to values concerning accomplishment, love, and competence of one sort or another. Lower income was particularly associated with greater importance assigned to cleanliness. Relationships across the five levels of income were not always monotonic, however. Most displayed curvilinear trends. But the Ns involved in the different income groups were relatively small, and because of this one should perhaps attend only to the gross differences in mean value importance.

Rokeach and Parker (1970) also found that being *clean* was the value that best distinguished the rich from the poor. They also found that the value that next best distinguished the rich from the poor was *a comfortable life,* with the poor

TABLE 6-11. Median Rankings and Composite Rank Orders of Terminal Values in Relation to Income Levels of Heads of Households from 1972 and 1973 Adelaide Surveys

	1972 Survey						1973 Survey					
Income:	Less than $2,000	$2,000 –3,999	$4,000 –5,999	$6,000 –7,999	Over $8,000	p	Less than $2,000	$2,000 –3,999	$4,000 –5,999	$6,000 –7,999	Over $8,000	p
Terminal Value — N	20	33	37	18	18		25	39	81	25	28	
A comfortable life	11.00(12.5)	6.75(5)	11.17(14)	13.67(15)	12.50(13)	.05	11.21(13)	11.30(13)	9.38(11)	8.75(10)	12.00(13)	—
An exciting life	14.33(18)	11.93(15)	13.83(16)	10.25(13)	13.00(14.5)	.05	12.83(14)	14.63(16)	12.28(14)	12.25(15)	11.50(11)	—
A sense of accomplishment	11.00(12.5)	10.25(11)	8.75(10)	4.00(2)	4.33(3)	.01	9.75(10)	9.30(11)	8.50(9.5)	7.50(6)	4.40(3)	.01
A world at peace	3.67(2)	5.25(3)	2.93(2)	7.67(9)	4.00(2)	—	4.17(2)	2.83(2)	5.25(2)	8.17(8)	9.00(10)	.001
A world of beauty	9.00(10)	11.92(14)	10.70(12)	9.75(11)	9.00(11)	.05	10.75(12)	11.70(14)	12.65(16)	10.63(14)	11.60(12)	—
Equality	7.50(6.5)	8.17(9)	10.83(13)	9.67(10)	9.00(11)	—	10.50(11)	8.13(7.5)	9.50(12)	13.17(16)	13.40(16)	.01
Family security	2.00(1)	1.54(1)	2.42(1)	2.75(1)	2.00(1)	—	1.94(1)	2.44(1)	2.71(1)	1.70(1)	2.29(1)	—
Freedom	8.00(9)	6.83(6)	6.13(4)	7.00(7)	5.50(4.5)	—	7.30(6)	5.25(3)	5.68(4)	8.17(8)	6.00(4)	—
Happiness	6.00(4)	5.10(2)	3.95(3)	6.33(4)	5.50(4.5)	—	4.50(3)	5.30(4)	5.30(3)	4.75(2.5)	3.50(2)	—
Inner harmony	7.67(8)	8.50(10)	8.36(9)	6.50(5.5)	9.00(11)	—	8.75(8.5)	7.63(5)	7.93(7.5)	8.17(8)	7.00(6)	—
Mature love	11.67(14)	10.75(12)	7.88(6)	10.00(12)	7.25(7)	.05	13.25(15)	8.13(7.5)	8.50(9.5)	7.25(5)	7.67(8)	.01
National security	10.50(11)	11.17(13)	9.75(11)	12.00(14)	13.00(14.5)	—	8.75(8.5)	10.38(12)	10.70(13)	9.83(12)	13.33(15)	.05
Pleasure	13.50(17)	13.69(17)	13.38(15)	14.67(16)	14.00(16)	—	13.38(16)	12.88(15)	12.50(15)	10.50(13)	13.00(14)	—
Salvation	13.00(15.5)	15.58(18)	14.90(17)	17.10(18)	16.00(18)	—	14.30(18)	15.25(18)	15.83(18)	17.17(18)	17.07(18)	—
Self-respect	4.67(3)	8.13(8)	8.13(8)	6.50(5.5)	8.50(9)	—	8.38(7)	7.90(6)	7.93(7.5)	6.75(4)	7.50(7)	—
Social recognition	13.00(15.5)	12.75(16)	16.36(18)	15.00(17)	15.00(17)	.05	13.88(17)	15.13(17)	14.36(17)	15.21(17)	14.60(17)	—
True friendship	6.50(5)	6.90(7)	8.10(7)	7.50(8)	8.00(8)	—	6.50(4)	8.50(9)	7.32(5)	9.75(11)	8.33(9)	—
Wisdom	7.50(6.5)	5.50(4)	7.10(5)	6.00(3)	6.20(6)	—	6.75(5)	8.58(10)	7.50(6)	4.75(2.5)	6.40(5)	—

Note. Lower numbers denote higher relative value. In each column the rank order of each median (low to high) is denoted in parentheses after the median. *N*s are for error-free rankings. Statistically significant *p* values from one-way analyses of variance are presented.
Source: Data are from Feather, 1975b.

TABLE 6-12. Median Rankings and Composite Rank Orders of Instrumental Values in Relation to Income Levels of Heads of Households from 1972 and 1973 Adelaide Surveys

Income: Instrumental Value	1972 Survey						1973 Survey					
	Less than $2,000	$2,000–3,999	$4,000–5,999	$6,000–7,999	Over $8,000	p	Less than $2,000	$2,000–3,999	$4,000–5,999	$6,000–7,999	Over $8,000	p
N	22	33	37	18	18		25	39	82	25	28	
Ambitious	11.33(13.5)	7.88(8)	9.83(12)	9.00(10)	11.50(15)	—	12.25(14)	10.30(13)	8.75(10)	6.50(4)	8.00(8.5)	—
Broad-minded	9.00(9.5)	9.75(12)	6.25(3)	7.00(5.5)	9.00(10.5)	—	5.25(4)	8.75(8)	6.57(3)	5.50(3)	7.00(6)	—
Capable	10.25(11)	6.83(4)	6.90(5)	8.50(8)	8.00(5.5)	—	8.50(8.5)	9.75(11)	7.56(6)	7.25(5)	3.43(2)	.05
Cheerful	8.20(8)	8.50(9)	10.17(14)	10.67(13)	8.67(7)	—	5.42(5)	10.75(15)	9.71(13)	11.63(14)	8.00(8.5)	.01
Clean	4.40(2)	7.50(6.5)	8.75(11)	12.67(16)	9.00(10.5)	.001	10.25(12)	6.13(3)	7.33(4.5)	8.25(8)	12.67(16)	.01
Courageous	9.00(9.5)	10.25(13)	6.50(4)	6.00(3)	8.00(5.5)	—	4.75(3)	9.25(10)	7.33(4.5)	10.13(12)	7.50(7)	.05
Forgiving	5.67(4)	6.50(3)	7.88(7)	7.00(5.5)	7.00(4)	—	7.75(6)	6.83(5)	8.33(9)	9.50(11)	11.00(14)	—
Helpful	6.50(5.5)	7.38(5)	8.13(8)	9.00(10)	6.75(3)	—	8.83(10)	8.75(8)	8.00(7.5)	11.88(15.5)	10.00(11.5)	—
Honest	2.60(1)	2.75(1)	2.90(1)	2.00(1)	2.00(1)	—	3.83(1)	2.92(1)	2.89(1)	2.17(1)	3.33(1)	—
Imaginative	15.00(17)	15.32(18)	15.92(18)	12.33(15)	12.00(16)	.01	14.42(17)	15.10(18)	14.25(18)	13.90(17)	12.75(17)	—
Independent	8.00(7)	11.25(14)	12.25(15)	6.50(4)	9.00(10.5)	.05	8.50(8.5)	10.17(12)	10.20(14)	9.25(10)	10.50(13)	—
Intellectual	15.33(18)	12.83(17)	13.63(17)	14.33(17)	13.00(17)	—	14.13(16)	11.25(16)	13.75(16)	11.25(13)	10.00(11.5)	.05
Logical	12.67(16)	11.50(15)	8.50(9)	10.00(12)	9.00(10.5)	.05	13.75(15)	10.58(14)	11.40(15)	11.88(15.5)	6.75(5)	.01
Loving	5.50(3)	7.50(6.5)	7.38(6)	9.00(10)	9.00(10.5)	—	7.83(7)	6.25(4)	8.00(7.5)	7.50(6)	6.00(4)	—
Obedient	11.00(12)	12.17(16)	12.75(16)	14.50(18)	16.00(18)	—	15.21(18)	12.83(17)	14.00(17)	14.75(18)	15.80(18)	—
Polite	11.33(13.5)	8.92(10)	9.88(13)	11.25(14)	11.00(14)	—	9.17(11)	7.50(6)	9.69(12)	8.50(9)	12.33(15)	—
Responsible	6.50(5.5)	4.38(2)	4.83(2)	5.33(2)	2.80(2)	—	4.25(2)	5.50(2)	5.00(2)	4.83(2)	4.40(3)	—
Self-controlled	12.25(15)	9.50(11)	8.63(10)	7.50(7)	9.00(10.5)	—	10.75(13)	8.75(8)	9.40(11)	7.63(7)	9.50(10)	—

Note. Lower numbers denote higher relative value. In each column the rank order of each median (low to high) is denoted in parentheses after the median. *N*s are for error-free rankings. Statistically significant *p* values from one-way analyses of variance are presented.
Source: Data are from Feather, 1975b.

assigning this value greater importance. In the 1972 Adelaide survey there was a suggestion of this difference, but not in the 1973 Adelaide survey. In addition Rokeach and Parker discovered a tendency for more affluent members of their sample to assign higher importance to values concerning accomplishment, love, and competence, which is consistent with some of the differences to be noted in Tables 6.11 and 6.12. But there were some differences that occurred in the Adelaide surveys that did not occur in the Rokeach and Parker survey, and vice versa.

The differences in results are probably due to a variety of reasons. The sample used by Rokeach and Parker was a much larger national sample involving adult Americans over 21 years of age, the surveys being administered in 1968 by the National Opinion Research Center (for a summary of other findings from this survey, see Rokeach, 1973). Because of the size of the sample it was possible to conduct analyses over a much wider range of incomes than was possible in the two Adelaide surveys ($15,000 and over at the higher end). Moreover, the American survey was more heterogeneous with respect to age than were the two Adelaide samples. Hence, some of the differences obtained by Rokeach and Parker could be age-related, higher incomes being associated with older respondents, and older respondents having different value priorities than younger respondents (see earlier discussion in this chapter). Obviously, one needs to control for age as well as other demographic variables when looking at the relationship between value priorities and income levels. Finally, the Rokeach and Parker survey was conducted at the national level whereas the present study sampled respondents from one large Australian city. Given these various differences and the further possibility of some cross-cultural variation in value priorities between Australia and the United States (see Chapter 8), it is perhaps surprising that the results reported in Tables 6.11 and 6.12 were as similar to those of Rokeach and Parker as they were.

These similarities suggest that the poor (and the rich) may encounter similar problems and undergo somewhat similar socialization experiences wherever they are in the more affluent, Western societies—these similarities crossing national boundaries. It may happen that the poor come to place more value on what they feel they lack or are denied, or on what to them are significant and enduring problems in their lives. Confronted with poorer living conditions and lacking other material benefits that come with prosperity, they may see cleanliness and a comfortable existence as very salient issues whereas the more affluent, taking these things for granted, are thereby freed to focus upon other sources of value. The complete causal picture is probably a lot more complex than that, however, and would also involve socialization effects that relate to important differences across social classes in the way parents bring up their children, especially in what they teach them to value (see also Kohn, 1969). Obviously, we need research that looks in detail at the process of value acquisition across different social classes at the family level (for a related study examining income levels and ideology, see Huber and Form, 1973).

CONCLUDING REMARKS

This chapter has reported data from a fairly wide cross section of respondents in one large Australian city—concentrating upon *intergenerational* comparisons in particular. The pattern of findings has turned out to be remarkably consistent, although the specific set of causal factors that underlie the pattern is obviously complex.

In attending to intergenerational comparisons, we do not mean to minimize the similarities and differences that may also occur at the *intragenerational* level —within generations rather than between them. Despite their common exposure to general historical trends and events, people from within the same age group are obviously subject to many different socializing influences depending upon their family background, their social class, their sex, the type of occupation they pursue, and so on. In dealing with value priorities one therefore needs to look not only at the variation across generations (as we have done in this chapter) but also at the variation within generations in relation to the major socializing influences (as in our attempt above to relate the value priorities of heads of households to social class, using income as the index). What is clearly needed in the future are large-scale national surveys that look at variables such as age, income, education, sex, occupation, and so forth in combination, and with regard to their complex interactions, in order to determine their contributions to variations in value priorities among individuals.

In the next chapter we turn to more specialized groups: student activists and juvenile delinquents. In the latter case, we move once more in the direction of investigating the degree to which value systems match those attributed to others.

7. Special Groups: Student Activists
and Delinquents

IN THE LAST CHAPTER we were concerned with generational comparisons. Now, still within the context of investigating values in different segments of society, let us turn from rather heterogeneous samples to two groups that are similar in the sense that they are both made up of young people who are at odds with society. One—the student activists—rejects certain social norms, values, and practices and advocates different ones; the other—the delinquents—breaks the law to the degree that its members are temporarily "removed" from society and sent to a training center.

THE STUDENT PROTEST MOVEMENT
OF THE 1960s

The worldwide emergence of student protest movements in universities in the 1960s has been discussed in a flood of publications too numerous to be listed here. In an excellent synthesis, Lipset (1972) has reviewed much of the relevant theory and evidence about the development of student activism in the sixties and has provided a useful historical perspective showing that it is by no means a uniquely modern phenomenon but has occurred throughout history.

MOTIVATING AND FACILITATING CONDITIONS

In tracing some of the sources of student activism, Lipset draws from both sociological and psychological analyses, and his account demonstrates both the fascination that social scientists have displayed in the phenomenon and the complexity of the underlying determinants. He discusses the following

152

factors that have been referred to as sources of student protest: the changing political climate of the 1950s and 1960s that involved a moving away from cold war politics, the interest in civil rights for Negroes, and the spread of opposition to the Vietnam War; the tendency for students to be especially responsive as a group to political events and to the need for social change; the discrepancies between generations that are produced in times of rapid social change; and the possible "de-authorization" of the older generation. Many commentators on student activism have noted that rebellion may be particularly likely to occur in adolescence with its strains, uncertainties, and frustrations and with youth's need to establish a personal identity and to determine an adult role. Students as a group are sociological adolescents, occupying marginal positions in society. They are people in transition, still largely dependent upon their families for support and on the faculty for their advancement. In an environment that is relatively removed from the mainstream of society, they are involved in a meritocratic system where they compete with their peers and prepare for future roles in the world outside.

In this unique environment they are able to reflect upon the discrepancies that are evident between egalitarian values and the inequalities that clearly exist within society. They bring to the university attitudes, beliefs, and values shaped by their families, by their peers, and by other influences. At least as far as the children of the intelligentsia are concerned, many of them have attended elementary and secondary schools that emphasize play and spontaneity, creativity, and lack of restraint. As young people, they tend to be romanticized and even glorified by their elders and to have ideals that have not been tempered by experience with imperfection.

Lipset also deals with student activism as an expression of a need for a distinct youth culture with its own differentiating attributes and ways of viewing the world—a subculture that displays an enthusiastic, idealistic, impatient, and romantic style together with symbols of membership. He recognizes that, within the universities, student values and faculty values in the social and political spheres are often closely related. Intellectuals, in their demand for freedom of inquiry untrammeled by established authority and in their nurturance of an open and critical stance toward evidence and issues, strike chords to which the young can resonate. At the same time the increasing distance between faculty and students as universities grow and as faculty members assume new roles creates an impersonal, unsatisfying environment where faculty-student interactions are not frequent enough to enable the sort of learning that follows from positive identification with a warmly regarded teacher. The university environment may then contain the seeds for discontent.

These various sources of student protest may be regarded as general *motivating* factors, and they constitute a complicated web. Lipset also points out that there are factors in the students' situation that *facilitate* mass activity. These include the greater availability of students for new political movements because they are at an age when they are less likely than adults to have made political and ideological commitments or to be identified with agents and institutions supporting the status quo. At their stage of development, the ground may be fertile for the seeds of conversion. Further, as young people, students have fewer responsibilities. They are less likely to have spouses or jobs to worry about. Their behavior is probably viewed more tolerantly by their elders, within a culture that is fairly permissive toward youth. Hence, they can stretch the limits further, and behave in ways that would not be permitted in other groups. The ecology of a university, usually with large numbers of people in a small area, makes communication easier and facilitates mobilization for action.

When one adds to these motivating and facilitating factors some important precipitating issues that raise questions of great moral significance, issues such as civil rights for underprivileged groups and intervention in the Vietnam War, then one has a set of conditions that are explosive enough to cause some young people to rebel.

WHO ARE THE ACTIVISTS?

What sorts of students become activists? Lipset's account is also helpful here. He says that the most general conclusion that can be drawn is that

> leftist children are largely the children of leftist or liberal parents. The activists, particularly, are more radical or activist than their parents, but both parents and children are located on the same side of the spectrum. (p. 80)

Thus, the political orientations of parents are especially important in understanding the political behaviors of their children and these political orientations may differ in their social class relationships across countries. In the United States, for example, student activists in the 1960s tended to come from relatively privileged families with left-wing or liberal orientations. These left-wing orientations found a great deal of their backing among

> a well-educated segment of the affluent engaged in intellectual and welfare occupations, and among members of traditionally progressively disposed religious groups, particularly the liberal Protestant denominations and the Jews. (Lipset, 1972, p. 80)

In other countries, however, where leftist, socialist, and liberal political orientations may be more characteristic of the workers, one would expect that student activists would be more likely to come from less privileged families.

Some evidence (Friedman, Gold, & Christie, 1972) suggests that the leftist or liberal family background of American student activists may be more apparent in the *early* stages of the student protest. As more members are recruited into the protest movement and the ground of the movement is enlarged, the family differences between activists and nonactivists may become attenuated. With extension of the effects of the movement in the United States and Australia, one might expect to find greater representation of working-class youth among the activists of the 1970s, as contrasted with the more privileged youth of the 1960s. But the activist value systems from the more affluent youth would be tempered by those value systems that the less privileged already hold so that the outcome for working-class youth would be a blend of the old with the new rather than a complete transformation of their value systems. The extent to which change occurs would also depend upon the dominant ethos of the situation in which the newly recruited members work and the pressures that emanate from their peers and family. Kasschau, Ransford, and Bengtson (1974) discuss these issues and provide evidence consistent with the view that old and new values have blended in rather subtle ways among American working-class youth, and that this blend varies according to whether these youth are in college or not in college.

Lipset notes that studies have shown that student activists on the whole, within a university, are more often found in the social sciences, in the humanities, and in the more pure theoretical fields of science—in that order—than in the more vocational, professional, and experimental fields. These differences may relate more to selective entry of students into these fields, however, than to the effects on students of exposure to these fields (see also Chapter 5). They may also relate to the amount of time students have to engage in protest since students in vocational, professional, and experimental fields may have limited time available outside of their studies.

In describing student activists some theorists have distinguished between different types of protest. Lipset (1972, p. 104), for example, notes the differences between the radical and renunciatory tendencies among youth, the radical involving action against the system and the renunciatory involving the disowning of society. Keniston (1967) differentiates student deviants into the "alienated," whose orientations are apolitical, romantic, and aesthetic, and the "activists," whose orientations are political, humanitarian, and universalistic. Similar distinctions have been made by others.

Some research workers have analyzed the family background, and psychological health, academic performance, and personality characteristics of students in the protest movement, in some cases making the distinction between the radicals and the renouncers. In his review Lipset (1972, p. 109) concludes that the evidence on the academic success and psychological health of left-wing activists is somewhat contradictory. He does not view student activists through rose-colored glasses. While obviously sympathetic with some of their ideals, he argues that many of the self-identified "radicals" in the American movement were close to total alienation from the rational and political world, displaying renunciatory rather than radical tendencies and, in their style of action, often coming close to the political tactics of the extreme right. Their focus was upon the ends rather than the means; the "ethic of absolute ends" was dominant rather than the "ethic of responsibility." In many cases, impulsiveness and expressiveness were conjoined in the pursuit of worthy ideals but without careful consideration of the ethics and long-term effectiveness of the political actions involved in the attempt to achieve these absolute ends.

These observations by Lipset have to be qualified, however, in view of the fact that the activists may not be a homogeneous group in their level of moral reasoning. Haan, Smith, and Block (1968) in an important study using the Kohlberg Moral Judgment Scale—a test based upon Kohlberg's analysis of developmental stages in moral reasoning (Kohlberg, 1969)—found strong associations between political protest, social action, and an advanced stage of principled moral reasoning (Stage 6 in Kohlberg's scheme). They also discovered that, among the protesters, there were some who showed an earlier stage of premoral reasoning (Stage 2). But young people who showed conventional moral reasoning in response to the moral dilemmas in Kohlberg's test tended to be inactive as far as protest was concerned. Fishkin, Keniston, and MacKinnon (1973) found that holding a radical versus conservative ideology tended to be associated with moral reasoning at both ends of the continuum of moral development (the premoral and principled stages). Conservatism, however, was associated with Stage 4 conventional moral reasoning of the law-and-order type.

These two studies suggest that the activist group may not be homogeneous in regard to where people are located along Kohlberg's continuum of moral development. The activist group may contain some people who are at an advanced stage in their moral reasoning—involving either a contractual, legalistic orientation relating to the welfare of the total community (Stage 5) or a more advanced use of principles that are organized around the abstract concepts of equity, universality, and justice (Stage 6). And the activist group may also contain people who are at a relatively early stage of preconventional moral reasoning—involving egocentric, instrumental thinking (Stage 2). Fishkin, Keniston, and MacKinnon (1973, p. 117) speculate that the latter individuals may be more likely to become involved in the more violent and revolutionary forms of action. The studies also show that the non-activist and more conservative people are more frequently found at the intermediate stages of moral development—involving either conformity to conventional role expectations (Stage 3), or a more advanced concern with community morality, conventional standards of behavior, and law-and-order (Stage 4).

There is an obvious need for studies that relate the relative importance of the terminal and instrumental values from Rokeach's lists to the stages of moral reasoning that different individuals have attained (see Rokeach, 1973, p. 82, for mention of one such study by McLellan, 1970). In the present context, however, the main point is to caution against treating activists as a homogeneous group as far as their level of moral development is concerned.

A recent study by Kerpelman (1972) also cautions against simplified views of the student activist, especially the tendency to see him as some sort of psychological superman. Kerpelman studied both activists and nonactivists and sorted the students into three different levels of ideology (left, middle, and right). This 2 × 3 sampling design was conducted on three different campuses, all students completing a battery of tests concerned with demographic information, abilities, values, and personality. Among other differences, Kerpelman found that activists (whether of the left or right) tended to be higher on autonomy than nonactivists. Left wing students (both activists and nonactivists) tended to be lower on authoritarianism and they showed more humanitarian, moral concern than right wing students (activists and nonactivists alike). Activists of the left were not found to be unique or special in the psychological sense. As Kerpelman (1972) puts it:

> personal qualities usually imputed to student left activists characterize the involved generally (no matter what their level of political involvement) . . . only on lack of "Authoritarianism," a combination of personality characteristics, did the left activists stand out psychologically from the other groups. On the "Autonomy" factor, interestingly, the left activists and the right activists stood together. In not one of the many separate demographic, intelligence, or personality measures, however, were student left activists appreciably different from any other subgroup, nor were right activists, nor were any activism–ideology subgroups. (p. 117)

FUTURE EFFECTS OF THE PROTEST MOVEMENT

It is likely that the effects of the protest movements of the 1960s will continue as the young men and women who took part in them move into various positions within society. For they will bring with them their own orientations to the tasks they are required to perform, orientations that will be modified by their own life experiences, by their adjustments to the realities of biological and psychological change that occur as one grows older, and by the unique historical events that they encounter. Like a river one's life carries some of its own past with it, but is modified by new currents and by new demands that are made upon it. In regard to the student activists of the 1960s Lipset (1972) argues that

> as they grow older they will become *relatively* less responsive to new change-directed thrusts than those who follow them through the university. . . . even though American politics and morals may continue to "liberalize" over time, the relative relationship of the older to the younger remains "conservative." In this sense, societies like our own, which have a built-in process of enormous social change, also always have a generation gap of some magnitude, particularly between those living in the encapsulated, experiment-oriented campus, and those outside. (pp. 262–263)

The contribution that each generation makes to social change is not easy to determine since social change is influenced by a complex set of factors. It would be simplistic to assume that youthful ideals are inevitably translated into social reform. So much depends upon the degree to which the new values are widely shared among members of a generation or age-cohort, and the opportunities that are available for promoting and actualizing these values in the context of the structures and institutions within society.

There have been several recent discussions of the impact of youth and generations on social change (in Chapter 6 we referred to the collection of papers in two recent issues of the 1974 *Journal of Social Issues*). These discussions draw upon two main approaches: the structural-functionalist model (Eisenstadt, 1956, 1963; Parsons, 1963) and the generational unit model (Mannheim, 1952). The structural-functionalist model argues that intergenerational conflict is a function of how different age groups are integrated into society. As Eisenstadt (1963) puts it

> age serves as a basis for defining the cultural and social characteristics of human beings, for the formation of some of their mutual relations and common activities, and for the differentiation and allocation of social roles. (p. 24)

The generational unit model assumes that belonging to the same age group and background are similar in that

> both endow the individuals sharing with them in a common location in the social and historical process, and thereby limit them to a specific range of potential experience, predisposing them for a certain characteristic mode of thought and experience, and a characteristic type of historically relevant action. (Mannheim, 1952, p. 291)

Mannheim goes on to argue that

> Youth experiencing the same concrete historical problems may be said to be part of the same actual generation; while those groups within the same actual generation which work up the material of their common experience in different specific ways, constitute separate generational units. (1952, p. 304)

There may be several generational units competing with one another within the one generation but all share a similar location and common destiny in history. For example, Laufer and Bengtson (1974) describe four generation units that they see as emerging from the oppositional culture of the 1960s, each having a distinct approach to social transformation. They call these generation units radicalism, bohemianism or freakism, communalism, and revivalism. Each generation unit has its distinctive mode of behavior but each unit is a response to the social and cultural forces of the time. Braungart (1974) has compared the structural-functionalist and generational unit models of social change and Katz (1974), more generally, has discussed a range of factors that influence social change.

In the context of discussions of the youth generation of the 1960s it is important to remember that the activist movement was by no means widespread but was largely confined to college campuses. In speculating about social change, therefore, one needs to look at other generation units within the youth generation of the 1960s and not base predictions solely upon a limited sample of college youth. Some studies are now beginning to appear that concern the fate of student activists some years after they left the university. Fendrich (1974) presents evidence that suggests that the college activists of the early 1960s that he studied in 1971 had retained their distinctive attitudes and values even today. Activists in his sample were concentrated in a limited range of occupations in the public sector (knowledge, social service, and creative occupations) rather than in the private sector of the economy. Following our previous discussion (Chapter 3), we can speculate that they chose to work in environments that supported their value systems, perhaps having found that opportunities for expressing their political commitments were restricted in other contexts, such as industry and business. Thus, they had not begun that long march through *all* the institutions of society that some of their leaders predicted.

THE VALUES OF STUDENT ACTIVISTS

One would expect on the basis of the preceding discussion that student activists would have different value priorities when compared with those students not involved in political protest. A recent study in the Flinders program by Ellerman (1975) addressed itself to this issue. On the basis of a comprehensive review of the literature and his own intuitions and experience (he was a participant in the protest movement himself), Ellerman made a number of predictions about the relative importance activists would assign to the terminal and instrumental values from the Rokeach Value Survey when compared with nonactivists. We will summarize his predictions and briefly present the main reasons for them.

PREDICTIONS

In regard to the terminal values Ellerman expected that student activists, unlike the student nonactivists, would give more importance to these values: *an exciting life, a sense of accomplishment, a world at peace, a world of beauty, equality, freedom, mature love,* and *true friendship.* But he expected them to assign less importance to the following terminal values: *a comfortable life, family security, national security, pleasure, salvation,* and *social recognition.* These predictions followed from considerations about the characteristics of student activists that could be distilled from past research and personal experience. The activist, therefore, was seen as more likely than the nonactivist to reject materialist values, to want to escape from boredom and to seek excitement, to be concerned with accomplishing important social change, to strive for peace and freedom from violence, to be interested in aesthetic values, and a world of beauty, to be strongly concerned with working for a universalistic goal of equality, to reject total immersion in family life, to emphasize freedom as embodied, for example, in democratic methods and in personal living, to want sexual and spiritual intimacy, to downgrade national security with its implications of potential violence, to de-emphasize hedonistic and leisurely pursuits, to be skeptical of conventional religion, to be relatively unconcerned with social recognition and the approval of others (particularly conventional society), and to seek strong bonds of affiliation and friendship with others.

In regard to the instrumental values Ellerman expected that in comparison with student nonactivists the activists would assign more importance to the following values: being *broad-minded, forgiving, helpful, honest, imaginative, independent, loving,* and *responsible.* He expected them to assign less importance to being *ambitious, clean, obedient, polite,* and *self-controlled.* Again these predictions were based on an interpretation of results of previous studies of student activists and from personal intuition and experience, some factors involved in these predictions being similar to those already given for the terminal values. The activist was seen as more likely than the nonactivist to reject conventional career aspirations and competition, to be open-minded and less authoritarian, to be relatively unconcerned with cleanliness, to show humanitarian concern as demonstrated in his helping behavior and forgiveness, to value sincerity and honesty, to favor the use of imagination, to value self-expression and self-actualization, to stress self-reliance and autonomy, to emphasize loving and affectionate relationships with others, to question authority and uncritical obedience to it, to diminish the importance of middle-class conventions such as politeness, and to show a strong concern for social responsibility and dependability.

SUBJECTS AND QUESTIONNAIRES

To test these predictions Ellerman conducted a postal survey of 255 activist students. This activist sample consisted of 48 students (43 males and 5 females) who had been arrested by police during the moratorium demonstration in Adelaide in September 1970; 177 young men who had notified the Victorian Draft Resistors Union that they had publicly refused to register for National Service selection (conscription for military service); and 30 students (26 males, 4 females) who held membership in various clubs, committees, or student government organizations that were involved in a variety of activities concerned with student protest. The response rates from these three groups were not high. Twenty-one persons (44 percent) from the moratorium group replied; 58 persons (33 percent) from the public noncompliers group replied; and 13 persons (43 percent) from the formal activist groups replied. Hence, a total of 92 respondents constituted the entire activist sample. Given the length of the questionnaire (completed anonymously), the sensitive and controversial issues it addressed, and the suspicious attitudes many activists have toward questionnaires, very high response rates were not expected.

Questionnaires were also sent through the post to a control group consisting of 297 students (201 males, 96 females) chosen at random from a complete list of all students enrolled at Flinders University in 1970 (approximately a 1-in-7 sample). One hundred and nineteen persons from this group replied (40 percent). In his report, Ellerman (1975) gives more details of the samples and procedures used.

The questionnaire consisted of five main parts. Part A posed questions seeking biographical information; Part B consisted of Form E of the Rokeach Value Survey; Part C presented eight concepts (yourself, Australia, father, technological progress, mother, American intervention in South Vietnam, sex, and politics), each of which had to be rated on a set of 11 bipolar adjective scales according to the usual procedure for the semantic differential (Osgood, Suci, & Tannenbaum, 1957); Part D contained items designed to assess attitudes toward five issues (the war in Vietnam, conscription for military service, political party allegiance, social change, and drugs) in regard to self and in regard to how respondents thought their father, mother, and most of their friends would answer the questions; and Part E consisted of open-ended questions on three topics: respondent's ideology and criticisms of the present social system, methods of social change that should be used to implement these goals, and a subjective report on the important formative influences on the respondent's own attitudes.

AVERAGE VALUE SYSTEMS OF ACTIVISTS AND NONACTIVISTS

How did the activist and control respondents differ in the priorities they assigned to the terminal and instrumental values. Table 7.1 presents the median rankings of the terminal values for the activist and control groups together with the results of simple, one-way analyses of variance on the transformed rankings for each value. Table 7.2 presents similar information in regard to the instrumental values.

Most of Ellerman's predictions were confirmed. As predicted, activist respondents ranked the following values significantly higher in importance than did the control respondents: *a world at peace, a world of beauty, equality, freedom,* and being *helpful, imaginative,* and *loving.* Also, as predicted, they ranked the following values significantly lower in importance than did the control respondents: *a comfortable life, family security, national security, salvation,* and being *ambitious, clean, obedient,* and *polite.* These differences are apparent when one compares the medians across groups. In addition, the activists ranked being *courageous* as more important on the average than did the controls, but they ranked *happiness,* and being *capable, cheerful,* and *responsible* as less important on the average than did the controls. These differences were also statistically significant. Altogether 20 of the 36 values showed significant differences in their average rankings between activists and controls. Virtually all of these significant findings also occurred when analyses were run for males only in the activist and control groups, a procedure that was considered worth conducting since the activist sample was predominantly male.

TABLE 7-1. Median Rankings and Composite Rank Orders of Terminal Values for Activist and Control Groups

Terminal Value	Prediction	Activist (A)	Control (C)	p
		N 79	113	
A comfortable life	C > A	14.82 (16)	13.32 (15)	< .001
An exciting life	A > C	10.13 (12)	9.36 (11)	–
A sense of accomplishment	A > C	8.19 (9)	8.55 (9)	–
A world at peace	A > C	2.97 (1)	5.90 (3)	< .01
A world of beauty	A > C	8.42 (10)	10.75 (13)	< .001
Equality	A > C	3.31 (2)	7.05 (8)	< .001
Family security	C > A	10.95 (13)	9.75 (12)	< .05
Freedom	A > C	3.35 (3)	5.50 (1)	< .001
Happiness	–	9.05 (11)	6.28 (6)	< .001
Inner harmony	–	6.50 (6)	6.45 (7)	–
Mature love	A > C	4.86 (4)	6.19 (5)	–
National security	C > A	16.38 (17)	15.32 (17)	< .01
Pleasure	C > A	12.71 (14)	13.26 (14)	–
Salvation	C > A	17.01 (18)	15.63 (18)	< .01
Self-respect	–	7.93 (8)	8.92 (10)	–
Social recognition	C > A	14.38 (15)	15.16 (16)	–
True friendship	A > C	5.83 (5)	5.71 (2)	–
Wisdom	–	6.63 (7)	6.05 (4)	–

Note. Lower numbers denote higher relative value. In each column the rank order of each median (low to high) is denoted in parentheses after the median. A > C means that activists were predicted to assign higher importance to this value than controls, and C > A means the reverse. Ns are for error-free rankings. Statistically significant p values from one-way analyses of variance are presented.
Source: Data are from Ellerman, 1975.

In discussing these results Ellerman suggests that they show certain broad dimensions on which activists and nonactivists differ, most of which we have already noted in the preceding section. Thus activists when compared with nonactivists seemed to display the following general themes in their value priorities: greater humanitarian concern, romanticism, and aesthetic sensitivity; greater emphasis upon political and social goals of a peaceful and democratic nature, together with a stronger commitment to standing up for one's own beliefs; less importance assigned to materialist and hedonistic concerns and to security in general; less concern with authoritarian and conventional forms of behavior and with orthodox religion; and less emphasis upon competitive striving.

OTHER DIFFERENCES BETWEEN ACTIVISTS AND NONACTIVISTS

Ellerman's survey also produced a wealth of other statistically significant findings, some of which can be briefly summarized. Thus, activists were more likely than nonactivists to be males, to be studying for Arts degrees than for

TABLE 7-2. Median Rankings and Composite Rank Orders of Instrumental Values for Activist and Control Groups

Instrumental Value	Prediction	Activist (A)	Control (C)	p
		N 80	109	
Ambitious	C > A	15.33 (16)	12.17 (15)	< .001
Broad-minded	A > C	6.00 (5)	4.88 (2)	–
Capable	–	9.44 (11)	7.17 (6)	< .01
Cheerful	–	10.63 (14)	8.06 (7)	< .01
Clean	C > A	15.44 (17)	14.14 (17)	< .001
Courageous	–	4.63 (3)	8.25 (8)	< .001
Forgiving	A > C	6.57 (6)	6.10 (3)	–
Helpful	A > C	4.67 (4)	8.75 (9.5)	< .001
Honest	A > C	2.93 (1)	3.64 (1)	–
Imaginative	A > C	7.44 (7)	11.25 (14)	< .001
Independent	A > C	7.80 (9)	9.28 (12)	–
Intellectual	–	7.57 (8)	9.42 (13)	–
Logical	–	9.75 (12)	8.95 (11)	–
Loving	A > C	4.40 (2)	6.13 (4)	< .05
Obedient	C > A	16.46 (18)	15.77 (18)	< .05
Polite	C > A	14.29 (15)	12.35 (16)	< .01
Responsible	A > C	8.22 (10)	6.79 (5)	< .05
Self-controlled	C > A	10.13 (13)	8.75 (9.5)	–

Note. Lower numbers denote higher relative value. In each column the rank order of each median (low to high) is denoted in parentheses after the median. A > C means that activists were predicted to assign higher importance to the value than controls, and C > A means the reverse. *N*s are for error-free rankings. Statistically significant *p* values from one-way analyses of variance are presented.
Source: Data are from Ellerman, 1975.

Science degrees, to be in later years of their courses, to live away from home, to have been arrested or convicted for politically motivated offenses, to have attended more protest demonstrations, to believe that activism would increase and spread to other sectors of the population, to list more criticisms of present society, and to belong to political groups both on-campus and off-campus and be more involved in them. Activists also tended to have a slightly lower level of academic performance than nonactivists, though Ellerman says this difference may be due to variation in the assessment procedures used in different institutions rather than to differences in the groups themselves. In any case, the North American evidence on grades is somewhat confused, as Lipset indicates (1972, p. 109). Earlier studies showed that leftists tended to have higher grades but this alleged superiority was based upon self-reported grades and disappeared when actual grades were compared.

Activists and nonactivists did not differ significantly in the mean status of father's occupation. These means were 3.72 and 3.84 respectively for the activist and nonactivist groups—using the scale devised by Congalton (1969) to measure the perceived prestige of occupations in Australia (scored 1 to 7 in the direction of *decreasing* prestige). These means suggested that, on the average, both activists and nonactivists tended to come from middle-class families.

The responses of the activists and nonactivists were compared with respect to how they rated the eight concepts—yourself, Australia, and so forth—in Part C of the questionnaire, using 11 bipolar adjective scales. The responses to each scale were coded 1 to 7 in the positive direction of the dimension assumed to be involved in that scale: positive evaluation, competence, power, or activity. Total scores for each respondent were obtained for each dimension using the following scales (as noted in parentheses): evaluation (*good-bad, admirable-deplorable, worthless-valuable*), competence (*incompetent-competent, successful-unsuccessful*), power (*powerful-powerless, delicate-rugged, intense-mild*), and activity (*quiet-restless, quick-slow, active-passive*). Total evaluation scores could range from 3 to 21; total competence scores from 2 to 14; total power scores from 3 to 21; and total activity scores from 3 to 21. The mean scores on each dimension regarding each of the eight concepts that were rated are presented in Table 7.3 for activist and nonactivist respondents.

The following differences were statistically significant: Activists rated themselves as less competent ($p < .01$) and rated father as lower in power, competence, and activity ($ps < .01$) than did the control respondents, but there were no differences between these groups in their assessments of mother on these dimensions. Activists rated Australia less favorably and lower in competence, power, and activity (all $ps < .001$) than did control respondents. They were also less favorable toward technological progress ($p < .01$) and American intervention in South Vietnam ($p < .001$) and rated both of these concepts lower in competence ($ps < .001$ and $< .05$ respectively). Activists rated the two concepts American intervention in South Vietnam and politics higher in power ($ps < .001$ and $< .01$ respectively) and the former higher in activity ($p < .001$). Finally, the activists assigned higher evaluation ratings to sex than did the nonactivists ($p < .01$).

When the remaining attitude information was analyzed (Part D of Ellerman's questionnaire involving five political and social issues) there was a consistent trend for activists to endorse positions that were more liberal, leftist, and radical when compared with the control group, especially in regard to the issues of the war in Vietnam, conscription for military service, preferred political party, and social change. The activists also saw their parents and most friends as further to the left on these issues when activist and control groups were compared on how they answered the attitude items for father, mother, and friends. Ellerman's results also showed that children generally assigned themselves less conservative positions on most of the issues than they assigned to their parents, a result that is consistent with the differences in conservatism across generations described in the previous chapter. In addition, however, it appeared that the activists viewed themselves as more different from their parents (in the liberal or radical direction) than the control respondents did

TABLE 7-3. Mean Scores of Activist and Control Respondents for Evaluation, Competence, Power, and Activity for Each of Eight Concepts

		Dimensions			
		Evaluation	*Competence*	*Power*	*Activity*
Concept	Group	(Range, 3–21)	(Range, 2–14)	(Range, 3–21)	(Range, 3–21)
Yourself	Activist	14.7	10.0	13.2	14.6
	Control	15.0	10.7	13.3	14.5
Australia	Activist	10.7	6.4	10.6	9.1
	Control	15.0	8.7	12.0	11.4
Father	Activist	15.4	10.1	13.3	12.6
	Control	16.4	11.2	15.0	14.0
Technological	Activist	13.8	8.4	16.0	16.8
progress	Control	15.3	9.9	15.5	16.8
Mother	Activist	16.3	9.8	11.9	13.4
	Control	17.0	10.4	12.0	13.3
American inter-	Activist	3.7	3.8	17.0	16.3
vention in	Control	7.9	4.5	15.1	14.7
South Viet-					
nam					
Sex	Activist	19.1	9.7	14.9	14.9
	Control	18.1	10.1	15.0	14.9
Politics	Activist	12.2	6.6	15.6	13.9
	Control	11.4	6.7	14.2	13.1

Note. Higher scores mean more positive evaluation, greater competence, more power, and more activity.
Source: Data are from Ellerman, 1975.

in relation to theirs. Thus, the evidence supported Lipset's conclusion (stated previously) that leftist children tend to have leftist or liberal parents, but the activists are relatively more radical or activist than their parents—when compared to the nonactivists. All of the differences just described are illustrated in Table 7.4, which presents data for the attitude item concerned with the war in Vietnam.

In summary, it can be seen that many of Ellerman's findings were consistent with those found in studies conducted in other countries as reviewed by Lipset (1972)—most of which have been conducted in the United States. Of particular interest were the striking differences in value priorities provided by the activist respondents when compared with the control group, most of which supported—on the basis of a well-researched assessment procedure, the Rokeach Value Survey—the various hypotheses and findings concerning the characteristics of student activists that have been presented by other research workers and analysts (for example, Bettelheim, 1969; Erikson, 1970; Feuer,

TABLE 7-4. Percentage of Activist and Control Respondents Endorsing Positions for Self, Father, Mother, and Most of Friends Regarding the War in Vietnam

Ratings for	Group	No response 0	Attitude Position *Pro* 1	2	3	4	5	*Anti* 6
Self								
	Activist	0.0	0.0	0.0	0.0	4.3	45.6	50.0
	Control	2.5	3.4	1.7	5.0	40.3	42.0	5.0
Father								
	Activist	3.3	6.5	9.8	14.1	28.3	35.9	2.2
	Control	11.8	7.6	9.2	24.4	26.9	20.2	0.0
Mother								
	Activist	6.5	5.4	0.0	9.8	31.5	44.6	2.2
	Control	9.2	2.5	7.6	18.5	38.7	22.7	0.8
Friends								
	Activist	3.3	0.0	1.0	2.2	15.2	46.7	31.5
	Control	6.7	1.7	1.7	6.7	33.6	44.5	5.0

Note. For activist group, $N = 92$; for control group, $N = 119$.
Source: Data are from Ellerman, 1975.

1969; Flacks, 1967; Geller & Howard, 1972; Katz & Georgopoulos, 1971; Keniston, 1967, 1968, 1971, 1973; Kerpelman, 1972; Lipset, 1972; Sampson, 1967).

ROKEACH'S LAW OF POLITICAL ACTIVISM

In the context of Rokeach's own work, the value differences found by Ellerman are particularly interesting inasmuch as they support Rokeach's "law of political activism," which he states as follows:

> A more extreme regard for either one or both of the two political values, *equality* and *freedom,* is a minimum condition for sustained political action and is also a minimum consequence of political action. (1973, p. 211)

It is clear from Table 7.1 that activists ranked both *equality* and *freedom* very high in their list of priorities among the terminal values (second and third in importance on the average) and only slightly lower than *a world at peace,* to which they assigned top priority on the average. But *equality* and *freedom* were only two values among several that differentiated activists from controls. The complete picture revealed a much more extensive set of differences.

THE INTERGENERATIONAL EVIDENCE

As we have noted, Ellerman's results on the attitudinal positions of respondents and the positions they attributed to their parents on important social and political issues suggested both intergenerational similarities and intergenerational differences, children seeing their parents as somewhat similar to themselves in attitudes but rather more conservative, and activists reporting especially liberal or radical positions. Whether the parents' own positions were *actually* in the same direction as those of their children cannot be answered from Ellerman's study as parents themselves did not answer the questionnaire. Children's statements about their parents' attitudes could obviously be in error. Nevertheless, several studies of political socialization have indicated the important role of the family as a transmitter of political attitudes—notably in regard to voting behavior (Sears, 1969). For example, in commenting upon his own research on the acquisition of political values during adolescence, Adelson (1970) writes that "it is patently clear that the political outlook of the parents, particularly when it is strongly felt, tends to impress itself firmly on the politics of the child" (p. 10).

It would be incautious, however, to claim that the family dominates all other influences in transmitting political attitudes to the young. Perhaps it does when the child is quite young and more under the control of his parents. But, as Connell (1972) has pointed out, many past investigations in this area leave much to be desired methodologically, and in those studies worth considering pair-correlations between family members in regard to political and social attitudes tend to be rather low—about .20 (see also Friedman, Gold, & Christie, 1972). Where similarities occur between generations they may also reflect the influence of a common set of external factors, such as similar information from the mass media to which all family members have been exposed or secular trends and events that both generations have experienced. And differences between family members may likewise reflect different external influences that affect different generations, such as the outside peer groups with which each generation has contact, and differential exposure to particular trends and events that affect one generation more than the other. As we have noted before (Chapter 6), one requires *longitudinal* studies to separate out the effects of familial socialization from the effects of peer groups, mass media, secular events, life-cycle changes, and other influences on attitudes and values— studies that involve data collection from family members and from different age-cohorts over a period of years, that repeat the procedures at different points in history for new generations, and that probe the same divisions in the life-span.

Granted these cautions, however, one can still endorse Adelson's (1970) complaint that many popular commentators have uncritically accepted the view that there is a very wide "generation gap" in many areas of attitudes, values, and behavior (for example, in political, social, and sexual attitudes, and in general values). This view Adelson sees as oversimplified and sentimentalized, based upon limited samples of some of the more visible, vivid, and voluble young, especially those from elite college campuses. These young people cannot be taken as representative of youth in general. Indeed, when one examines the student protest of the 1960s it is clear that it was not an age-group phenomenon. As Lipset (1972, p. 38) has pointed out, one must consider other generation-units (to use Mannheim's term) who may have quite different attitudes even though they belong to the same age-cohort. In fact, opinion surveys conducted in North America and dealing with the relationship of age as such to opinion about the Vietnam War showed that from 1965 to 1971 respondents in the 21-to-29-year-age group were less likely to oppose the war than their elders. Those 50 years of age and older were more likely to consider that participation in the war was a mistake. Young people became more negative toward the war as it went on, but so did older people (Lipset, 1972, pp. 38–39). Other researchers have also found no evidence to support the view that in the late 1960s the young opposed the Vietnam War and the old supported it (Converse & Schuman, 1970; Rosenberg, Verba, & Converse, 1970). One can be seriously misled by focusing upon data from only one segment of an age-cohort (for example, student youth). One needs to look at various segments of the one generation in addition to comparing different generations, as we noted in the last chapter.

Recent evidence reported by Yankelovich (1974) suggests that there has been a dramatic change in the values and beliefs of young people between the late 1960s and the early 1970s. The study included interviews with 3,522 American youths conducted in the late spring of 1973. Two samples were interviewed, both involving youth from 16-to-25 years of age. The first sample contained 1,006 college students drawn from a representative selection of the country's two-year and four-year colleges and universities. The second sample was of 2,516 young people and was based upon a national probability sample of all households in the country with household members between the ages of 16 and 25 years. The results of the interviews were compared with similar data collected from surveys conducted in 1967, 1969, and 1971.

Yankelovich (1974) summarizes the major differences in the beliefs and values between the late 1960s and the early 1970s as follows:

> [In the early 1970s as contrasted to the later 1960s] The campus rebellion is moribund. . . . An almost total divorce takes place between radical politics and new life styles. . . . A central theme on campus: how to find self-fulfillment *within* a conventional career. . . . Lessening criticism of America as a "sick society." . . . Wide and deep penetration of Women's Liberation precepts

is underway. . . . Violence-free campuses; the use of violence even to achieve worthwhile objectives, is rejected. . . . The value of education is strongly endorsed. . . . The younger generation and older mainstream America move closer together in values, morals, and outlook. . . . The gap within the generation narrows. Noncollege youth has virtually caught up with college students in adopting the new social and moral norms. . . . The new sexual morality spreads both to mainstream college youth and also to mainstream working class youth. . . . The work ethic appears strengthened on campus but is growing weaker among noncollege youth. . . . Criticisms of some major institutions are tempered on campus but are taken up by the working class youth. . . . Criticism of the universities and the military decreases sharply. . . . Campuses are quiescent, but many signs of latent discontent and dissatisfaction appear among working class youth. . . . Concern for minorities lessens. . . . No clear-cut political center of gravity: pressures in both directions, left and right. . . . The New Left is a negligible factor on campus: the number of radical students declines sharply. . . . College students show greater acceptance of law and order requirements. . . . There are few signs of anger or bitterness and little overt concern with public attitudes toward students. (pp. 3–5)

These abrupt changes on United States college campuses from the late 1960s to the early 1970s provide fascinating material for sociologists to explain. No doubt some of them are due to the removal of an important precipitating cause of activism: the Vietnam War. Some of them probably also relate to the worsening economic climate in the early 1970s where, particularly on campuses, young graduates are no longer assured of the type of employment they prefer but are confronted by a highly competitive job market. Over and beyond these specific factors, however, one sees the gradual diffusion of beliefs, attitudes, and values throughout wider and wider segments of the population, new ideas that came from a relatively small but active section of vocal college youth spreading further and further afield, some ideas being accepted and some rejected as people consider them and relate them to their own social conditions and their own life-styles. Yankelovich (1974) argues that a new set of values, incubated on the nation's campuses in the 1960s, has now spread to the entire youth generation. These new values involve moral norms dealing with sex, authority, religion, and obligations to others; social values concerned with money, work, family, and marriage; and a concern with self-fulfillment. In reacting to the survey findings as a whole, Yankelovich (1974) concludes that if there are emerging patterns, then

> they are the story of the transmission of the New Values from the campus to the mainstream of American youth, the efforts of both college and noncollege youth to find a satisfactory means of blending the New Values with older, more traditional beliefs, and the search for new modes of adaptation to the highly institutionalized structure of American society. (p. 7)

One sees in this process a synthesis of the new with the conventional as new ideas diffuse throughout the population and are weighed in the balance along with the realities of situational pressures and pre-existing cognitive structures—

as we noted previously in relation to the study by Kasschau, Ransford, and Bengtson (1974). And one also sees change occurring for different segments of the population at different times—as if the sweep of social change hits different points in its curve for people in different parts of the social structure. These data therefore remind us of the importance of looking at continuity and change in value systems for different segments of the same generation (*intragenerational* comparisons) as well as between generations. The same age-cohort may contain different generation-units depending upon where people are located in the strata of society (see Laufer & Bengtson, 1974).

As far as *intergenerational* comparisons are concerned, those who proclaim that the generations are falling apart also usually assume incorrectly but romantically that all good and important ideas emanate from the young and that the young are alienated from their elders and cannot communicate with them. In so doing, these commentators forget the seminal role of the older, middle-aged generation in providing leadership and statements of ideology, and ignore the evidence that most children have generally close and friendly relationships with their parents (Bengtson, 1970; Campbell, 1969; Offer & Offer, forthcoming). Proponents of the view that there is a wide generation gap also tend to develop extreme and overgeneralized images of youth, images that are usually simplified, often romantic, and perhaps projective of adult wishes, that miss the complexity of human variety and of social change and that ignore the important continuities between generations. Thus, we return to a familiar *leitmotiv,* a theme that empasizes both similarity and difference in attitudes and values across generations and that calls for analytic studies of the agencies and products of socialization across the life-span. The same type of study should also be conducted within generations, for each stage in the life-cycle.

THE FAMILY CONTEXT OF THE ACTIVIST

Ellerman's semantic differential data convey an interesting clue about the family context of the activist since, as we have seen (Table 7.3), activists were more likely than control respondents to rate the concept of father low on scales concerned with competence, power, and activity—but similar differences were not obtained when the corresponding ratings for mother were compared between the two groups. In discussing this result Ellerman refers to Feuer's (1969) hypothesis that an essential precondition to activism is the "de-authorization" of the elders of any generation, a diminution of their power and authority by the young. The lower ratings for father provided by the activists may be evidence for de-authorization selectively applied to the male parent. Ellerman also suggests that these differences in ratings may be consistent with Keniston's (1968) observation that his sample of activist leaders often reported their fathers to be involved, idealistic, and principled, but, at the same time, weak and acquiescent because they had failed to act on their principles. In a recent contribution Wood (1974) also argues that many student activists may have been acting out radical political values derived from their parents, yet they were in conflict with their parents initially for the simple reason that their parents did not live up to their values in their behavior.

It would be worthwhile in future studies to obtain information about the value priorities of the parents of activist and control respondents using the Value Survey, for then one would be able to investigate the degree of discrepancy in value systems between different family members and to compare these measures of discrepancy across activist and control groups. Such data might further clarify Feuer's (1969) analysis of protest in terms of the conflict of generations. One might indeed discover more intergenerational value clash among activists, particularly when sons' value systems were compared with the value systems of their fathers. But one might also discover a fair amount of intergenerational similarity in the ranking of important values together with a heightened concern among activists about the disjunction between the values their parents hold and the degree to which these values are reflected in behavior. As we will see, information about the value systms of parents was obtained in the study of male juvenile delinquents, to be described in the next section. We should note that there have been a number of studies and speculations about the family situation of student activists (see, for example, Block, Haan, & Smith, 1969; Flacks, 1967; Haan, Smith, & Block, 1968; Keniston, 1967; Lipset, 1972, pp. 102–104; Wood, 1974), but we need more sophisticated and detailed information about the value systems of parents in relation to those of their children, and how discrepancies between values and behavior are viewed by each.

THE NEED FOR MORE GENERAL INQUIRIES

A fertile line of inquiry would involve comparing the value systems of activists with those of the important value-promoting institutions within society with whom they have contact. One source of influence to include in this more general inquiry would be the university or college environment—especially with regard to the values it is seen to represent. With family and peer group comparisons added, one would then be able to construct a fairly complete matrix that summarized similarities and differences in value systems between activists, peers, family members, educational institutions, and other relevant individuals, groups, and social environments. These discrepancies could relate both to actual value systems and to attributed value systems. The analysis of this discrepancy matrix might provide significant clues for understanding social protest in connection with where the large discrepancies exist, which are the important ones, and what the activist does about them. As will be discussed in later chapters, such a matrix would also be of use in other ways—as, for example, in the study of social conflict and immigrant assimilation at the level of beliefs, attitudes, and values.

Marked discrepancies in value systems may correspond to the seeds of discontent, particularly when these discrepancies pertain to important values. Whether or not these seeds flourish or die would depend upon the nature of the environment and the degree to which it is nurturant and tolerant of different points of view. In inhospitable environments where protest is inhibited by various sanctions, the seeds may wither. A young person employed by a large business organization, for instance, who sees his values as quite discrepant from its competitive and materialistic values may have little opportunity for protest, and his own solution to the discrepancy might be to seek employment elsewhere. But in more nurturant environments (such as universities and colleges) where different viewpoints are more likely to be tolerated, the seeds may survive. For some young people the discontent associated with discrepancies may then spill over into active protest. The institution may itself become the target of protest if its values are seen as divergent in important ways from the members' own value commitments. In other cases the mode of resolution may involve not protest but renunciation of the institution and a search for more congenial environments, some of which may involve relative alienation from society in general (for example, joining a commune). And, of course, as we have noted previously (Chapter 5) there may be other modes of resolution, apart from protest or renunciation, that individuals may adopt in handling important discrepancies. This is not to say that value discrepancy is the sole motivating factor in student protest. Clearly it is not. The picture is a lot more complicated than that, as we have seen. But it is to say that sophisticated studies of value discrepancies between student activists and other people, groups, and institutions within society may provide worthwhile information in the future about some of the underlying dynamics of student protest.

In the next section we discuss another form of behavior that also involves young people at odds with society: juvenile delinquency.

THEORETICAL APPROACHES TO JUVENILE DELINQUENCY

Just as student protest may be related to a clash in values, so is it possible that one factor involved in delinquency may be a discrepancy between the values of juvenile offenders and the perceived values of other individuals and groups. Again we must caution against overgeneralization. Most treatments of the causes of juvenile delinquency stress the complexity of the problem and refer to myriad factors that are associated in varying degrees with delinquency. Theories may appeal to psychological, sociological, biological, or other determinants (or a mixture of all of them). Many of these theories have been reviewed before (for example, Bordua, 1961; Cohen & Short, 1971; Gibbons, 1970; West, 1967), and no attempt will be made to cover them in this chapter.

Our interest is in approaches to the problems of juvenile delinquency that suggest that value conflict may be a factor in it, and there are a number of theoretical contributions from both sociology and psychology that do point in this direction. For example, in his seminal work *Delinquent Boys,* Cohen (1955) argued that some working-class boys may develop delinquent sub-cultures as a response to problems they encounter when they are evaluated in terms of middle-class standards. Many of these problems are concerned with status. Delinquent subcultures may arise as solutions to shared problems of low status among working-class youths, problems that become salient in the class-room where there is usually competition against middle-class peers for recognition by adults. As Cohen (1955) states:

> Certain children are denied status in the respectable society because they cannot meet the criteria of the respectable status system. The delinquent subculture deals with these problems by providing criteria of status which these children *can* meet. (p. 121)

Working-class delinquents, then, may be seen as reacting against such middle-class values as ambition, individual responsibility, talent, asceticism, rationality, courtesy, and self-control—against notions of proper behavior for which they have been inadequately socialized. Instead, they develop in their own subcultures other standards for status in terms of which the valued be-haviors tend to be nonutilitarian, malicious, and negativistic, dominated by short-run hedonism instead of by long-term goals, and where the group is seen as autonomous and having its own solidarity.

Yinger (1965) goes further and argues that, although the concept of a distinctive subculture is a valuable one, implying the transmission of norms through processes of socialization among members of a subsociety, one also needs the concept of a *contraculture.* This concept, he says, involves

> the creation of a series of inverse or countervalues (opposed to those of the surrounding society) in the face of serious frustration or conflict. . . . Use of this concept in place of subculture seems appropriate wherever the normative system of a group contains, as a primary element, a theme of conflict with the values of the total society; wherever personality variables are directly involved in the development and maintenance of the group's values; and wherever its norms can be understood only by reference to the relationships of the group to a surrounding dominant culture. (p. 231)

Yinger argues that the set of countervalues is a response to ambivalence and that many other groups, apart from delinquent ones, possess contracultural qualities.

For Cloward and Ohlin (1960), there is a common value commitment to "success" among low-class boys, where success largely involves materialist advancement. However, these boys are at a competitive disadvantage in comparison with their middle-class counterparts. They may not have access to legitimate or conventional means for attaining success or they may, for one reason or another, perceive their chances of succeeding to be very low. They may, therefore, experience a large gap between what they are led to want in terms of the commonly shared success ethic and what they expect will actually occur. This disjunction between aspiration and reality may prompt them to explore nonconformist and illegal means of attaining their ends. The specific behaviors that develop will depend upon the *opportunity structures* available in the community. Where, for example, there is a tradition of organized, criminal networks one might see the development of criminalistic gang subcultures, the delinquent boy becoming the budding gangster who is later integrated into adult criminal organizations. In other cases the deviant behavior may take the form of "conflict" (as in fighting between gangs) or of a "retreatist" disengagement (as in the subculture of the drug addict).

Another explanation of gang behavior has been advanced by Miller (1958). He believes that the structure of working-class life is sufficient in itself to bring about delinquent behavior and that it is not necessary to appeal to a reaction against middle-class norms and values to explain delinquency. According to Miller, a common structural pattern in lower class society is a female-based household—one in which the mother and/or other adult females provide stability within the family unit. This structure may create problems of sex-role identification, anxieties about masculinity that can be reduced by membership in male adolescent peer groups that have their own territory on city streets. These working-class youth sense their material and social deprivation and their behavior reflects certain focal concerns or values that include "trouble," "toughness," "smartness," "excitement," "fate," and "autonomy." The boy who avoids trouble, demonstrates bravery, lives by his wits, seeks excitement, maintains his independence, and who sees his life as dominated by forces over which he has little control, displays these focal concerns in his behavior. In including excitement as one of the focal concerns, Miller echoes an earlier characteristic noted by Thrasher (1927), who described the exhilaration and satisfaction that often accompanies delinquent acts—a different sort of emphasis from the rather grim picture of protest and rebellion implied in Cohen's analysis of delinquent subcultures (Bordua, 1961).

Other theorists have also questioned the view that the delinquent is a person committed to an oppositional culture, in revolt against the norms and values of others rather than expressing his own individual concerns, which are products of his own socialization. Matza (1964) points out that this image does not ring true for most delinquents he encountered and interviewed. They are less alienated from the wider society and not so uncompromising in their opposition to middle-class values as some sociologists would have us believe. Rather than opposing the dominant values, they may seek to evade some of them by selecting and extending trends or "subterranean values" that are already present in the wider culture (Matza & Sykes, 1961). These subterranean values may not be publicized to the extent that other more conventional values are. They may involve, for example, a search for excitement, a willingness to bend the rules, a pursuit of hedonistic fun, a tolerance for certain kinds of aggression —all of which can be extended and raised to a level where they become antinormative. The delinquent may adopt some of these less publicized but widespread values in intensified form. But he may also behave conventionally as well. As Matza (1964) puts it:

> The delinquent transiently exists in limbo between convention and crime, responding in turn to the demands of each, flirting now with one, now the other, but postponing commitment, evading decision. Thus, he drifts between criminal and conventional action. (p. 28)

It can be seen that concepts of norms and values are central to all of the sociological theories just described—whether they be the values that the delinquent brings with him from his own social class and family background or the values that he adopts as he moves into a new subculture or contraculture. These various theories suggest, therefore, that empirical studies are needed in which the own-value systems of delinquents are compared with those of other groups in society in order that one would be able to discover those sources of important discrepancies in value systems that might be correlated with delinquent behavior. We made a similar suggestion in relation to the future investigation of factors that might be associated with student protest. In the field of delinquency, however, sociological theory has tended to outpace careful empirical analysis of the normative systems of delinquent boys in relation to those of other groups and segments of society. There has been too much conjecture and not enough hard evidence to permit the testing of competing theories. This is a pity because it is possible that some of the sociological approaches to delinquent behavior might contain the seeds for more general theories of collective deviance—theories that might also be appropriate to the analysis of student protest (Wasburn, 1973).

What does the psychologist tell us about the underlying causes of delinquent behavior? Most explanations center on dynamics of the family situation and some also postulate basic personality characteristics or dimensions in terms of which, it is argued, delinquent behavior can be understood (for example, Eysenck, 1964; and reviews by Schuessler & Cressey, 1950; Waldo & Dinitz, 1967). Focus upon the family situation usually involves attention to interaction, to the quality of parental care, to child-rearing practices, and to the effects of parental deprivation (for a review see West, 1967). More attention has been given to maternal care and deprivation than to the role of the father. Psychologists have also attempted to classify different types of delinquents (for example, Glueck & Glueck, 1970; Jesness, 1962; Quay, 1965) and to isolate early signs that can be used to predict future delinquent behavior (for example, Glueck & Glueck, 1950, 1959). Again, however, the literature is too voluminous to summarize. What is surprising is the virtual absence of any studies that attempt to relate the value systems of delinquents to those of their parents and other members of their family.

Why might such studies be useful? Presumably delinquency, like student protest, can be viewed in both psychological and sociocultural terms. One can agree with Yinger (1965) that theories of delinquent behavior should be field-oriented, taking both person and situation into account. In moving toward a field theory of delinquency it may turn out that the concept of value will serve an important integrative role. Because it spans both psychological and sociological theory, this concept may be an important means of bridging the gap between the wider views of normative pressures, as they occur across different molar levels of social structure and within different social institutions, and the more specialized treatments of socialization and social influence that are concerned with processes at the molecular level. The molecular level of analysis deals with how individuals are modified through both their experience in the small groups to which they belong and to which they relate and through the mass media to which they are exposed and to which they selectively attend. In particular, one would expect the study of values at the family level to emphasize not only the effects of the sociocultural context as broadly conceived, but the internal, complex dynamics of family interaction. The family is an important transmitter of social values. A focus upon values and normative development and change would therefore help to integrate both sociological and psychological approaches to the study of delinquency.

PREDICTIONS

A study from the Flinders program conducted by Feather and Cross (1975) relates to some of the issues just raised. This study dealt with persistent, hard-core delinquent boys who were in Training Centers in metropolitan Adelaide, and also involved a control group of matched nondelinquents for comparison. The following predictions were tested: If one can assume that persistent juvenile offenders are a group somewhat at odds with society and with their parents, and as a group developing their own rules and standards within their subculture or contraculture, then one would expect to find that their own value systems would be more discrepant from the perceived value systems of their parents than would be the case for a nondelinquent group. Note that this is not to say that value discrepancy would not occur between nondelinquents and their parents. As we saw in the previous chapter there are some marked differences in value priorities across generations. But the discrepancy in value systems may be more pronounced for delinquents and it may be qualitatively different, involving distinct clusters of values not involved in the generational differences for nondelinquents. Moreover, it may vary according to whose value systems are involved in the comparison—for example, child compared with father or child compared with mother.

A second prediction was that one might expect parents to disagree about basic values to a greater degree in the delinquent's home than in the non-delinquent's home. This prediction was based upon an assumption that has had a good deal of empirical support, namely, that the family situation tends to be less stable and more disturbed for delinquents than for nondelinquents (for example, Andry, 1960; Glueck & Glueck, 1962).

A third prediction was based upon the assumption that interpersonal attraction is likely to be a positive function of the degree of similarity between persons in their beliefs and attitudes (for example, Byrne, 1971; Feather, 1966). That is, the more similar people are in important characteristics, the more likely it is that they will be attracted to one another. Therefore, it was predicted that both delinquents and nondelinquents would evaluate their parents more favorably the closer their own value priorities matched the value systems they attributed to their parents (see also Beech, 1967).

SUBJECTS

The juvenile offenders studied were 82 boys from two juvenile institutions in Adelaide. One of these institutions (McNally Training Center) catered for older boys above the age of 15; the other institution (Brookway Park Junior Boys Reformatory) catered for younger boys up to the age of about 15 years. There were 43 boys ranging in age from 15 years to 17 years 7 months who were tested at McNally; the remaining boys ranging in age from 12 years to 15 years 9 months were tested at Brookway Park. Thus, the investigation sampled a fairly wide age range (12 to 18 years approximately). Most of the boys were multiple offenders, committed to the institutions by the local courts.

The control group involved 82 boys from secondary schools in Adelaide who were matched individually with boys in the delinquent groups on the basis of age and socioeconomic status of father or mother or both (where applicable). Geographic location was also taken into account in the matching by selecting control respondents from three secondary schools in three main areas of delinquency concentration in Adelaide (Cross, 1972). A fairly successful matching was achieved. Mean age for both delinquent and control groups was 15 years 3 months. The measure of status of father's occupation was based upon each respondent's description of his father's occupation in a questionnaire that followed the Value Survey. As in previous studies, the scale devised by Congalton (1969) for the prestige rankings of occupations in Australia was used to code the descriptive statements (scored 1 to 7 in the direction of *decreasing* prestige). Mean status of father's occupation was 5.90 for the delinquent group and 5.03 for the control group. So the fathers of the juvenile offenders were involved in quite low prestige occupations, slightly lower in prestige on the average than were the occupations of fathers of the matched control respondents and much lower in prestige than were the occupations of fathers of other respondents tested in the Flinders program (such as the fathers of the student activists). As in previous studies (for example, Ferguson, 1952) boys in the delinquent group reported significantly ($p < .05$) more siblings in their family (mean $= 5.47$) than did boys in the control group (mean $= 2.38$). They also reported more siblings older than themselves (mean $= 3.59$ for delinquent group; mean $= 1.74$ for control group; $p < .05$), but there were no differences between the groups in regard to religious affiliation.

The use of a matched control group in studies such as the present one carries its own risks because the more one matches on relevant variables such as social class and education, the more one is likely to decrease the possibility of discovering differences in the dependent variable being observed if that dependent variable is also a function of the variables involved in the matching. One is dealing with a complex interrelated network of variables and simple matching may lose some of the systemic characteristics of the causal process. Moreover, matching on a number of variables may produce a control group that contains a large proportion of either potential delinquents or undetected delinquents.

Nor should one lightly assume that an incarcerated delinquent group itself is representative of a heavily delinquent group generally. As Gold (1970, and personal communication) has argued on the basis of North American evidence, a lot of heavily delinquent youth are never caught and, if they are caught, they may not be referred to the courts. If they are referred to the courts the chances are that they will not be incarcerated. If they are incarcerated the court's decision might reflect the use of some subjective criterion not always consistently applied (see also Cohen & Short, 1971). The Adelaide study dealt with persistent juvenile offenders rather than with those who did not repeat their mistakes. A different pattern of causal factors may be associated with hardcore delinquency than with casual, once-only offences (West, 1967). But one should bear in mind Gold's caution about treating an incarcerated group as representative of delinquent youth in general. There is a lot of arbitrariness in the process whereby a youth ends up in an institution and one should be aware of the implications of this arbitrariness when interpreting results.

PROCEDURE

The details of test procedure are contained in the reports by Cross (1972) and Feather and Cross (1975). Testing occurred during a four-week period in April and May 1972, and all tests were completed under anonymous conditions. In the schools teachers were not present when the test was administered but in the institutions it was customary procedure that staff always be in attendance. The instructions and format of the tests were identical for both delinquent and control groups.

Considerable attention was given to making the instructions simple and meaningful. The experimenter (Cross) explained that the tests were part of an educational survey and demonstrated, by using the blackboard, the ranking procedure that would be used in the Value Survey in relation to a list of ordinary words such as cars, food, girls, parties, and TV. He also explained the two lists of terminal and instrumental values by using an expanded description on charts which were placed at the front of the class. For example, *an exciting life* was described as "an active life, a life that isn't boring, a life that's always on the move," *clean* was described as being "neat, tidy, well-kept," and *self-controlled* as being "restrained, self-disciplined, when the heat's on you keep your cool." Finally, the experimenter demonstrated, again using the blackboard, the sort of rating scale that respondents were to employ in providing favorability ratings concerning their parents later in the questionnaire.

Two forms of the test were randomly distributed so that approximately half the respondents ranked the terminal values in their order of importance (40 delinquents, 40 controls), and the remainder ranked the instrumental values (42 delinquents, 42 controls). Respondents were told that there were two forms of the test but that, because of time limitations they would not do both (only one or the other). They had to provide *three* sets of rankings for whatever list of values they had been given—one for self, one for mother, and one for father. The order in which these three sets of rankings were to be provided was counterbalanced across respondents, using the six possible orders with approximately equal frequency. Form E of the Rokeach Value Survey was employed. The general instructions printed on the title page of the Value Survey repeated the main points that the experimenter had made in his verbal preamble, and also requested respondents to take the test seriously, to give their own true opinions and answers, and to work quickly and quietly. Detailed instructions for the actual ranking procedure corresponded to those used in other studies involving Form E (described in earlier chapters) with slight modifications to meet the fact that values were also ranked for mother and father as well as for self (Cross, 1972).

When they had provided their rankings respondents filled out an Information Sheet designed to obtain background information (age, religion, father's occupation and so on). The last two items on this questionnaire dealt with attitudes toward mother and father. The first question asked: How well do you think you get on with your mother? and the second question asked: How well do you think you get on with your father? Respondents answered each of these questions by putting a cross on a 5-inch rating scale divided into eight equal parts and labeled "Get on very well" at one extreme, "Do not get on at all" at the other extreme, and with the labels "Moderately or fairly well," "Average," and "Not very well" at equal distances along the scale. These ratings were scored from 1 to 8 with a high rating denoting high favorability.

ANALYSIS OF INDIVIDUAL SIMILARITY INDEXES

Three similarity indexes were obtained for each respondent, one indicating the similarity of his own value rankings to those he attributed to his mother, one indicating the similarity of his own value rankings to those attributed to his father, and one indicating the similarity of value rankings attributed by him to his mother and father. In each case the index was a Spearman rank-order correlation coefficient, and, like the similarity indexes used in the study of value similarity and school adjustment (Chapter 4), they were calculated for each individual and were not correlations between averaged data. The means of these similarity indexes are presented in Table 7.5 for the delinquent and control groups.

TABLE 7-5. Mean Similarity Indexes for Delinquent and Control Groups

| | Similarity Indexes | | | | | |
| | Terminal values | | | Instrumental values | | |
Group	Self-Mother	Self-Father	Mother-Father	Self-Mother	Self-Father	Mother-Father
Delinquent	0.20	0.24	0.27	0.19	0.26	0.34
Control	0.35	0.42	0.54	0.14	0.24	0.36
F[a]	4.02	6.37	16.69	0.46	0.09	0.07
df	1,77	1,78	1,77	1,82	1,81	1,81
p	<.05	<.05	<.001	N.S.	N.S.	N.S.

Note. If a parent was not alive or not present in the family, subjects were asked to rank for an adult substitute of the same sex who had helped to look after them.
[a]F values are from simple one-way analyses of variance comparing each similarity index between delinquent and control groups. N.S. means "not statistically significant".
Source: Data are from Feather & Cross, 1975.

One-way analyses of variance indicated that in the case of the terminal values all of the similarity indexes were significantly lower for the delinquent group than for the control group, as predicted. But when similarity indexes relating to the instrumental values were compared there were no significant differences between the two groups. Thus, respondents' own value systems were more discrepant from those they attributed to their parents among the delinquent boys than among the nondelinquent boys. And the value systems attributed to mother were more discrepant from the value systems attributed to father for the delinquent group than for the control group; that is, there was more "value clash" in regard to the parents of the delinquent boys. But these differences related only to the terminal values, not to the instrumental values. Thus, it was at the level of the general goals, the terminal values, that predictions concerning differences in value systems were confirmed, the gap between parents and their children and between the parents themselves being greater for the delinquent boys. Note, however, that all of the mean similarity indexes were positive. Thus, there were also general similarities in the value systems of the children and their parents, at least as these value systems were perceived by the children.

Table 7.5 also shows that there was a regular increase in the size of the similarity index as the comparison of value systems shifted from self compared with mother, to self compared with father, to mother compared with father. This increase occurred in both the delinquent and the control groups and in relation to both terminal and instrumental values. Analyses of variance showed that differences in the three types of similarity indexes for the two groups combined were highly significant for both the terminal values ($p < .01$) and the instrumental values ($p < .001$). On the average, therefore, the value systems attributed to mother and father were less discrepant than those attributed to self and father, and to self and mother in that order.

AVERAGE VALUE SYSTEMS AND ANALYSES OF SINGLE VALUES

The average orders of importance (median rankings) assigned to the values by the delinquent and control groups are presented in Tables 7.6 and 7.7 for the terminal and instrumental values respectively. To investigate differences in the rankings of *single* values, a series of 2 × 3 analyses of variance were conducted on the rankings following the normal curve transformation. The first factor in each analysis was group (delinquent versus control) and the second factor was type of ranking (self, mother, father). Subsequently, generational differences (self versus mother, self versus father) and parental differences (mother versus father) were explored in further analyses. In view of the large number of comparisons made, an effect was not accepted as significant unless it was at the .01 or .001 level. These various analyses allowed for the fact that the design of the study involved repeated measures, respondents providing three types of ranking.

The 2 × 3 analyses showed that boys in the delinquent group tended to assign greater importance to *an exciting life, national security,* and being *clean* than did boys in the control group. The control group saw *happiness, wisdom,* and being *responsible* as relatively more important than did the delinquent group. These differences were main effects, that is, they occurred when all three types of ranking were combined.

When generational differences were examined, both mother and father were seen as assigning relatively more importance to *a comfortable life, family security,* and being *clean* and *polite* than did the boys themselves in both the delinquent and control groups. The delinquent and nondelinquent boys ranked *an exciting life, freedom, mature love, true friendship,* being *courageous,* and being *imaginative* as relatively more important for themselves than for their parents. There were some generational differences involving only one parent. In comparison with the boys' own priorities mother was seen as assigning relatively

TABLE 7-6. Median Rankings and Composite Rank Orders of Terminal Values for Delinquent and Control Groups in Relation to Self, Mother, and Father

Terminal value	Delinquent group			Control group		
	Self	Mother	Father	Self	Mother	Father
N	40	39	40	40	40	40
A comfortable life	6.50 (6)	4.88 (2)	4.00 (2)	10.80 (12)	5.50 (3)	5.00 (3)
An exciting life	5.33 (4.5)	9.83 (10)	8.00 (7)	5.00 (4)	15.00 (17.5)	12.33 (15)
A sense of accomplishment	11.00 (14)	11.38 (16)	7.75 (5)	11.00 (13)	10.25 (10)	8.50 (9)
A world at peace	8.75 (10)	8.50 (8)	8.00 (7)	5.50 (5)	7.33 (6)	7.00 (6)
A world of beauty	12.17 (17)	11.25 (14)	10.40 (11)	12.60 (15)	10.60 (12)	13.00 (16.5)
Equality	10.00 (12)	10.75 (11)	10.33 (10)	9.00 (9)	9.00 (9)	8.67 (10)
Family security	8.67 (9)	4.75 (1)	2.50 (1)	10.33 (11)	1.00 (1)	1.20 (1)
Freedom	2.86 (1)	5.25 (3)	7.00 (4)	2.82 (1)	7.43 (7)	6.00 (4)
Happiness	7.67 (7)	5.88 (4)	6.00 (3)	3.67 (3)	4.40 (2)	4.75 (2)
Inner harmony	11.50 (15)	10.83 (12)	11.50 (16)	10.00 (10)	10.75 (13)	11.00 (13)
Mature love	5.00 (2.5)	11.30 (15)	10.50 (12.5)	6.50 (7)	8.67 (8)	7.75 (7)
National security	10.80 (13)	13.10 (18)	11.00 (14)	14.83 (17)	15.00 (17.5)	12.25 (14)
Pleasure	5.00 (2.5)	6.25 (5)	10.50 (12.5)	8.67 (8)	10.33 (11)	10.00 (11)
Salvation	15.38 (18)	12.38 (17)	14.75 (18)	16.00 (18)	12.00 (15)	15.20 (18)
Self-respect	9.33 (11)	11.13 (13)	12.00 (17)	12.57 (14)	11.00 (14)	10.80 (12)
Social recognition	11.67 (16)	9.42 (9)	11.40 (15)	14.00 (16)	13.00 (16)	13.00 (16.5)
True friendship	5.33 (4.5)	7.17 (7)	8.00 (7)	3.50 (2)	5.71 (4)	8.25 (8)
Wisdom	8.25 (8)	6.50 (6)	8.75 (9)	6.25 (6)	7.00 (5)	6.40 (5)

Note. Lower numbers denote higher relative value. In each column, the rank order of each median (low to high) is denoted in parentheses after the median.
Source: Data are from Feather & Cross, 1975.

TABLE 7-7. Median Rankings and Composite Rank Orders of Instrumental Values for Delinquent and Control Groups in Relation to Self, Mother, and Father

Instrumental value	Delinquent group			Control group		
	Self	Mother	Father	Self	Mother	Father
N	42	42	41	42	42	42
Ambitious	5.00 (2)	5.00 (3)	1.63 (1)	5.17 (1)	7.67 (8)	3.00 (1)
Broad-minded	7.80 (8)	9.00 (9)	8.50 (9)	5.75 (2)	13.00 (13.5)	9.00 (9.5)
Capable	7.00 (6)	8.67 (7)	9.10 (11)	9.50 (11)	9.50 (11)	6.00 (4.5)
Cheerful	5.86 (3)	10.25 (12)	7.17 (4)	7.50 (6)	9.25 (10)	11.75 (14)
Clean	4.38 (1)	3.80 (1.5)	4.81 (2)	12.50 (18)	3.80 (2)	7.00 (6)
Courageous	6.67 (4)	9.86 (11)	11.17 (15)	8.50 (8)	13.86 (16)	12.00 (15.5)
Forgiving	7.00 (6)	7.33 (6)	7.50 (6.5)	9.00 (10)	7.25 (7)	9.40 (11)
Helpful	8.33 (9)	6.00 (5)	7.50 (6.5)	11.67 (16)	6.00 (5.5)	8.67 (8)
Honest	9.00 (10)	5.75 (4)	7.75 (8)	6.75 (5)	4.33 (3)	6.00 (4.5)
Imaginative	12.00 (17)	13.86 (18)	11.50 (16)	10.80 (14.5)	14.67 (18)	15.20 (18)
Independent	10.50 (13)	12.25 (15)	12.38 (17)	10.33 (12)	14.00 (17)	12.00 (15.5)
Intellectual	11.67 (15)	11.40 (14)	10.83 (14)	8.67 (9)	13.50 (15)	9.00 (9.5)
Logical	12.00 (17)	12.75 (17)	13.08 (18)	10.50 (13)	13.00 (13.5)	10.33 (12)
Loving	7.00 (6)	3.80 (1.5)	6.83 (3)	6.67 (3.5)	2.40 (1)	5.00 (2)
Obedient	12.00 (17)	12.57 (16)	10.50 (12.5)	12.00 (17)	9.75 (12)	12.33 (17)
Polite	11.00 (14)	9.33 (10)	7.38 (5)	10.80 (14.5)	5.50 (4)	8.00 (7)
Responsible	9.86 (12)	8.75 (8)	10.50 (12.5)	6.67 (3.5)	6.00 (5.5)	5.56 (3)
Self-controlled	9.33 (11)	11.00 (13)	8.75 (10)	8.40 (7)	9.00 (9)	10.75 (13)

Note: Lower numbers denote higher relative value. In each column, the rank order of each median (low to high) is denoted in parentheses after the median.
Source: Data are from Feather & Cross, 1975.

more importance to *salvation,* and being *helpful, honest,* and *loving,* while father was seen to place relatively more emphasis upon *a sense of accomplishment* and being *ambitious.* But being *broad-minded* and *independent* were ranked as relatively more important for self than for mother. These generational differences closely resembled those obtained when parents answered the Value Survey themselves, as in the surveys described in the previous chapter (see Table 6.6). In the present case, there was evidence of more emphasis from both parents on values relating to material prosperity, the security of the family, and conventional rules of conduct in comparison with their sons, whereas the boys themselves assigned higher importance to values relating to freedom, independence and imagination, affiliative relationships, and an active, adventurous stance toward life.

When parental differences were considered, mother was seen as assigning relatively more importance to *salvation,* and being *clean* and *loving* than father. Father was seen as giving higher priority to *an exciting life, a sense of accomplishment,* and being *ambitious* and *intellectual* than mother. These differences may relate to the overlapping and distinctive roles of the parents in the family situation—the mother being seen as the main purveyor of moral and religious values, and the father as relatively more concerned with those values that relate to making one's way in the world—with activity, competence, and accomplishment.

There were similarities as well as differences, however, between mother and father in the way they were seen to assign importance to the values, and between parent and child. We have already noted that the similarity indexes tended to be positive, suggesting that there was some overlap in value systems. But Table 7.5 shows that parents were seen as more similar in their priorities than the children were to each parent alone. The generation gap was wider than the parental gap.

There were also some significant interactions in the 2 × 3 analyses of variance that qualify certain of the main effects between delinquent and control groups that we have just noted. Two of these interactions, involving the values *family security* and *clean,* were highly significant ($p < .01$ and $< .001$ respectively). There was little difference between the delinquent group and the control group in the relative importance assigned to *family security* in regard to their own priorities. But the relative importance of this value to parents was seen as much higher by respondents in the control group than by respondents in the delinquent group (see Table 7.6 medians). The delinquents may have been responding in terms of family situations that were for them less secure and stable, where the quality of family care was inferior in certain respects.

Some support for this interpretation came from responses to a question on the Information Sheet. Whereas 95 percent of the boys in the control group answered yes to the question, "If both parents are alive, do they live together?" only 70 percent of the boys in the delinquent group gave this answer. This difference was statistically significant ($p < .001$). Thus, evidence was obtained of a greater incidence of reported separation in the families of the delinquent group, a common finding in delinquency research. Note, however, that in a national survey and in an interview study of teen-agers in Flint, Michigan, results suggested that broken homes did not always produce more delinquent youngsters than intact homes (Gold, 1970; Haney & Gold, 1973). In fact, boys raised only by their mothers were among the least delinquent in the Flint and national samples. Intact homes involving the natural mother and a stepfather were conducive to more frequent and more serious delinquent behavior for both boys and girls. And having delinquent friends and getting poor grades at school were more important reasons for delinquency for boys than whether their homes were broken or intact. Clearly, the causal web is complex and differences in the importance assigned by delinquents and controls to values such as *family security* need to be followed up by detailed study of the family setting, moving from rather gross, molar variables, such as separation or intactness, to more subtle analyses of types of separation and intactness and the quality of child care. One obvious further step in the present study would be to explore whether the differences obtained for *family security* still occurred when only delinquents and controls from intact homes were involved in the analyses.

In regard to the relative importance assigned to being *clean,* the rankings attributed to mothers of subjects in the delinquent and control groups differed very little, high importance being common to both groups. The largest difference occurred between the boys themselves in relation to their own rankings, the delinquent boys placing being *clean* at the top of their priorities (on the average) and the boys in the control group placing this value at the bottom of their list (Table 7.7). Why this marked difference? At least three interpretations are possible. The high value assigned to being *clean* may reflect the working-class backgrounds of most of the delinquent boys. We saw in the last chapter that lower income groups tend to assign more importance to being *clean* than higher income groups (see Table 6.12). But this interpretation fails to explain why this value was ranked so low by the matched control group, because one basis for the matching was the father's occupation. A second interpretation is that the delinquent's family situation may be more harsh and authoritarian. There is some evidence (Feather, 1971*d*) that high relative importance assigned to being *clean* may be linked to authoritarianism. In the last chapter we also noted that a high value placed upon cleanliness seemed to be associated with ethnocentric attitudes. Perhaps the early socialization of the juvenile offender is such as to emphasize cleanliness so that, in his eyes, cleanliness does indeed come to bear some relationship to godliness and becomes associated with positive evaluations of self, negative evaluations of outsiders, and strong, authoritarian judgments. A final interpretation is that, as a result of their contact with social workers, parole officers, staff workers at their institutions, and other institutional personnel, persistent juvenile offenders in time may come to incorporate beliefs about what factors cause their behavior and about the attitudes and values that they *ought* to express in the situations to which they are exposed. In a study such as the present one it is difficult to disentangle what the boys actually believe from what they consider ought to be expressed. This problem is a general one that we will return to in the final chapter. In the present context, it is possible that the delinquent boys placed being *clean* high in their priorities because that is what they thought their institutions would stress, given the emphasis on tidiness in most institutions.

One would expect that a correctional institution would have some effects on the values of the inmates over time, given the fact that the environment approximates to a "total institution" in Goffman's sense (Goffman, 1961). Such effects would be related not only to the influence of the institutional staff but, perhaps more importantly, to that of the other inmates. For example, Hautaluoma and Scott (1973), in a cross-sectional study of 107 young male inmates at a federal correctional institution in the U.S.A., found that there was decreasing acceptance by the inmates over time of values concerning religiousness, honesty, achievement, and kindness. But there was increasing acceptance of values concerning independence and loyalty. There was little evidence of a change toward socially acceptable values as the inmates neared release, contrary to the results of some other studies. The total institution might therefore promote and support some general changes in value priorities involving a downgrading of some moral and competence values—social influence coming from the incarcerated themselves. The total institution might also provide normative influences from the staff (for example, cleanliness) which the inmates may perceive as "ought" requirements but which they may or may not internalize as guides to their own conduct or as goals toward which they should strive. As in the schools (Chapter 5), there are different sources of social influence, and some (such as the inmates' own reference groups) would be expected to have more impact on values than other sources of influence.

Two other interactions were also significant but at a lower level ($p < .05$). Although little difference resulted in the relative importance assigned to *an exciting life* by the delinquent and control boys in relation to themselves, boys in the delinquent group saw their parents as placing more emphasis on this value than did boys in the control group. And, although boys in the control group tended to rank *wisdom* as more important for themselves and for their fathers than did boys in the delinquent group, both groups assigned similar rankings to this value when mother's priorities were recorded.

Finally, being *courageous* was ranked much higher in importance for the mothers of the delinquent boys than for the mothers of boys in the control group ($p < .001$).

The differences noted above provide interesting new evidence about the ways in which delinquents and nondelinquents differ, not only in their own value priorities but also in their perceptions of their parents' values. Previous studies have focused upon variables such as extraversion and neuroticism (Eysenck, 1964); needs for dominance, aggression, and exhibition (Thompson & Gardner, 1969); values from the Allport-Vernon-Lindzey scale (Conger &

Miller, 1966); and other personality characteristics assumed to distinguish delinquents from nondelinquents. The differences evident in Tables 7.5 and 7.6 are consistent with some of these previous findings in that they suggest a less stable, less secure, more restless life-style among the delinquents and their families. They bear little similarity at the level of specific values to results obtained by Cochrane (1974) in a study comparing delinquent and nondelinquent boys also using the Value Survey. On the basis of his results Cochrane concluded that his delinquent groups displayed a greater emphasis on short-term personal values and less emphasis on long-term social values. Differences in the samples tested, the procedures used, and the conditions of testing could account for the divergence in results between his study and the present one (Feather & Cross, 1975).

The present results add an important new dimension to the total picture by indicating parental differences as well. It is of obvious importance to investigate parental characteristics in the families of delinquents and nondelinquents, and the way in which each parent is perceived by the child. Yet this investigation is seldom pursued and where it is pursued attention is usually concentrated on the mother rather than the father. We urgently need further investigations that take account of both family structure and family process so that family interactions and their effects on personality development and social behavior can be evaluated. These studies should examine not only parental deprivation, and demographic variables, such as family size and social class, but also interpersonal relationships within the family and the quality of child care, taking both parents into account—the father as well as the mother (Andry, 1960; Grygier, Chesley, & Tuters, 1969; Riege, 1972). They should attempt to obtain objective information about the family situation as well as examine subjective or perceived impressions, because in families where there is considerable parental strain perceived impressions (such as attributed value systems) may not be accurate reflections of reality but systematic distortions that may exaggerate differences. And these studies should not treat the family as an entity encapsulated from society but influenced by the social and economic forces therein—relating the family to the wider context of the particular social milieu in which it is located (West, 1970).

VALUE SIMILARITY AND ATTITUDES TOWARD PARENTS

We now turn to an examination of those results that concern attitudes toward parents and value similarity. Were respondents' attitudes toward their parents related to the degree to which their value systems were similar to those they attributed to parents? The detailed results are presented in the original paper (Feather & Cross, 1975). They showed that there was some tendency for the favorability ratings to correlate positively with the corresponding similarity indexes, but the results were not strong. Only a few of the positive correlations were statistically significant. Strongest support for the hypothesis that the extent of value match would be positively related to favorability ratings came from the positive correlations between the self-father similarity index for the terminal values and the attitude toward father. These correlations were statistically significant for both delinquent and control groups, and they showed that the attitude toward father tended to be more favorable the more a respondent's terminal value system matched the terminal value system he attributed to his father. One can speculate that, since the father would be the focal model in the identification process for boys, then the similarity-attraction relationship would therefore be more likely to occur with regard to him. On this argument, one might expect in future studies to find stronger evidence for a similarity-attraction relationship among girls in relation to their mothers than their fathers.

The self-mother and self-father similarity indexes were positively correlated as were the measures of attitudes toward mother and father. That is, the more similar a respondent's value system was to that he attributed to his mother, the greater the similarity of his value system to that he attributed to his father. And the more favorable his attitude toward his mother, the more he viewed his father favorably.

The delinquent and control groups did not differ significantly in their ratings of favorability to either mother or father, although one might have expected less favorable attitudes among delinquents in regard to father (Glueck & Glueck, 1950; Medinnus, 1965). Note, however, that only two questions concerning attitudes toward mother and father were employed and that they were not particularly subtle ones.

In summary, we can say that the predictions about differences between delinquent and nondelinquent boys in the extent to which there were generational and parental discrepancies in value systems were confirmed, at least for the terminal values. When single values were compared between delinquents and nondelinquents several differences were obtained, not only in their own value priorities but also in the rankings they reported for each of their parents. Finally, the favorability ratings toward the fathers of delinquent and nondelinquent boys tended to relate positively to the degree to which the boys' terminal value systems were similar to those they attributed to their fathers.

COMPARISON OF STUDENT ACTIVIST AND DELINQUENT VALUE SYSTEMS

When one compares the average value systems of student activists and delinquents (terminal values: Table 7.1 with Table 7.6; instrumental values: Table 7.2 with Table 7.7) certain differences are obvious. The student activists assigned much higher importance to *a world at peace, a world of beauty, equality, inner harmony,* and being *helpful, honest, imaginative, intellectual,* and *loving* than the juvenile offenders. The delinquents assigned much higher importance to *a comfortable life, an exciting life, pleasure,* and being *ambitious, cheerful,* and *clean* than did the student activists. Table 7.8 presents the five most important and the five least important terminal and instrumental values for each group. There it can be seen that the degree of overlap between the two groups was quite small. The student activists were much more concerned with general social goals, with honest, imaginative, and intelligent ways of

TABLE 7-8. Five Most Important and Five Least Important Values for Student Activists and Delinquent Groups for Both Terminal and Instrumental Value Sets

Terminal Values	
Activists	
Most important:	*A world at peace, equality, freedom, mature love, true friendship*
Least important:	*Pleasure, social recognition, a comfortable life, national security, salvation*
Delinquents	
Most important:	*Freedom, pleasure, mature love, an exciting life, true friendship*
Least important:	*A sense of accomplishment, inner harmony, social recognition, a world of beauty, salvation*
Instrumental Values	
Activists	
Most important:	*Honest, loving, courageous, helpful, broad-minded*
Least important:	*Cheerful, polite, ambitious, clean, obedient*
Delinquents	
Most important:	*Clean, ambitious, cheerful, courageous, capable, forgiving, loving*
Least important:	*Polite, intellectual, imaginative, logical, obedient*

behaving, and with prosocial modes of conduct than were the delinquents. We have seen that these concerns have been noted in many other descriptions of the characteristics of student activists. The delinquent boys placed much more emphasis on immediate hedonistic concerns, stimulus-seeking, material comforts, and with being ambitious, cheerful, and clean than did the student activists. Some of these concerns relate directly to the theories of delinquent behavior described previously where the search for excitement, for short-term hedonistic goals, and for the material comforts of life have been mentioned by various authors in describing the behavior of delinquent boys.

These results therefore indicate that some basic differences existed between the juvenile offenders and the student activists in their average value systems. This should not be overly surprising. The two groups came from different parts of the social structure and had consequently undergone different socialization experiences. The delinquent boys were more likely to have come from lower-class families; the student activists, in contrast, usually had middle-class or upper-class family backgrounds. In addition, the delinquent boys were younger than the student activists and the environments in which each group existed were quite different. Student activists do not generally live in relatively depressed or lower status urban areas (unless they move to them for political and social reasons). They have the benefits of better living conditions than do delinquents, and they promote their protest in the relatively benign environment of the college or university campus.

Many of the differences in value priorities that we have just described between the predominantly male group of student activists and the group of delinquent boys were also evident when the average value systems of each group were separately compared with those of other males of roughly similar age who were tested in other studies in the Flinders program—for example, male students entering Flinders University in 1969 and 1970 (Feather, 1970*b*, 1971*b*), male students tested at the Mitchell College of Advanced Education (Feather & Collins, 1974), boys tested in the Adelaide secondary schools survey (Table 5.5), and sons tested in the two Adelaide surveys (Tables 6.3 and 6.4). So the average value systems of these two groups were fairly distinctive, each group having priorities that set it apart.

These comparisons provide interesting supplements to the intergenerational evidence that we have described. They show that there can be marked differences in value priorities when comparisons are made at a *horizontal* level—across groups of roughly similar age. The intergenerational comparisons were at the *vertical* level—across groups that differed in age. The horizontal comparisons again remind us that people of similar age may come from quite different segments of the social structure, may live in vastly different environments, may have undergone radically different socialization experiences, and may be involved in different generation units. They are subject to quite different demands, satisfactions, frustrations, and disappointments depending upon where they are located in the structure of society. As people cope with the realities of life, they may view some values as more salient and relevant than others, some values as having at least some chance of being expressed or achieved but not others, and some values but not others as involved in a complex balance of contradictions with the acts they must perform in order to cope with social pressures and to satisfy their basic needs. And what for some are important values may not even exist within the life-space of others. The picture is not a simple one and the complex ways in which values emerge and are expressed at different levels of the social structure cannot be denied.

The classic analysis of Merton of the effects of a disjunction between dominant societal goals and the institutionalized means of attaining these goals may be helpful in understanding some of the differences that we have found between the value systems of activists and delinquents (Merton, 1968; 1971; for subsequent related approaches see Coser & Rosenberg, 1969). Indeed, Merton's analysis has had an important impact upon theories of deviant behavior (for example, on crime and delinquency: Cohen & Short, 1971; Cloward & Ohlin, 1960). Merton argues that American society sets up certain superordinate goals among which a very important one is achievement or success defined by a high material standard of living. These general goals affect people's aspirations and the very way in which they define success and failure. Different segments of society, however, differ in their ability to realize their aspirations by means that are defined by the society as legitimate. Where there is a large disjunction between these societal goals and the institutionalized means, a condition of *anomie* prevails, regulative norms break down, and people adopt other means that pay off or work. Under conditions of anomie, delinquency and crime rates are assumed to be high. Where the general societal goals and the institutionalized means are more congruent one would expect these rates of deviant behavior to be lower.

General societal values are therefore assumed to inform members of a society about what their aspirations should be, but these aspirations are often unreal ones for many people who are disadvantaged because of their race, social class, sex, age, and so on. Thus the low income, poorly educated person in American society may be told that success is the Holy Grail, the pot of gold at the end of the rainbow, and that he should strive hard to better his status (betterment being measured by material rewards). But the social realities are such that he has little chance of progressing very far up the ladder. In the face of this discrepancy between aspiration and reality, such a person might resort to illegitimate means learned in the subcultures with which he is associated (Cohen, 1955; Cloward & Ohlin, 1960). He accepts the dominant goals of his culture, but rejects the legitimate means of obtaining them. As Cohen and Short (1971, p. 128) point out, this type of theoretical analysis fails to explain some acts of crime and delinquency that do not seem to be concerned with the acquisition of worldly possessions (for example, certain crimes of violence and property destruction), but it does make sense of some illegal acts in which the offender seems to be intent upon improving the extent of his material resources.

There is some support in Table 7.8 for this interpretation (if one can assume that success measured in material terms and in terms of hedonistic outcomes is an important goal in Australian society) because the juvenile offenders tended to upgrade materialist, action-oriented, and hedonistic values (*a comfortable life, an exciting life, pleasure*) together with competitive striving (being *ambitious*), and to downgrade being *honest* when compared with the activists and with other groups of young Australians tested in the Flinders program.

In terms of the same framework one might view student activists as rejecting some of the dominant societal goals (such as material success), substituting others in their place, and using either legitimate or illegitimate means to attain these alternative goals. Those employing legitimate means presumably would have chosen to pursue their substitute goals from within the system through attempts at reform; those adopting illegitimate means may have chosen to attempt to achieve their goals by overturning the system through rebellion. The social critics might not reject all of their society's goals. Indeed, they may have ambivalent attitudes toward some of them and also toward some of the institutionalized means.

Like the delinquents, the means adopted by the activists would depend upon the subcultures to which they belonged and the opportunities these subcultures offered for learning and performing instrumental behaviors relevant to their goals. For both delinquents and activists the means adopted would also depend upon the extent to which social controls were operative. On university campuses, for example, strict disciplinary measures are often difficult to enforce and noninstitutionalized means, supported by a significant proportion of the student subculture, might therefore become more likely.

Again there is some evidence in Table 7.8 to support these conjectures. Clearly, the activists were substituting alternative values of a humanitarian, politically liberal, and self-actualizing sort and downgrading materialist and competitive values. But they assigned being *honest* a very high priority in their rankings.

In a recent contribution Merton (1971, pp. 829–833) has distinguished between two forms of deviant behavior, both forms having in common a significant departure of behavior from social norms. The two forms are nonconforming behavior (as in student activism) and aberrant behavior (as in delinquency). The distinction is of interest for it supplements our previous discussion and generalizes some of the differences between student activists and juvenile delinquents that we have just been considering within the framework of Merton's ideas.

According to Merton the two forms of deviant behavior can be distinguished as follows: The nonconformer publicly announces his dissent, whereas the aberrant tries to hide his departures from the norms; the nonconformer challenges the legitimacy of the norms he rejects or the way the norms are applied in particular circumstances, whereas the aberrant is likely to acknowledge the legitimacy of the norms he violates; the nonconformer attempts to change the norms he is denying, whereas the aberrant is more concerned with escaping from the sanctioning force of the existing norms; conventional members of the social system tend to acknowledge that the nonconformer is departing from prevailing norms for disinterested purposes, but the aberrant's departures are seen as serving self-interest; the nonconformer tends to appeal to an allegedly higher morality and may claim legitimacy because he is drawing upon certain superordinate or ultimate values that have been denied in social reality, whereas the aberrant is seen to be concerned not with the higher social interest but with his own ends.

This analysis can be seen as developing the earlier treatment of patterns of behavior that might occur under conditions of anomie. Thus, nonconforming behavior develops somewhat the pattern of behavior previously called "rebellion," whereas aberrant behavior encompasses what Merton previously called "innovation," "ritualism," and "retreatism" (Merton, 1968). These two forms of deviant behavior are still considered in terms of the theory of an anomie-and-opportunity structure; as Merton (1971) summarizes:

> Varying rates of particular kinds of deviant behavior result from socially patterned discrepancies between culturally induced aspirations and differentials in access to the opportunity structure for moving toward those aspirations by use of legitimate means. (p. 826)

In the present case, therefore, we can interpret the values and behaviors of the two groups of young people—the student activists and the juvenile offenders—in very general terms in relation to whether they accepted or rejected some or all of the dominant values of their society and whether their aspirations once formed were pursued by legitimate or illegitimate means. We can add to the picture the further distinctions between nonconformers and aberrants that have just been described. And we can note that the problems that each group confronted and the particular solutions they adopted were related to where they were located in the social structure. This location would affect the socio-economic realities of their lives and the way in which they were socialized with respect to their beliefs, attitudes, and values. It would also provide different types of subcultures to which they might be exposed (for example, the student subculture versus the streetcorner gang) and different probabilities of access to desired goals, some goals being readily available to some people but not to others. And it might also provide differences in the likelihood of negative sanctions when rules are broken. Embedded in different environments, therefore, our groups differed in their value priorities and behaved in different ways.

Were there ways in which the activist and delinquent groups were alike? The most obvious shared characteristics were the relatively high priority both groups assigned to being *courageous* and the relatively low priorities they gave to being *responsible* and *self-controlled* compared with other groups of young males tested in the Flinders program. These three values all concern modes of conduct and have in common a stress on acting in defense of one's own beliefs and a movement away from self-disciplined, predictable, reliable, and more controlled ways of behaving. That both groups were similar in these respects but different from their nonactivist, nondelinquent peers is perhaps to be expected. Although the two groups were marching to different drummers, moving toward different terminal goals, they both shared a strong commitment to action without high regard for the inhibitions of control and restraint.

Let us now turn to a consideration of a final group of studies from the Flinders program—those pertaining to people from different cultures. Some of these studies are of a descriptive nature. We will discover that many of the ideas concerning person-environment fit and, in particular, value discrepancy that have emerged in previous chapters can also be applied to other areas, especially to those of cross-cultural interaction and the subjective assimilation of immigrant groups.

8. The Comparison of Value Systems across Cultures

IN THE NEXT TWO CHAPTERS we present the results of studies from the Flinders program on people from different cultures. Two main classes of study will be reported. In the first class the respondents live in different countries and those from one culture may be assumed to have had little contact with those from the other culture. Rokeach (1973, pp. 89–94) has already described some relevant studies that fall into this class and has compared the average value systems of Americans, Canadians, Australians, and Israelis. In this chapter, we will extend his comparisons and add some new information from a developing country, Papua New Guinea.

The second class of study involves migrant groups, people from one culture who have chosen to move to a new or host culture, bringing with them common sets of background experiences that relate to the history and societal characteristics of the culture they have left. These migrants are confronted with the complex problem of adapting to a new society. In Chapter 9 we will explore what this adaptation involves, giving particular attention to the subjective assimilation of migrant children, the second generation, as they make their way in the new society.

THE CONCEPT OF CULTURE

In distinguishing between these two classes of study we are identifying the term "culture" in a very general sense with nation or country. Some of the comparisons to be discussed relate to people from the United States and Australia, people from Papua New Guinea, and people whose parents have migrated to Australia from the Ukraine and from Latvia. Each of these countries is assumed to have a different culture, though it is recognized that some cultures may be more similar than others.

Sociologists and anthropologists have puzzled over the meaning of the term "culture"—see, for example, the discussion by Frey (1970, pp. 178–179). Their various analyses do not lead to any firm conclusions about the meaning of the term, which is used in different ways by different people. Perhaps it would be more fruitful to define culture generally and then to describe how one might approach the analysis of different cultures. At a very abstract level of analysis, a culture can be thought of as a social system that possesses identifiable and interdependent structures or institutions. A culture is associated with a common set of shared beliefs, attitudes, and values among its members, these orientations being reflected not only in the behavior of individuals, but also in societal organization and functioning. A bias toward certain core societal values, however, still allows variations to exist in the orientations of individuals, in particular across different segments of the social structure. A culture is not fixed and unchanging. It corresponds to a dynamic system, modified by trends and events across history. Yet, it preserves some constancy in its outward forms and central values over time. It may share some characteristics with other cultures, but have other characteristics that are unique to itself.

Comparisons between cultures, therefore, involve comparisons between social systems and their objective and subjective correlates, and they can proceed in various ways. One could refer, for example, to structural and demographic characteristics of the culture. These would bear upon such aspects as the amount and type of stratification—as indicated by the differentiation of status, social class, power, and social roles. One could also refer both to the number of distinct subcultures and languages that can be identified within the culture as a whole and to the characteristics of the population with respect to such variables as age, education, sex, religion, income level, and so on. Or one might be more interested in describing the culture in terms of some of its basic institutions and how they function; the family, the legal system, the political system, religion, the military, the schools, the trade unions, the bureaucracy. Using this approach, one might then attempt to abstract from each culture the traditional norms, values, and other distinctive aspects of the culture as a whole, setting them within both a comparative and a historical context. No doubt there are other ways of describing cultures, many of which have been the concern of sociologists and anthropologists. The important point is that the analysis of cultures, involving as it does the analysis of social systems, is exceedingly complicated and part of this complexity is due to problems in defining the concept itself and what it includes.

Cross-cultural comparisons can be approached from many different perspectives using a wide variety of methods from different areas of social science. These approaches include survey methods; documentary analysis; impressionistic observation; statistical analyses of aggregate data; simulation; content analyses; case studies based upon clinical techniques, participant observation, and key informants; structural and dimensional analyses; and various forms of experimental and quasi-experimental procedures (Frey, 1970). And, as we have seen, cross-cultural comparisons can focus upon many different aspects of cultures. Yet a comparison of value systems would appear to be especially germane, particularly if one takes a functionalist point of view and regards cultures as dynamic social systems whose development and modification involve the adaptation of institutions to central value systems—systems that are themselves relatively stable but still subject to gradual change as institutions make adjustments to new trends and conditions with resultant effects upon the subsequent course of socialization (Lipset, 1963a and b; Parsons, 1960a and b). One need not be associated with a functionalist position, however, to be interested in the study of values cross-culturally. Values and value systems are important concepts in virtually all analyses of social or national character, whether these values be considered as central reference frames underlying the way in which societies function, as complex products of historical, economic, technological and other forces, or as both.

The most informative cross-cultural studies are those that compare a set of cultures on a large number of different variables. One would hope to include more than two cultures in the sample set so that one has adequate grounds for coming to conclusions about what is unique about each culture. Such *multi-cultural* studies, once rare, are now becoming more common. The two studies to be described here were not multicultural. Like many other comparative studies, they were *bicultural*. Multicultural research is exceedingly expensive and beyond the resources of one investigator. With the careful collection of relevant data by investigators in different countries (for example, by administration of the Value Survey and other measures to national samples, supplemented by careful behavioral observations and analyses of social structures and social institutions), one might hope in time to assemble enough reliable information to enable multicultural studies of value priorities. But one cuts the cloth according to the resources available, and so our comparisons were limited ones.

Both of our studies involved respondents with a good command of the English language. Consequently, we were able to avoid the problems that arise when one has to translate a survey involving abstract concepts into a different language. Nevertheless, some difficult problems of research design and data interpretation still remain when one compares different cultures in regard to their value priorities—as might be expected from the complex nature of the concept of culture itself. We will first discuss some of these problems before turning to the research evidence.

METHODOLOGICAL AND INTERPRETATIVE ISSUES

There have been several recent discussions of the difficulties that confront the research worker who plans to conduct cross-cultural investigations (see, for example, Armer & Grimshaw, 1973; Berry, 1969; Brislin, Loner, & Thorndike, 1973; Cole & Scribner, 1974; Dawson, 1971; Frey, 1970; Frijda & Jahoda, 1966; Triandis, 1972; Warwick & Osherson, 1973*b;* Whiting, 1968). After reading these analyses of the pitfalls that confront the cross-cultural psychologist one wonders whether the task he sets himself can ever be conducted in such a way as to lead to strong inferences about cross-cultural similarities and differences, or whether his findings, despite care in research design and data collection, will always be open to more than one interpretation. Yet, as most authors point out, there are many gains to be had from cross-cultural research, not the least of which are the possibilities it offers for sharpening and clarifying concepts, for covering a much wider range of dependent and independent variables, for testing the generality of theories, for suggesting more parsimonious explanations, and for providing the salutary impact on the researcher of getting him outside his cultural shell so that he becomes "more aware of both cultural differences and his own assumptions, whether in defining concepts, deciding on the suitability of a research method, or interpreting his findings" (Warwick & Osherson, 1973*a,* p. 11). A further benefit comes with the realization that cross-cultural research, like most social science, profits from a readiness to employ a variety of methods in searching for meaningful answers to questions. In practice this usually means that progress follows from multidisciplinary collaboration in joint research programs calling upon the unique skills of the psychologist, the sociologist, the historian, the geographer, the anthropologist, the economist, and others.

THE PROBLEM OF APPROPRIATENESS OF MEASURES

In discussing the use of test instruments and research procedures in cross-cultural investigations, the questions of *appropriateness* and *equivalence* are of great importance. Armer (1973) describes these two aspects of the research process in the following way:

> A major methodological problem facing comparative sociological research is the *appropriateness* of conceptualizations and research methods for each specific culture. Appropriateness requires feasibility, significance, and acceptability in each foreign culture as a necessary (but not sufficient) condition for insuring validity and successful completion of comparative studies. . . . Since the emphasis on appropriateness of methods in each particular society ultimately means that methods are rarely, if ever, phenomenally identical across societies because of variation in social-cultural conditions, comparativists must inquire whether there is sufficient *equivalence* [italics added] in the research concepts and methods to permit meaningful comparisons across societies. Even if the concepts and methods in different societies are outwardly identical, the meanings or implications may not be. (pp. 50–51)

It should be clear that the problems of appropriateness and equivalence are not unique to cross-cultural investigation. The same questions arise whenever comparisons are made within a society, for example as between different income groups, people of different ages, males and females, or just between different individuals.

Let us first consider the Rokeach Value Survey in regard to its appropriateness for use in cross-cultural research. Questions that can be raised in this context are: What other procedures are available? Do Rokeach's two lists of values provide a reasonably extensive sample of possible values, or have important values been left off the list? Are these values meaningful and within the range of experience of most members of the population?

On the first question let it be said that, when one surveys the literature, alternative procedures designed to assess values and value systems vary a lot in their appropriateness for cross-cultural research. Triandis (1972, pp. 76–83) describes some of the main procedures that have been employed cross-culturally and these include the Allport-Vernon-Lindzey Study of Values, Kluckhohn's classification of value-orientations (Kluckhohn, 1951; Kluckhohn & Strodtbeck, 1961), Morris's "Paths of Life" (Morris, 1956), the self-anchoring striving scale developed by Cantril (1965), and various projective tests and specially tailored questionnaire items. In developing our research program it seemed to us that Rokeach's Value Survey was a great improvement over these alternative approaches, many of which are quite restricted in the number of values they sample. We have described some of the other advantages of Rokeach's procedure in Chapter 2.

In regard to the remaining questions it will be recalled that when Rokeach selected his two lists of terminal and instrumental values he aimed at samples of values that were reasonably comprehensive and universally applicable. It is always possible to question whether he achieved that aim. One might argue that important values have been left off the list, or that most of the values represent concerns that are typical of middle-class Western societies, or that some end-states or modes of conduct that are more "negative" might have been included—and no doubt some of these arguments could be supported with examples. Yet, when one looks at the lists, it is apparent that the values included in them cover a fairly wide range. Moreover, the different structural analyses reported in Chapter 2 show that one cannot readily reduce the two sets of terminal and instrumental values to a more limited number of dimensions or clusters. One is encouraged to the view that these lists should prove useful in cross-cultural research, particularly with English-speaking respondents who have had a sufficient level of education so that they can understand the instructions and the concepts involved.

In less developed and more primitive societies, however, and with groups with low verbal comprehension, use of the Rokeach Value Survey may be inappropriate and misleading, even following careful attempts to present the concepts in a meaningful way. In the first place, some of the value labels may not be understood by respondents or they may even be irrelevant to the society or group being studied. In these cases, respondents may deal first with the values they know and respond to the others randomly or on the basis of irrelevant criteria. Second, in some cultures different from our own, respondents may have difficulty with the basic operation of ranking. The procedure of arriving at a linear order involving abstract concepts may be outside their range of experience and the instructions may also be beyond them. Obviously, in such instances, other procedures will have to be developed based upon careful analyses of the range of concerns or values within the society and thoughtful appreciation of the appropriate ways of obtaining information about these concerns. This latter problem of how to *retrieve* the information will call for close observation of the normal repertoire of tasks that members of the society perform in their daily lives (Cole, Gay, Glick, & Sharp, 1971; Cole & Scribner, 1974).

In all applications, we assume that the Value Survey (where appropriate) will be supplemented by other measures and observations of the culture itself. Otherwise, interpretations of the value rankings will be simplistic and perhaps quite misleading.

THE PROBLEM OF EQUIVALENCE OF MEASURES

The problem of achieving *equivalence* is perhaps more difficult. Warwick and Osherson (1973a) discuss four types of equivalence: conceptual equivalence, equivalence of measurement, semantic equivalence, and sampling equivalence. When one employs the Rokeach Value Survey one can attempt to control the measurement side of the operation: the procedures employed in selecting respondents, the standardization of the conditions of testing, and the form in which the data are analyzed. Equivalence of methodology might then be assumed in terms of the same objective procedures and criteria used in the different cultures. For example, one might use the same method of sampling, the same instructions and test materials, the same types of interviewers, the same context in which testing occurs, the same time of testing, and so on.

One can be misled by objective criteria, however, even in fairly concrete aspects of method. Use of such nominal criteria does not necessarily guarantee that one has achieved functional equivalence of meaning. Let us take an example. Suppose that the sampling of respondents involves some form of stratification of which income level is one ingredient. One might then be able to compare responses of those within a defined income level (say, $4,000 to $6,000) across cultures. But obviously, this income level, though objectively defined, may have quite different significance depending upon the standard of living within a country. The same sort of problem arises when one attempts to define the poverty level in different countries. Identical objective criteria may disguise important real differences between cultures. In different countries those who suffer poverty may have quite different average income levels. Much careful research may be required to achieve equivalent indicators. Identity does not guarantee equivalence.

The problem of equivalence becomes especially difficult when the test situation involves (as it usually does) the use of language whether in oral or written form. How does one organize the situation in such a way that basically the same *meanings* are being conveyed by the instructions and by the item content across different cultures? This problem is acute when procedures developed in one language have to be translated into the language of another culture. Various ways of dealing with the problem of conceptual equivalence when languages differ have been proposed, including back-translation, and these procedures have been widely discussed (see, for example, Frey, 1970). Running through these discussions is a stress on the need to employ concepts that are salient to the cultures that are being compared, the need to have advance familiarity with the cultures being studied, and the need to conduct qualitative pretests of the items to be used in the interview (Deutscher, 1973; Warwick & Osherson, 1973*a*).

Some specialized procedures have been worked out for assessing conceptual equivalence when items or survey questions are used. For example, Schuman (1973) has described a technique using random probes in which respondents "explain a little" what they had in mind when making their choices on a set of items randomly selected from the interview schedule for each respondent. Przeworski and Teune (1973) have proposed an identity-equivalence procedure where indicators contain some items that are identical in all the cultural units and some that are specific to local conditions. And others have suggested use of multidimensional procedures and factor analysis in which the relationships between item responses are analyzed in order to discover whether there are similar underlying structures and dimensions across cultures (as with some of the research using semantic-differential procedures, Osgood, 1964). Some of these latter techniques have been discussed in Brislin, Lonner, and Thorndike (1973).

Frey (1970) has also described ways of demonstrating equivalence both in conceptualization and measurement across cultures or systems. One is the approach through *unidimensionality* or homogeneity where items may be shown to tap the same attitudinal universe within each culture (or system), and predominantly only that universe (he gives the Przeworski and Teune identity-equivalence procedure as an example). The other is the approach through *validation* where one determines, according to some theoretical base, that items predict in similar ways to other designated variables in each culture (or system). Frey (1970) summarizes these procedures as follows:

> In the unidimensional approach, a core equivalence is asserted on the basis of showing that the *same set of items* (formally identical) hangs together across systems, i.e., that the items exhibit similar, nonrandom patterns of relationship *among each other* without regard to system. In the validational approach, equivalence is asserted on the basis of demonstrating that *different system-specific sets of items* all measure a variable which is similarly and predictably related to *designated other variables* in each system. (p. 286)

In countries where the same language is spoken the problem of conceptual equivalence may not be so important when items refer to *concrete* objects or events within the everyday experience of the respondents. Yet the kinds of procedure just described are also relevant in this case since identical words in English, for example, may be given different interpretations and have different implications across English-speaking cultures, particularly if the words are abstract and not easily tied to specific objects or events in the real world. The values in the Rokeach Value Survey fall into this class. They are abstract terms that may be interpreted differently both between and within cultures, the interpretation being related to complex patterns of implications.

Let us take the value *equality* as an example. In the Value Survey this terminal value is accompanied by the descriptive phrase, "brotherhood, equal opportunity for all." Now *equality* may have different meanings in different cultural contexts and these differences may be reflected in the way social institutions function within a society and in the patterns of beliefs, attitudes, and behaviors that are characteristic of its members. Rokeach's short defining phrase may be quite appropriate in the United States where equality as a value does carry with it implications of equal opportunity to make one's way in life and equal treatment of individuals. This special character of the meaning of equality is emphasized by Lipset (1963*a*). He argues that the two basic values working through American society are equality and achievement, where equality means respect for others, simply because they are human beings, and equal opportunity. Every person should have an equal chance to do well, to push ahead and achieve success by his own efforts. But, as Lipset (1963*a*) notes, "the American concept of equality, which focuses on opportunity and the quality of social relations, does not demand equality of income" (p. 321). As Potter (1954) states:

> The American ideal and practice of equality . . . has implied for the individual . . . opportunity to make his own place in society and . . . emancipation from a system of status. . . . [T]he American . . . has traditionally expected to find a gamut running from rags to riches, from tramps to millionnaires. . . . [E]quality did not mean uniform position on a common level, but it did mean universal opportunity to move through a scale which traversed many levels. (pp. 91–92)

The conjunction of equality and achievement in American society obviously results in the paradox that individual competitive striving for success determines inequalities of various kinds, as some are able to move up the achievement ladder and gather the rewards that come with successful accomplishment whereas others, not so fortunate, are left behind.

Equal opportunity is also valued in Australia but social historians, sociologists, and other commentators on the Australian way of life have noted that the concept of equality has other characteristics as well. Many of their views have been covered by Encel (1970*a*) in his analysis of equality and authority in Australia. An early contribution was made by Hancock (1930), who explored the influence of the equalitarian outlook throughout politics, economics, culture, and manners in Australian life. He noted that a crucial assumption of Australian society was a "fair and reasonable" standard of living for everyone. This assumption was accompanied by a distrust for special excellence and a dislike of authority and status seekers. Encel remarks upon the frequently noted tendency for equalitarianism to be associated with anti-intellectualism in Australia, a connection that has also been explored by Hofstadter (1963) in relation to American society. Encel also notes that the "mythology of the spectacular career"—the Horatio Alger myth—is much less evident in Australian society than it is in America. Hancock's metaphor of 40 years ago still has a grain of truth in it when he states that Australian democracy

> is properly anxious that everybody should run a fair race. It is improperly resentful if anybody runs a fast race. Indeed, it dislikes altogether the idea of a race, for in a race victory is to the strong. Its solicitude is for the weak, and its instinct is to make merit take a place in the queue. (p. 183)

Perhaps, however, Hancock's metaphor was overstated even for the times he was describing. Success in some walks of life has always been admired in Australia (especially in sport). And the value of achievement has probably gained a lot of ground since Hancock wrote (Taft & Walker, 1958), along with changes in social structure (Mayer, 1964), and other rapid developments in the direction of greatly increased complexity and sophistication within Australian society. Encel (1970a) sums up these ideas by stating that

> the conception of equality which prevails in Australia is one which places great stress on the enforcement of a high minimum standard of material well-being, on the outward show of equality and the minimisation of privileges due to formal rank, and almost by implication restricts the scope for the unusual, eccentric, or dissenting individual. (p. 56)

He goes on to show how equality and bureaucracy are conjoined in Australian life in a paradoxical manner:

> Constitutional liberalism, which thinks in terms of uniform general laws, would create a set of bureaucratic rules to enforce equal treatment. . . . Herein lies the paradox of egalitarianism in Australia: the search for equality of the re-distributive kind breeds bureaucracy; bureaucracy breeds authority; and authority undermines the equality which bred it. (p. 57)

It is evident, from this brief discussion of what the term "equality" implies in the United States and Australia, that a value defined by some descriptive label may have different meanings and implications in different societies. And the same point applies to the other values on Rokeach's lists. The meaning of the term cannot be divorced from the culture. Identical words may suggest different meanings. Each word carries with it a residue of culturally unique associations, although that should not imply that it has no common aspects of meaning across cultures. Each word is embedded in a structure of implications and these structures may have both common and unique segments across cultures, as they may also have between people and groups from the same culture. A major requirement in cross-cultural research is, therefore, to discover in what ways the same words are uniquely interpreted in different cultures as well as in what ways they share common meanings across cultures.

How does Rokeach deal with this issue of conceptual equivalence? He gives four main answers (Rokeach, 1973, pp. 49–51). First, one could take a strict behaviorist stance and treat each value as a specific stimulus to which the person responds. In this case what is important is the degree to which the response is predictable and replicable and how it relates to other objectively defined circumstances and behaviors. The focus is upon regularities that can be subjected to public scrutiny. The search for *subjective* meaning is seen as leading one into an unproductive byway unless private experience can somehow become public knowledge.

Second, if one is concerned with connotative meaning, one can measure it with Osgood's semantic differential technique (Osgood, Suci, & Tannenbaum, 1957), using bipolar adjective scales to rate each value along dimensions of evaluation, potency, and activity. A study by Homant (1969) did just this and found that the correlations between the evaluative (good-bad) dimension of the semantic differential and the value rankings were fairly high. Rokeach takes these results as suggesting that the value rankings may be measuring essentially the same kind of connotative meaning as that measured by Osgood's evaluative factor.

Third, there is evidence (Rokeach, 1973, pp. 31–32) that reliability coefficients are virtually unaffected when one leaves out the defining phrases for each value in the Value Survey. Moreover, systematic relationships between values and attitudes and values and behavior still appear at much the same level irrespective of what form of the Value Survey is employed. Rokeach (1973) concludes: "If the values employed in the Value Survey were semantically tyrannical, meaning different things to different people, significant results of a systematic kind would not be possible" (p. 50).

Finally, Rokeach argues that the *psychological significance* that a particular value has for a person is far more important than its semantic meaning. This psychological significance relates to how the value is ranked in relation to other values. For example, Rokeach (1973, Chap. 6) found evidence from content analyses of their writings to suggest that both Hitler and Lenin ranked *freedom* low on their scale of values. He asks: Does *freedom* mean the same thing to Hitler and to Lenin? Rokeach believes that *freedom* has different psychological significance for Hitler and Lenin because Hitler ranked *equality* low whereas Lenin ranked it high. He interprets this difference as follows:

> These findings suggest that in Hitler's case, the denial of *freedom* by the state is a weapon to coerce inequality; in Lenin's case, the denial of *freedom* by the state is also a weapon, but a weapon to coerce equality. Thus, the psychological significance of *freedom,* or its denial, is obviously different for

Hitler and for Lenin, even though both rank it equally low and even though it may be semantically identical to both. . . .

. . . In the final analysis, it is probably scientifically more fruitful to be concerned with the concept of psychological significance than with the question of the semantic meaning of values. (Rokeach, 1973, pp. 50–51)

We would argue that studies of the semantic meaning of terminal and instrumental values are required and should be conducted. Thus, one might ask what associations do people have to the abstract verbal labels? Can they provide synonyms and opposites for them, and define them in fairly detailed ways, or is their understanding more limited? And what, if any, is the common core of meaning for each value across individuals, groups, and cultures?

One would also be concerned with how the value rankings interrelate among each other across cultures and whether the matrix of interrelationships implies similar underlying structures and dimensions in each culture. In Chapter 2 we showed that there were indeed certain similarities between the results of Rokeach's analyses of the structure of terminal and instrumental values in the United States (based upon factor analysis) and the results we obtained in Australia (based upon nonmetric multidimensional procedures). This focus upon the basic structure of values across cultures is similar to the approach used by Osgood (1964) in testing the generality of the factor structure of semantic differential scales across cultures. It relates to Frey's (1970) "approach through unidimensionality," although it is clear that in the case of both the Rokeach Value Survey and the semantic differential more than one dimension is involved.

More important, however, is evidence that responses to the value labels on Rokeach's lists are involved in regular patterns of relationships with *other* variables or criteria within each culture, patterns of relationships that are similar or the same across different cultures. For, if one discovers such evidence, then it indicates that the values appear to be functioning in equivalent ways across cultures. Tests for functional equivalence are in the nature of the "approach through validation" (Frey, 1970), and typically they involve defined criteria and some overall theory or conceptual scheme that enables one to work out various sets of implications and to test them empirically. In the early stages of inquiry this theory might be quite "low level," but as the inquiry proceeds and more observations are made it may become quite sophisticated.

Let us take an example. One might predict that individuals who assigned high importance to both *freedom* and *equality* would be more likely to have liberal attitudes and to engage in social protest than those who ranked these values further down the list. If this prediction were confirmed in different cultures, then one has evidence of functional equivalence through validation. The values are similarly related to defined criteria on the basis of some theoretical formulation. One might also predict that cultures where both *freedom* and *equality* are ranked high on the average will tend to have different forms of political and social institutions than cultures where, for example, both *freedom* and *equality* are assigned low priority on the average. Again, if this prediction were confirmed, one would have evidence for functional equivalence but at the societal level. One would hope to collect many pieces of evidence of different kinds to support a case for functional equivalence.

Of course, one can expect differences as well as similarities. Patterns of relationships involving value rankings and specified criteria may have something in common and also something unique. We might find, for example, that in both the United States and Australia, people who assigned high importance to *equality* might insist on equal political rights and equal pay for equal work regardless of sex. But, we might find that in Australia a high priority assigned to *equality* implied some demand for redistribution of income so that the rich would help to provide for the poor, whereas this same demand might not be observed quite so strongly in the United States. In the United States, we might find that a high priority assigned to *equality* implied that the educational system should be structured in particular ways to allow for equal opportunity and equal treatment of individuals whereas the same implication might not be observed quite so strongly in Australia. These examples are somewhat oversimplified because they consider one value rather than sets of values. One would expect that other values in addition to *equality* would be involved in some of the relationships just mentioned. But the main point is that patterns of implication might not completely overlap across cultures. The strategy of attempting to discover the similarities and differences in these patterns across different cultures should enable one to specify what is distinctive about each culture and what it shares with other cultures with respect to how its values operate.

The procedure for demonstrating the degree of equivalence in concepts and methods that we have just discussed also applies to different sections of the same society—as between different social classes, different age groups, different sexes, and so on. *Freedom,* for example, may have different implications for the young than for the old, although some implications would be shared across ages. Comparisons of value priorities across societies should, therefore, also take into account the fabric of variation within societies. The search for cross-cultural similarities and differences in values, therefore, opens up the analysis of the ways in which values operate in each culture separately.

There is no denying that the type of comparative study implied by the preceding discussion will involve sophisticated, costly, and time-consuming methodologies as well as complicated (and perhaps as yet uninvented) forms of statistical analysis. Yet one should not dodge the complexity of social science. One immediate practical implication is that we should attempt to formulate testable theories about how values might operate at the individual and societal levels; we should then specify, given the theoretical framework, the criteria to which value rankings and value systems should relate. The networks of relationships that emerge from empirical studies would then reflect upon the theoretical formulation. These networks could be compared across cultures. Such comparisons would tell us what different cultures have in common and in what respects they are unique when the functional significance of values is the focus of concern.

As we have noted, the search for meaningful patterns based upon a variety of multiple indicators will involve interdisciplinary cooperation. This joint effort is essential if one is to achieve a valid assessment of values and a deeper understanding of their meaning in relation to the complex structure of the societies being studied.

This general approach to the cross-cultural study of values represents an "ideal," one not yet achieved in practice. In the next section we will describe studies that compare the median rankings of particular groups across cultures, where these groups can be considered to be roughly equivalent in terms of other criteria. A valuable strategy in this type of approach is to "slice" the society in different ways so as to discover whether the differences in average value rankings, found when groups chosen on the basis of one set of criteria are compared, are also discovered when groups chosen on the basis of other criteria are compared. If adolescents in Country A rank *true friendship* higher on the average than do adolescents in Country B, does this difference also occur when other age groups are compared across the two countries, assuming that sampling procedures and measurement techniques have been equated? Does the difference also appear when stratification is on the basis of income rather than age? And so on. The strategy is analogous to looking for a "main effect" across cultures—differences that stand out regardless of how one slices the pie.

CROSS-CULTURAL COMPARISONS: AUSTRALIA AND THE UNITED STATES

PAST RESEARCH

Rokeach (1973, pp. 89–93) has compared the median value rankings for both sets of terminal and instrumental values across four groups of college men from the United States, Australia, Israel, and Canada. In describing value differences among the four countries, his comparison, like one made in an earlier discussion of results obtained in the initial stages of the Flinders program (Feather, 1970b), refers to hypotheses proposed by Lipset (1963a and b).

In making his comparisons Lipset used the concept of "pattern variables" developed by Parsons (1951, 1960a). Four pattern variables were used in the analysis: achievement-ascription, universalism-particularism, specificity-diffuseness, and equalitarian-elitist. These variables are described by Lipset (1963a and b) as follows:

> According to the achievement-ascription distinction, a society's value system may emphasize individual ability or performance or it may emphasize ascribed

or inherited qualities (such as race or high birth) in judging individuals and placing them in various roles. According to the universalism-particularism distinction, it may emphasize that all people shall be treated according to the same standard (e.g., equality before the law), or that individuals shall be treated differently according to their personal qualities or their particular membership in a class or group. Specificity-diffuseness refers to the difference between treating individuals in terms of the specific positions which they happen to occupy, rather than diffusely as individual members of the collectivity. . . . [According to the equalitarian-elitist distinction] a society's values may stress that all persons must be given respect simply because they are human beings, or it may stress the general superiority of those who hold positions of power and privilege. (pp. 209–211)

Lipset is careful to point out that "no society is ever fully explicable by these analytic concepts" (p. 211). According to Parsons (1951):

In a very broad way the differentiation between types of social systems do correspond to this order of cultural value-pattern differentiation, but *only* in a very broad way. Actual social structures are not value-pattern types, but *resultants* of the integration of value-patterns with the other components of the system. (p. 112)

Parson's list of pattern variables includes some that, for reasons of parsimony, Lipset did not use in his cross-cultural comparisons. Pattern variables can, of course, be employed in other types of comparison as well as cross-cultural ones, as in the comparisons involving different subsystems within a culture.

With reference to the four pattern variables selected, Lipset (1963*a*) concludes:

Australia differs from the United States in being slightly more equalitarian, but less achievement oriented, universalistic, and specific. It also seems less universalistic and more equalitarian than Canada, but it is difficult to estimate the differences on the other two polarities. Canada differs somewhat from the United States on all four dimensions of equalitarianism, achievement, universalism, and specificity, while Britain in turn is less oriented toward these values than Canada. (p. 249)

This conclusion was based upon impressionistic evidence to be found in a considerable number of writings about each country, to which Lipset refers in his discussion. But he believes that these differences in value patterns may help to account for other important differences between these four stable and highly developed democracies (as, for example, in their political and educational systems), and that they may be related to the sequence of historical events involved in the development of each democracy.

The comparisons made by Rokeach (1973) between the median rankings of terminal and instrumental values across the four groups of United States, Australian, Israeli, and Canadian college men lent some support to Lipset's speculations about American, Australian, and Canadian value differences, but some discrepancies also resulted. The reader is referred to Rokeach's discussion for details (Rokeach, 1973, Tables 3.18 & 3.19). Our purpose here is to update the Australian and United States comparison by including more recent evidence.

AVERAGE VALUE SYSTEMS FOR AUSTRALIAN AND UNITED STATES GROUPS

Tables 8.1 and 8.2 present the median rankings of the terminal and instrumental values respectively for the following groups of respondents: (1) male respondents tested at Flinders University in 1969 (Feather, 1970b, and Chapter 3) and at Michigan State University—the Australian and American college men involved in Rokeach's comparisons; (2) heads of households (predominantly male) and wives tested in the 1972 and 1973 Adelaide surveys referred to in Chapter 6; and (3) males and females tested in United States surveys conducted in 1968 and 1971 by the National Opinion Research Center (Rokeach, 1973, 1974; Chapter 2). Details of these various samples have been given in earlier chapters of this book, as noted. The Australian and American groups to be compared obviously cannot be considered equivalent in regard to the way in which they were obtained and they differ in other respects as well. Nevertheless, these groups are as close as we can get to comparable samples at the present time. Systematic cross-cultural research in the future should be able to do a lot better.

We cannot provide direct statistical tests of the significance of differences between the Australian and United States data. We can, however, compare the median value rankings between roughly comparable groups (Flinders male students versus Michigan State male students; Adelaide heads of households versus American adult males; and Adelaide wives versus American adult females), looking for consistent differences between all of these groups. Some obvious and consistent differences did occur. Irrespective of which groups were being compared, the Australian respondents tended to rank the following values higher in importance than did the Americans: *an exciting life, a world of beauty, inner harmony, mature love, true friendship, wisdom,* and being *cheerful, loving, honest* and *responsible,* although some of the differences in the medians were quite small. Also irrespective of which groups were being compared, the Americans tended to rank the following values higher in importance than did the Australians: *a comfortable life, salvation,* and being *ambitious.*

There were also some interesting reversals. Flinders male students ranked *equality* higher in importance and both *family security* and *happiness* lower in importance than did Michigan State male students, but these differences were in the other direction when the Australian and American adult groups were compared.

Some differences occurred either between the student groups or between the adult groups, but not for both. Flinders male students ranked being *broad-*

TABLE 8-1. Median Rankings and Composite Rank Orders of Terminal Values by Male Students at Flinders University and Michigan State University and by Respondents Tested in Adelaide and U.S. Surveys

Terminal Value	Male Students		Australian (Adelaide) Surveys				United States Surveys			
	Flinders University	Michigan State University	1972		1973		1968		1971	
			Heads	Wives	Heads	Wives	Males	Females	Males	Females
N	279	169	140	139	226	219	665	744	687	743
A comfortable life	12.6(13)	10.3(11)	11.4(14)	13.4(14)	10.6(13)	12.1(14)	7.8(4)	10.0(13)	9.2(9)	11.7(13)
An exciting life	9.2(11)	10.8(12)	13.1(15)	13.9(15)	12.7(15)	13.6(15)	14.6(18)	15.8(18)	14.6(17)	15.6(18)
A sense of accomplishment	6.3(4)	7.1(5)	9.1(9)	9.1(10)	8.2(9)	9.8(11)	8.3(7)	9.4(10)	9.3(10)	9.8(12)
A world at peace	8.2(9)	9.3(10)	4.3(2)	2.8(2)	5.1(3)	2.6(2)	3.8(1)	3.0(1)	3.2(1)	2.6(1)
A world of beauty	13.0(15)	14.4(18)	11.0(12.5)	10.6(12)	11.9(14)	11.0(12)	13.6(15)	13.5(15)	12.8(15)	12.4(14)
Equality	9.0(10)	12.3(13)	9.2(11)	10.0(11)	9.9(11)	9.3(10)	8.9(9)	8.3(8)	8.0(6)	7.4(4)
Family security	9.5(12)	8.1(7)	2.1(1)	2.4(1)	2.4(1)	2.1(1)	3.8(2)	3.8(2)	4.0(2)	4.4(2)
Freedom	4.9(3)	4.7(1)	6.6(5)	8.4(9)	5.9(4)	6.7(4)	4.9(3)	6.1(3)	5.1(3)	5.5(3)
Happiness	7.5(7)	6.2(2)	5.4(3)	5.4(3)	5.0(2)	4.1(3)	7.9(5)	7.4(5)	7.6(4)	7.8(8)
Inner harmony	7.7(8)	8.8(9)	8.3(8)	6.8(5)	8.0(8)	8.3(9)	11.1(13)	9.8(12)	11.0(13)	9.5(11)
Mature love	6.6(5)	7.4(6)	9.2(10)	7.0(7)	8.6(10)	8.1(8)	12.6(14)	12.3(14)	11.4(14)	12.4(15)
National security	13.9(17)	13.8(17)	11.0(12.5)	11.3(13)	10.3(12)	11.2(13)	9.2(10)	9.8(11)	9.0(8)	8.9(9)
Pleasure	12.7(14)	13.1(15)	13.7(16)	14.7(17)	12.8(16)	13.6(16)	14.1(17)	15.0(16)	14.3(16)	15.1(17)
Salvation	15.9(18)	13.4(16)	15.4(18)	14.0(16)	15.5(18)	15.5(18)	9.9(12)	7.3(4)	10.9(12)	7.6(6)
Self-respect	7.5(6)	7.0(4)	7.6(7)	6.8(6)	7.7(6)	7.2(6)	8.2(6)	7.4(6)	7.9(5)	7.4(5)
Social recognition	13.7(16)	12.9(14)	15.0(17)	16.0(18)	14.2(17)	15.4(17)	13.8(16)	15.0(17)	14.6(18)	15.1(16)
True friendship	4.9(2)	8.7(8)	7.3(6)	8.4(8)	7.8(7)	7.3(7)	9.6(11)	9.1(9)	9.4(11)	9.5(10)
Wisdom	4.7(1)	6.8(3)	6.5(4)	6.3(4)	7.5(5)	6.9(5)	8.5(8)	7.7(7)	8.9(7)	7.7(7)

Note. Lower numbers denote higher relative value. In each column the rank order of each median (low to high) is denoted in parentheses after the median. *N*s are for error-free rankings.
Source: For male students data are from Feather, 1970b and Rokeach 1973; for American adults data are from Rokeach, 1973; 1974.

TABLE 8-2. Median Rankings and Composite Rank Orders of Instrumental Values by Male Students at Flinders University and Michigan State University and by Respondents Tested in Adelaide and U.S. Surveys

Instrumental Value	Male Students		Australian (Adelaide) Surveys				United States Surveys			
	Flinders University	Michigan State University	1972		1973		1968		1971	
			Heads	Wives	Heads	Wives	Males	Females	Males	Females
N	279	169	142	137	228	219	665	744	687	743
Ambitious	7.8(6)	6.4(3)	9.8(13)	12.2(14)	8.7(8)	11.6(14)	5.6(2)	7.4(4)	5.4(2)	8.0(6)
Broad-minded	4.6(2)	6.7(4)	8.3(7)	8.5(10.5)	6.7(3)	7.6(5)	7.2(4)	7.7(5)	7.1(4)	7.8(5)
Capable	8.2(8)	7.5(5)	8.4(9)	8.6(12)	7.7(6)	7.7(6)	8.9(8)	10.1(12)	8.7(6)	10.3(12)
Cheerful	8.5(9)	12.0(15)	9.3(10)	8.4(8)	9.4(11)	8.0(8)	10.4(12)	9.4(10)	11.0(13)	9.8(10)
Clean	13.9(17)	14.1(17)	8.4(8)	7.9(7)	8.1(7)	8.6(10)	9.4(9)	8.1(8)	10.2(11)	9.0(9)
Courageous	8.7(10)	8.4(8)	8.2(6)	7.6(6)	7.7(5)	8.5(9)	7.5(5)	8.1(6)	8.0(5)	8.2(8)
Forgiving	9.3(11)	10.5(12)	7.2(3)	5.5(4)	8.7(9)	7.0(4)	8.2(6)	6.4(2)	8.8(7)	5.9(2)
Helpful	10.2(13)	11.9(14)	7.6(4)	6.9(5)	9.7(13)	7.9(7)	8.3(7)	8.1(7)	9.2(9)	8.0(7)
Honest	4.0(1)	5.2(1)	2.7(1)	2.6(1)	2.9(1)	2.6(1)	3.4(1)	3.2(1)	3.3(1)	3.2(1)
Imaginative	11.5(15)	10.8(13)	15.1(18)	15.4(18)	14.3(18)	15.1(18)	14.3(18)	16.1(18)	14.5(18)	15.8(18)
Independent	7.9(7)	7.7(6)	9.6(12)	11.4(13)	9.9(14)	10.3(13)	10.2(11)	10.7(14)	9.9(10)	10.4(13)
Intellectual	10.6(14)	8.5(9)	14.2(17)	13.1(16)	12.9(16)	14.1(16)	12.8(15)	13.2(16)	12.5(15)	12.9(15)
Logical	9.9(12)	8.3(7)	10.3(15)	12.8(15)	11.5(15)	12.2(15)	13.5(16)	14.7(17)	12.8(16)	13.9(17)
Loving	7.5(4)	9.1(11)	7.8(5)	5.4(2)	7.2(4)	4.8(3)	10.9(14)	8.6(9)	10.6(12)	7.3(4)
Obedient	15.3(18)	15.0(18)	12.9(16)	13.7(17)	14.2(17)	14.7(17)	13.5(17)	13.1(15)	13.4(17)	13.2(16)
Polite	12.1(16)	13.2(16)	10.2(14)	8.5(10.5)	9.6(12)	9.9(12)	10.9(13)	10.7(13)	11.2(14)	10.8(14)
Responsible	5.2(3)	5.9(2)	4.9(2)	5.5(3)	5.2(2)	4.8(2)	6.6(3)	6.8(3)	6.2(3)	6.7(3)
Self-controlled	7.7(5)	8.6(10)	9.5(11)	8.5(9)	9.0(10)	9.0(11)	9.7(10)	9.5(11)	9.2(8)	10.0(11)

Note. Lower numbers denote higher relative value. In each column the rank order of each median (low to high) is denoted in parentheses after the median. Ns are for error-free rankings.
Source: For male students data are from Feather, 1970b and Rokeach, 1973; for American adults data are from Rokeach, 1973; 1974.

minded higher in importance and being *intellectual* lower in importance than did Michigan State male students. These differences, however, were not apparent in comparisons of the adult survey data. And there was a tendency for the American adult groups to rank *freedom* higher in importance than did the Australian adult groups, but this difference was not evident when the student groups were compared.

If we concentrate on the consistent differences, that is, on the "main effects" or those differences that occurred generally, then the American groups emerge from these comparisons as more materialistic, more achievement-oriented, and more orthodoxly religious ("*salvation*-minded") than the Australian groups. Rokeach (1973, p. 91) noted these differences and they also occurred when comparisons involved Americans with Israelis and Canadians. The stronger concern with achievement (or ambition) among the Americans is consistent with Lipset's (1963*a*) analysis. He places the American character within an historical context and argues that

> Two themes, equality and achievement, emerged from the interplay between the Puritan tradition and the Revolutionary ethos in the early formation of America's institutions. . . . [T]he dynamic interaction of these two predominant values has been a constant element in determining American institutions and behavior. (p. 101)

Although the Australian student group tended to assign higher importance to *equality* than did the American student group (consistent with Lipset's analysis), this difference was reversed in the adult samples. But the differences were not large and it would be foolish to generalize about them.

Further support for the higher emphasis upon achievement in American society is provided by the results of the survey on explanations of poverty described in Chapter 6. Comparison of the American data (Feagin, 1972) with those obtained from the Adelaide heads of households (Feather, 1974*b*) showed that both samples saw the following reasons as relatively important ones: lack of thrift and proper money management, sickness and physical handicaps, lack of effort by the poor, low wages in some businesses and industries, lack of ability or talent among poor people, and loose morals or drunkenness. Both samples saw bad luck as the least important reason for poverty. However, the Americans were more likely to blame poverty on the poor themselves, appealing to some "Protestant ethic" type of reason (lack of effort, lack of ability, loose morals and drunkenness) more than did the Australians. In America, apparently, the poor were more likely to be seen as not having made the most of their opportunities because of flaws within themselves. Australian adults also tended to blame the poor themselves for their present status, but not to quite the degree that the Americans did. The Australian adults saw sickness and physical handicaps as a more important reason for poverty than did the Americans. They were also more likely to blame poverty on lack of good schools and exploitation by rich people than were the Americans. For both samples younger respondents were more likely to endorse structural explanations of poverty (those relating to the socioeconomic factors) than were older respondents (see Chapter 6, Table 6.9).

The value data for the Australian respondents (Table 8.1 and 8.2) showed that they placed more emphasis upon peace of mind, an active life, and a cheerful approach to life than did the Americans. Perhaps the most interesting differences to surface were those that pointed to the Australians' higher concern with affiliation at the level of close interpersonal relationships—*mature love, true friendship,* being *loving*—especially *true friendship.* When Lipset assigned Australians the highest rank for equalitarianism, he may have been confusing equality with values that imply close affiliation. One's equals are not necessarily one's friends, and vice versa. Presumably, one could value equality highly, yet place a low value on friendship. The two values are not the same and can be distinguished. They did, in fact, emerge on opposite sides of a dimension involving personal versus social values in the analyses reported in Chapter 2, *true friendship* being more personal in nature and *equality* more social.

Within the context of Australian society the emphasis upon friendship and close companionship probably links up with the common assumption that Australians (especially working-class males) regard "mateship" as an important value. The stereotype relates to the expectation that one will be loyal to one's mates, not deserting them in an emergency, and it supports conformity to group norms within the outwardly masculine culture.

Many visitors to Australia and writers on the Australian ethos have referred to this concern with mateship. One could provide many examples. Encel (1970a) refers to some of them. He quotes (p. 54) an Australian trade-union paper in 1892 as stating "Socialism is being mates" and notes that the German sociologist Pfeffer, who visited Australia in the 1930s, reported that "what foreigners miscall 'materialistic trade union sentiment' is the true offspring of evangelical brother-love" (p. 85).

Among Australian historians both Ward (1958) and Clark (1963) have written about mateship. Ward, in particular, sees it as part of the Australian legend and traces its origins and development in relation to the characteristics of the early settlers, particularly the itinerant pastoral workers in the outback who had to contend with a harsh environment without much benefit of family life and who came to be romanticized in folklore, stories, and ballads. In time, the legend was generalized to other working-class males who were seen as distinctively Australian types involved in a culture emphasizing mateship and a lack of deference to established authority. Like all legends, it has some basis in reality and, also like other legends, it may influence behavior by providing a normative framework for action.

Ward discusses the development of the Australian legend in terms of the "frontier hypothesis" of the American historian Turner (1920). In Australia during the 19th century, the itinerant pastoral worker was the frontiersman who had a disproportionate influence on ideas about the "typical" Australian. Ward shows, however, that there were important differences between the Australian frontiersman and his American counterpart:

> The loneliness and hardships of outback life, as on the American frontier, taught him the virtues of cooperation, but his economic interests, unlike those of the American frontiersman, reinforced this tendency towards a social, collectivist outlook. By loyal combination with his fellows he might win better conditions from his employer, but the possibility of becoming his own master by individual enterprize was usually but a remote dream. (pp. 226–227)

Both frontiers promoted a national outlook and both promoted "democracy," but this term had a different meaning in the two countries. According to Ward,

> for the American the implicit meaning of "democracy" tended to be freedom to make his own way to the top by his own individual efforts, and regardless of his fellows. The implicit meaning of the word for the Australian frontiersman tended to be freedom to combine with his mates for the collective good, and the discomfiture of "those wealthy squatters" (the large land-holders). Thus the Australian labour movement has been, and continues to be, much more collectivist in outlook as well as much stronger, relatively, than the American. And collectivist and socialist ideas are much more widely tolerated, if not accepted, in Australian society generally, than they are in America. (p. 227)

Similarly, Clark writes that in the early days of Australian rural settlement

> the bush workers were groping towards quite a different set of values. Ignorant of the consolations of religion, untouched by the traditions and conventions of European society, they looked for a comforter to offset the loneliness of their lives and to protect them against its dangers. They found it in mateship. . . . The same conditions promoted a belief in equality and the habit of judging a man by his performance rather than his inheritance. Prepared to stand by each other in anything, the bushmen were at the same time morbidly suspicious of the newcomer or the intruder who might upset their monopoly of labour, or disturb their way of life. The sentiments of mateship tended to be reserved for the native-born, and the ideals that were the off-spring of their loneliness and isolation became in turn forces to strengthen their provincialism and their xenophobia. (pp. 109–110)

One would expect that other influences, as well as those deriving historically from the rural proletariat, would also have contributed to stereotypes about the Australian national character. Often overlooked, for example, is the fact that Australian settlement has always been highly urbanized. At the present time, most Australians live in a few large cities along the coast. It would be surprising if the city and suburban life that most Australians experience did not significantly contribute to their views of national character (Clarke, 1970). But such influences and their effects on national stereotypes still remain to be explored systematically. It is also to be expected that these stereotypes have become a lot more complex and differentiated as Australia has developed and matured as a nation during the present century—coming to terms with the massive changes and historical events that have occurred over the past 70 years, becoming more urbanized and industrialized, and taking in a vast number of new immigrants after the Second World War. With all these changes, however, the data presented in Table 8.2 indicate that in the early 1970s mateship in the guise of *true friendship* still remains a unique part of the image, as people describe their own values. Rokeach (1973, p. 92) found that this value was also ranked higher in importance by the Australian student group in comparison with the Israeli and Canadian student groups, so it appears to be a distinctively Australian emphasis.

It would take us too far afield to present a historical and sociological interpretation of other value differences between Australia and the United States —fitting the differences we have noted into a historical and sociological context with detailed description of the structural and functional characteristics of each nation and the important formative influences. Moreover, a lot of the relevant material concerning American society has been presented by Lipset (1963a, b), and for Australian society by Encel (1970a). Both authors have compared the two societies, Encel being rather critical of Lipset's use of pattern variables. Encel's analysis is particularly rich in describing the complex nature of equality and inequality in Australian society and the bureaucratic character of social and political organization (see also Davies & Encel, 1970). Lipset's analysis makes an important contribution in the way it examines the interaction of basic values with social institutions and trends in American society over the years, and in its use of cross-cultural comparisons. Both discussions remind us of a point made earlier, namely, that in interpreting similarities and differences in value importance across cultures, one needs to consider how each value is defined in each culture, how it relates to other values, and how it functions or operates within the societies being compared. Otherwise, one might end up with a simple and misleading picture, overlooking the complexity and richness of each culture and the unique ways in which values emerge in each and are expressed. Typically, this kind of research approach is beyond the scope of one man and calls for an interdisciplinary team of experts. The value profiles obtained from such procedures as the Value Survey, therefore, have to be supplemented by other information if they are to illuminate cross-cultural similarities and differences. They are frameworks that can be used as a basis for further building.

ANALYSIS OF SIMILARITY COEFFICIENTS

In comparing the average value systems in Tables 8.1 and 8.2 one should not overlook the similarities between Australians and Americans. Table 8.3 presents similarity coefficients (Spearman rhos and Kendall taus) obtained from intercorrelating the median rankings in the 10 columns of Tables 8.1 and 8.2.

TABLE 8-3. Similarity Coefficients Comparing Median Rankings for Australian (Adelaide) and U.S. Samples

Group	Male Students		Adelaide Adults				United States Adults			
	1 Flinders	2 Mich. State	3 1972 Heads	4 1972 Wives	5 1973 Heads	6 1973 Wives	7 1968 Males	8 1968 Females	9 1971 Males	10 1971 Females
Male Students										
1. Flinders		.87 (.69)	.68 (.51)	.62 (.40)	.68 (.51)	.66 (.48)	.35 (.20)	.32 (.22)	.36 (.24)	.25 (.17)
2. Michigan State	.80 (.65)		.73 (.55)	.70 (.47)	.79 (.61)	.74 (.55)	.57 (.39)	.49 (.36)	.54 (.37)	.39 (.27)
Adelaide Adults										
3. 1972 Heads	.58 (.41)	.34 (.24)		.95 (.87)	.99 (.94)	.98 (.92)	.74 (.58)	.71 (.61)	.80 (.63)	.68 (.55)
4. 1972 Wives	.48 (.34)	.15 (.14)	.94 (.84)		.94 (.84)	.95 (.86)	.67 (.51)	.68 (.54)	.73 (.57)	.65 (.50)
5. 1973 Heads	.73 (.59)	.55 (.41)	.82 (.70)	.76 (.63)		.98 (.92)	.77 (.60)	.72 (.63)	.82 (.66)	.69 (.58)
6. 1973 Wives	.66 (.50)	.37 (.30)	.95 (.85)	.91 (.82)	.87 (.75)		.73 (.56)	.71 (.62)	.80 (.64)	.69 (.56)
United States Adults										
7. 1968 Males	.64 (.47)	.62 (.48)	.76 (.63)	.61 (.49)	.79 (.67)	.67 (.57)		.83 (.72)	.94 (.86)	.81 (.68)
8. 1968 Females	.57 (.40)	.40 (.31)	.86 (.73)	.79 (.65)	.81 (.65)	.78 (.64)	.92 (.78)		.86 (.73)	.96 (.88)
9. 1971 Males	.74 (.55)	.72 (.56)	.74 (.60)	.57 (.45)	.82 (.70)	.68 (.56)	.98 (.92)	.86 (.73)		.91 (.80)
10. 1971 Females	.66 (.47)	.40 (.30)	.92 (.80)	.87 (.76)	.84 (.69)	.88 (.74)	.83 (.71)	.96 (.89)	.80 (.66)	

Note. Similarity indexes for average terminal value systems are above the diagonal; similarity coefficients for average instrumental value systems are below the diagonal. Similarity coefficients not in parentheses are Spearman rhos; similarity coefficients in parentheses are Kendall taus. Higher similarity indexes indicate greater similarity between the average value systems involved in the comparison.

Higher coefficients imply greater similarity between the pair of average value systems involved in the comparison.

Table 8.3 shows that all of the similarity coefficients were positive, that is, some degree of overlap occurred between the average value systems in all comparisons. The highest coefficients were obtained when average value systems from groups within the *same culture* were compared (the triangular matrices in Table 8.3). These comparisons were possible only for the adult groups, there being more than one adult group in each culture. (Similar comparisons for different Australian student groups to be presented in the next section also demonstrated high within-culture similarity.)

Table 8.3 shows further that coefficients based upon cross-cultural comparisons for the *same age* groups were also relatively high (the single coefficients for male students, the large rectangular matrices for adults). The lowest coefficients were obtained when comparisons were made between different age groups, that is, between students compared with adults (the smaller rectangular matrices). This latter finding is consistent with the age effects described in Chapter 6 when average value systems were compared across generations.

One might expect higher similarity indexes for *student* groups from different countries than for youth or adults chosen on the basis of national samples. Students to some extent constitute an international subculture. One would expect them to be similar in many respects and to be subject to many similar influences across nations—more so than are adults or nonstudent youth from different countries. It is not surprising, therefore, that the similarity indexes comparing the average value systems of Flinders males with Michigan State males were relatively high.

When one looks at the medians for the individual values (Tables 8.1 and 8.2) it is evident that the age effects that occurred in regard to Australian and American groups were similar for both, and similar to those noted in Chapter 6 across generations. Thus, Australian and American adults assigned more importance than the students to such values as *family security, national security,* and being *clean* and *polite.* The students in both cultures assigned more importance than did the adults to such values as *an exciting life, freedom, pleasure, true friendship,* and being *broad-minded* and *imaginative.*

Moreover, there were sex differences in the relative importance assigned to particular values similar to those noted previously, and these differences tended to occur in both the Australian and American adult groups. For example, inspection of the medians shows that males in both cultures assigned higher importance to such values as *a comfortable life, an exciting life, pleasure,* and being *ambitious* and *logical,* whereas the females saw such values as *a world at peace, inner harmony, salvation,* and being *forgiving* and *loving* as more important. These differences, together with the others that we noted, must be taken with the proviso that some of the smaller ones may not be statistically significant, because we were unable to conduct the appropriate tests, not having all available data. The consistencies provide important evidence for some functional equivalence of the values across the two cultures. For despite differences in the nature of the samples, the ways in which they were selected, when they were tested, and so on, the values behaved in predictable ways for the Australian and American groups.

Given the fact that both cultures are stable, affluent, well-developed democracies, and alike in other respects, it would have been surprising if no overlap in average value systems had been discovered. In the next section we turn to a more extreme comparison, one that compares the value systems of Australian students with those from the developing nation of Papua New Guinea.

CROSS-CULTURAL COMPARISONS: AUSTRALIA AND PAPUA NEW GUINEA

The study described below was initiated in 1971 to obtain information about the value systems of Papua New Guinea students enrolled in tertiary and training programs and to compare them with those of Australian secondary and tertiary students. Some basic differences in their value systems were anticipated. The predicted differences followed from two main lines of argument, the first relating to general speculations about the effects of affluence and education on societies, the second relating to a consideration of some aspects of the history and traditional culture of Papua New Guinea.

VALUES AND STAGE OF NATIONAL DEVELOPMENT

If, as Rokeach (1973) argues, values have a motivational base, then one should be able to make predictions about the relative importance of different values—providing reasonable assumptions about the relative strength of underlying needs can be made. In less affluent, newly independent, developing countries, such as Papua New Guinea, one might expect that values concerned with security, material comfort, conventional forms of religion, and conformity would assume greater importance. The reasoning here is that security, safety, and other needs related to survival would be especially salient in a country emerging into nationhood, initiating independent forms of government, and seeking to establish a stable economy and peaceful and mutually advantageous relations with its neighbors. Where a nation has been established for many years, however, and has moved beyond the complex and uncertain stages of newly acquired nationhood to affluence and stability, then survival, security, and safety needs would be likely to be less salient. Under these conditions one might anticipate values related to love, competence, and self-actualization to receive greater emphasis. On the basis of this argument it was expected that Australian students would assign more importance to these values because they belong to a stable and affluent nation that has now been in existence as a commonwealth for a considerable time.

It should be apparent that the argument just presented draws an analogy between the needs of nations and the needs of individuals in a very general, speculative way. Both nations and individuals cope with needs that emerge at various levels and have to be satisfied to some degree before others can be attended to. Just as people on low incomes and in reduced material circumstances would be more concerned than the affluent members of a society with meeting basic survival and security needs (Chapter 6), so it is argued that new nations seeking their own forms of identity, their own modes of unification and political organization, and their own economic strength and independence may have similar priorities compared with nations that have achieved economic and political stability and a high standard of living. In talking about nations, of course, we are talking about people. And in talking about new nations we are considering the kinds of concerns that become relatively dominant in people's minds as their country passes through those periods of uncertainty and change that accompany the emergence of independent nationhood. Obviously, such assumptions draw upon Maslow's (1954) theory of a hierarchy of needs, some of which have to be at least partially satisfied before other higher-order needs can become prepotent, and on Rokeach's (1973) discussion (referred to in Chapter 1) of how values and needs might be linked.

The argument is also related to Cantril's discussion of the stages of development through which nations proceed—a discussion that is based upon the results of a series of studies presented in his book, *The Pattern of Human Concerns* (Cantril, 1965). In these studies people in different countries were asked about their hopes and fears for the future, both in regard to themselves and their country. They also provided aspiration estimates by using a ladder device that Cantril calls the "self-anchoring striving scale." Information was obtained from a wide range of different countries which included Westernized nations, large underdeveloped nations, samples from the Middle East, three Caribbean nations, and the Philippines. Cantril (1965) concludes that "the concerns of people are patterned largely according to the phases of development they are in both culturally and ontogenetically within their society" (p. 301). He distinguishes between a number of phases of national development: (1) Acquiescence to circumstances; (2) Awakening to potentialities; (3) Awareness of the means to realize goals; (4) Assurance and self-reliance; (5) Satisfaction and gratification, with the promise of continued development. The developing nation of Papua New Guinea can probably be placed at the second phase and moving into the third phase, whereas Australia would be at the fifth phase of Cantril's scheme. Cantril also assumes that there are certain universal demands that human beings everywhere impose on the society in which they live. They include demands for survival, security, order, enrichment, improvement, choice, freedom, identity and integrity, personal worth, an anchoring set of values, and a sense of confidence that their society will be able to fulfill their aspirations. This set of demands is obviously similar to the set of needs described by Maslow.

HISTORY AND CULTURE OF PAPUA NEW GUINEA

Thus, one can argue that different needs, concerns, and values become prepotent depending upon each nation's stage of development. It should also be possible, however, to develop predictions about cross-cultural similarities and differences in values and value systems from a careful analysis of the history, social institutions, and traditional culture of the societies being compared. Some characteristics of Australian society have already been noted, especially mateship. A detailed analysis of the history and culture of Papua New Guinea is far beyond our scope and resources (see Ryan, 1972). However, one can provide some general information. Geographically, Papua New Guinea is directly north of Queensland, Australia, and takes up the eastern half of the large island of New Guinea. It is a country with high mountain ranges, river valleys, and coastal plains. According to the 1971 census, the total population was just under 2½ million, with about 2,435,400 indigenous people and 54,500 non-indigenous people (or expatriates) living in Papua New Guinea. The rural population is especially concentrated in the highlands where there is much agriculture and where native villages can be seen studding the ridges and the valleys. There is also a concentration of population in the major cities of Port Moresby, Lae, Rabaul, Wewak, Madang, and Goroka, which are the main commercial centers (Ward, 1970). Among the indigenous population there is a multiplicity and diversity of languages and most of them are languages of small to very small speech communities (Wurm, 1970). The two major *langue franche* are Police Motu and Pidgin, the latter being used more widely than the former.

New Guinea was one of the last unexplored regions of the world. The western part of the large island was annexed by the Dutch early in the nineteenth century but now belongs to Indonesia. Following pressure from Australia, the eastern coast across from Queensland was first claimed by the British in 1884 and became known as British New Guinea and later on as Papua. While British New Guinea was being proclaimed, the Germans were laying claim to the north-east. The north coast and the large northern islands became known as German New Guinea. In 1906 British New Guinea became the Australian Territory of Papua and in 1914 Australian troops occupied German New Guinea. Following a mandate granted by the League of Nations, Australia was given power to administer what had been German New Guinea and so, by the early 1920s, both Papua and the Mandated Territory of New Guinea were under Australian administration. In subsequent years, as the more remote areas became better known, there was a gradual extension of administration stations to outlying districts (Nelson, 1970). Parts of the country were invaded and occupied by the Japanese in the Second World War. After the war Australia provided a single administration for Papua and New Guinea, the latter territory being governed under a trusteeship agreement with the United Nations.

Papua New Guinea is now experiencing rapid political and socioeconomic change, the effects of which are diffusing toward more remote parts of the country. Politically, there has been a movement toward independence. In 1974, Papua New Guinea achieved internal self-government, although independence is not yet complete because Australia continues to retain certain rights and responsibilities. Complete independence is expected to occur later in 1975. In recent years expenditure on public health and education has increased considerably. Even so, less than 50 percent of primary (elementary) school age children do in fact attend primary school and the tapering-off into high school is even more dramatic. A large majority of the school attenders are males. There are technical and vocational schools as well as primary schools and high schools, and several teacher training colleges, most of which are associated with Missions. There is a university in Port Moresby and an institute of technology in Lae. The educational system is gradually expanding (Rumens, 1970).

The Missions have had an important influence from the nineteenth century onwards. They were established in various regions throughout the country, especially by the Lutheran and Roman Catholic churches. Dickson (1970) states that

> The Missions were primarily evangelical; they presented a simplified evangel to meet the needs of an unsophisticated people and a multiplicity of languages; and they did this while the non-missionary contact was becoming increasingly secular and increasingly sophisticated. . . . The work of the Missions in translation, education, and, to a degree, even medicine, was designed to win Christian adherents. . . . The Missions tended to permeate the whole life of the village with their message and its expected behaviour patterns. In all of these activities the missionary purpose was primarily the creation of Christian communities, not the re-building of village life. Missionary attitudes varied from authoritarian to paternalistic and the positive response, at least superficially, from acquiescence to obedience. (p. 22)

PREDICTIONS

How might the various influences just discussed affect the value priorities of the indigenous population? It is possible to make some "educated guesses." One would expect that the strong missionary influence would promote a basically conservative outlook in matters of morality, and that this influence would also be reflected in relatively high importance assigned to conventional religious values such as *salvation*. Further, one would expect that the extended family system of relationships in Papua New Guinea and the concern with equalitarian distribution of material possessions within this system would result in high importance being given *equality* and to values concerned with respect for authority. As with Australian groups, one might expect *true friendship* to rank relatively high for Papua New Guinea students, but for different reasons—for example, special bonds between members of the extended family and between those speaking the same language from among the many languages that exist ("one-talks" or, in Pidgin English, "wantoks"). These, and other possible differences, were investigated in the study now to be described (Feather & Hutton, 1974).

In our minds also was the possibility of acquiring information about values that could be used in a long-term investigation of value changes that might occur following independent nationhood in Papua New Guinea. Value systems obtained from tertiary students after political independence could be compared with those determined in the 1971 test program to discover whether there were general changes that could be related to intervening events. Hence, a long-term goal was to use the Value Survey as a social indicator at different points in time in a modest way, with full awareness of the difficulties in establishing equivalent samples and procedures over a period of years (Frey, 1970)—and the fear that, with limited budgets, these problems could not be solved.

SUBJECTS AND PROCEDURE

The details of the 1971 Papua New Guinea survey have been presented previously (Feather & Hutton, 1974). What follows is a summary of the main procedures and results. Respondents were obtained from a number of different sources involving the University of Papua New Guinea at Port Moresby, the Institute of Technology at Lae, five teachers' colleges throughout the Territory (Balob, Gaulim, Goroka, Madang, Vunakanou), the Vudal Agricultural College, the Local Government Training College at Vunadidir, and the Administrative College at Port Moresby. In addition, a number of school inspectors and headmasters in Papua New Guinea were also tested. Respondents from the last three sources were of more mature age. All others were in their first year of post-secondary study, most having completed Form 4, the fourth year of high school. The institutions they attended were in five different areas: Port Moresby, Lae, Madang, Rabaul, and Goroka. Three, all teachers' colleges, were under the direct influence of a church group, these being Balob (Lutheran), Gaulim (United), and Vunakanou (Catholic). Respondents attending the various institutions came from all parts of Papua New Guinea. The average ages of respondents in these institutions ranged from 17.79 to 20.69 years (Feather & Hutton, 1974, p. 94).

There were about four times as many males as females in the sample, reflecting community attitudes about the education of females. All respondents were fluent in the English language.

Two forms of the Value Survey were used. In some institutions Form D (the gummed-label form) was administered with the usual instructions. In other institutions, due to a shortage of copies of Form D, another form of the Value Survey was used, one that involved printing each value with its accompanying descriptive label on a small card. The 18 cards for the terminal values and the 18 for the instrumental values then had to be sorted in their order of importance for self (see Feather & Hutton, 1974, p. 95). This form of the Value Survey, designated Form S, was rather similar to Form D in that it required sorting and rearranging the values. Respondents seemed to experience little difficulty with either form.

In addition to completing the rankings, respondents provided information about their age, course of study, religion, clan, home subdistrict, and district. The latter information was used to classify each respondent as to length of contact with expatriate (mainly white) influence, the classification being based upon the year an administration station was established in the subdistrict (Hutton & Rumens, 1974). Persons in subdistricts where stations were set up before 1920 were classified as having long contact, after 1920 as having short contact. The results of analyses comparing value rankings in relation to religion and length of expatriate contact have been presented in the original report and will not be described here.

All questionnaires were completed anonymously, code numbers being used. The testing was conducted by psychologists who had been thoroughly briefed beforehand about procedure.

AVERAGE VALUE SYSTEMS FOR AUSTRALIAN AND PAPUAN NEW GUINEA STUDENTS

The median rankings of the terminal values and the instrumental values for Papua New Guinea respondents are found in Tables 8.4 and 8.5 respectively. These average value systems were fairly representative of those from all 12 groups surveyed. Factor-analytic evidence revealed that general similarities existed in average value systems across all 12 groups, but the evidence also suggested a distinction between "academic" and "administrative" groups in the case of the instrumental values (for details, see Feather & Hutton, 1974).

Also presented in Tables 8.4 and 8.5 for comparison purposes are the average value systems (medians) obtained from students in the 1970–1971 Adelaide secondary schools survey (Chapters 4 and 5), the average value systems of students entering Flinders University in 1970 (Chapter 3), and the average value systems of students who were tested in 1971 at the Mitchell College of Advanced Education (Chapter 3).

The four sets of median rankings in Tables 8.4 and 8.5 were compared using Spearman's rho and Kendall's tau to test the degree of similarity. The results are presented in Table 8.6, and they clearly show that the average value systems

TABLE 8-4. Average Value Systems and Composite Rank Orders for Terminal Values for Four Groups of Students

| | Papua New Guinea Students | Australian Students | | |
| | | Secondary Schools | Flinders University | Mitchell CAE |
Terminal Value	N 1116	1408	404	506
A comfortable life	9.59 (11)	11.62 (13)	13.06 (14)	13.00 (15)
An exciting life	11.69 (13)	8.83 (10)	10.33 (12)	12.17 (12)
A sense of accomplishment	12.44 (15)	7.37 (7)	6.80 (7)	7.63 (10)
A world at peace	2.89 (1)	5.42 (2)	6.70 (6)	4.57 (1)
A world of beauty	13.25 (18)	12.19 (14)	11.96 (13)	12.55 (13)
Equality	4.69 (2)	7.41 (9)	7.00 (8)	7.28 (9)
Family security	6.55 (5.5)	7.38 (8)	8.88 (10)	6.92 (7)
Freedom	6.03 (3)	5.45 (3)	5.43 (2)	6.00 (4)
Happiness	8.34 (9)	6.30 (4)	6.06 (4)	5.48 (2)
Inner harmony	10.56 (12)	9.34 (11)	7.13 (9)	6.78 (6)
Mature love	12.98 (17)	7.21 (6)	6.58 (5)	6.29 (5)
National security	6.55 (5.5)	13.45 (16)	14.28 (16)	12.67 (14)
Pleasure	12.77 (16)	12.36 (15)	13.54 (15)	13.40 (16)
Salvation	7.51 (8)	15.23 (18)	16.17 (18)	14.21 (17)
Self-respect	11.81 (14)	10.44 (12)	8.92 (11)	8.74 (11)
Social recognition	8.38 (10)	14.27 (17)	15.00 (17)	14.74 (18)
True friendship	6.20 (4)	4.99 (1)	4.70 (1)	5.67 (3)
Wisdom	7.36 (7)	6.72 (5)	5.55 (3)	7.15 (8)

Note. The lower the median the higher the relative value. The rank orders of the medians (low to high) are denoted in parentheses. Ns are for error-free rankings.

Source: Data are from Feather & Hutton, 1974.

TABLE 8-5. Average Value Systems and Composite Rank Orders for Instrumental Values for Four Groups of Students

Instrumental Value	Papua New Guinea Students	Australian Students		
		Secondary Schools	Flinders University	Mitchell CAE
	N 1128	1438	404	509
Ambitious	6.69 (5)	7.53 (4)	8.32 (7)	10.70 (13)
Broad-minded	10.21 (13)	6.84 (3)	5.74 (3)	6.75 (5)
Capable	10.04 (12)	9.07 (8)	9.36 (10)	9.33 (9)
Cheerful	9.67 (11)	8.24 (6)	9.48 (12)	8.10 (7)
Clean	12.69 (15)	10.16 (14)	12.67 (17)	10.73 (14)
Courageous	8.74 (8)	10.06 (13)	8.90 (8)	10.02 (11)
Forgiving	8.31 (7)	9.66 (12)	7.84 (5)	6.29 (4)
Helpful	5.30 (2)	9.27 (10)	8.96 (9)	7.90 (6)
Honest	4.27 (1)	3.64 (1)	3.21 (1)	2.69 (1)
Imaginative	14.46 (18)	13.90 (18)	12.52 (16)	13.85 (18)
Independent	12.73 (16)	9.49 (11)	9.38 (11)	9.98 (10)
Intellectual	10.36 (14)	12.81 (17)	10.52 (14)	13.08 (16)
Logical	13.55 (17)	11.14 (15)	10.45 (13)	11.50 (15)
Loving	9.25 (9)	8.86 (7)	6.68 (4)	4.74 (2)
Obedient	6.46 (4)	11.63 (16)	14.86 (18)	13.49 (17)
Polite	7.04 (6)	9.11 (9)	11.68 (15)	10.18 (12)
Responsible	6.43 (3)	4.49 (2)	4.87 (2)	5.40 (3)
Self-controlled	9.54 (10)	8.03 (5)	8.17 (6)	8.47 (8)

Note. The lower the median the higher the relative value. The rank orders of the medians (low to high) are denoted in parentheses. *N*s are for error-free rankings.
Source: Data are from Feather & Hutton, 1974.

within one culture were more similar than were the average values systems across cultures (just as they did when the Australian and American data were compared in Table 8.3). The indexes obtained from comparing the three Australian groups were uniformly high, especially for the terminal values; those obtained from comparing each Australian group with the total Papua New Guinea group were much lower, indicating marked differences in the average orders of importance assigned to the two sets of values cross-culturally.

TABLE 8-6. Similarity Indexes Comparing Average Value Systems for Papua New Guinea Students and Three Australian Groups

Group	Group			
	1	2	3	4
1. Papua New Guinea Students		.41 (.25)	.33 (.20)	.40 (.26)
2. Secondary School Students	.51 (.37)		.96 (.87)	.93 (.78)
3. Flinders University Students	.45 (.33)	.79 (.62)		.90 (.75)
4. Mitchell CAE Students	.49 (.35)	.78 (.63)	.87 (.70)	

Note. Similarity indexes for average terminal value systems are above the diagonal; similarity indexes for average instrumental value systems are below the diagonal. Similarity indexes not in parentheses are Spearman rhos; similarity indexes in parentheses are Kendall taus. Higher similarity indexes indicate greater similarity between the average value systems involved in the comparison. In the columns, 1 = Papua New Guinea students, 2 = Adelaide secondary school students, 3 = Flinders University students, 4 = Mitchell CAE students.
Source: Data are from Feather & Hutton, 1974.

What were these differences? When one examines the medians of particular values in Tables 8.4 and 8.5 certain obvious discrepancies in the medians can be noted. If we focus upon the largest differences and those that occurred consistently when the Papua New Guinea group was compared to *all* three Australian groups, then the following effects were apparent, all of which were statistically significant: Among the terminal values, the Papua New Guinea students gave higher priorities to *a world at peace, equality, national security, salvation, social recognition,* and *a comfortable life,* and they assigned much less importance to *happiness, inner harmony, self-respect, a sense of accomplishment, mature love,* and *a world of beauty* than did the Australians. Among the instrumental values, the Papua New Guinea students assigned higher importance to being *helpful, obedient,* and *polite,* and much lower importance to being *loving, self-controlled, broad-minded, independent,* and *logical* than did the Australians.

INTERPRETATION OF VALUE DIFFERENCES

These differences suggest that the Papua New Guinea students were more concerned with some general social values, and with orthodox religious values and values implying deference to authority, than were the Australian students.

But the Australians assigned more emphasis to personal, humanistic types of values than did the Papua New Guinea students. As predicted, many of the differences were consistent with the assumption that, in a less affluent, developing country moving into nationhood, safety and security needs would be more salient and values related to these needs would assume greater importance. The following values relating to security, material comfort, conventional forms of religion, and conformity, some of which may be a reflection of stronger safety and security needs, were all ranked higher in importance by the Papua New Guinea students: *a comfortable life, a world at peace, national security, salvation,* and being *polite* and *obedient*. In a study involving male Israeli students, Rim (1970) also found high importance assigned to *a world at peace* and *national security* by his respondents. Unlike the Papua New Guinea students, however, the Israelis gave very low priority to what Rokeach calls the two main Christian values, *salvation* and being *forgiving,* and higher priority to values concerning intellectual competence (being *capable, intellectual,* and *logical*). There were other differences as well in average value priorities between the two groups of Papua New Guinea and Israeli students which we will not pursue but which make sense in terms of what we know about the two nations. The interesting similarity is in the high importance assigned by both nations to *a world at peace* and *national security*. Israel is also a relatively new nation, though its stressful position vis-à-vis its neighbors is in extreme contrast to the peaceful relationships that Papua New Guinea enjoys.

In a stable, affluent country such as Australia, on the other hand, other needs would presumably become more salient, and values related to these needs would assume greater importance. This assumption was also supported. Thus, *happiness, inner harmony, self-respect, a sense of accomplishment, mature love, a world of beauty,* and being *loving, self-controlled, broad-minded, independent,* and *logical* were all ranked higher by the Australians. These values appear to be more closely related to needs concerning love, competence, and self-actualization which, according to Maslow (1954), would be more likely to become prepotent once the more basic physiological and safety and security needs have been satisfied.

So too, some of the obtained differences may be seen to be related to particular characteristics of the two cultures, involving their history and traditions. The higher priority given to *salvation* by the Papua New Guinea students, for example, would be a reflection of the strong church influence on schooling and within the community generally (Rowley, 1965). The missions were still teaching 55 percent of the schoolchildren by 1969, and before 1951 they had controlled practically all education (Rumens, 1970). The effect of the church may also be evident in the relatively high importance assigned by the Papua New Guinea students to certain other values (for example, being *helpful, polite,* and *obedient*). But these differences could also be related to traditional modes of conduct both in the extended family system of relationships and in group affiliations based upon use of the same language system—the wantok (one-talk). In these interpersonal networks there is an emphasis upon obligations to others, orderliness, and respect for authority. It is likely that deference to authority as suggested by the high priorities assigned to being *polite* and *obedient* might also be a product of the types of subservient roles to which indigenes in a colonial society are often assigned in relation to expatriates. There is now, however, a movement toward "localization," that is, toward filling higher status and more responsible positions with indigenes. The importance of *social recognition,* of being admired and respected by others, is well embedded in tradition—as in, for example, the "big man" leadership system considered to be characteristic of some Melanesian groups (Finney, 1971). The lower importance of being *self-controlled* among the Papua New Guinea students is probably reflected in a greater tendency for their culture to encourage public expression of emotion when compared with Australian mores.

The relatively high importance assigned to *equality* by the Papua New Guinea students may reflect a general concern with egalitarian distribution of material goods, a sharing of possessions, which is also part of the fabric of the extended family system. Moulik (forthcoming) recently discussed this strong social norm of egalitarianism as it relates to material objects. He argues that it may have inhibitory effects on entrepreneurial activity and economic development. In this regard, the relatively low priority given by the Papua New Guinea students to values relating to achievement (such as *a sense of accomplishment,* being *independent*), which one might also expect to be associated with economic development (McClelland & Winter, 1969), is rather interesting. The relatively high priority assigned to *equality* (and to *social recognition* and *national security*) may also reflect the kinds of concern that develop in a country moving into independent nationhood and desiring unity. One would expect thoughts about brotherhood, about winning the respect of others, and about national unity to become especially salient in people's minds when old bonds are being severed and independence achieved. *True friendship* was also ranked high by the Papua New Guinea group, but not quite so high in relative importance as by the Australian students.

The above discussion again underscores the complexities of interpreting cross-cultural differences in values. It points up the necessity of taking account of a whole network of factors having to do with the societies involved. Any interpretation of the Papua New Guinea results should also take into account the unique situation of most tertiary students in this newly independent nation, especially the rapid changes they have experienced. As Nelson (1972) points out:

> The Niuginian tertiary student rarely avoids stress. Many have moved quickly through three value systems: a village community, a mission or administration boarding school and a secular university. Both the village and the mission may have held him within a closed society while they taught their pervasive explanations of the natural and supernatural world. Mission teaching in the Territory has been doctrinally conservative: a few missions warn

departing students of the heresy of evolution. The student's experience at the University forces him to abandon or modify two sets of values but there is no third set to be picked up; he is in the first generation of Niuginians to be given tertiary education in the Territory. Students grope for a role and an ideology in their past, their present experience and in the echoes of Frantz Fanon, black power, and Australian student behavior. Not surprisingly few students have spoken consistently and confidently on fundamental issues. (p. 181)

There is plenty of evidence from the comparisons that have just been made to support this emphasis on the rapidly changing situation of Papua New Guinea students and the different sources contributing to their value priorities.

TWO METHODOLOGICAL POINTS

Two points remain to be discussed. The first concerns the "appropriateness" of the Value Survey for use in a country such as Papua New Guinea, so different in many respects from the United States where the test was developed. Tests and questionnaires that have been constructed and used in affluent, Western democracies may not be relevant in other countries whose culture and circumstances are so different. In the present case some teachers in the tertiary institutions visited in Papua New Guinea wondered, for example, if their students would understand the meaning of values such as *inner harmony, mature love,* and being *broad-minded*. Others thought that some other values such as *generosity, loyalty,* and *justice* might be included on the lists. Other values distinctive to Papua New Guinea and perhaps also appropriate to other non-Western societies might also be added. As for comprehension, it might be necessary to expand the explanation of some values so that they are better understood (as in the study of delinquent boys described in Chapter 7). One would also hope to investigate what effects failure to comprehend a particular value or values has on the ranking procedure. Are such values relegated to the bottom of the list? These problems obviously need further study. But, as we have argued before, both lists provided by Rokeach do cover a fairly wide range of values. They should provide useful indicators of cross-cultural differences in future comparative research among people who have had a reasonable standard of education. And clearly, one needs a common yardstick in making comparisons, or at least a fair degree of overlap in items and procedures, though items may have to be separately validated in each culture.

A second point concerns the possibility that respondents in the Papua New Guinea samples may have tended to answer in more concrete terms than the Australian students, ranking "concrete" values higher in importance than the more "abstract" (and perhaps less understood) values (Mulford & Young, 1973). This interpretation assumes that the values provided by Rokeach can be scaled in terms of a dimension of concreteness-abstractness. Clearly this is an empirical question and one that calls for precise specification of what is meant by concreteness-abstractness in relation to values. It may be very difficult to provide this specification, however, and to operationalize it, because values are typically defined as abstract concepts. Moreover, when one examines the values ranked high in importance by the Papua New Guinea students, several of them appear to be quite abstract (for example, *equality, freedom,* and being *honest*)—assuming again that it is indeed possible to distinguish degrees of abstractness where values are concerned.

More generally, Cole and Scribner (1974), on the basis of a review of cross-cultural experimental studies of the conceptual processes (mainly classification), have concluded that:

> *Abstract* and *concrete* have been used in a rather loose manner to designate a number of different operations, which do not always co-vary . . . it is clear that experimental findings do not allow the conclusion that in general the thinking of any group of people is, or is not, abstract. (p. 121)

So much depends upon how the information is retrieved from individuals, on the familiarity and form of the stimulus materials, and the specific domains from which the items are drawn.

Finally, it should be noted that despite the differences between the Papua New Guinea group and the Australian students in some of their value priorities, there were also similarities. The cross-cultural similarity indexes presented in Table 8.6 were all positive and some values had similar average ranks for all groups (for example, *freedom, pleasure,* being *responsible* and *capable*).

SOME POSSIBLE FUTURE RESEARCH

In future research it would be useful to extend the inquiry to other groups in Australia and Papua New Guinea. One might investigate students beyond their first year of tertiary studies and also look at the value systems of expatriate Australians in Papua New Guinea to see how discrepant these value systems are from those of the indigenous population. Provided that appropriate procedures could be developed, it would be worthwhile to extend the inquiry from well-educated samples to the community at large (even to the village level in Papua New Guinea) and, as in the Australian-American comparison, to look at values in relation to age differences within Papua New Guinea. Some recent studies have looked at wider segments of the population. Harrison (1974) reports research with a Pidgin version of the Kluckhohn value-orientation test (Kluckhohn & Strodtbeck, 1961) with three Papua New Guinea groups and concludes that it is an adequate vehicle for further comparative work. Joyce (1974) administered value-related items to two groups of high school students that were contrasted in their physical and social environments. His results supported the conclusion that the two groups differed in some of their basic values. Hicks (1974) has investigated the vocational interests and values of some Australian high school students in Papua New Guinea, the values being assessed using the Allport-Vernon-Lindzey Study of Values. And Young, Schubert, and Jacka (1974) used the approach developed by Cantril (1965) to study the hopes and fears of Papua New Guineans in the period immediately prior to self-government. In their study, first year students at Port Moresby Teacher's College, who had been extensively trained prior to their actual field work, interviewed people in their home villages which were mainly along the Papua coast. On the basis of the results these investigators concluded that

> Papua New Guineans have strong hopes for economic development but that they see disunity, particularly tribal fighting, or inter-regional hostilities as the greatest threat to this goal. Some fear too early moves towards political independence and others fear that independence will not come soon enough. There is a desire for strong and effective leadership. . . . Both personal hopes and personal fears centered around personal economic advancement in jobs, possessions or education, and around the problems of family life in Papua New Guinea today. There was little room for concern about happy leisure time, recreation or concerns about acceptance by others, personality development and the like, concerns which are more common in affluent developed countries. (pp. 60–61)

These conclusions are consistent with the implications of some of the value differences that we presented earlier when discussing the results of the Feather and Hutton study.

It is encouraging to see this development of research on values in Papua New Guinea and the use of different assessment procedures for different samples of the population—procedures that involve both structured and less structured approaches. It would be foolish in research of this kind to use only one method for assessing values. One needs to be flexible to meet local conditions. There may be occasions where less structured procedures, that allow respondents the free opportunity of providing information about their own values, may be more valid and informative than procedures, such as the Value Survey, where the sets of values are specified in advance. Given the resources, one would hope to use a variety of appropriate assessment techniques and, at the same time, observe actual behavior assumed to reflect value priorities.

The study of values in developing countries such as Papua New Guinea is of great social relevance, especially in furthering our understanding of the problems that are involved when people from different cultures coexist in a developing society and what the implications are for adaptation when there are discrepancies in the value systems of these different groups. As we will argue in the next chapter in the context of migrant assimilation, large discrepancies in value systems between different groups may make it difficult for them to adapt to one another. In fact, one way of reducing the possibility of social conflict would be to strive to achieve some agreement on basic values among different segments of a developing society (and perhaps of any society).

CONCLUDING REMARKS

The studies reported in this chapter have shown that the Value Survey is a useful instrument in cross-cultural research, even when the societies being compared are very different in political, socioeconomic, and other cultural characteristics, and in their stage of national development. Cross-cultural comparisons are fraught with difficulties. But information about value differences may suggest other lines of inquiry in the direction of filling in the details of the broad structural picture implied by the value priorities. These studies would involve social scientists from a range of interrelated disciplines looking in detail at the social process and structure within society in relation both to the present realities and to the background of past history and tradition.

In time, given the possibility of conducting valid and accurate surveys across nations, one should be able to compare a large set of nations with respect to their average value priorities and, by multidimensional and other related procedures, to discover how nations cluster together and in what ways they are similar and different in their average value priorities—just as we were able to investigate the structure of average value systems in the Adelaide schools survey (Chapters 4 and 5). This type of information might have important implications at the international level when supplemented by other information about the societies. A minimum level of similarity or congruity in basic values may be an important condition for international relationships that are relatively free of conflict. The same approach could be used to investigate the structure of value systems within the same society, working with its different segments and trying to isolate basic structural dimensions that enable one to describe similarities and differences between groups.

In the next chapter we extend our description of cross-cultural studies to look at the value priorities of migrant groups who have settled in Australia. In particular, we will be concerned with the degree of subjective assimilation that has occurred among the second generation.

9. Subjective Assimilation in Immigrant Groups

MIGRANTS ARE CONFRONTED with the problem of settling into a new country, with the task of adjusting to new physical and social environments that may differ in many ways from those they have left behind. In the previous chapter we treated nations as separate entities; here the groups to be compared are people living within the one nation—Australia—who have different cultural backgrounds. One important question with which we will deal is the degree to which a minority migrant group comes to resemble the host society it has entered. (For a useful summary of some of the literature on Australian immigration, see Price, 1970b.)

There is an immense literature on migrant assimilation. Historically, it is one of the earliest questions to which sociologists addressed themselves. In a very general sense the problem of assimilation is ubiquitous in society. Any person entering a new physical and social environment is confronted with it. The individual who changes his occupation, the child who shifts to a different school, the woman who assumes a vocational role after raising a family, the rural worker who moves to the city—all are involved in the process of adapting to new environments and becoming absorbed into a new community.

The person coming from another country is of special interest, however, because he has made an abrupt and decisive change in his situation. He has moved from a country where he was socialized as a child and has detached himself from the social roles he previously performed. He has left behind the various primary and secondary groups to which he belonged, some of which involved family and friends. In so doing he has narrowed his field of social participation and given up some of his major frames of reference for testing his attitudes, beliefs, and values. He has exchanged the security that comes with habitual forms of daily activity forged over time in familiar circumstances for the insecurity that accompanies any movement into new and strange territory. He has many new adjustments to make: finding a home and job; making new acquaintances; becoming accepted into new groups; learning new skills; achieving some structure or meaningful organization of his new experience—in general, absorbing the new culture so that he can settle down to a reasonably well-adjusted existence within the set of contraints that the culture imposes. In the course of the process the beliefs, attitudes, and values that he brought with him may be modified as he establishes new reference groups and is influenced by people whom he likes and respects.

It should be obvious that the assimilation process is a complex one and that any general theory of what it entails would have to draw its concepts from many different areas of social psychology and sociology. Minority-majority group relations, social learning, stereotyping, the function of groups, prejudice, the development of norms, role theory, attitude change, social motivation, and discrepancy theory are but a few of the many relevant areas. It seems foolish at this stage to hope for a single, well-articulated, comprehensive theory of the assimilation process. Instead, it is more useful to focus upon different aspects of assimilation and to develop theories that apply to each while at the same time being alert to relationships between the different aspects. This type of approach is facilitated by discussions in the literature that identify various stages, aspects, or facets of the assimilation process. To a consideration of some of these approaches we now turn.

STAGES OR ASPECTS OF THE ASSIMILATION PROCESS

Three approaches will be briefly mentioned, the first by Eisenstadt (1954), the second by Gordon (1964), and the third by Taft (1965).

Eisenstadt (1954) analyzes migratory movements in relation to the motivation to migrate, the social structure of the actual migratory process, and the absorption of the migrants into the social and cultural framework of the new society. Of particular interest are his statements about the process of absorption. This process is seen as including three different though closely connected phases: the acquisition of skills, the performance of various new roles, and changes in the self-concept in which new sets of values are acquired and tested out in relation to the new roles that are available. The entire process, therefore, involves "re-socialization," not unlike the basic process of socialization in any society. With migrants, however, the process starts with certain givens, "the groups, and their role expectations, within which the migratory process took place" (Eisenstadt, 1954, p. 7). These primary basic groups which are there at the outset of migration, and which may include family and friends who also migrated, are assumed gradually to become transformed and interwoven into the social structure of the receiving country. In this way the migrant's roles become institutionalized, values and aspirations develop that are compatible with those of the absorbing society, and the restructuring of previously held values and aspirations may occur. With these changes formation of new channels of communication with the wider society also occurs, along with new orientations toward wider spheres of activities and extension of social participation beyond the initial small primary groups.

Eisenstadt points out that this process is not always either smooth or successful. The social structure into which the migrants gradually move has certain expectations regarding them, makes certain demands on them, and offers certain possibilities with which the migrants have to come to terms. The host society thereby imposes formal and informal constraints on the process. Its expectations, demands, and possibilities may be incompatible with the migrant's own attempts to change and with the migrant's own aspirations. But it nonetheless sets limits to what he can do and how far he can go.

Of particular interest in Eisenstadt's analysis is his discussion of the criteria one might employ to gauge the degree to which migrants have been fully absorbed within the new society. He refers to three criteria: acculturation, personal adjustment, and institutional dispersion. *Acculturation* "is concerned principally with the extent to which the immigrant learns the various roles, norms, and customs of the absorbing society" (p. 12). The second criterion takes as an indication of successful adaptation evidence of good *personal adjustment* as inferred, for example, from low rates of suicide, mental illness, crime, delinquency, family upheaval, and so on. The third criterion relates to "the extent of the immigrants' dispersion or concentration within the various institutional spheres of the society" (p. 13), it being assumed that full absorption has occurred when the migrant group populates the society's institutions and ceases to have a separate identity.

This third index, *institutional dispersion* and dissolution of the migrant group, is seen by Eisenstadt as the principal evidence that full absorption has taken place, but he points out that in reality this criterion is never satisfied. Usually large-scale migration affects a country's "institutional contours" and a pluralistic structure or network of substructures arises so that total dispersion does not occur but different groups coexist, with some roles in common, with some roles unique, and with each group maintaining some degree of separate identity. This pluralistic structure enables both overlap and identity, universal and particular roles, and it involves some constraints on the alternative roles available to individuals. Eisenstadt contends that the emergence of a pluralistic structure may be accompanied by different types of tension within it on the part of both the migrants and the "old" inhabitants. He goes on to apply his analysis to research on the absorption of migrants in Palestine and Israel.

Gordon (1964) examines assimilation into American life. Like Eisenstadt, he assigns special importance to the structural aspects of assimilation—to the degree to which migrants have been able to move beyond the primary groups that are part of their ethnic communities into groups that are contained within the new society. He distinguishes seven different but interrelated subprocesses of assimilation. These are: (1) *cultural* or *behavioral assimilation* (acculturation), where cultural patterns have changed toward those of the host society; (2) *structural assimilation,* where large-scale entry of migrants into cliques, clubs, and institutions has occurred within the host society, on a primary group level; (3) *marital assimilation,* where extensive intermarriage has taken place; (4) *identificational assimilation,* where migrants have developed a sense of people-hood based exclusively on the host society; (5) *attitude receptional assimilation,* where social relations involve an absence of prejudice toward members of the migrant group; (6) *behavior receptional assimilation,* where no discriminatory behavior is shown toward members of the migrant group; and (7) *civic assimilation,* where conflict between migrants and the host society is absent over issues concerning values and power.

Gordon goes on to apply his analysis to three views of assimilation that at various times have been discussed in relation to American life. One view argues that the logic of assimilation should be adaptation to a core society and culture in which the migrant renounces his own culture and accepts the values and behavior of the Anglo-Saxon core group (the "Anglo-conformity" goal). Another view argues that the goal should be a merger of Anglo-Saxon peoples with other migrant groups by intermarriage and cultural blending to create a new indigenous American type (the "melting-pot" goal). The third view takes as its goal the preservation of the communal life and significant aspects of the culture of migrant groups within American society while at the same time ensuring that migrants have the usual rights and privileges of American citizen-ship and encouraging them to participate in the political, economic, and cultural life of the community as a whole (the "pluralistic society" goal). Gordon believes that the present American situation does in fact indicate a high degree of *structural pluralism:*

> The most salient fact . . . is the maintenance of the structurally separate sub-societies of the three major religious and the racial and quasi-racial groups, and even vestiges of the nationality groupings, along with a massive trend toward acculturation of all groups—particularly their native born—to Ameri-can culture patterns. (p. 159)

Of the seven subprocesses in assimilation Gordon believes that cultural assimilation or acculturation is likely to be the first to occur and, for some migrants it may be as far as their assimilation goes. But special status is assigned to structural assimilation. Gordon expresses its importance as follows:

> Once structural assimilation has occurred, either simultaneously with or subsequent to acculturation, all of the other types of assimilation will naturally follow. . . . Structural assimilation, then, rather than acculturation, is seen to be the keystone of the arch of assimilation. The price of such assimilation, however, is the disappearance of the ethnic group as a separate entity and the evaporation of its distinctive values. (p. 81)

Thus, intermarriage, the development of a sense of national identity, reduction in prejudice and discrimination, and changes in attitudes, beliefs, and values in the direction of congruence with the host society are all rendered more likely once structural assimilation begins to occur. More generally, Gordon believes that "group life and social structure constitute the matrix in which cumulative psychological states are embedded, . . . the latter cannot be thoroughly understood without reference to the former" (p. 233). This sentiment is surely one with which most social psychologists and sociologists would agree.

In Australia, Taft (1965) has also treated assimilation as a multifaceted process. He lists the following five aspects, each of which may be analyzed in terms of their *dynamics,* which involve motivation (the desired state) and conation (or what the migrant does to bring about his state), and in terms of their *achievement,* which may be considered either as perceived or actual. The five facets are as follows: (1) *cultural knowledge and skills,* in which the migrant learns the language, learns new roles, and acquires knowledge of the history and culture of his host society; (2) *social interaction,* in which the migrant is socially accepted and interpersonal contacts occur; (3) *membership identity,* in which the migrant is granted formal membership in groups within the host society; (4) *integration into new groups within the host society,* in which the migrant assumes some status within the new society and is granted attendant roles, privileges, and rights; and (5) *conformity to group norms,* in which the migrant adopts the values, frames of reference, and role perceptions of the host society; performs roles according to its norms; and conforms to its norms in appearance and expressive behavior. Taft also presents some ecological conditions that he considers relevant to each facet.

This multifacet analysis has been used in a general way in research at the University of Western Australia and elsewhere, involving migrant groups of various nationalities; a program that has also employed cumulative scaling and factor-analytic procedures in an attempt to identify basic aspects of the assimilation process (Taft, 1965). Taft indicates that his interest is primarily psychological with particular reference to the attitudes, reference groups, identifications, satisfactions, and personality of individual migrants.

Taft's multi-facet approach is similar in many ways to the analyses of the assimilation process provided by Eisenstadt and Gordon. In each case there is reference to acculturation, structural assimilation, the performance of new roles, and changes in the beliefs, attitudes, and values of the migrant. And these various aspects of assimilation are not to be thought of as independent, but as interrelated. All three approaches stress the realities of the structured nature of society. The migrant does not enter a homogeneous mass but a social field that is organized and stratified in various ways. This social field sets the range of possibilities and provides a plurality of different groups (work groups, church groups, leisure-time groups) in which members of the host society customarily participate in varying degrees. The extent to which the migrant has become assimilated is very much determined by his success in being accepted into some of these groups and assuming a role and a status in each. Finally, all three approaches distinguish between changes that occur at the surface and can easily be identified (such as increased skill in employing the language idiom of the host society), and changes that are more central or basic (such as a restructuring of the attitudes and values that the migrant brought with him to the host society).

We have concentrated upon these three analyses of assimilation for it is important to see the process in its complexity. The same considerations may be seen to apply when other forms of assimilation apart from migrant assimilation are explored. The changes that occur in a student's values, for example, when he enters a college or university and encounters a new environment will be a function of what he brings with him to the situation, the constraints imposed upon him by the situation, and the degree to which he is able to find membership in new groups that may come to achieve reference status for him. In discussing value change in Chapter 5 we pointed to the significance of reference groups and other important sources of influence within the new community. Values do not function in a vacuum. They are closely related to a person's psychological makeup and to information that flows to him from his environment, especially from the groups to which he relates and from people whom he likes and respects.

SUBJECTIVE ASSIMILATION

The studies now to be described pertain to the internal or subjective changes that can be assumed to occur in the cognitive sphere as the migrant's values, attitudes, and ways of thinking come to resemble those of members of his host culture. This internal or *subjective assimilation* involves the "psychological life" of the migrant and can be distinguished from more peripheral aspects of assimilation in which changes are obvious to an outside observer. It should be apparent that a migrant may be externally assimilated, in the sense that, to an outside observer, he behaves like members of his host group, but not assimilated in the subjective sense because he still retains the attitudes, values, and ways of thinking that he brought with him. And he may still consider himself as not yet identified with the host culture. This point should be obvious from the three analyses of assimilation that have just been presented; it is also one that has been made by a number of other authors (for example, Johnston, 1965, 1972). As we have seen, subjective assimilation should be looked at as one aspect (albeit a very important one) of a complex chain of events that may occur over time as a migrant becomes more and more a part of the host society.

POST-WAR IMMIGRATION TO AUSTRALIA

The two studies to be reported in this chapter involved Ukrainians and Latvians. Most Ukrainian and Latvian migrants arrived in Australia as refugees between 1948 and 1951 under a resettlement program organized by the Commonwealth government and the International Refugee Organization (IRO). They were part of the mass immigration to Australia that followed World War

II—a flow that differed from previous immigration in that it involved a high proportion of non-British migrants. Price (1970*b*) reports that about 58 percent of new settlers arriving between 1947 and 1969 were of non-British stock. The Ukrainians and Latvians were part of some 200,000 refugees who arrived in the immediate post-war years. They were followed in later years by an influx of migrants from southern Europe, particularly from Italy and Greece. Price (1970*a*) gives the following estimates of the ethnic origins of persons who came to Australia between July 1947 and June 1970 with the intention of settling: British Isles, 1,086,500; Italy, 337,700; Greece, 200,000; Netherlands, 140,600; Yugoslavia, 136,800; Germany, 121,300; Malta, 68,400; Other East Europe, 220,600; Others, 334,100.

The new immigrants to Australia have had an important influence on post-war Australian society. As Borrie (1972) puts it:

> They manned great national projects like the Snowy Mountains Scheme; they provided a great part of the labour force for new mineral enterprises; they helped to build houses, offices, and industrial buildings; they made the nation's steel; and they became the workhorses of the burgeoning motor industry. But, above all, they settled in the major cities, often forming substantial ethnic groups, restructuring national customs in their adopted environment, keeping alive their native languages, yet rubbing shoulders with Australians, being influenced by Australian culture—often through the participation of their children in Australian schools—and at the same time influencing by their presence and activity a remarkably homogeneous and at times slightly suspicious Australian society. (p. vi)

The impact of immigrants on Australian society has been studied in a number of publications notable among which is the series *Immigrants in Australia* sponsored by the Academy of the Social Sciences in Australia. The literature on Australian immigration is now quite extensive (Appleyard, 1965; Borrie, 1959; Johnston, 1965, 1972; Jones, 1967; Kunz, 1971; Martin, 1965 1972; Price, 1963, 1970*a*, 1970*b*; Richardson, 1967; Zubrzycki, 1968—and this is only a selection of available publications).

The Ukrainian and Latvian refugee groups have not received a great deal of attention from research workers. Latvians in Canberra have been studied by Jaunzems and Brown (1972). On the basis of their study they conclude:

> The Latvians have become integrated into the Australian community by a process of adaption, without loss of a separate national identity as Latvians. The majority are naturalised, have good English, are materially satisfied, and have at least some Australian friends and a generally favourable attitude to Australians. Despite this they continue to regard themselves as 'Latvians,' they commonly interact with other Latvians, and many prefer to speak Latvian at home. (p. 67)

Martin (1972) has provided a detailed sociological account of fourteen refugee groups in Adelaide—including Ukrainians and Latvians—focusing upon their formal group organization, the extent of structural pluralism, and the degree to which these ethnic minorities have been able to remain as distinct structures within the community, maintaining their own identity. She conducted a "multbet" classificatory analysis (Lance & Williams, 1967) of the 14 Adelaide minorities using all of the manageable data that she could obtain about them— information that she presents throughout her book. Four "like" clusters of minority populations emerged and one of them included Ukrainian, Latvian, Estonian, Polish, and Lithuanian ethnic groups. So there is evidence to show that the Ukrainian and Latvian communities are similar in their structures and functions within the wider Adelaide community.

Some information about numbers of Ukrainians and Latvians in Australia and in Adelaide will help to set the scene for the two studies to follow. Analysis of the 1971 national census data showed that 12,450 people listed their birthplace as the Ukraine and 14,478 listed their birthplace as Latvia. Of these there were 1,949 Ukrainians and 2,218 Latvians from urban Adelaide. The total population of urban Adelaide at that time was 809,482.

With this background information, let us now turn to a description of the two studies of subjective assimilation.

THE UKRAINIAN STUDY

PREDICTIONS

The first study to be discussed had two focuses. In the first place it was concerned with the value systems of second-generation Ukrainian migrants and their relation to those of their parents and the wider Australian community. It is well recognized that the effects of assimilation are more likely to be evident among second generation migrants than among their parents. It is reasonable to assume that adult migrants have ways of living and basic values and attitudes that, for various reasons, are often difficult to change. Their children are in a better position to learn the new ways and to move toward the culture of the host society. Typically, these children have become acculturated and, in the school situation and also in leisure-time and other activities, have experienced some structural assimilation, mixing with children of the host society and being accepted into various peer groups. On these grounds one would expect the value systems of migrant children to more closely resemble those of members of their host culture than would the value systems of their parents.

This hypothesis could be tested by comparing the value systems of a group of children from migrant Ukrainian families and the value systems of their parents, first with each other and then with those of Australian children and their parents. In this way it was possible to examine the similarity between the value systems of migrant Ukrainian parents and their children, and Australian parents and their children. Evidence was thereby obtained about the extent of value assimilation that had occurred in the migrant parents and in their children.

The second focus of the investigation was on parent-child similarities and differences in values and value systems. The study provided, therefore, another source of evidence about generational effects, adding to the evidence we have already described in Chapters 6 and 7.

Finally, as a secondary aim the study explored differences in *ethnocentrism* between the migrant groups and their Australian counterparts. Some authors (for example, Allport, 1954) have commented on the tendency for minority groups to be suspicious of outgroups. It was possible to examine this question by using the Australian Ethnocentrism Scale designed by Beswick and Hills (1969, 1972).

SUBJECTS AND PROCEDURE

Full details of our sampling and procedure have been reported by Wasyluk (1971) and by Feather and Wasyluk (1973b). All of the testing was carried out by Wasyluk, himself a second-generation Ukrainian migrant, who conducted the present study as part of his honors program. One group of respondents consisted of Australian male and female students (members of the Adelaide University Science Association) and their families, including both parents and siblings over 15 years of age willing to participate in the study. The second group comprised Ukrainian male and female students (members of the Ukrainian Students Association) and their families, including both parents and any siblings over 15 years of age who were willing to participate. These samples obviously cannot be taken as representative of Ukrainian migrants and Australians in general. It is usually very difficult to get a representative sample of a migrant group, however, and one has to do the best with groups that one has access to, providing as much information as one can about their distinctive characteristics. In all, considering just students and parents, 184 respondents participated in the study: 54 Australian students, 41 Australian parents, 50 Ukrainian students, and 39 Ukrainian parents.

The student samples were recruited with the help of leaders of the two student organizations. These respondents completed a questionnaire that took about 40 to 45 minutes to answer. Testing was conducted under group conditions with the usual request to respondents to work quietly and not to discuss aspects of the questionnaire among themselves. When they had finished the questionnaire the students took sufficient copies home for their parents and other members of the family who were more than 15 years of age. They were cautioned against prompting family members while these members were completing the questionnaire, and they were asked to return the questionnaire as soon as possible (50–60 percent of the Ukrainian and Australian parents completed the questionnaire). It was made clear that all responses would be treated in strictest confidence. All questionnaires were completed anonymously, code numbers being used. Only the data from students and parents would be considered in presenting the results. A higher response rate from the parents would have been preferred, and therefore we should view their results with appropriate caution.

The questionnaire contained items on age, sex, place of birth, length of time in Australia if foreign born, education, and present employment. Thirty-eight of the Ukrainian students were born in Australia, the remainder coming to Australia at a very early age (from two to four years of age). As in some of the other studies we have described, the occupations of fathers were coded for status according to the scale by Congalton (1969), occupations being rated from 1 to 7 in the direction of *decreasing* prestige. Fathers in the Australian families had occupations of higher prestige (mean = 4.00) than did fathers in the Ukrainian families (mean = 5.59), and the difference in means was statistically significant ($p < .01$). However, this difference should be interpreted along with the fact that some of the migrants had a professional status in their own country that they were not able to maintain in Australia.

When the initial items had been answered, respondents completed Form E of the Rokeach Value Survey according to the usual procedure. They then completed the Australian Ethnocentrism Scale (Beswick & Hills, 1969). This test contains items tapping five areas of attitudes derived from Levinson's theory of ethnocentrism (Adorno, Frenkel-Brunswik, Levinson, & Sanford, 1950), namely, stereotyped positive imagery and submissive attitudes regarding ingroups, intolerance of ambiguity and inflexibility, favoring a hierarchical society and suppression of outgroups, segregation within Australia, and rejection of groups outside Australia. Ethnocentrism was not defined as prejudice against particular racial groups, but as a general tendency to discriminate against any possible outgroup that might include aborigines, criminals, Asians, communists, migrants, or Australians. There were 32 items in the test, half of them positive and half negative, presented in mixed order. Possible responses to the items were "Strongly agree," "Agree," "Disagree," or "Strongly disagree" keyed to scores of 5, 4, 2, and 1 respectively with a score of 3 given for no response to an item (no responses being discouraged, however). A total score was obtained by adding those for the 16 positive items expressing an ethnocentric position and then subtracting the sum of the scores on the sixteen negative items expressing the opposite position. Hence, scores could fall in the range +64 (maximum ethnocentrism) to −64 (minimum ethnocentrism).

AVERAGE VALUE SYSTEMS FOR AUSTRALIAN AND UKRAINIAN RESPONDENTS

Tables 9.1 and 9.2 present the median ranks of terminal and instrumental values for the four groups. As in previous analyses these average value systems were compared for similarity using Spearman's rho and Kendall's tau. These similarity indexes, presented in Table 9.3, show that the average terminal values

TABLE 9-1. Median Rankings and Composite Rank Orders of Terminal Values for Ukrainian Students, Australian Students, Ukrainian Parents, and Australian Parents

Terminal Value	Students		Parents		Significant Effects
	Ukrainian	Australian	Ukrainian	Australian	
N	48	53	36	39	
A comfortable life	11.50 (13)	13.83 (15)	7.00 (5.5)	13.31 (14)	A, B
An exciting life	11.00 (12)	7.63 (10)	14.50 (18)	14.07 (16)	B
A sense of accomplishment	6.83 (6)	6.25 (4.5)	11.50 (13)	7.88 (9)	—
A world at peace	8.20 (10.5)	7.13 (8)	5.33 (3)	5.88 (4)	—
A world of beauty	12.80 (16)	10.30 (13)	11.75 (14)	13.38 (15)	—
Equality	7.60 (9)	7.30 (9)	10.00 (11.5)	9.50 (11)	—
Family security	6.40 (3)	9.06 (12)	1.78 (1)	2.75 (1)	A, B
Freedom	6.50 (4.5)	5.93 (2)	6.00 (4)	6.75 (5)	—
Happiness	4.33 (1)	5.50 (1)	5.00 (2)	5.75 (3)	—
Inner harmony	7.00 (7.5)	6.92 (7)	7.83 (7)	7.83 (8)	—
Mature love	8.20 (10.5)	6.50 (6)	12.50 (16)	8.70 (10)	B, AB
National security	15.00 (17)	14.69 (17)	7.00 (5.5)	11.50 (12)	B
Pleasure	12.17 (14)	13.50 (14)	14.25 (17)	14.10 (17)	—
Salvation	15.67 (18)	15.92 (18)	8.75 (9)	12.50 (13)	B
Self-respect	6.00 (2)	7.70 (11)	8.33 (8)	6.88 (6)	—
Social recognition	12.50 (15)	14.30 (16)	12.00 (15)	15.28 (18)	A
True friendship	6.50 (4.5)	5.94 (3)	10.00 (11.5)	7.10 (7)	A, B
Wisdom	7.00 (7.5)	6.25 (4.5)	9.40 (10)	5.25 (2)	A

Note. The lower the median the higher the relative value. The rank-order of each median (low to high) is shown in parentheses. "A" effects refer to Ukrainian versus Australian. "B" effects refer to students versus parents. Ns are for error-free rankings. Alpha level is $p < .01$.

Source: Data are from Feather & Wasyluk, 1973b.

TABLE 9-2. Median Rankings and Composite Rank Orders of Instrumental Values for Ukrainian Students, Australian Students, Ukrainian Parents, and Australian Parents

	Median Rankings				
Instrumental Value	Students		Parents		Significant Effects
	Ukrainian	Australian	Ukrainian	Australian	
N	46	52	34	38	
Ambitious	10.71 (14)	11.40 (14)	9.00 (7.5)	12.67 (15)	—
Broad-minded	5.71 (3)	5.33 (2.5)	9.00 (7.5)	9.50 (10.5)	B
Capable	9.20 (10)	9.25 (11)	7.33 (4)	8.20 (5)	—
Cheerful	9.50 (11)	7.67 (7)	12.00 (16)	8.50 (7.5)	A
Clean	13.67 (17)	14.38 (17)	8.00 (5)	9.67 (12)	B
Courageous	9.00 (8)	8.40 (8)	9.00 (7.5)	9.50 (10.5)	—
Forgiving	8.00 (5.5)	6.75 (6)	6.50 (3)	9.33 (9)	—
Helpful	8.00 (5.5)	8.67 (9)	9.00 (7.5)	10.17 (13)	—
Honest	3.50 (1)	2.33 (1)	1.67 (1)	2.20 (1)	—
Imaginative	10.00 (13)	13.00 (16)	15.44 (18)	15.29 (18)	B
Independent	9.00 (8)	6.40 (5)	9.33 (10)	11.50 (14)	B
Intellectual	9.67 (12)	10.33 (13)	10.00 (13.5)	13.20 (16)	—
Logical	11.33 (16)	9.00 (10)	10.00 (13.5)	8.50 (7.5)	—
Loving	5.50 (2)	5.75 (4)	9.40 (11)	5.50 (3)	—
Obedient	14.67 (18)	15.00 (18)	13.00 (17)	13.50 (17)	—
Polite	11.00 (15)	12.40 (15)	10.40 (15)	8.00 (4)	—
Responsible	7.80 (4)	5.33 (2.5)	6.00 (2)	4.00 (2)	A
Self-Controlled	9.00 (8)	9.29 (12)	9.50 (12)	8.33 (6)	—

Note. The lower the median the higher the relative value. The rank-order of each median (low to high) is shown in parentheses. "A" effects refer to Ukrainian versus Australian. "B" effects refer to students versus parents. Ns are for error-free rankings. Alpha level is $p < .01$.
Source: Data are from Feather & Wasyluk, 1973b.

of the two groups of students were very similar. So were the average value systems of the two groups of parents (rhos of .77 and .70 respectively, taus of .66 and .55 respectively). However, the average priorities of the Ukrainian students for the set of terminal values were much more similar to those of the Australian parents than to those of their own Ukrainian parents (rhos of .79 and .42 respectively, taus of .59 and .29 respectively). On the other hand, the average priorities of the Australian students for the terminal values were much more similar to those of the Australian parents than to those of the Ukrainian parents (rhos of .65 and .15 respectively, taus of .46 and .12 respectively). The data suggest, therefore, that so far as terminal values are concerned, Ukrainian students were more similar to their host culture than to their own parents.

TABLE 9-3. Similarity Indexes Comparing Median Rankings across Groups

	Students		Parents	
	Ukrainian	*Australian*	*Ukrainian*	*Australian*
Students				
Ukrainian		.77 (.66)	.42 (.29)	.79 (.59)
Australian	.89 (.75)		.15 (.12)	.65 (.46)
Parents				
Ukrainian	.57 (.43)	.54 (.42)		.70 (.55)
Australian	.51 (.39)	.56 (.41)	.44 (.36)	

Note. Similarity indexes for average terminal value systems are above the diagonal; similarity indexes for average instrumental value systems are below the diagonal. Similarity indexes not in parentheses are Spearman rhos; similarity indexes in parentheses are Kendall taus. Higher similarity indexes indicate greater similarity between the average value systems involved in the comparison.
Source: Data are from Feather & Wasyluk, 1973*b*.

The pattern of similarity indexes in Table 9.3 for the terminal values can be fitted to an ordered-metric scale as indicated in Figure 9.1. To do so assumes that similarity indexes can be coordinated to scaled distances so that groups that are similar or close together have a high similarity index whereas groups that are dissimilar or far apart on the scale have a low similarity index. The particular solution presented in Figure 9.1 was based upon the centroid solution

FIGURE 9-1. Ordered-Metric Scale Representing Similarity between Australian Students and Parents and Ukrainian Students and Parents in Their Average Terminal Values

0	Ukranian Students	.555		Ukrainian Parents
Australian Students	.361	Australian Parents		1

Source: Figure is from Feather & Wasyluk, 1973*b*.

of the delta method for representing order-metric scales, using the Spearman rho coefficients as similarity indexes (Coombs, 1964, chap. 5, sec. 6). The scale presented in Figure 9.1 shows that the four groups can be ordered in a particular way and that some metric information can be obtained given the assumptions of the centroid solution. The most dissimilar groups were the Australian students and the Ukrainian parents (furthest apart). Ukrainian parents and Ukrainian students were next in dissimilarity, and so forth, and Ukrainian students and Australian parents were most similar (closest together) in regard to the average value systems for the terminal values.

When one turns to the results for the instrumental values, again it is apparent that the average value systems of the Australian and Ukrainian students were very similar, much more so than were those of their parents (rhos of .89 and .44 respectively, taus of .75 and .36 respectively). The four cross-correlations were all at about the same level (rhos of .57, .54, .51, and .56; taus of .43, .42, .39, and .41). These data suggest that Ukrainian students were very similar to Australian students in the priorities they assigned instrumental values, but no more similar to Australian parents than to their own. Ukrainian and Australian parents were rather dissimilar in the priorities they assigned instrumental values.

It was again possible to fit the pattern of similarity indexes in Table 9.3 for the instrumental values to an ordered-metric scale, using the same procedure as before. The solution, presented in Figure 9.2, shows that Australian parents and Ukrainian parents were most dissimilar (furthest apart), Australian parents and Ukrainian students were next in dissimilarity, and so forth, and Australian students and Ukrainian students were most similar (closest together) in regard to average value systems for the instrumental values.

FIGURE 9–2. Ordered-Metric Scale Representing Similarity between Australian Students and Parents and Ukrainian Students and Parents in Their Average Instrumental Values

0	Australian Students	.639	Ukrainian Parents
Australian Parents	.444	Ukranian Students	1

Source: Figure is from Feather & Wasyluk, 1973*b*.

In general, therefore, our comparative analyses of similarity indexes supported the prediction that subjective assimilation to the host culture would be most evident in the second generation. The Ukrainian students were very similar to the Australian students in their average value systems, more so than the Ukrainian parents were to the Australian parents. As we have argued, this greater similarity among the children is to be expected. The children of migrants growing up in a host society can learn its language, discover its institutions, move into its groups, and absorb the culture in a wide variety of settings. Their parents are more restricted in what they can do, often not possessing the language of the host culture and resistant to change in old habits and ways of thinking.

What kinds of values were the Ukrainian students assimilating to? The details about specific values can be found in Tables 9.1 and 9.2. There it can be seen that the average orders of preference for the Australian students were very similar to those obtained with adolescent student groups in the studies we have described in previous chapters (see Table 5.12). In the present case the Australian students saw *happiness, freedom, true friendship, a sense of accomplishment,* and *wisdom* as most important among the terminal values and *a comfortable life, social recognition, national security,* and *salvation* as least important. The four most important instrumental values for the Australian students were being *honest, broad-minded, responsible,* and *loving,* and the four least important were being *polite, imaginative, clean,* and *obedient.* The corresponding highest and lowest terminal and instrumental values for the Ukrainian students showed a high degree of overlap with those of the Australian student group (see Tables 9.1 and 9.2).

ANALYSIS OF SINGLE VALUES

A 2 × 2 analysis of variance was applied to the transformed ranks for each value with country of origin (Ukrainian versus Australian) as the first factor (A) and generation (parent versus student) as the second factor (B). Tables 9.1 and 9.2 list the significant main effects and interactions using an alpha level of $p < .01$ or lower. There it can be seen from inspecting the medians that the following values were ranked as more important by Ukrainian respondents when compared with Australian respondents irrespective of whether they were parents or students (significant main effects of the country of origin factor—A effects): *a comfortable life, family security,* and *social recognition.* The Australian respondents ranked the following values as more important: *true friendship, wisdom, cheerful,* and *responsible.* When the rankings of parents were compared with the rankings of their children, regardless of country of origin (significant main effects of the generation factor—B effects), the following values were ranked as more important by the students: *an exciting life, mature love, true friendship, broad-minded, imaginative,* and *independent.* Their parents ranked these values as relatively more important: *a comfortable life, family security, national security, salvation,* and *clean.* There was one significant interaction (AB effect) due to the fact that Ukrainian parents ranked *mature love* much lower in importance than Australian parents, whereas the students were more similar in their rankings of this value. Again, most of the differences just mentioned are reflected in differences in the respective medians.

When a less conservative alpha level was employed ($p < .05$), the following additional effects became significant, of which some were main effects from the analysis and others were interaction effects: Ukrainian parents saw *national security* as more important than did any of the other three groups; students assigned more importance to *a sense of accomplishment* and being *cheerful* than did their parents; parents saw being *honest* (marginally), *obedient,* and *responsible* as relatively more important than did their children; Ukrainian parents placed *wisdom* and being *loving* especially low in importance relative to the other three groups; Australian parents regarded being *polite* as much more important than did the other three groups. Again these differences are reflected in the median rankings, but some of them were marginal.

Analyses of variance of sex differences in regard to particular values showed similar effects to those described in previous chapters (see Table 5.11). Thus, males ranked the following values higher in importance than did females: *a comfortable life, an exciting life,* and *pleasure.* Females saw *salvation,* and being *honest* and *loving* as relatively more important than did males. All these effects were significant at $p < .01$ or $p < .05$.

In summary, there was evidence that Ukrainian families (parents and students) seemed to assign more importance to values that related to various forms of security and respect whereas their Australian counterparts gave relatively more attention to affiliative values, a mature understanding of life, and to being responsible and cheerful. This Australian emphasis corresponds to that noted in the last chapter when Australian value priorities were compared with those of American groups. The greater importance assigned to security (nation and family) by the Ukrainians can be understood in terms of their more stressful history and their experience as refugee migrants. Their concerns are doubtless communicated to their children. The family unit may be viewed, then, as an especially significant source of psychological comfort in a new and somewhat alien culture, particularly by the parents.

The parent-child or generational differences echoed those reported in previous chapters. They will not be discussed further except to say that, as in the corresponding Australian-American age effects described in the last chapter, they were strong enough to appear despite differences in national backgrounds. These various results suggest that the generational differences we have uncovered may have considerable cross-national applicability, at least where cultures are not too dissimilar in the demands made upon and the roles expected from individuals of different age groups.

ANALYSIS OF ETHNOCENTRISM SCORES

A final source of information about subjective assimilation concerns social attitudes, in this case ethnocentrism or general negative attitudes toward outgroups. The mean scores on the Australian Ethnocentrism Scale are presented in Table 9.4.

When a $2 \times 2 \times 2$ analysis of variance was applied to the total ethnocentrism scores with sex, country of origin, and generation as factors in the analysis, the following statistically significant main effects emerged: Parents had significantly higher total ethnocentrism scores than their children ($p < .001$) irrespective of whether respondents came from Ukrainian or Australian families. Parents and children from Ukrainian families had higher total ethnocentrism scores than their Australian counterparts ($p < .05$). Males did not differ significantly from females in total ethnocentrism scores nor were any of the interactions statistically significant.

TABLE 9-4. Mean Total Ethnocentrism Scores for Ukrainian Students, Australian Students, Ukrainian Parents, and Australian Parents

	Male	Female
Ukrainian students	−17.34	−22.84
Australian students	−27.25	−20.42
Ukrainian parents	.75	1.59
Australian parents	− 4.50	− 6.90

Source: Data are from Feather & Wasyluk, 1973*b*.

Similar analyses were applied to the scores on individual items from the Australian Ethnocentrism Scale that concerned three main groups: Aborigines, Communists, and Asians. The results showed that in nearly all cases the parents were significantly more ethnocentric than were their children. The Ukrainian respondents were especially ethnocentric toward Communists, with Ukrainian parents showing the greatest antagonism toward this political group—a not unsurprising result considering that many of these parents were refugees who had fled their homeland and had a realistic basis for their attitudes (Borrie, 1959). Quite apart from particular antagonisms, however, it is possible that migrant groups may be rather suspicious of outgroups in general (Allport, 1954)—a view that might be especially prevalent among the older first-generation migrants who have left familiar territory to enter a strange and somewhat alien world. As we have pointed out, these older migrants have greater problems of assimilation than their offspring, and, in their search for security and peace of mind, they may be particularly sensitive to what they perceive to be threats from without.

The generational differences in ethnocentrism resemble those reported for conservatism in Chapter 6. Indeed, an examination of the items in the Conservatism Scale (Wilson & Patterson, 1968) shows that a number of them relate to outgroups (for example, mixed marriage, apartheid, white superiority, colored immigration). Factor-analytic studies of the Conservatism Scale at the item level have provided evidence for a factor involving ethnocentric attitudes (Feather, 1975*a;* Wilson, 1973*c*). One way of conceiving of ethnocentrism, therefore, would be to regard it as an aspect of a general conservatism syndrome that is more apparent among older people.

Again, however, one needs to be careful in interpreting generational differences, particularly when they are based upon cross-sectional evidence and not on longitudinal studies. The interesting question to be answered in the future is whether individuals become more ethnocentric as they grow older (that is, whether they undergo a cognitive change tied to the aging process) or whether the parent-child differences in ethnocentrism were due to other factors. A leading candidate would be different levels of education. Beswick and Hills (1969) have noted the strong effect of education on ethnocentrism, the more highly educated person being more tolerant of outgroups. In the present study the students were highly educated in comparison with their parents, and the generational differences obtained in total ethnocentrism scores could therefore be due to educational differences. They could also be a result of not just age and educational effects, but of a whole set of different experiences (for example, war and its aftermath, economic frustrations) that the parents had undergone.

The same argument applies to generational differences in value priorities, conservatism, and other social attitudes—as we noted in Chapter 6. Clearly, if we are to disentangle some of these alternative interpretations, we need sophisticated longitudinal studies that are begun at different points in time and that include different age cohorts.

In summary, the Ukrainian study provided evidence supporting the expectation that second-generation migrant children would display more advanced subjective assimilation than do their parents. It also uncovered further evidence for generational differences. This was a fairly straightforward descriptive study without any pretense at theoretical or methodological sophistication, but of value in its own right because it opened up territory that has not been sufficiently explored in the past. The study to be described in the next section was able to build upon it and to introduce rather more sophisticated and theoretically relevant procedures.

THE LATVIAN STUDY

PREDICTIONS

The Latvian study went further than the Ukrainian in a number of important respects. It included various measures of different aspects of assimilation, such as acculturation, ethnic identity and identification, structural assimilation, and subjective assimilation, and it examined the effect of attending an ethnic school on these assimilation measures. It was also concerned with how each group (Latvian and Australian) perceived the value priorities of the other and the degree to which these perceptions were accurate reflections of reality. In contrast with the Ukrainian study, parent-child differences were not explored.

The Latvians in Australia have not been subject to a great deal of study (for some recent information, see Jaunzems & Brown, 1972; and Martin, 1972).

Like the Ukrainians, they represent a refugee migrant group, most of them arriving as displaced persons in 1949 and 1950. Since then there have been very few additions to their number. As refugees and with strong national identification many of these immigrants see themselves as keepers of a national heritage that they believe is being destroyed in their homelands (Dunsdorfs, 1968; Veidemanis, 1963). Taft (1965, p. 67) noted that in Australia adult Latvian and Lithuanian migrants had least identification with Australia when compared with other migrant groups. Kukurs (1968) found that Latvians in Canberra had strong ethnic identification. This ethnic consciousness finds an outlet in the Saturday schools established by Latvians in Australian capital cities. These schools have operated outside of the Australian education system, pupils meeting in Latvian community centers and even in private homes. Each Saturday morning during the Australian school year pupils are taught Latvian language, literature, and aspects of Latvian history and geography. The schools can be seen as a practical expression of parental concern with the maintenance of the ethnic identity of their children, their main aim being to develop Latvian literacy and ethnic consciousness. Martin (1972) estimates that approximately 33 percent of Latvian children were attending these ethnic schools. (She also provides background information about Latvian immigration to Australia and sociological information concerning the Latvian community in Adelaide.)

It might be expected that the Latvian children who attend these schools would be less assimilated in relation to Australian society than the Latvian children who do not. This circumstance would seem logical for at least two reasons. First, the ethnic school itself might have an effect, countering the assimilation process. Second, children attending the ethnic school would be more likely to come from families that are less assimilated than are those of the nonattenders, with less group contacts within the Australian community and with greater anxiety about preserving their Latvian identity and identification and the language and cultural heritage of their homeland. It would be difficult to disentangle the effects of the school from the effects of the family, and the study we will describe made no attempt to do so. It was simply interested in comparing a group of Saturday school attenders with a group of Saturday school nonattenders on a variety of assimilation measures, many of which relate to Gordon's discussion of stages in the assimilation process (Gordon, 1964). As in the Ukrainian study, however, the main focus of interest was on subjective assimilation, especially in regard to values and social attitudes. The Rokeach Value Survey was again employed as the basic research instrument. In addition, subjective assimilation was assessed according to degree of Australianism (Taft, 1965) and conservatism (Wilson & Patterson, 1968)—both scales describing social attitudes.

Of particular interest was the degree to which the two groups of young second-generation Latvians (Saturday school attenders and nonattenders) could *accurately* perceive the value systems of their Australian peers of the same age and, vice versa, the degree to which a group of young Australians could accurately perceive the value systems of the "New Australians" of their own age. One would expect some tendency for increased assimilation to be mirrored in greater accuracy of perception of the other's values, both from the migrants' point of view and from the host point of view. Accurate perception would seem the reasonable accompaniment of structural assimilation that affords greater opportunities for social interaction and enables belief to be tested against reality. Even so, however, structural assimilation could be hindered by prevailing stereotypes, difficult to dislodge even in the face of strong conflicting evidence.

SUBJECTS AND PROCEDURE

Full details of both the samples and the procedure used in the study have been provided by Rudzitis (1972) and by Feather and Rudzitis (1974). The Latvians who were tested were all second-generation immigrants and, with one exception, were all born in Australia. Altogether 96 Latvians were tested but 9 were excluded from the sample for having only 1 Latvian parent. There remained 87 Latvian adolescents with Latvian parents. Of these, 59 had attended the Latvian Saturday or ethnic school in Adelaide (the "attenders") and 28 had never attended the school (the "nonattenders"). There were 28 boys and 31 girls in the group of attenders; their mean age was 15.22 years with a range from 13 to 17. Thirteen boys and 15 girls were in the group of nonattenders, and their mean age was 15.18 years with a range from 13 to 17. Most of the Latvians (84 percent of the attenders, 61 percent of the nonattenders) belonged to the Lutheran Church, and most of the remainder were Catholics. The mean status of occupations of fathers was 5.00 for both the attenders and the nonattenders, using the scale devised by Congalton (1969) described previously (scored 1 to 7 in the direction of *decreasing* prestige). The attenders had taken courses at the Saturday school for a mean of 6.6 years with a range of 1 to 10 years. Seventy-seven of the Latvian children were contacted at 16 high schools in Adelaide, the remainder being tested in the Latvian Community Center or in their own homes. The 16 high schools covered most of the Adelaide metropolitan area.

A total of 71 Australian children were tested. Of these, 19 had to be excluded because they had immigrant parents, because they had left school, or for some other reason. That left 52 Australian adolescents with Australian parents and, with one exception, all had been born in Australia. The Australian group consisted of 27 boys and 25 girls; their mean age was 15.69 years with a range from 13 to 17. There was no dominant religious affiliation among the group, although most respondents were associated with a Protestant church (Methodist, Church of England, or Lutheran). Using the Congalton index, the mean status of the fathers' occupations was 3.76, indicating that the occupations of the Australian fathers were, on the average, higher in prestige than were the occupations of Latvian fathers. The difference in means was statistically significant

(p < .001). The Australian respondents were obtained from various youth organizations (for example, boy scouts, girl guides, youth camps, YMCA, church groups) covering a wide area of Adelaide.

Testing of respondents (both Latvian and Australian) was organized by Rudzitis, himself a second-generation Latvian migrant, who conducted the present study as part of his honors program. He was assisted in the actual test- ing by high-school teachers and supervisors who had been thoroughly briefed about correct procedure. All testing was conducted during July, August, and September 1972, in group sessions. All respondents completed the questionnaires anonymously with the usual request to read the instructions carefully, to work quietly, and to give their own true answers.

Two versions of the questionnaire were used, one for the Latvian respon- dents and one for the Australian. Both versions began with Form E of the Rokeach Value Survey in its usual form, respondents being asked to rank the two sets of values in their order of importance in regard to self, that is, to note their own priorities. The Latvian respondents were then asked to rank the two sets of values according to how they thought Australians of their own age would rank them. Similarly, the Australians were asked to rank the two sets according to how they thought New Australians of their own age would answer them. The "own" rankings were obtained before the "others" rankings because it was thought that the rankings for self would provide a meaningful reference frame for judgments of the value systems of the other. Because of the small number of Latvians in Australia, asking the Australians to rank the values for Latvians would have been too specialized and inappropriate. Instead they were asked to rank for New Australian migrants in general.

In summary, therefore, the Latvians provided two different sorts of rankings for each set of values—one relating to their own priorities and then one relat- ing to the perceived Australian priorities, their own rankings preceding the perceived rankings. Similarly, the Australian group provided two different types of rankings for both sets of values—first their own and then their per- ceived rankings for New Australians.

Following the Value Survey respondents completed the Australianism Scale developed by Taft (1962, 1965) as a measure of assimilation to Australian society. The test consists of 28 items to each of which the respondent can agree or disagree. The items cover a variety of topics and, according to Taft (1965), analysis of the item responses highlights some representative Australian values with which migrants must come to terms:

> Compared with European immigrants, Australians appear to value con- formity of behaviour more than individual self expression and, in the same vein, many superficial contacts rather than fewer but more intimate ones; they place more stress on the equality of social classes as a principle, but are less tender-minded concerning human relationships (sacrifice humans for a principle, children have no obligation to look after their parents, for example); finally, the Australians are less pessimistic about the future of mankind than are the immigrants and more secure about their own future. (p. 16)

In addition to the Australianism Scale, respondents also completed the Conservatism Scale (Wilson & Patterson, 1968) and a set of especially tailored items. These three sections of the questionnaire were presented to respondents in counterbalanced order to control for order effects.

The Latvian version of the questionnaire contained 10 special items designed to assess various aspects of assimilation. For the first seven of these items the respondent had to choose one of five possible anwers that were scored from 1 to 5 in the direction of increasing assimilation to Australian society. In the following description of items, the assimilation scores for the five alternatives to each item are shown in brackets. These scores were not, of course, included in the items as presented to respondents; they are presented here for the reader's information.

Three items were concerned with the respondent's *ethnic identity* as perceived by himself, by his parents, and by his friends. Each item was phrased as a question. In the case of own identity, for example, the question was: "Generally, do you think you are: Completely Latvian [1]? More Latvian than Australian [2]? Half Latvian-half Australian [3]? More Australian than Latvian [4]? Completely Australian [5]?" *Ethnic identification* was investigated by the question: "Generally, would you prefer to be Completely Latvian [1] . . . ?" and so on, the alternative responses being the same as those for the three identity items. One item was concerned with *ethnic origins of friends:* "Would you say that you have: All Latvian friends [1]? More Latvian than Australian [2]? Half Latvian-half Australian [3]? More Australian than Latvian [4]? All Australian friends [5]?" Another related to the ability to speak the *ethnic language* and still another to the preferred use of this language: "Can you speak Latvian: Very Well [1]? Well [2]? Reasonably Well [3]? Badly [4]? Not at all [5]?" and "When you have a choice do you: Speak Latvian only [1]? Speak more Latvian than English [2]? Speak Latvian and English equally [3]? Speak more English than Latvian [4]? Speak English only [5]?" Finally, two items asked for a listing of Latvian and Australian *organizations and groups* to which the respondents belonged (sports teams, scouts, folk-dancing groups, school clubs, hobby associations, and so forth). And one item asked respondents if there were any *preferred countries* in which they would like to live more than Australia. The items were not grouped according to the classification just described but were presented in mixed order.

The Australian version of the questionnaire also contained some especially apropos items. Three items corresponded to three in the Latvian version. One asked for a listing of Australian group memberships, one for a listing of New Australian group memberships, and one for a listing of countries of residence in preference to Australia. The remaining two items are described in the original reports (Feather & Rudzitis, 1974; Rudzitis, 1972). Again the items were presented in mixed order.

Finally, all respondents (Latvians and Australians) provided biographical information concerning place of birth, date of birth, sex, religious affiliation, suburb of residence, particular school attended, father's occupation, and nationality of parents. They were also asked whether (and if so, when) they had ever attended the Latvian school.

AVERAGE VALUE SYSTEMS FOR AUSTRALIAN AND LATVIAN RESPONDENTS

The median rankings by the Australians and Latvians of the terminal and instrumental values, both in relation to own priorities and the perceived priorities of the other, are presented in Tables 9.5 and 9.6 respectively. Table 9.7 presents the Spearman rank-order correlations (rhos) between these average value systems and, in parentheses, the corresponding values of Kendall's tau. As before, these coefficients may be regarded as similarity indexes, higher coefficients implying greater similarity between average value systems.

The size and pattern of the similarity indexes in Table 9.7 permit the following conclusions. First, the *own* average value systems of respondents were similar irrespective of whether respondents were Latvians or Australians, and this similarity was rather more pronounced for the set of terminal values than for the set of instrumental values (compare the triads of similarity coefficients for own priorities above and below the diagonal). Among the terminal values, respondents from all three groups ranked *a world at peace, freedom, happiness,* and *true friendship* as among their most important values and *national security, pleasure,* and *salvation* as among their least important values (see Table 9.5). Among the instrumental values, respondents from all three groups ranked being *honest, broad-minded, responsible,* and *loving* as among their most important values and being *obedient* and *imaginative* as among their least important (see Table 9.6). These highest and lowest priorities are similar to those we have noted before for adolescent respondents in Australia. There was no consistent evidence from comparing these similarity indexes that the own priorities of the Latvian school nonattenders were more similar to those of their Australian peers than were the own priorities of the Latvian school attenders, a difference that one might expect if the nonattenders were more assimilated.

Second, both groups of Latvians *perceived* the priorities of Australians of their own age in quite similar ways for both the terminal and instrumental values. Thus, irrespective of whether they attended a Saturday school or not, the Latvians were in fair agreement regarding the average value priorities of the Australians (rhos of .86 and .82, taus of .72 and .67 for the terminal and instrumental values respectively).

Third, the Australians appeared to be more successful in judging the own priorities of the New Australians than were the Latvians in judging the own priorities of their Australian peers. For the average terminal value systems the relevant comparisons are rhos of .52 and .65 (taus of .37 and .47) compared with rhos of .30 and .41 (taus of .26 and .28). For the average instrumental value systems the relevant comparisons are rhos of .54 and .65 (taus of .39 and

TABLE 9-5. Median Rankings and Composite Rank Orders of Terminal Values for Latvian and Australian Groups in Relation to Own Priorities and Perceived Priorities of Other Group

| | Latvian Groups | | | | Australian Group | |
| | School Attenders | | School Nonattenders | | | |
Terminal Value	Own	Perceived Australian	Own	Perceived Australian	Own	Perceived New Australian
N	59	51	28	28	51	48
A comfortable life	9.50 (8.5)	5.58 (3)	11.00 (12.5)	5.67 (4)	13.50 (17.5)	9.50 (10)
An exciting life	8.13 (6)	3.93 (1)	8.00 (8)	6.00 (5.5)	10.50 (12)	12.67 (17)
A sense of accomplishment	9.30 (7)	6.63 (5)	8.25 (9)	10.33 (10)	8.21 (8)	9.00 (8.5)
A world at peace	5.25 (3)	5.88 (4)	4.33 (2)	4.67 (2)	3.93 (1)	5.50 (1)
A world of beauty	10.83 (14)	11.63 (14)	11.00 (12.5)	10.67 (11)	10.88 (13)	11.67 (16)
Equality	9.50 (8.5)	8.63 (10)	5.67 (3)	6.50 (7.5)	6.93 (6)	6.20 (5)
Family security	10.06 (12)	12.10 (15.5)	7.00 (6)	13.00 (16)	8.38 (9)	5.75 (3)
Freedom	5.50 (4)	4.30 (2)	4.00 (1)	4.00 (1)	6.17 (4)	6.00 (4)
Happiness	4.79 (2)	7.75 (9)	6.33 (4)	6.50 (7.5)	5.63 (3)	7.00 (6)
Inner harmony	9.70 (11)	11.10 (13)	10.33 (11)	12.00 (13.5)	7.50 (7)	10.00 (11.5)
Mature love	9.56 (10)	6.88 (6)	9.50 (10)	11.00 (12)	8.50 (10)	11.50 (15)
National security	12.70 (16)	14.25 (17)	13.00 (15)	14.00 (17)	13.25 (16)	10.33 (13)
Pleasure	10.75 (13)	7.25 (7)	13.33 (16)	6.00 (5.5)	13.13 (15)	10.60 (14)
Salvation	16.25 (18)	16.19 (18)	13.80 (17)	16.67 (18)	13.50 (17.5)	13.25 (18)
Self-respect	11.70 (15)	12.10 (15.5)	12.33 (14)	12.33 (15)	10.21 (11)	9.00 (8.5)
Social recognition	14.17 (17)	9.08 (11)	14.67 (18)	9.00 (9)	12.50 (14)	8.00 (7)
True friendship	4.75 (1)	7.70 (8)	6.60 (5)	4.80 (3)	4.30 (2)	5.57 (2)
Wisdom	6.75 (5)	9.79 (12)	7.50 (7)	12.00 (13.5)	6.83 (5)	10.00 (11.5)

Note. The lower the median the higher the relative importance of the value. In each column the rank order of each median (low to high) is denoted in parentheses after the median. *N*s are for error-free rankings.
Source: Data are from Feather & Rudzitis, 1974.

TABLE 9-6. Median Rankings and Composite Rank Orders of Instrumental Values for Latvian and Australian Groups in Relation to Own Priorities and Perceived Priorities of Other Group

| | Latvian Groups | | | | Australian Group | |
| | School Attenders | | School Nonattenders | | | |
Instrumental Value	Own	Perceived Australian	Own	Perceived Australian	Own	Perceived New Australian
N	59	53	28	28	52	50
Ambitious	8.38 (7)	6.08 (4)	6.00 (3)	6.00 (3.5)	9.25 (9)	4.25 (1)
Broad-minded	4.13 (1)	4.79 (2)	7.50 (4)	5.00 (2)	7.33 (5.5)	6.50 (4)
Capable	8.75 (9)	7.42 (6)	8.00 (5.5)	7.67 (8.5)	10.00 (11)	7.00 (6)
Cheerful	8.50 (8)	6.38 (5)	9.25 (9)	4.83 (1)	8.00 (8)	10.75 (15)
Clean	10.50 (14)	11.38 (16)	11.00 (15.5)	12.00 (16.5)	11.63 (15)	10.50 (13.5)
Courageous	12.10 (15)	5.75 (3)	11.00 (15.5)	7.67 (8.5)	10.33 (13)	8.50 (7)
Forgiving	7.50 (6)	11.30 (15)	11.00 (15.5)	11.00 (15)	7.33 (5.5)	11.00 (16)
Helpful	9.50 (10)	10.58 (14)	9.50 (10)	9.00 (11)	7.75 (7)	8.75 (8.5)
Honest	5.42 (2)	10.50 (12.5)	5.60 (2)	7.00 (6.5)	5.80 (2)	6.75 (5)
Imaginative	12.50 (16)	9.75 (10)	15.00 (18)	8.33 (10)	13.00 (16.5)	10.50 (13.5)
Independent	9.83 (11)	4.38 (1)	9.00 (8)	6.00 (3.5)	9.40 (10)	6.33 (3)
Intellectual	13.06 (17)	9.83 (11)	10.00 (11.5)	10.00 (12.5)	13.20 (18)	9.75 (11)
Logical	9.93 (12)	10.50 (12.5)	11.00 (15.5)	10.00 (12.5)	11.50 (14)	9.83 (12)
Loving	6.21 (5)	9.30 (9)	8.00 (5.5)	7.00 (6.5)	5.00 (1)	9.33 (10)
Obedient	13.90 (18)	14.50 (18)	10.50 (13)	14.75 (18)	13.00 (16.5)	12.40 (18)
Polite	10.10 (13)	13.56 (17)	8.67 (7)	12.00 (16.5)	10.25 (12)	12.20 (17)
Responsible	5.79 (3)	8.17 (8)	5.00 (1)	6.50 (5)	6.00 (3)	6.00 (2)
Self-controlled	5.92 (4)	7.88 (7)	10.00 (11.5)	10.60 (14)	7.25 (4)	8.75 (8.5)

Note. The lower the median the higher the relative importance of the value. In each column the rank order of each median (low to high) is denoted in parentheses after the median. Ns are for error-free rankings.
Source: Data are from Feather & Rudzitis, 1974.

TABLE 9-7. Similarity Indexes Comparing Median Rankings Across Conditions

	Own Priorities			Perceived Priorities of Other Group		
	1	2	3	4	5	6
Own Priorities						
1. Latvian School Attenders		.86 (.70)	.81 (.67)	.67 (.53)	.69 (.52)	.52 (.37)
2. Latvian School Nonattenders	.68 (.48)		.87 (.66)	.46 (.37)	.52 (.41)	.65 (.47)
3. Australians	.93 (.80)	.63 (.40)		.30 (.26)	.41 (.28)	.70 (.51)
Perceived Priorities of Other						
4. Perceived Australian by (1)	.36 (.26)	.34 (.22)	.25 (.15)		.86 (.72)	.20 (.17)
5. Perceived Australian by (2)	.54 (.42)	.60 (.43)	.46 (.33)	.82 (.67)		.45 (.34)
6. Perceived New Australian by (3)	.54 (.39)	.65 (.48)	.44 (.30)	.71 (.55)	.69 (.62)	

Note. Similarity indexes for average terminal value systems are above the diagonal; similarity indexes for average instrumental value systems are below the diagonal. Similarity indexes not in parentheses are Spearman rhos; similarity indexes in parentheses are Kendall taus. Higher similarity indexes indicate greater similarity between the average value systems involved in the comparison. In the columns, 1 = Average own value priorities of Latvian School attenders, 2 = Average own value priorities of Latvian School nonattenders, 3 = Average own value priorities of Australians, 4 = Average perceived value priorities of Australians by Latvian School attenders, 5 = Average perceived value priorities of Australians by Latvian School nonattenders, 6 = Average perceived value priorities of New Australians by Australians.
Source: Data are from Feather & Rudzitis, 1974.

.48) compared with rhos of .25 and .46 (taus of .15 and .33). In terms of the average priorities of the other, then, the Australians were more accurate judges than were the Latvians.

Fourth, the Australians more accurately perceived the own priorities of the Latvian school nonattenders than those of the Latvian school attenders. The relevant comparisons are rhos of .65 and .65 (taus of .47 and .48) for the terminal and instrumental values, compared with rhos of .52 and .54 (taus of .37 and .39). Correspondingly, the Latvian school nonattenders more accurately perceived the own priorities of the Australians than did the Latvian school attenders. The relevant comparisons are rhos of .41 and .46 (taus of .28 and .33) for the terminal and instrumental values respectively, compared with rhos of .30 and .25 (taus of .26 and .15). Both of these results suggest greater assimilation of the Latvian school nonattenders if one uses *accuracy of perception of the other's values* as an index of degree of assimilation.

ANALYSIS OF SINGLE VALUES

So far we have been concerned with the degree of similarity between average value systems. As in the other studies that have been discussed, differences in the relative importance of particular values across conditions were investigated, using the analysis of variance applied to the transformed rankings. The significant findings from a series of these analyses have been presented by Feather and Rudzitis (1974). Certain consistent patterns of results may be summarized here. When respondents' own rankings were compared with those they assigned to the values of the other group (Australian or New Australian), there was a consistent tendency to upgrade the importance they assumed the others would assign to *a comfortable life, pleasure,* and *social recognition* when compared with their own priorities. They also tended to downgrade the importance they assumed the others would assign to *wisdom* and being *polite* and *self-controlled* in comparison with their own priorities (see Tables 9.5 and 9.6). Apparently, the respondents tended to regard others as being more concerned with the good life and with being approved of, and less concerned with a mature understanding of life, with courtesy, and with restraint than they were themselves. However, while the Latvians perceived *family security* as less important for their Australian peers than for themselves, the Australians perceived *family security* as more important for New Australians than for themselves. Thus, there was common recognition of the importance of *family security* for migrant groups, a basic source of security for migrants adjusting to a new society.

When the rankings of the perceived values of the other group were compared to the rankings of own values actually assigned by that group, a considerable amount of misperception was evident, particularly by the Latvian groups and more so by the Saturday school attenders. This result is not surprising, given the differences in similarity indexes we have described previously. Both groups of Latvians assigned greater importance to the following values for their Australian peers than the Australians did themselves in their own rankings: *a comfortable life, an exciting life, pleasure,* and being *imaginative.* The Latvians assigned lower importance to the following values for their Australian peers than the Australians did themselves in their own rankings: *family security, inner harmony, salvation, wisdom,* and being *forgiving.* Some other discrepancies or "errors" in perception were not shared by both groups, and these were especially in evidence in the Latvian group of Saturday school attenders. For example, this group tended to exaggerate the importance for their Australian peers of *social recognition,* and of being *courageous* and *independent.* But they underestimated the importance for their Australian peers of *true friendship* and of being *honest.* Again these differences can be seen by reference to Tables 9.5 and 9.6.

The Australian respondents assigned greater importance to the following values for New Australian peers than both groups of Latvians did themselves in their own rankings: *social recognition* and being *courageous.* They assigned lower importance for their New Australian peers than both groups of Latvians did themselves in their own rankings to *an exciting life* and *wisdom.* Again there were discrepancies or "errors" in perception not applying to both Latvian groups, but especially evident in comparisons involving the Latvian school attenders. For example, the own priorities of this group were particularly discrepant from the priorities assigned by the Australian respondents to their New Australian peers in regard to being *ambitious* (overestimated in importance by the Australians) and being *forgiving* (underestimated in importance by the Australians).

Finally, simple one-way analyses of variance of the transformed rankings for each value across the three groups (Latvian school attenders and non-attenders and the Australians) in regard to *own* priorities showed a complete absence of significant differences (setting a conservative alpha level of .01 for significance) for both individual terminal and individual instrumental values. Thus, not only were the average value systems fairly similar across the three groups when own priorities were involved (see Table 9.7) but the average rankings (transformed) for *each* value were also rather similar when respondents provided their own priorities of importance.

ANALYSIS OF QUESTIONNAIRE ITEMS

The results so far reported have concerned value systems and particular values. Table 9.8 compares the Latvian school attenders with the Latvian school nonattenders on several of the items from the Latvian version of the questionnaire, and includes the results of simple one-way analyses of variance of the item scores. As noted on page 253 for each item (scored 1 to 5) a higher

TABLE 9-8. **Percentage of Respondents for Different Categories of Assimilation and Mean Item Scores of Latvian Saturday School Attenders and Nonattenders on Items from Questionnaire**

	Percentage of Respondents for Different Item Categories					Mean Item Score	Significance Level (p)
Item	Assimilation: 1 Low	2	3	4	5 High		
Ethnic Identity							
Perceived by Self							
School attenders	1.6	44.0	35.5	16.9	1.6	2.73	<.001
School nonattenders	0.0	10.7	21.4	50.0	17.8	3.75	
Perceived by Parents							
School attenders	28.8	42.3	15.2	11.8	1.6	2.15	<.001
School nonattenders	10.7	14.2	21.4	32.1	21.4	3.39	
Perceived by Friends							
School attenders	1.6	22.0	30.5	33.8	11.8	3.32	<.001
School nonattenders	0.0	3.5	10.7	35.7	50.0	4.32	
Ethnic Identification							
School attenders	10.3	31.0	41.4	13.8	3.4	2.69	<.01
School nonattenders	3.5	14.2	42.8	7.1	32.1	3.50	
Ethnic Origins of Friends							
School attenders	0.0	15.5	46.6	31.0	6.9	3.29	<.001
School nonattenders	0.0	3.5	7.1	67.8	21.4	4.07	
Ethnic Language Ability							
School attenders	28.8	44.0	22.0	5.0	0.0	2.03	<.001
School nonattenders	0.0	10.7	28.5	10.7	50.0	4.00	
Preference							
School attenders	3.3	8.4	30.5	52.5	5.0	3.47	<.001
School nonattenders	0.0	0.0	3.5	32.1	64.2	4.61	

Note. For details of the low-to-high, 1-to-5 columns, see page 253.
Source: Data are from Feather & Rudzitis, 1974.

score represents increased assimilation in the Australian direction. It is apparent from Table 9.8 that the Latvian school nonattenders showed more evidence of assimilation over all of the items. In regard to *ethnic identity* they were more likely to see themselves as toward the Australian pole and thought that their parents and friends would see them that way too. They were more likely to express a preference for being toward the Australian pole (*ethnic identification*), and to state that they had more Australian than Latvian friends (*ethnic origins of friends*). They were also more likely to indicate low ability in speaking Latvian (*language ability*) and to prefer to speak English rather than Latvian (*language preference*).

Among the Latvian school nonattenders 82 percent of the group memberships reported were Australian compared with 38 percent by the Latvian school attenders. All of the Australian respondents reported memberships with Australian groups. Among the Latvian school nonattenders, 36 percent stated they would prefer to live in countries other than Australia. The corresponding percentages for the Latvian school attenders and the Australian respondents were 56 percent and 35 percent respectively. All of these differences supported the expectation that Latvian school nonattenders would be more assimilated in the Australian direction.

ANALYSIS OF AUSTRALIANISM AND CONSERVATISM SCORES

Finally, simple one-way analyses of variance showed that the two Latvian groups and the Australian group did not differ significantly in regard to Australianism or conservatism scores (see Table 9.9), although the Australian-

TABLE 9-9. Mean Australianism and Conservatism Scores of Latvian and Australian Respondents

Test	Means			Significance Level
	Latvian School Attenders	*Latvian School Nonattenders*	*Australians*	*p*
Conservatism	36.64	39.32	37.75	N.S.
Australianism	28.58	30.29	31.94	N.S.

Note. N.S. means "not statistically significant".
Source: Data are from Feather & Rudzitis, 1974.

ism means were in the expected direction. Taft (1965, p. 80) reports mean Australianism scores of 35.6, 26.4, and 22.0 for the following respective samples: 61 Australian-born male foremanship trainees; 75 male Dutch migrants in Australia from 5 to 9 years; and 42 "assorted" migrants enrolled in a Victorian adult education course. The means in Table 9.9 are well within this range. The mean conservatism scores reported in the table are also quite similar to those obtained for children tested in the 1972 Adelaide survey (Chapter 6; Table 6.8).

DISCUSSION OF RESULTS

When we examine all these results as a whole the picture that develops is of two groups varying in degree of assimilation—the group of Latvians who did not attend Saturday schools being further along the path of assimilation than the group of Latvians who did. This greater degree of assimilation was evident both in its more visible forms (such as membership in groups, country of preference, ethnic origin of friends, language ability and preference) and in its more subtle and private aspects (such as perception of ethnic identity and identification). In terms of our earlier discussion of stages of assimilation, the Latvian school nonattenders showed more acculturation, more identificational assimilation, and more evidence of structural assimilation. Those Latvians who did attend or who had attended Saturday schools had not advanced as far through Gordon's levels of assimilation, nor for that matter were they as far along the road in terms of the analyses of Eisenstadt or Taft discussed earlier. They were more likely to possess bilingual skills and to prefer using the Latvian language; more likely to be formally associated with Latvian groups and organizations and, within more informal networks, with their Latvian friends; more likely to perceive themselves as Latvian and to see their parents (especially) and their friends (less firmly) as perceiving them as Latvian; and more likely to prefer being Latvian.

Yet, as we have just seen, the results revealed a paradox. Both Latvian groups were similar to each other and to Australians of their own age regarding social and political attitudes or opinions as indicated by the Australianism and Conservatism scales and in regard to the average rankings assigned to terminal and instrumental values on the Rokeach Value Survey when the respondents ranked the values according to their own priorities. In the Ukrainian study we also found that the average own value systems of young second-generation migrants were very similar to those of a group of Australians of comparable age (see Table 9.3). But it is still a puzzle why the two Latvian groups were similar to each other on measures of their own opinions and values but so different in other respects, as indicated by their responses to the tailored items on the questionnaire.

One answer to the puzzle may involve subtle differences in procedure. The response alternatives for the tailored items usually referred to host and migrant groups. Hence, on these items the question of assimilation was very focal and the expected differences between groups were obtained. In contrast, on the Australianism and Conservatism scales respondents were not asked to compare themselves with other groups (Australian or New Australian). Nor was their initial response to the Value Survey one involving comparison with other groups because respondents first had to rank their own values. Only subsequently did they rank the values of the other group and this requirement was not foreshadowed in the instructions. Therefore, when respondents were ordering the values in terms of their own priorities, comparison with another group was not focal. Future studies could make these comparisons more focal by deliberately setting respondents the task of relating themselves to other groups. For example, they might be asked to tell whether they considered a particular value was more important for themselves than for the host group, about the same in importance for both, or less important for themselves than for the host group.

Even with changes in methodology, however, one might still find that the similarities outweighed the differences in regard to attitudes and average value systems. Recently, Johnston (1972) has shown that Polish, British, and German second-generation immigrants in Perth (Western Australia) seem to have rapidly assimilated to their host society and appear to function less as a "bridge generation" with a distinctive subculture than do similar groups in North America.

But it would be wrong to conclude at this point that the Latvian groups responded to the Value Survey in the same way. There were indeed subtle differences between the two Latvian groups in subjective assimilation, but at the level of how *accurately* migrant and host groups could perceive the other group's values. Overall, as we have seen, the Australians were better judges of New Australian average own value systems than the Latvians were of Australian average own value systems. And, as we have also noted, the Latvian school nonattenders were more accurate judges of Australian values than were the Latvian school attenders. Moreover, the Australians were more accurate judges of New Australian values when their average judgments were related to the own value systems of the Latvian school nonattenders than to those of the Latvian school attenders. It is likely that the greater social interaction of the Latvian school nonattenders, as shown in the greater frequency of Australian friends they had (Table 9.8), provided more opportunity for these Latvians and their Australian peers to learn about each others' attitudes and values leading to more accurate reciprocal perceptions of value systems. The Latvian school attenders, on the other hand, further removed from Australian society, might have been more willing to echo stereotyped viewpoints about Australians passed on to them by their families and the ethnic groups to which they belonged, views that were more likely to be inaccurate.

It is probable, of course, that the young Australian would misperceive the actual value priorities of his own society to some extent, and that the young Latvian would also misperceive the actual priorities of his own Latvian peers. Stereotyped views of national characteristics are common in societies and are not always easy to disconfirm, given the fact that one's experience with people and groups is usually restricted to a limited sample. It was not possible to obtain information on the perceived priorities of one's own society (Australian or Latvian) in the present study, though such information would be useful in the future.

The Latvian study just described shows one way in which inaccurate perceptions of the values of others may come about and one would expect these inaccuracies to become even more pronounced as segregation of the migrant group from the host society increased. The segregation in the Latvian study was mild and based upon the preservation of national identity. It simply involved attendance at an ethnic school once a week. But segregation can be much more pronounced, as in some large American cities where blacks and whites still attend schools that are basically separate. In these cases the black child in a segregated school may grow up with false perceptions of the values and other characteristics of his white peers, and the white child in a segregated school may similarly develop inaccurate perceptions of his black peers—simply because neither group has had the opportunity to interact with the other in realistic settings. This type of educational experience at school ill equips children to deal with the realities of life once they leave school and work in the wider context of society. Exactly the same argument has been used against separate education of the sexes (see Chapter 5) and to justify coeducation, and it is equally applicable to other characteristics (such as race) that differentiate people. One hopes that, in educating the young, opportunities will be provided for them to learn about other people on the basis of face-to-face interaction. In that way their judgments have some basis in reality and are not distortions formed in an artificially segregated environment. These issues are important because a great deal of social unrest involves action based upon inaccurate and oversimplified views of reality.

ASSIMILATION AND ACCURACY OF JUDGMENT

Programmatic research has the advantage of providing the opportunity for replication of previous findings, as we have seen throughout this book. Also, each successive study often raises new questions and suggests new procedures that might be used in future investigations. We have already noted some implications that issue from the Latvian study. Now we turn to some additional general considerations.

Future studies of subjective assimilation, in which immigrants make judgments about the beliefs, attitudes, and values of both groups and individuals within their host society—or about the host society itself—would do well to include procedures that enable the *accuracy* of these judgments to be checked. The same need to obtain "objective" measures has been mentioned in previous chapters—for example, in regard to the school situation, the values of parents and siblings, and so on. In the context of assimilation studies, the degree to which judgments about aspects of the host society are accurate may be an important index of degree of assimilation. Veridical or accurate judgments should become more frequent both as acculturation progresses and as the migrant moves into more and more groups within the host society, becoming acquainted with more and more people.

One would expect other indexes of assimilation to correlate with accuracy of judgments, particularly when the judgments relate to rather subtle and complex aspects of the host society. Measures of personal adjustment, as indexed by the frequency of emotional disorders, suicide rates, family upheaval, and so on, may be related to how accurately the migrant has come to know his host society in its various aspects. This is so for a variety of reasons. A new environment often appears strange and threatening, frustrating and difficult. It is inevitable that in the early stages a newcomer will make mistakes in adjusting to the new situation in which he finds himself. But the only way to eliminate the errors that occur is for him to interact with the new environment in its many physical and social aspects. In this way novel information is received and processed, new cognitive structures are developed, and old ways of thinking are modified. Gradually, as the environment becomes known with increasing accuracy, new meanings are acquired and mistakes that were made in the early stages of adjustment become less frequent. This process cannot continue if the immigrant retreats from the new environment and isolates himself from its social groups and institutions. He then becomes a stranger in alien territory, not part of the host society and no longer a member of the old one, rootless because the new soil has not been explored and assimilated, a misfit because the essential learning about a new environment has not occurred. In such instances judgments about the host society may be seriously in error. Moreover, the anxiety and despair that accompany social isolation and anomie may be reflected in distorted perceptions that are a function of personal fears and wishes rather than accurate reflections of reality.

This grim picture of the rootless immigrant has probably been overdrawn. Yet many first-generation migrants come to know very little about their host society. They retain their native language, modes of dress, past habits, and so on, and they receive support from primary groups whose members come from the same country and live in close proximity in the same city area. They may be relatively happy in this shared community of people with similar backgrounds and ways of thinking, leaving it to their children, the second-generation immigrants, to move into the host society and assimilate its characteristics. Thus, one would expect measures of poor adjustment and evidence of inaccurate perception of characteristics of the host society to be positively related when migrants lack primary groups to which they can relate—either groups involving migrants like themselves, people from the host community, or both.

The possibility of using accuracy of judgment as an index of the degree of assimilation extends beyond the area of migrant assimilation to any situation in which a person is confronted with a new environment. When a child moves to a new school, a person takes a new job, two people get married, a new environment is entered. To make accurate judgments about it does not necessarily mean, however, that a person likes the new situation and is satisfied with it. As we saw in Chapter 4, measures of happiness and satisfaction with a specific environment relate to how well one's own personal characteristics match those that the environment is seen to demand or promote. It would be important, however, to discover how far this relationship is a function of the degree to which the measure of goodness of fit involves realistic estimates and is not a serious distortion. One's successful adaptation must take account of the realities of life. A realistic measure of goodness of fit would depend upon how accurately a person could judge both his own characteristics and the commensurable aspects of the environment in question.

Measures that permitted the accuracy of respondents' judgments to be checked would not present a problem when it came to characteristics that are publicly observable and easily specifiable. For example, a migrant's judgment that he can speak the language of his host society fluently and with good knowledge of its idiom is not too difficult to verify. But a problem does exist when judgments about abstract and subtle aspects of self and of the social environment are involved. How can one tell, for example, that a person's judgments about his own values and the values of others are accurate pronouncements about the real state of affairs?

One answer to this question is to observe behavior in relevant situations. If a person claims *equality* takes precedence over other values, for example, is his dedication to it demonstrated in the way he acts in situations where equality is a basic consideration? Does he act in a consistent manner to promote equality? Or do his actions belie his verbal statements? In the same way one can check the accuracy of his judgments about other people by seeing what they do in situations where one would expect the relevant attribute being judged to be an important influence on behavior. Such an approach necessitates assumptions about how what is being judged (values or whatever) would influence what people do in concrete situations. And this process is by no means a simple one to conceptualize because beliefs, attitudes, and values often bear complex relationships to actual behavior.

In judgments about others, the others themselves can be asked to report their own beliefs, attitudes, values, or whatever it is that is the object of concern. Then the judgments *about* others can be related to the judgments made *by* them in order to check on accuracy. In the Latvian study, for example, not only did we obtain judgments from the Latvian respondents about the value priorities they believed Australians of their own age to have, but we also asked the Australians what indeed their own value priorities were. We could then relate perceived rankings to actual rankings.

Similar procedures have been used by Newcomb (1961, 1963) in testing his A-B-X model of systems of orientations, in the context of the acquaintance process. Orientations correspond to attitudes and attractions—to evaluative relations in a general sense. According to Newcomb (1961):

> *La condition humaine,* as we view it, is such that individuals continually face a three-pronged problem of adaptation. Each of us must somehow come to terms, simultaneously, with the other individuals and groups of which our interpersonal environment is constituted, with the world that we have in common with those persons and groups, and with our own, intrapersonal

autistic demands. Were it not for this ever-present triple confrontation, problems of strain and balance would not arise. (p. 259)

Single orientations in individual and collective systems may change under the impact of new information from the environment (*reality* forces). The systems themselves are under constant influence to remain stable so that strain and imbalance are kept to a minimum (*balance* forces). Consequently, the development of interpersonal attraction is seen by Newcomb as a complex product of preexisting orientations and information exchange in which the participants discover the extent to which their attitudes toward mutually relevant and important issues and toward other persons are similar. The *system* of attitudinal relations or orientations involving self (A), other (B), and object (X) may be modified by reality forces, but it retains its tendency toward stability and balance, although the situation is complicated if the interpersonal relations are negative (Newcomb, 1968). Systems of orientations are therefore influenced by new information and are subject to the internal cognitive dynamics of the individual in the service of the achievement of stable structures. Presumably, the system components correspond more accurately to reality as the person processes more and more relevant information. Newcomb's results did in fact indicate that his subjects tended to become more accurate in their judgments of others over time as acquaintance progressed (Newcomb, 1961).

Accuracy of knowledge about the host society, then, may turn out to be a useful index of a migrant's degree of assimilation, both at the external (or easily observable) level and at the level of internal or subjective assimilation. It should be positively related to measures of both acculturation and structural assimilation. Under certain conditions already discussed, inaccurate judgments about the host society may also be accompanied by evidence of poor personal adjustment. Yet a person can make quite accurate judgments about his host society in its various aspects, but not yet feel identified with it. His primary identification is elsewhere; he still feels he belongs to the country he left. In time, however, this identification may change, given increased opportunities for social interaction through structural or institutional dispersion and the likely consequent modification of the migrant's beliefs, attitudes, and values toward those of his host society. In general, therefore, one would expect the various indexes of assimilation to correlate positively, an increase in one (say, structural assimilation) being accompanied by an increase in another (say, accuracy in judgment).

THE VALUE-DISCREPANCY MATRIX

It follows from the preceding discussion that future studies of the individual in relation to his various social environments would profit by including both "subjective" and "objective" measures, investigating both the perceived and actual situation, the *beta* press and the *alpha* press (Murray, 1938). In the case of values, procedures could be designed that enabled a *value-discrepancy matrix* to be constructed, a matrix that summarized the discrepancies between a person's judgments of his own value priorities, his judgments about the value systems of others in the defined social environment, their judgments of his value priorities, and the actual value systems of these others as reported by themselves.

An important part of the procedure in developing this value-discrepancy matrix would be specifying who is to be included from the person's social field. Clearly, the individuals or groups should be known to the person making the judgments about them, and they in turn should also be familiar with him to enable reciprocal judgments to be made. Hence, an initial task would be the careful analysis of the structure of the social environment under consideration in order to discover its various agents of influence within it, and which of these influences are the important ones for the person. Agents of influence outside of the immediate social environment being considered might also be included, for some of these outside agents may serve as important reference groups.

The analysis of such matrices should assist our understanding of the individual's assimilation to and satisfaction with the various social environments he encounters in his daily life. It should also provide useful information about the degree of concordance in value systems and the clustering of value systems within social environments.

CONCLUDING REMARKS

This discussion of the two studies of assimilation from the Flinders program concludes the actual presentation of research findings from this program. In the next and final chapter, we will attempt to summarize the main contributions that have emerged from this series of studies. We will also examine some aspects of the assessment procedure and we will discuss some further theoretical issues.

10. Recapitulation and Final Discussion

IN THIS FINAL CHAPTER we take up certain general theoretical considerations. But before doing so, it is appropriate to recapitulate some of the theoretical and methodological points that have been raised in the preceding chapters and to summarize some of the major findings.

RECAPITULATION

THE VALUE SURVEY

The program of research that has been described has dealt mainly with the *cognitive* domain, with the world of thought and feeling as expressed in the order of priorities assigned to values by respondents and in their responses to various questionnaires on attitudes. We have said little about the world of *action*, of behavior in concrete situations. That is a deficiency we will attempt to remedy later in this chapter. The world of action brings us face to face with the problem of deciding upon a conceptual framework for the analysis of motivated behavior.

Within the cognitive domain we have focused upon values and, secondarily, upon more specific attitudes and beliefs. Rokeach's discussion of the nature of values was taken as a useful starting point to clarify the major concepts and to introduce the primary method of assessment—the Value Survey (Rokeach, 1973). This approach to the measurement of values and value systems was adopted as the best procedure currently available for our purposes.

The decision to use the Value Survey was made in full realization that, like most forms of psychological assessment, it poses questions and presents limitations. For example, it constrains subjects to a standard set of items (values) rather than requiring them to describe their own values without constraint. Some would consider this restriction an advantage—especially in those comparative studies where it is appropriate to use the Value Survey as a common yardstick. Others would argue that the procedure might suggest values to respondents that are not part of their cognitive world—values that they have not given much thought to previously. That is, certain values on the lists may not exist in any "psychological" sense for a person until his attention is drawn to them, and his responses to these values might therefore be artificial. As we noted, the Value Survey's ipsative quality creates certain difficulties in data analysis. Also, respondents may resent having to rank values in a linear order without being allowed to assign equal ranks to some of them. And some people might consider that important values have been left off the lists, whereas others might object to the defining phrases. Moreover, to increase the reliability of measurement, one might prefer that the Value Survey had more items relating to each value rather than only one verbal label plus a defining phrase. The usefulness of distinguishing between terminal and instrumental values might also be questioned, just as one might be curious about the range of meanings the same value label elicits for different people. And one might wonder about the degree to which responses can be affected by social desirability and situational demands.

Indeed, some research workers may prefer to work with other sets of values that also span a wide range. At present, however, the main alternative assessment procedures to Rokeach's cover only a limited set of values. For example, the Allport-Vernon-Lindzey "Study of Values" measures the relative strength of only six basic values: theoretical, economic, aesthetic, social, political, and religious, suggested by Spranger's *Types of Men* (1928)—see Allport, Vernon, and Lindzey (1951).

It can be argued, however, that some self-descriptive tests that were designed to measure other variables, such as needs, are in fact tapping value priorities in a fairly comprehensive way. The Edwards Personal Preference Schedule (EPPS) was based upon Murray's (1938) classification of human needs. Atkinson and Litwin (1960), however, have contended that it may in fact be measuring values rather than needs, providing information about the relative value assigned by respondents to achievement, deference, order, exhibition, autonomy, affiliation, and so on.

The general question of how one arrives at a set of basic values and which appropriate values to include in this taxonomy can be answered only after careful theoretical and empirical inquiry. Such an inquiry would compare alternative ways of classifying values with respect to how well they can be integrated into theoretical systems that enable a comprehensive account of the role of values at the personal and social level. Some value classifications may be more fertile than others, both theoretically and empirically, permitting the development of clearly stated theories that can be applied to a wide range of phenomena. New values may be added to these taxonomies contingent upon their success in improving the power of explanation.

The formulation of the initial lists would depend upon one's theoretical proclivities and on the range of phenomena one is interested in accounting for. Some lists of values, for example, may be closer to the person pole than to the social pole, concerned more with the dynamics of human personality than with the analysis of social process. Values corresponding to Murray's (1938) list of needs would carry with them this relative focus upon personal concerns. Rokeach's lists, however, are less oriented toward the person pole because they include many social values as well. Indeed, Rokeach (1973, p. 25) argues that one should be able to compile a comprehensive list of values by identifying the major institutions within a society and their role in the maintenance, enhancement, and transmission of values. Further, Rokeach's lists contain other theoretical distinctions (such as that between terminal and instrumental values) relating to a general framework concerned with belief systems, just as other lists of values are usually presented within the context of an overall system (as with the Allport-Vernon-Lindzey classification). Clearly, one's theoretical commitments constrain the final taxonomies that emerge.

These various issues suggest future areas of theoretical and empirical inquiry, some of which would pertain to the Value Survey itself. Yet for all that we would endorse Rokeach's (1973) conclusion about it that

> the instrument that has been developed to measure values is simple and economical and can be employed to describe the values of virtually all people who can read at a certain minimal level of proficiency. (p. 323)

We can appeal to an old pragmatic aphorism: "The proof of the pudding is in the eating." The Value Survey has turned out to be a very useful instrument in many different contexts, as is attested to by the impressive range of studies reported by Rokeach in *The Nature of Human Values* and by the program of research described in the present monograph. Moreover, we have found it especially useful in its present form for studying a person's own value systems in relation to *attributed* value systems—and that was a further important reason for our decision to use it. No doubt it can be built upon and improved as an assessment device. But we leave that task to others.

STRUCTURAL DISCREPANCY AND PERSON-ENVIRONMENT FIT

Our stance has differed from Rokeach's. We have been more concerned with investigating values and value systems within a general theoretical framework that emphasizes a person's adaptation to the various environments to which he may be exposed and his attempts to resolve discrepancies between his own personal characteristics and commensurate environmental characteristics perceived to be present in the immediate situation. It was assumed that persons tend to seek environments that best fit their own personal characteristics and that they are more likely to feel happy and satisfied with such environments than would be the case if there was a significant degree of mismatch.

It was recognized that the range of environments from which a person can select is usually limited by many factors outside of his control but that, within that range, there should be a tendency for him to gravitate toward the best person-environment fit where discrepancies are kept to a minimum. This general approach has an analogue in the interest shown by students of animal behavior in the question of species' selection of and adaption to natural habitats. In this literature the Darwinian principle of natural selection is invoked along with other mechanisms that allow for the effects of experience.

An approach that emphasizes the match between organism and environment implies the need to specify the boundaries of the environment being considered. As far as humans are concerned, is it the family situation, the school situation, the work situation, and so on? Can the environment be clearly defined and distinguished from other environments? In research with humans is it the objective environment discovered by a procedure entailing public observation and consensus or is it the perceived environment, the situation as structured and reported by the individual? Having defined the particular environment under consideration, one then needs to conduct a careful analysis of organismic and environmental characteristics with a view to identifying those that are *commensurate* and can be related, using the concept of goodness of fit. We noted that several properties of both person and situation can usually be abstracted. These include personal needs and the situational resources pertinent to these, personal abilities and the situational requirements that must be met, and at a higher level of analysis personal values and the opportunities the environment provides for satisfying these values. Finally, in investigating adaptation in terms of person-environment fit, it is essential to go beyond the molar principle and to identify the underlying processes involved. Adaptation poses a question that has to be answered by detailed consideration of how an organism learns, how it is motivated, how it perceives the world around it, how it thinks, and so on. If this final step is not taken, the appeal to organism-environment fit as an explanatory principle is specious and empty.

In our program of research we have focused upon the value systems that people report to be their own and the value systems that they attribute to particular environments (for example, the school situation). These two commensurate sets of values were related to one another to determine their degree of similarity, that is, how closely the priorities matched. We chose to investigate values because they are ubiquitous concepts, appearing in conceptual analyses from many different areas of social science and human concern, and because they enable integration to be achieved between the individual and society. As we have just noted, there are other properties of persons and environments that could be investigated, some of which may be more basic and more crucial for selection and adaptation than values. We think in particular of the primary needs and the built-in capacities and acquired skills of organisms in relation to the resources and difficulties that environments provide. Values are higher-order concepts than these. They are products of a considerable amount of experience in social interaction and of exposure to sources of information. But they are also key concepts in social inquiry.

In dealing with defined environments we recognized that a person exists in overlapping situations. His environments include both physical and social objects, and these environments can be considered objectively, using agreed-upon measures, or subjectively from the point of view of the person. We decided to concentrate upon the *perceived* environment rather than the objective environment in the belief that it is important to deal with the meanings that individuals assign to stimulus input, in this case with the value priorities they perceived as being promoted by the environments they were asked to consider. It was recognized, however, that to complete the picture one would need to obtain information about the *objective* environment or, more accurately, about those sources in the environment that influenced the sorts of attributed value priorities that individuals provided. We were not able to undertake this task ourselves, however; we were not able to chart those environmental sources of information that affect the way in which a person perceives environmental value systems. Given the resources and time available, we concentrated mainly upon attributed value systems. But clearly the task of filling in the links should be undertaken in the future. One does not want to encapsulate the research within individual "life-spaces." One also wants to discover how the perceived environment came to be that way.

ABSTRACT AND PERCEIVED STRUCTURES

With this general approach it was possible to consider the concept of person-environment fit and its relationship to choice of environment and personal adjustment in terms of certain concepts that had been developed previously. These concepts relate to the ways in which cognitive structures become organized and the effects of discrepancies between them (Feather, 1971*a*). In this earlier work, which was an outcome of a long program of studies applying the principle of balance (Heider, 1958) to the analysis of communication effects, causal attribution, and recall (see Feather, 1967*b*, 1969*b*, 1970*a*, for representative publications), the person is viewed as an active processor of information, seeking to achieve order and stability from complex information input. As a result of this processing of information the person is assumed to develop organized cognitive structures or schemata that are abstract summaries of experience, relatively stable over time, but modifiable in the face of new information.

These abstractions from reality, or *abstract structures* as they are called, are assumed to serve as basic underlying referent structures having an "oughtness" quality about them. For instance, a person might develop a model of what typically occurs when people react to communications or how people usually attribute causation for success or failure (Feather, 1969*a*, 1971*a*). These models are assumed to function as normative theories about what ought to be the case, to be abstractions that capture the "common thread" running through many discrete but related experiences (as in interpersonal communication situations or achievement situations where causal inference is involved). In the examples provided in the earlier paper (Feather, 1971*a*), the abstract structures were assumed to be *balanced* according to Heider's principle, but we recognized that other forms of cognitive organization may also occur.

It should be obvious that the concept of abstract structures applies to both the physical and social environments and the way in which experience with them is represented cognitively. Abstract structures are seen as transcending particular situations which, while not identical, have some general characteristics in common (for example, they incorporate reactions to communications, ascriptions of causality, perception of certain physical properties, or whatever). Though abstract structures are considered to be relatively stable they are not seen as invariant. Rather, it is assumed that they are subject to modification in the light of persistent discrepant input and that they become more finely articulated with wider ranges of experience.

This general cognitive approach also assumes that information coming in from the environment at any given time will be perceived as organized and that the *perceived structure* arising from stimulus input will be checked against the corresponding transituational abstract structure. In many cases, both structures will coincide and the individual will not experience strain. In the physical world of objects, for example, one sees a picture hanging straight on a wall and that perception is congruent with the general expectation or abstraction that pictures should hang straight and not be askew. In other cases, however, discrepancies may arise between perceived structures and underlying abstract structures. In the social world of communication, a highly respected and well-liked information source delivers, apparently of his own free will, a communication on a mutually relevant issue that is diametrically opposed to one's own viewpoint. Cases such as these involve cognitive discrepancies between perceived and abstract structures. These discrepancies are usually accompanied by some experienced strain and by attempts to resolve them.

A number of possible ways that a person might use to resolve these cognitive discrepancies were noted. The resolution might be achieved by cognitive adjustments in which the perceived structure was somehow modified, if indeed such modification can take place. In the physical world, perceptions tied to physical objects would be difficult to modify or reinterpret. One cannot change one's perception of a picture that hangs crookedly on the wall even though the sight of it is discordant. In the social world, however, it is often easier to reinterpret immediate reality. The trusted communicator who sends dissonant information may be seen as coerced to do so or his message may be reinterpreted so that it fits existing cognitions within the form of organization that has been established.

In other cases resolution of discrepancies might be achieved by changes in the basic abstract structures as these discrepancies persist or recur. Or they might be resolved by overt action, such as seeking new information or getting out of a particular situation. These possible modes of resolution were discussed in a previous paper (Feather, 1971*b*) and related forms of adjustment have been dealt with in theories that assume individuals prefer cognitive consistency—such as balance theory, dissonance theory, symbolic psychologic theory, and congruity theory (for an extensive review of these approaches see Abelson et al., 1968).

Within the context of this general approach it was possible to view the value systems reported by people as their own as *abstract* structures and the value systems they attributed to particular environments as *perceived* structures. One could then examine the extent of discrepancy between these two sets of value systems (own and perceived) and speculate about ways in which discrepancies might be experienced and resolved in real situations. The research that we reported focused upon educational choice and educational adjustment, using students from secondary and tertiary institutions. Evidence showed that students tended to select educational environments that were congruent with their own value systems, and that they were more likely to be happier and more satisfied with these environments as congruence increased. The problem of value change was also considered in relation to the resolution of cognitive discrepancies, although the research reported was not explicitly designed to test the speculations that emerged from this discussion.

SOME THEORETICAL QUALIFICATIONS

We noted qualifications to this broad theoretical approach along the way, recognizing that we were using discrepancy theory in a very general manner as a sort of framework to which we could relate sections of our research program. It is clear, for instance, that one's choice of environments and one's satisfaction with a defined environment are related to many factors of which the value match is only one. As we pointed out the value match is probably less important than some other commensurate characteristics of persons and environments that should be congruent if successful adjustment is to be achieved. Moreover, the discovery of a relationship between the degree of value match and other dependent variables should be taken not as the end of the inquiry but as a starting point for further investigation of what factors might underlie the relationship. In the case of the generally low correlations obtained between degree of value match and reported happiness and satisfaction, for example, one could argue that part of the positive affect comes from the fact that some consistency or lack of discrepancy has been achieved. Hence the strain that is assumed to be associated with inconsistent or discrepant states of affairs is reduced. But we certainly do not mean to imply that the comfort of consistency is the only factor involved. Probably more important is the fact that in a value-congruent environment the individual can expect his important values to be supported and satisfied. What he values tends to be confirmed and rewarded. His value-related actions are reinforced. And of course other explanations of the positive relationship may be valid. Thus, our general framework does not hold up consistency as the sovereign principle underlying relationships between the value match and other dependent variables. It is likely to be only one of many factors that produce the relationships, and perhaps not a particularly important one.

We have noted certain other qualifications to our use of the principle of person-environment fit, a principle that we have explored at the cognitive level in relation to discrepancy theory. In the first place, it is possible that minor discrepancies between own and perceived value systems may be motivating in themselves, the individual being attracted to situations that are slightly novel or different. The likelihood of selecting the slightly discrepant situation rather than the perfect match would depend upon how far one had to sacrifice the possibility of satisfying important values, however. One might be willing to follow one's curiosity when discrepancies pertained to relatively unimportant values, but not those central to the self.

A second qualification is that to assume that value systems attributed to the environment may be treated as perceived structures may be an oversimplification. Where a person reports on his work situation or the school environment, for example, he may be reporting fairly general and stable views of the environment that are based upon a good deal of experience and that are relatively resistant to change. As such, these attributed value systems may be more in the nature of abstract structures. Thus, the research that we described comparing own value systems with the perceived value systems of the school may perhaps be conceptualized more accurately as involving discrepancies between abstract structures relating to the person and abstract structures relating to the defined environment.

Third, we noted that a person exists in a number of environments, some of them overlapping. The dissatisfactions that come from a poor value match in one situation (such as the work environment) may be compensated for by satisfactions arising elsewhere (as within the family situation). A person may tolerate some degree of mismatch in values in a situation because other characteristics (for example, abilities and job requirements) fit together well and are associated with positive rewards, absence of negative sanctions, and so on.

Fourth, choice of and adjustment to environments take place in a context that includes factors (both facilitating and inhibiting) over which a person has little or no control. One does not have unlimited choice, for instance, but is restricted to a range of alternatives that has to do with such factors as economic means, geographical location, and so on. The selective migration to a new environment that better fits one's personal characteristics, then, is often just not possible.

Fifth, it was recognized that some discrepancies are more significant than others and that their significance is a function of the degree to which the mismatch encompasses both values that are especially important to the individual and the extent to which the perceived environmental value systems are promoted by highly respected, trustworthy, legitimate, well-liked, or "positive" sources. The question of what makes a value have salience for an individual is a complicated one to answer. We noted various antecedents of value formation at the beginning of this book. A complete treatment would take one into the areas of socialization and social influence, with detailed consideration of the important socializing agents and reference groups at different stages of the life-cycle. We have not attempted this fine-grain analysis, but we would encourage research in this area. Progress will depend upon the combined efforts of many, including psychologists from the developmental, social, and personality areas.

THE IMPORTANCE OF MAPPING VALUES

The studies reported in the first part of the book, dealing with educational settings, suggest some of the correlates of value systems discrepancy that might be looked at in the future in the wider context of societal processes. The correlates that were of interest there (choice of environment, satisfaction with environment, and value change) are crucial ones to investigate. To these three we could add others—interpersonal communication and influence, changes in specific beliefs and attitudes, differences in interpersonal attraction, the nature of group memberships, the selective seeking and processing of information, and so on. All these correlates should also reflect processes concerned with the resolution of discrepancies in value systems. And no doubt there are other possible correlates that could be investigated in future research.

Other studies concentrated more on a *mapping* of value systems for different segments of society and in different cultures. Similarities and differences in value priorities were thereby noted between males and females, parents and children, different income groups, student activists and nonactivists, delinquents and nondelinquents, Australians and Americans, Australians and indigenous people from Papua New Guinea, and Australians and migrant groups—Ukrainians and Latvians—assimilating to Australian society. For the most part the similarities and differences were reported, sometimes with a brief comment about their implications. In some analyses the degree of value match was explicitly related to certain specified dependent variables. For example, in the delinquency study, childrens' attraction to their parents was looked at in relation to the degree to which their value systems were similar to those they perceived their parents to have. Most of the studies in the second part of this book, however, centered on the identification of similarities and differences in value priorities between different groups, not with discovering empirically the correlates of discrepancies in value systems.

It would be wrong to underestimate the importance of discovering just where the similarities and differences in value priorities lie between individuals, groups, organizations, institutions, and cultures. These similarities and differences also have to be accounted for, whether in terms of socialization and the processes of social influence, or in terms of the selective migration of people (where possible) to environments that best fit their personal characteristics, or whatever. The task of mapping value systems is a vital aspect of social inquiry and one that should be given more attention now that procedures for identifying value systems in different segments of society and across cultures are available—procedures that can be used to obtain value systems regarding both the self and the defined environments.

The mapping of values should also be a continuous project *over time,* for value systems are likely to be important "social indicators" related to many areas of human concern. We noted the intended use of the Value Survey in studying social change in a developing country (Papua New Guinea), and its use here was only one of many possible applications involving societal questions about values. We urgently require social indicators that reflect the subjective side of social change to supplement other more objective indicators such as those relating to economic indexes (Campbell & Converse, 1972).

SOME SUBSTANTIVE FINDINGS

Here we report in summary form some of the main substantive findings of the research program:

1. Studies of the test instrument (Chapter 2) provided information about the test-retest reliability of single values and of value systems. Over a five-week interval these reliability coefficients—on the basis of Rokeach's Value Survey Form E—averaged in the .60s for single terminal values, in the .50s for single instrumental values, in the .70s for terminal value systems, and in the .60s for instrumental value systems. The reliability coefficients (particularly for single values) were lower over a longer interval (2½ years), as one would expect given the increased likelihood that intervening events would determine certain changes in relative value priorities. Other studies of the test instrument revealed the following: that distributions of rankings of single values differed reliably in their dispersions, with similar dispersions being obtained in two separate samples; that whether or not the test was completed anonymously seemed to have little effect on the value rankings (though this conclusion was qualified); that average value systems were similar irrespective of whether each value was ranked in importance, rated for importance, or selected as the more important value from pair comparisons; and that the value sets could not easily be reduced to a few easily interpretable dimensions by factor-analytic, multidimensional scaling, or clustering procedures.

2. Studies of educational choice with incoming freshman university students showed a tendency among them to match their value systems to those attributed to the program of studies they entered (Chapter 3). Moreover, students in the last two years of secondary school reported greater satisfaction with various

aspects of the school situation and greater overall happiness with school the more their own value systems matched those they saw their school as promoting (Chapter 4). Thus, there was evidence that both choice and adjustment were related to the value fit.

3. Studies of secondary-school impact (Chapter 5) demonstrated few differences in the value priorities of children attending single-sex or coeducational secondary schools. Certain differences in the attitudes of these children were manifested, however, toward aspects of the school situation. Students in independent or private fee-charging schools had value systems that more closely matched the value systems they attributed to their schools than did students in state-controlled, government schools. Nonetheless, in all cases the value priorities of the students themselves were quite discrepant with the value priorities they saw their schools as promoting. A study of university impact on value systems over a 2½-year interval, using control groups, revealed systematic changes in value priorities over that time but a virtual absence of any change that could be attributed to the impact of the university per se (Chapter 5).

4. Two cross-sectional surveys in metropolitan Adelaide exhibited consistent differences between parents and their children (14 years of age and older) in the priorities each generation assigned to particular values and in their social attitudes (Chapter 6). Parents placed more stress upon values connected with family and national security, self-respect and responsibility, cleanliness and politeness, and competence; the children gave more emphasis to values associated with excitement and pleasure, equality and freedom, a world of beauty, friendship with others, and a broad-minded and imaginative style of thought. Parents also displayed more conservative attitudes and they were more likely to blame poverty on the poor themselves than were their children. These social attitudes were related to value priorities in the direction that one would expect.

5. Studies of special groups in society (student activists and juvenile offenders) also showed distinctive differences in value priorities when these groups were compared with controls and with one another (Chapter 7). Many of these differences were in line with prediction. For example, the student activists revealed greater humanitarianism, romanticism, and aesthetic sensitivity; they placed more emphasis upon self-expression and political and social goals of a democratic nature; and they gave less importance to materialist and competitive values when compared with nonactivists. Some findings, such as the relatively high priority assigned by juvenile offenders to being *clean,* provided suggestive leads for future research. And some results of a structural nature were of special interest. For instance, the terminal value systems of juvenile offenders were more discrepant from those they attributed to their parents than were the terminal value systems of nondelinquents, but this difference in degree of discrepancy did not apply to the instrumental value systems. The student activist and delinquent groups displayed some large differences in value priorities when the two groups were compared with each other, but both groups were alike in assigning a relatively high priority to being *courageous* and relatively

low priorities to being *responsible* and *self-controlled* when compared with other male groups.

6. In other studies that were basically descriptive in their orientation, value systems were compared between respondents in Australia and the United States, and between respondents in Australia and Papua New Guinea (Chapter 8). Distinctive differences were noted and related to previous discussions of these societies (for example, to the assumed importance of "mateship" in Australian society and to the emphasis that has been assigned to equality and achievement as distinctive values in the United States).

7. Two studies pertaining to subjective assimilation compared the value systems of Ukrainian and Latvian immigrants with those of Australian controls, information being obtained from both children and parents in the Ukrainian study and from the children of Latvian families in the second study (Chapter 9). In general, the value systems of the second-generation immigrants (the children) were fairly similar to those of their Australian counterparts. Generational differences found in the Ukrainian study were consistent with those found in the two Adelaide surveys and in the delinquency study where subjects reported their parents' value systems. One finding from the Latvian study was of particular interest: Latvians who attended an ethnic school usually had less accurate perceptions of the value priorities of their host country than did Latvians who did not attend it, and, correspondingly, the Australian respondents judged the value systems of the Latvian nonattenders more accurately.

8. Throughout the book differences in value priorities were also noted as between males and females (Chapter 5) and across different income levels (Chapter 7).

This brief, general, and selective summary of some of the main results of the Flinders program is obviously incomplete and does not contain the appropriate qualifications noted in the text where each result was discussed. The summary also focuses upon differences between groups and, in the interest of brevity, ignores the similarities that also exist, some values being ranked uniformly high in relative importance by most groups (such as *a world at peace, freedom,* and being *honest*) and some being ranked uniformly low (*social recognition, salvation,* and being *imaginative*). Similarities are also important to remember.

FURTHER STUDY OF THE TEST INSTRUMENT

In the course of describing the studies presented in this book certain methodological issues were discussed, some of which can be summarized briefly. We recognized the need to explore the Value Survey further as a test instrument. A number of issues were raised: the reliability of single values and of value systems; the effects of presenting the values in different ways (ranking, rating, pair comparison) and in different orders; the question of the degree to which situational demands might influence the responses given in the direction of enabling the person answering the Value Survey to achieve rewards and avoid punishments; and the nature of the dimensions that might underlie responses to the two sets of terminal and instrumental values.

To these issues we would add three more. First, there is a need to study in detail the procedures that individuals employ in arriving at their two sets of rankings so that one finds out more about how they approach the task. Careful observations of individual performances might tell us about common procedures that people use in arriving at their rankings, about sources of difficulty in ranking, about the comparative processes involved, and so forth. Do respondents start at the ends and work toward the center, that is, ranking the most important and least important values earlier than they rank the intermediate values? Or do they tend to rank straight down the list from most important to least important? Do they discriminate between just a few values (perhaps those at the begining, the end, or both) and find the remaining values difficult to rank? To what extent are there individual differences in the procedures used? These questions are clearly relevant to the choice one would make of any procedure to transform rankings. In the Flinders research program we used a normal curve transformation on the assumption that values ranked at the extremes were more discriminable than those assigned intermediate ranks. This assumption was based on prior practice (Hays, 1967). It was also supported by some evidence (Chapter 2) and nonsystematic observations of how respondents approached the task. But more systematic and detailed studies of the ranking procedure are clearly called for. Such studies may also lead to an improvement in the test itself and better understanding of the cognitive processes that are involved in answering it.

Second, we need further study of the meanings assigned by respondents to the different values and the extent to which there is functional equivalence of responses across individuals, groups, and larger collectivities. Such questions are especially important in cross-cultural research, as we have noted, but they also apply in intrasocietal investigations that compare samples from different segments of society where respondents can be expected to differ in their background of socialization.

Third, we need to account for the different patterns of results between terminal and instrumental values, noted both by Rokeach (1973) and in various chapters of the present monograph. The correlations involving terminal values were often found to be higher than those involving instrumental values, whether in test-retest reliability studies, investigations of the correlates of value system discrepancy, or whatever. Rokeach (1973, p. 34) has advanced some possible reasons for the tendency for terminal value reliabilities to be higher than instrumental value reliabilities. He suggests that the terminal values may be learned earlier and thus become stabilized at an earlier age in the individual's development. He also suggests that the terminal list may be a more complete list of values and that the individual may therefore be more certain of his terminal rankings than he is of his instrumental. Finally, according to Rokeach, the terminal values may represent ideas that are more distinctively different from one another than are the instrumental values. These possible interpretations could be investigated in further research.

More generally, the distinction between terminal and instrumental values requires further theoretical analysis and justification. We noted before that distinctions involving means versus ends are always somewhat arbitrary because means can become ends in themselves (one might strive to become an honest and responsible person) and ends may be seen as means to other ends (one might strive for salvation in order to achieve inner harmony). What is needed are theoretical models that explicitly make use of the distinction between terminal and instrumental values and that enable testable predictions to be made.

General theories are available that refer to means and ends and the possible disjunctions between them. In Chapter 7 we noted Merton's analysis of anomie and some of its implications for the study of deviant behavior (Merton, 1968). In this context, we found the comparison of juvenile delinquents and student activists in regard to both their terminal and instrumental value systems to be meaningful and suggestive. Much more needs to be done, however, to relate Rokeach's distinction between the two kinds of value systems to wider theoretical frameworks. Otherwise the distinction has little point. We will return to this issue in a later section on values and behavior where we conceive of values as sources of valences within the context of an expectancy-value theory.

SOME FURTHER PROCEDURAL ISSUES

In addition to those issues concerned with the Value Survey itself, some other suggestions about procedures can be recapitulated here. We recognized that it would be useful to supplement procedures that obtained own and attributed value systems with procedures that enabled checks to be made on the degree to which these value systems are accurate representations of reality. There are a number of possible ways of doing this. One would be to observe actual behavior that is assumed to be related to value priorities. Another possibility would be to construct a value-discrepancy matrix (as in the Latvian study) that also involves the judgments of others. This type of matrix should turn out to be especially helpful in the study of assimilation.

A further procedural suggestion dealt with the difficulty of interpreting cross-sectional evidence and the need to supplement it by longitudinal studies of value priorities for different age-groups studied at different points in history. Such longitudinal studies have certain built-in methodological problems (for example, sample attrition) and are very expensive to conduct. Yet if meaningful interpretations of obtained differences—such as between the value systems of parent and child—are to be made, they are essential supplements to cross-sectional, simultaneous investigations of different age cohorts.

We would also support the strategy of developing studies in the general domain of values that follow the types of recommendations advocated by Campbell and Fiske (1959) in their discussion of convergent and discriminant validation by the multitrait-multimethod matrix. This strategy would include the use of different measures of values (in addition to Rokeach's procedure) and the inclusion of measures of other "nonvalue" concepts. The choice of tests would *not* be a random selection but would be related to basic theoretical assumptions about what is being assessed and how it would be expected to relate to the dependent variables under consideration. These measures would sample a wide range of procedures—self-report, ratings by others, questionnaire items, direct behavioral measures, more indirect and less structured methods, and so on. By detailed analysis of the pattern of relationships obtained in research guided by the theoretical framework within which one is working and by the logical demands of the multimethod-multitrait procedure, it should be possible to learn more about the validity of the tests that one is using as well as about the adequacy of the conceptual framework within which one's research is embedded.

Our own approach has been guided by this strategy, though in practice it is a difficult one to conduct in a relatively complete way. Throughout this book we have referred to patterns of similarities and differences between correlation matrices, usually involving the correlations between average value systems. (Parenthetically, we would again note that such correlations, where they are based upon averages, should not be taken to indicate the likely size of correlations had they been computed for individuals. Yet these "ecological correlations" provide useful information in their own right, as we have seen.) We have no doubt that the procedure of systematically comparing obtained relationships according to the multimethod-multitrait approach could be taken a lot further than we have done. At least we have not relied upon single correlation coefficients but have focused on the whole pattern of relationships in cases where the pattern could be explored.

Finally, it should be obvious that the research program has included samples of respondents from many different populations and that not all of these samples can be considered random ones. Indeed, it is a rare occurrence in applied social research that one can obtain a random sample of respondents from some defined universe. Even in well-conducted surveys one is confronted with problems of varying response rates and, in longitudinal studies, these problems are increased due to loss of subjects.

Our approach to this question again drew upon discussions of the strategy of research by Campbell and his colleagues (Campbell & Stanley, 1963; Cook & Campbell, forthcoming; Winch & Campbell, 1969). They argue that the interpretation of empirical relations obtained from experiments and quasi-experiments embraces questions of *internal validity* (Did the experimental variable make a difference in the specific instance under investigation?) and *external validity* (To what extent can the effect be generalized to other populations, settings, treatment variables, and measurement variables?). One can list numerous factors that threaten the interpretation of an empirical relationship (Campbell, 1969; Winch & Campbell, 1969). One of these factors relates to *instability,* whether it be in terms of the unreliability of measures, fluctuations in the sampling of persons or components, and so on. The test of significance is seen as relevant to this particular threat. As Winch and Campbell (1969) state:

> The establishing of a statistically significant difference goes but one step toward establishing an interpretation of that difference. That step is to exclude the hypothesis of chance. . . . the decision as to the plausibility of chance is made by formal, objective, communicable, and reproducible procedures rather than by intuition. (p. 143)

In conducting tests of significance therefore, we have attempted to provide some evidence that might enable one reasonably to exclude the hypothesis of chance when interpreting empirically obtained differences and relationships.

But this is only one "threat" to interpretation. As Campbell and his colleagues point out there are many other threats to internal and external validity. In developing the Flinders research program we have deliberately attempted to remove some of these possible alternative interpretations of empirical results by sampling from many different populations, by designing studies so as to provide for the replication of previous findings in different contexts, and by using different kinds of test instruments. We had in mind not only Campbell's valuable advice about the design and interpretation of experiments and quasi-experiments but John Stuart Mill's classic analysis of causal inference with its emphasis upon the discovery of common causal factors amid varying circumstances, the signal amid the noise. And we have tried to describe our procedures fully so that readers can detect possible sources of bias and make their own interpretations of the data.

Thus, our emphasis throughout has been on *programmatic* research, distrusting the information gained from single or "one-shot" studies. We have tried to develop an integrated program of research, each study involving some new questions and providing some new set of findings, yet at the same time reflecting back upon what has been found before, usually with a different type of sample and with slightly different procedures. To use a metaphor, we have attempted to walk some of the many different roads that lead to Rome (Feather & Wasyluk, 1973a; Witton, 1973). In traveling these different roads we have become more confident about the nature of the territory surrounding our destination. And we have discovered that Rome itself is a complex and multi-faceted city.

In the remainder of the chapter we shall look at some new issues. The first is on the measurement of value climates, the second relates to values and stereotyping, and the third pertains to the various factors that might influence the value rankings that respondents provide in the test situation. The fourth issue deals with the relationship of values to action.

VALUE CLIMATES

THE VALUE DISCREPANCY MATRIX

We have seen in Chapter 9 that it is possible to construct a value-discrepancy matrix for specified groups or individuals by obtaining information about own value systems and attributed value systems from each of these groups or individuals. Categorizing people as A or B, one can obtain information about the own value systems of A, the own value systems of B, and the value systems attributed by A to B and by B to A. Further, one can obtain information about the value systems that A attributes to others categorized as As and the value systems that B attributes to others categorized as Bs. Of course, the matrix could include more than two categories. It could be extended to any number of groups or individuals who have some form of acquaintance or communication with one another.

Although we have stated the basis for constructing this matrix in abstract terms, the procedure can easily be made more concrete by imagining particular groups or individuals. For example, A could represent a group of Australians and B a migrant group; discrepancies between them could be gauged in terms of aggregate measures, such as the average value systems for each group. Alternatively, A and B might be individuals rather than groups, with discrepancies determined at the individual level. In the second instance, the value systems obtained would relate to self and to other, two particular individuals being the subject matter.

One could also include more complex types of attribution. One might want to find out A's judgment of how B would rank the values for A, and vice versa—that is, how other is perceived by self to rank for self. Several of the possibilities just mentioned have been discussed in the literature of social perception and interpersonal perception (Newcomb, 1961; Tagiuri & Petrullo, 1958; Warr & Knapper, 1968) although not in the context of the Value Survey.

The very general value-discrepancy matrix that is obtained from these kinds of procedures can be used to secure information about the extent to which attributed value systems are *accurate* appraisals of the real state of affairs. This information can be looked at in the context of general theories, such as those concerning the acquaintance process (Newcomb, 1961, 1963) and the assimilation process (Chapter 9), among others. We have argued that evidence of this nature should help to illuminate those types of theoretical approach that stress the individual's attempt to resolve cognitive discrepancies.

HOMOGENEITY IN OWN AND ATTRIBUTED VALUE SYSTEMS AMONG INDIVIDUALS

One can also construct matrices that provide information about *value climates* within a defined social environment. For instance, within a school setting one might obtain the *own* value systems of all individuals contained in that environment (schoolchildren, teachers, administrators, secretaries, and so forth) and then examine the degree to which these value systems are homogenous. By analyzing the matrix of similarity coefficients acquired from comparing the value systems of every individual with those of every other individual, one might be able to identify homogeneous clusters of individuals who are similar in the value systems that they report for themselves. One might find that schoolchildren tend to cluster together in terms of their reported value systems, that the teachers form another cluster, the administrators still another cluster, and so on. Some social environments might have many distinct clusters, as in the example of the school just presented or in a large industrial organization with a complex role structure. These would be environments with a *heterogeneous* or differentiated value climate. Other social environments might have few distinct clusters, as might occur in an exclusive club for top business executives or in a high level committee of a political party. These would be environments with a more *homogeneous* or less differentiated value climate.

One could also obtain a general measure of consensus among individuals in their own value priorities (that is, the degree of homogeneity in the value climate) by using the coefficient of concordance. Rokeach, for example, has provided some information about the degree of concordance between value systems for different religious groups and a nonreligious group (Rokeach, 1973, p. 37).

At the level of single values, the degree to which the ranks assigned to a particular value varied across individuals would provide some evidence of homogeneity. In this case one could use measures of dispersion to signify degree of homogeneity (see Table 2.3).

These procedures could also be used to explore the degree to which consensus existed among people about the value systems they see a defined social environment to be promoting, for *attributed* value systems may also differ in their degree of homogeneity. Like the value climate based upon the analysis of own rankings, the attributed value climate may also be more or less differentiated in its structure.

Once it is possible to specify the detailed *structure* of a value climate within a defined social environment on the basis both of own and attributed value rankings, one can then analyze and investigate the factors that determined this structure and the effects of the value climate on thought and action. In an industrial organization, for example, the study of the determinants of its particular value climate would have to consider at least the size of the organization and its role structure, the selection criteria for filling positions within that role structure, and the communication and influence attempts that occur within the organization. The effects of the value climate could be investigated in relation to measures of output and worker satisfaction, taking account of discrepancies between the structure revealed by analysis of own value systems and the structure revealed by analysis of attributed value systems at different levels of the organization. These questions (and similar ones that can be formulated in terms of person-environment fit) are important for the social psychology of organizations, and they deserve attention in the future (for a recent review of research on organizational climate see James and Jones, 1974).

VALUE SYSTEMS AND STEREOTYPING

THE NATURE OF STEREOTYPES

We have argued that when people rank the values in the Value Survey either in relation to themselves or for others they are drawing upon cognitive structures that have been developed over time to give meaning to experience. These structures that enable individuals to come to terms with the "blooming, buzzing confusion" of daily experience may involve stereotyped ways of thinking.

Stereotypes, which are relatively simple categorizations or generalizations about people or groups, are shared by many. As Brown (1965, p. 177) points out, they are not usually viewed as "exceptionless generalizations" by those who hold them, but as something more in the nature of tendencies or trends in which unique information about individuals is lost in the process of arriving at a modal generalization. Brown also suggests that when applied to nationalities, religions, or races, stereotypes usually include an evaluative component based upon one's own standards and culture. As a consequence, there tends to be a cultural absolutism about national, religious, and racial stereotypes.

Simple and sometimes inaccurate stereotypes may be more likely to occur when they relate to people about whom we know very little. On these occasions when we do make generalizations, we may be relying upon what others have said about those we are describing. With persons we know very well, we are more likely to rely upon our own experience, though our views again entail categorizing and some of the categories may be in error. Stereotyping in the sense of categorizing or generalizing from a sample of cases or from what others tell us is, of course, a normal part of information processing among humans. Stereotypes acquire misleading and dangerous overtones when they are accompanied by negative evaluations linked to ethnocentrism, cultural absolutism, and beliefs about innate superiority.

Stereotypes may be modified through direct experience with the people being categorized. They may also show considerable stability over time. They may be normative, representing the "appropriate" and "correct" way of think-ing about another group of people, or they may be nonnormative, representing vague and undefined views of others outside the realm of one's own experience. Stereotypes may be quite inaccurate judgments about reality (as we have stated), yet have some truth to them. Triandis (1971, p. 107) notes, for instance, that autostereotypes (the way a group of people looks at itself) are often very similar to heterostereotypes (the way other groups look at the group in ques-tion). He suggests that this similarity may occur because stereotypes contain a kernel of truth, or because each group learns the stereotypes that others have of it and then develops its autostereotypes to match, or because the groups possess shared or overlapping implicit personality theories that have similar implica-tions.

Campbell (1967) has argued that stereotypes tend to be organized around those traits or characteristics on which groups show relatively large differences. He analyzes various reasons that might account for the poor judgment associ-ated with stereotypes. Both Triandis (1971, pp. 102–112) and Campbell and his associates (Campbell, 1967; LeVine & Campbell, 1972) have contributed useful and insightful discussions of stereotyping, and the reader is referred to these sources for more detailed treatments of the stereotyping processes and for some of the research evidence. The extensive literature on racial prejudice and ethnic stereotypes is also relevant (Allport, 1954; Brigham, 1971; Brown, 1965; Tajfel, 1969) as is the literature on stereotyping and implicit personality theory (for example, Secord & Berscheid, 1963) and the recent interest in the process of stigmatization and the labeling of deviant behavior (Becker, 1963; Goffman, 1963; Schur, 1971).

STEREOTYPING THE VALUE SYSTEMS OF OTHERS

In the present context we must recognize that value systems attributed to individuals, groups, or social environments may involve a degree of stereo-typing, particularly when those making the attributions have had very little contact with those being judged. In a number of places throughout this book we have noted the importance of checking the accuracy of attributed value systems either by observation of value-related behavior in appropriate situations or by obtaining the reported value systems of the group being judged. Indeed, increased accuracy of judgment was seen as one way of indexing the degree of assimilation, assuming that more accurate knowledge of a host community would follow from contact with it and with opportunities to move into its component structures.

Some misleading stereotypes may be retained, however, even in the face of increased contact with those being judged, although actual experience with these others should produce some modifications. People may hold to their myths despite evidence that may disconfirm them. The appeal to myths may be more likely when what is being judged is diffuse and general, not easy to specify en masse, and far removed from the reality of individual experience. Judgments about national character, for example, are peculiarly difficult to make. When one judges national character for a society other than one's own, the assessments are usually based upon very limited information—unless one has had considerable direct experience with the society in question. When one judges the national character of one's own society, one has a flood of information coming from direct experience. Confronted with the task of seeking an abstraction under conditions of either limited information or overabundant information, a person might fall back upon the myths he has been taught. Indeed, in his analysis of the "Australian legend" Ward (1958) acknowledges that he is concerned with myths that may or may not be accurate representations of Australian life.

The form that stereotypes take and their persistence over time may be understood in terms of certain factors. These factors include the particular learning and socialization experiences that people have undergone, the coding processes that lead to simplified organized cognitive structures as individuals deal with multifaceted information, the social support that some stereotypes receive in the community, and the underlying needs and wishes that stereotyped responses may satisfy. Stereotypes that relate to values may be associated with the *idealization* of certain values. These idealized images, as they pertain to national character for example, may be resistant to change, passed on from generation to generation, embodied and exalted in folklore and literature, and reaffirmed at moments of collective stocktaking.

STEREOTYPES, THOUGHT, AND ACTION

Though they are faulty representations of reality, stereotypes are important in that they do influence thought and action in relation to the object stereotyped. Sometimes stereotypes are vague and ill-defined representations reflecting ignorance. At other times they may be viewed as outcomes of normative pressures. Indeed, some stereotypes seem to be characterized by normative proscriptions that connote the "proper" or "correct" ways of thinking about the object in question (Triandis, 1971). As we pointed out in discussing the results of the delinquency study (Chapter 7), one would like to be able to separate what people think *ought* to be the case in regard to value priorities from what *is* the case, disentangling the normative stereotype from objective reality. But this separation is not easily accomplished.

The myths, therefore, whether they be normative or nonnormative, may be expected to affect responses when values are ranked for self and when values are ranked for other groups or for defined social environments. The value rankings provided by our Australian respondents, for instance, may have been influenced by stereotypes that they held about the Australian national character as well as by stereotypes about sex differences and age differences in value priorities within society. Similarly, those choosing a School to work in within the university (Chapter 3) may have ranked their own values according to their stereotypes of what a "typical" humanities, social science, or science student *should* be like, thereby revealing their knowledge of the stereotype rather than their own personal priorities. More generally, people in any occupation or pursuit may report value priorities consistent with stereotypes about that occupation or activity rather than revealing their own preferences.

Often the normative stereotype may become internalized and refined, and individuals may genuinely believe that their value systems conform to what ought to be true. This may be so for a number of reasons. Throughout this book we have argued that people attempt in various ways to resolve cognitive discrepancies. When these discrepancies touch upon differences between one's own value priorities and what others of importance or influence assert ought to be the case, one is subject to pressures to resolve the discrepancies. We need not spell out again the motivational basis for these pressures or the various forms these resolutions might take. But one possible readjustment is a change in one's own value systems so that they are consistent with the normative requirements of one's important reference groups and with the value systems of those whom one likes and respects. The science student who assigns being *logical* a high priority in his own instrumental value system probably relates to a reference group of scientists he sees as valuing logical inquiry. His concern with being logical would be reinforced in the science environment he chose to work in where there would be rewards (both intrinsic and extrinsic) for approaching and solving problems in a logical way. His value priorities may even have shifted before he entered this environment so that they became more similar to the normative structure he expected to encounter—a process of anticipatory socialization (Rosenberg, 1957). In his case, "ought" became "is."

In other instances the value rankings reported by individuals may follow from compliance with normative requirements rather than internalization of value systems. Because of peer group pressures, some students may assign high importance to certain ideal values that relate to a political or social ideology— values such as *freedom* and *equality*. They may publicly report these values as their own, yet not accept them privately or behave in ways consistent with them. The normative structure has not been integrated into the self-concept; "ought" differs from "is."

The conditions under which social influence leads to basic changes rather than surface alterations in beliefs, attitudes, and values have been extensively examined (for example, see Kelman, 1961, 1974*b*). Where norms have become internalized and accepted as part of the self one would expect that value systems and actual behavior would be more closely integrated, a person's actions in many areas being consistent with the dominant values that he reports. For example, the science student who reports a distinctive pattern of value priorities in which scientific values are given prominence may act like a scientist in the research he conducts and the reports he writes. But where the value rankings involve compliance with a normative system at the level of verbal report without the further step of internalization, there may be only a tenuous relationship between the reported value priorities and behavior, a relationship that is limited to specific situations and that does not occur generally. Some people may rank being *honest* high in their priorities, complying with society's idealization of honesty. Yet these same people may behave in very dishonest ways. A science student may rank being *logical* as very important for himself because he thinks that is what is expected of him by his scientific peers. Yet he may behave illogically and unscientifically because he has never really internalized the scientific values. A politician may rank *equality* as very high in his priorities, being influenced by the fact that an emphasis on equality of opportunity is a basic part of the creed of his political party and essential for his political success. Yet outside of the political arena he may behave with elitism and care little about inequities.

It is reassuring to note that studies relating behavior to values have generally found significant effects in the directions that one would expect on a priori grounds (Rokeach, 1973, chap. 5). *Equality,* for example, was the value most predictive of behavior related to interracial relations, *salvation* was the value that best predicted churchgoing, and the intellectual values—*imaginative, intellectual,* and *logical*—best predicted whether one would become a professor. These studies suggest that at least some internalization of values had taken place among the subjects tested. Some of the results, however, are also open to the interpretation that respondents may have felt that they should report value priorities consistent with past behaviors or with their present roles, that is, they may have been subject to the well-known pressures to be consistent. This type of interpretation would be less likely to apply where studies were *predictive* (What behaviors would one expect to follow from these value priorities?) rather than *postdictive* (Given these behaviors what values would one expect to be associated with them?) and where the study procedures were unobtrusive, designed specifically to reduce the demand characteristics of the test situation (Webb, Campbell, Schwartz, & Sechrest, 1966). We will return to the question of values and action later in this chapter. But certainly it would be useful in future research to develop procedures that would enable one to determine the degree to which the value systems reported by respondents have been internalized and accepted as one's own.

Finally, the possible presence of value stereotypes when respondents rank the values for themselves or for specified groups, organizations, or larger collectivities might be detected by examining the degree to which value systems are similar across individuals and by exploring the structure of the value climate. A high degree of homogeneity among respondents in the value systems they reported might suggest stereotyping and this hypothesis could be tested by obtaining further information, using additional procedures. One should recognize, however, that a high degree of homogeneity might also indicate that respondents were all well acquainted with what was being judged and that they were able to report value systems accurately.

CONCLUDING REMARKS

In this section we have suggested that one of the factors influencing the rankings provided by respondents to the Rokeach Value Survey may be the stereotypes that they hold and share with others. In the course of one's own unique experience and with the opportunity to learn more about those whose value systems are being judged, these initial oversimplified views may become more refined and closer to the truth. Where the task of judging others is difficult, however, perhaps because of limited information or because of too much information or for other reasons, people may fall back upon shared myths. In time normative stereotypes with some refinements may become internalized and accepted as a person's true beliefs. In other cases, reported value systems may imply compliance rather than internalization, and action may be related to values only under special circumstances.

It will be noted that we have not discussed stereotypes in a disparaging way, as beliefs that people should avoid at all costs. While many of a person's values are learned in the course of his own behavioral experience as certain of his actions are rewarded by others (for example, the child is rewarded for behaving honestly, the political candidate is praised for advocating equality), there are situations where simplified conceptions about values are taken over from others without much questioning. This is most apt to occur if these others are judged by the community to be important and trustworthy sources of information or have a charismatic quality about them or constitute one's important reference groups. In childhood particularly, these "correct" ways of thinking derived from others may be quite simple ones having an absolute quality. As the child matures his sense of right and wrong becomes more sophisticated (Kohlberg, 1966, 1969) and the structure of his value systems better articulated. Over time the structure of values held by a person may become quite complex, and value systems may be integrated into social, ethical, and political theories about man. The value priorities learned in the course of one's own experience and those taken over from others are molded together to constitute frames of reference and guidelines for attitudes, action, judgments, justifications, self-evaluations, and so on. But in those instances where judgments are difficult to make, perhaps because of the very nature of what is being judged, the simple and often faulty stereotype may become an important source of a person's report about values.

DETERMINANTS OF VALUE RANKINGS

THREE SETS OF FACTORS INFLUENCING VALUE RANKINGS

What are some of the other important factors that might be expected to influence the ranking of values? On the basis of past experience with another assessment device—the projective measure of Need Achievement using thematic apperception—we can list three broad sets of factors that affect test responses: (1) contextual cues that are present when the test is administered; (2) cues that relate to the test material; and (3) personality characteristics of the respondents themselves.

One can think of many ways in which the *context* in which the Value Survey is administered may vary. Experimenters giving the test may differ in certain characteristics (in status, appearance, sex); testing may be conducted individually or in a group setting; the size and nature of the group may vary; responses may be anonymous or subjects may be asked to sign their names; the situation immediately prior to administering the test may be experimentally manipulated; and so on. It is important, however, to understand the *motivational significance* of the test setting. The Value Survey is not a subtle, unobtrusive measure, and responses to it should be looked at within the total goal structure of the person who is providing the rankings, particularly in regard to the possible consequences (rewards and costs) that may be associated with different ways of responding (see Chapter 2 and the section to follow).

Factors concerned with the *test material* itself are also of obvious importance. We have already noted some of them (such as the nature and scope of the value lists), especially in discussing the questions of appropriateness and equivalence in relation to cross-cultural research with the Value Survey (Chapter 8). For example, there might be other values that one would want to add to the lists and some that one might want to remove. Others might want to modify existing definitions of values (as in the delinquency study in Chapter 7), or develop additional procedures in testing respondents who are very different from North Americans or who have other special characteristics. Factors in this second class should not be restricted to substantive characteristics of the value sets, however, that is, to characteristics such as the number of values, the specific values included and their verbal labels, and so on. The response mode is also of obvious importance. In Chapter 2 we reported a study comparing ranking, rating, and pair-comparison modes. Other possibilities are worth exploring as well: asking the respondent to pick the five most important values and the five least important values; allowing tied ranks; investigating intransitivities when pair-comparisons are used. These alternative procedures have been discussed in the assessment literature (Dawes, 1972) and in the theory of data (Coombs, 1964).

The third set of factors—the *personality characteristics* of the subjects being tested—is also very important. One hopes that the rankings subjects provide correspond closely to their own true value priorities at the time of testing, and, in the case of attributed rankings, to their true beliefs about the value priorities of other persons, groups, organizations, and so on. Yet it would be naïve to pretend that this always occurs. As we have noted, subjects could fake their responses to make a good impression, depending upon the context. And in some cases they may provide simple stereotypes that do not correspond to the actual value systems. They may also differ in the ease with which they are able to deal with the stimulus material—an "ability" factor. Certain respondents might find the task of ranking abstract values a lot more complicated than others because the task of defining value priorities in a conscious manner is a novel one and the procedure invokes forced choice (ties are not allowed). Also, they may not have given much previous thought to some of the values, and they may not completely understand a few of them. The object of judgment (self or others) is usually a complex concept and not easy to describe in terms of a linear order of abstract terms.

Doubtless, other important personal characteristics can influence responses to the Value Survey. Among these are the immediate motivational concerns of people. Values ranked high in importance may sometimes reflect a preoccupation with reducing states of deficit, with striving for goals that are presently unattainable—as is suggested by the relatively high ranking assigned to being *clean* and to *a comfortable life* by lower income groups (Rokeach, 1973; Chapter 6). But personal concerns are only one of many possible motivational effects. As Rokeach (1973) points out:

> There are several reasons why a given value may be ranked high or low. A person may, for instance, rank a value high because he wants something he does not have (e.g., poor people rank *clean* high) or because he already has it and wants more of it (e.g., artists rank *a world of beauty* high and a professor ranks *a sense of accomplishment* high). A person may rank a value low because he is not mature enough to know about it or to appreciate it (e.g., young children rank *a sense of accomplishment* low), because he has it and therefore takes it for granted (e.g., affluent people rank *clean* low), or because he has neither had it nor wants it (e.g., most Americans rank *imaginative* and *intellectual* low). Thus, there are alternative reasons why a value may receive a high or low ranking. (p. 62)

VALUE RANKINGS AS INSTRUMENTAL BEHAVIOR

Classifying factors that influence test responses is initially useful in attempts to systematize, but ultimately one wants to explain these responses in terms of some theory of behavior. In responses to the Value Survey we are studying self-descriptive behavior and other-descriptive behavior. This behavior varies like any other (for example, locomotor actions), depending upon the characteristics of the immediate situation and the motivational concerns and the learning background of the people involved.

The Value Survey constrains respondents in the choices they are offered because it provides subjects with specific stimulus items that are to be ranked in relative importance. This procedure is in contrast with others, such as the Thematic Apperception Test (TAT), that allow subjects freedom to create their own responses in the form of a flow of imaginative thought. There the responses correspond to operant behaviors at the imaginal level.

Regardless of the degree to which responses are restricted, however, one should be able to treat test answers like any others—in terms of a conceptual framework that enables an explanation of present behavior and a prediction of future behavior. We have argued previously that the rankings that subjects provide in the Value Survey should be looked at within the context of instrumental action and related to the *expected consequences* of the rank orders, that is, to the desired rewards and goals that might be achieved (like getting a good job) or the threatening costs and punishments that might be circumvented (like avoiding the disapproval of a teacher). Since test responses may be viewed as instrumental actions, it should be possible to apply theories that pertain to instrumental action to their analysis. Classical test theory overlooks the fact that tests are not taken *in vacuo*. Responses to them can be interpreted according to theoretical assumptions about the determinants of action. And theories of action have now been developed to a sufficient level that permit one to apply them to the analysis of test responses. We will not attempt such an application in this monograph. But in the next section we will turn to an examination of value systems in relation to overt behavior—an analysis that is relevant to the issue we have just raised.

VALUES AND BEHAVIOR

ATTITUDES AND ACTIONS

Most of our discussion so far has dealt with the cognitive arena. With some exceptions, we have had little to say about values and behavior. We have skirted this issue, although in the last section we emphasized the importance of examining test behavior in terms of some theory of action. And earlier, in considering the effects of value discrepancy, we noted that individuals may seek new environments that better fit their value systems if such mobility is possible within the bounds of reality and if it does not increase discrepancies in other areas (such as between abilities and task demands). In other words, overt behavior as well as cognitive adjustments may allow some resolution of cognitive discrepancies.

The whole question of the interrelationships between behavior and cognitive concepts, like beliefs, attitudes, and values, is exceedingly complex. One can look at the effects of behavior on cognition (as in dissonance theory) and also at the conditions under which cognitions of various kinds lead to behavior. There has been increasing interest in this latter topic over the past few years in the discussions of attitude, especially since Festinger's (1964) article dealing with the need for research and theoretical thinking on the effects of attitude change on subsequent actions. Recent articles have summarized the relevant literature (Fishbein & Ajzen, 1972; Fishbein, 1973; Kelman, 1974a; Wicker, 1969), and we will not attempt to review this literature again.

Most discussions assume that a thorough conceptual analysis of the conditions under which attitudes predict behavior must take account of other variables in addition to attitudes. Fishbein and Ajzen (1974) argue for a conceptual framework that relates overt behavior to a behavioral intention that is assumed to be a function of three main variables: attitude toward the act, normative beliefs about performing the behavior, and motivation to comply with these perceived norms. And Rokeach (1968b, d) maintains that behavior is always a function of at least two types of attitude—attitude toward the object and attitude toward the situation—weighted according to their relative importance. In his view the relationship of value change to behavior change is bound up with the resolution of contradictions between important values. These contradictions are likely to implicate self-conceptions and to give rise to feelings of self-dissatisfaction, which the individual attempts to eliminate or reduce by cognitive and behavioral change in the service of self-maintenance and self-enhancement. Some other writers concerned with aspects of motivation have also shown increased interest recently in the self-concept—for example, Aronson (1968, 1972) and Nel, Helmreich, and Aronson (1969) in regard to dissonance theory, and Raynor (1974b) in regard to the arousal of achievement motivation. The whole field, of course, has a very long history (Gordon & Gergen, 1968; Wylie, 1968, 1974).

ACTION IN RELATION TO PERSON AND SITUATION VARIABLES

Our own thinking about the relationship between values and action has been influenced by our past attempts to conceptualize the determinants of behavior in terms of *expectancy-value* models. Some 15 years ago we first reviewed examples of this kind of approach (Feather, 1959a), and it has guided many of our research efforts especially in the areas of object preference (Feather, 1959b), achievement motivation (Atkinson & Feather, 1966), information-seeking behavior (Feather, 1967b), the confirmation and disconfirmation of expectancies (Feather, 1963, 1967c), and causal attribution for success and failure (Feather, 1969b; Feather & Simon, 1971; Simon & Feather, 1973). Mitchell (1974) has recently updated our earlier review of expectancy-value models (Feather, 1959a), providing examples especially relevant to organizational psychology.

A fundamental aspect of this approach has been a commitment to the view that any theory of action must include concepts that relate both to the person and to the situation, a point recognized long ago by Lewin (1935) in his famous programmatic equation, $B = F(P, E)$ or Behavior is a function of Person and Psychological Environment. And the concepts that we have found useful in dealing with the interaction of person and immediate situation are the concepts of motive, expectancy, and incentive value.

In an earlier study of persistence, for example, we emphasized that the analysis of persistent behavior should take account of a set of motivational tendencies differing in strength and relating to the set of activities available to a person (Feather, 1961). These tendencies would include those relating to the task he is working on and those relating to the alternatives that are present and to which he can turn. The study of persistence was, therefore, defined as a problem in explaining *change in activity* and the dynamics of change were conceived in terms of changes in the strength of tendencies aroused in the situation, the person performing that action for which the resultant tendency was maximal. The strength of each positive tendency to perform an activity that might be instrumental to attaining goals or rewards and the strength of each negative tendency *not* to perform an activity that might lead to punishments and costs were related to three sets of variables. These variables were the general *motives* that characterized the person—motives that were conceived as relatively stable personality dispositions; the situationally elicited *expectations* about the implications of each separate activity; and the values of the specific *incentives* (both positive and negative) that the situation provides (Feather, 1962). This analysis of persistence triggered a subsequent reconstruction of the theory of motivation (Atkinson & Birch, 1970) in which change in activity was seen as the central problem that any theory of motivation has to explain.

New concepts have been added to the analysis of behavior in achievement situations (choice, performance, and persistence) over the past few years (Atkinson & Birch, 1974; Atkinson & Raynor, 1974; Raynor, 1974*a;* Weiner, 1972). The commitment to an interactional analysis involving both person and situation, however, remains an essential part of the approach.

From this interactionist viewpoint, it follows that any model that attempts to relate action simply to general values alone is doomed to failure because it has left out of consideration the important role of the situation in which the behavior occurs. As we have seen, both Fishbein and Rokeach recognize the contribution that the immediate situation makes in their analyses of conditions that influence the relationship of behavior to attitudes. And sociologists have made similar points when discussing the ways in which values are expressed (Parsons, 1960*b,* p. 173; Williams, 1971, p. 132). By now the need for an approach that considers both person and situation variables in interaction is obvious. But the point still deserves emphasis (for recent discussions of interactionist approaches in the psychology of personality, see Bowers, 1973; Ekehammar, 1974).

EXPECTANCY-VALUE THEORY: VALUES AND MOTIVES

One can speculate about the possibility of conceptualizing the conditions under which values lead to action within the context of expectancy-value theory —a general class of theories that relate tendencies either to perform particular actions or not to perform them to the strength of *expectancies* that these actions will lead to specific outcomes and the *valences* (or subjectively perceived values) of these outcomes for the person. The valences may be positive (the outcome is seen to be attractive) or negative (the outcome is seen to be repulsive). The expectancies and valences are usually assumed to combine multiplicatively to determine the strength of tendencies. The final resultant tendency is assumed to be the sum of all the separate positive and negative component tendencies.

In this general approach—of which the analysis of persistence presented above was one example—motives are conceived to function as among the important determinants of valence, weighting the subjective attractiveness or repulsiveness of those specific outcomes that are relevant to the motives that have been activated in the situation. Success at tasks of increasing difficulty, for example, is assumed to increase more rapidly in subjective attractiveness for a person with a strong motive to achieve success than for a person with a weak motive to achieve success, assuming that the motive has been activated. Can values be assumed to function in the same way? Are motives and values related?

There are both conceptual and empirical grounds for assuming that values and motives may be related. At the conceptual level the general concept of motive is often defined in a manner that makes it hard to distinguish it from the concept of value. For example, McClelland's treatment of the motive concept is very similar in certain respects to Rokeach's concept of value. McClelland (1965) argues that

> all motives are learned. . . . [C]lusters of expectancies or associations grow up around affective experiences, not all of which are connected by any means with biological needs. . . . [M]otives are "affectively toned associative networks" arranged in a hierarchy of strength or importance within a given individual. (p. 322)

Values for Rokeach are also assumed to have affective components and to be arranged in hierarchies within individuals. Our concept of value structure (Chapter 1) also includes the idea of a network of associations linked to affect—the network being describable in various ways (for example, in regard to its degree of differentiation, integration, isolation, centrality, and so on).

French and Kahn (1962) also treat values (together with needs) as motives. They consider that both needs and values

> have the basic conceptual property of the ability to motivate goal directed behavior in the person by inducing valences (or incentive values) on certain environmental objects, behaviors, or states of affairs. (pp. 11–12)

For French and Kahn a value may function to control the need-induced behavior of each individual so that other members of the group are not harmed (for example, the control of aggression). But in other cases, a motivational system may have the properties of a need and also the properties of a value in that what a person *wants* to do corresponds to what he thinks he *ought* to do. French and Kahn consider that values have the ability to induce evaluations of good and bad and that this conceptual property does not apply to a need. But both values and needs function as motives in their ability to induce valences, which may be positive or negative.

Finally, as we noted in Chapter 1, Rokeach views values as the cognitive representation and transformation of needs and argues that the transformation also takes account of societal and institutional demands. According to Rokeach, the more long-range functions of values are to give expression to basic human needs. Ultimately values are in the service of the self in that they are employed in order to maintain and enhance self-esteem, and they do this by helping a person adjust to the world he lives in, by defending his ego against threat, and by enabling him to test and understand reality.

At the empirical level one might expect to find some of the values on Rokeach's list to be related to underlying personality dispositions or motives that have been shown to influence choice, performance, and persistence in laboratory studies—motives such as the motive to achieve success, the motive to win approval, the motive to affiliate with others, and the motive to gain power. Further, one would expect that the conditions leading to the development of motives and values and to their activation in specific settings would be very similar—or perhaps the same. Rokeach (1973, pp. 48–49) has reported evidence on the relationship of the relative importance of particular values to projective measures of *n* Achievement, *n* Affiliation, and *n* Power (Rokeach & Berman, 1971), but the correlations were all quite low though some were statistically significant. One would be pessimistic about the possibility of finding strong relationships, however, in view of the fact that "self-descriptive" versus "imaginative" procedures are involved. Previous studies generally have found low correlations when these two procedures have been applied to the assessment of the same or similar concepts (for example, to the assessment of *n* Achievement; see Atkinson & Litwin, 1960; McClelland, 1958).

Future research should not rest with attempts to discover similarities and differences between the two concepts at the level of the test instruments that have typically been employed. Blind empiricism has little to commend it. Far more important is the need for further conceptual analyses of the concepts of motive and value that draw out whatever similarities and differences may exist between them and whether each has a distinctive place in theories of behavior. Such analyses may show that motives and values are conceptually and functionally equivalent, having the same antecedents, the same interrelationships with other theoretical concepts, and the same consequents. Then again these analyses may uncover important differences.

Conceptual analyses need to be supplemented by empirical studies that test the theoretical implications of definitions and assumptions. It may turn out that motives and values are functionally indistinguishable in many of their effects and that there is a basic identity in the antecedent conditions underlying their development. If so, there would be little point in maintaining the distinction between the two concepts. Then again, one might find extensive overlap between them in their antecedents and consequents but still some distinctive differences that justified continuing to differentiate between them. Values, for example, are commonly held to be normative, to involve conceptions of what is desirable and undesirable. As such they serve as standards that are employed in many contexts where evaluation is a consideration (see, for example, Rokeach's definition of value given in Chapter 1, p. 12). No necessary connection seems to exist, however, between motives and normative evaluations of goodness and badness. The desired is not always the desirable; goodness and badness are not identical to pleasure and pain; sometimes "want" and "ought" coincide, but by no means always; and action often takes place in the absence of conscious evaluation.

Perhaps motive should be regarded as the more general concept to be used as one important variable in theoretical accounts of the determinants of the direction, persistence, and amplitude (or vigor) of sequences of purposive behavior—sequences that can be abstracted from the ongoing stream of activity. Values may then be seen as a particular class of motives: those tied to a normative base relating to an evaluative dimension of goodness-badness. Thus, motive would be the more inclusive concept and value would be a member of this general class. There may, therefore, be some motives that are not values but no values that are not motives. Clearly, we need further conceptual and empirical inquiry to resolve some of these issues. In the meantime, however, there is no reason why values should not be treated as basic personality characteristics similar and perhaps identical to motives, and integrated into expectancy-value models in the same way that motives have been included in the past (see, for example, Atkinson & Feather, 1966; Feather, 1967a).

EXPECTANCY-VALUE THEORY: EXPECTATIONS AND INCENTIVE VALUES

It should be noted that even if values can be mapped into expectancy-value theory as personality variables that are equivalent to motives, information would still be required about other variables if differences across individuals in their responses to a given situation are to be accounted for. Obviously, when working within the framework of expectancy-value theory one also requires information about the expectancies that a situation elicits and the specific incentives or outcomes (both positive and negative) it provides.

The concept of expectancy is especially important in capturing the idea that actions may have different implications, each of which is associated with some *perceived likelihood* of occurrence. The concept is particularly congenial to theorists who conceive of behavior in means-end terms where actions are seen as embedded in a structured network of possible outcomes—some of which are sequentially linked to others, depending upon the nature of the actions. The concept of expectancy applies to actions that are *available* within a person's repertoire of responses, that is, to responses he can perform. Some of these responses may be more available than others, more firmly entrenched as habits (Atkinson & Feather, 1966, pp. 362–363). Expectancies and the exercise of habits are both a function of past learning and present reality. One can conceive of a person's expectancy of succeeding and moving up the occupational ladder, for example, as a function of his record of successes and failures in the past—in his school, in his job, and in other relevant situations. And the responses he has available would be outcomes of what he has been able to learn in the course of his development within the social environments and subcultures to which he has been exposed.

Present reality may facilitate or hinder instrumental actions and, together with the legacy of the past, influence whether a response *can* occur within a given situation. It can also influence the strength of a person's *expectancy* (or subjective probability) that the action will be effective. With delinquent boys, for instance, expectations that they can achieve their ends by legitimate means may be quite low, but by illegitimate means quite high. Some of the necessary responses for achieving their ends by legitimate means may not be available within their repertoire of habits, but illegitimate responses may be available. Furthermore, their subculture may in various ways block the use of legitimate means and favor illegitimate means instead.

In addition to the variables just mentioned one must also include the value of the particular *incentives* (positive and negative) that influence behavior in any given situation. In some cases the strength of these incentives will be a function of one's expectations. For example, the positive incentive value of success and the negative incentive value of failure both depend upon the degree to which one expects to succeed or fail, success having higher positive value the lower one's subjective probability of success, and failure having higher negative value the lower one's subjective probability of failure (Atkinson & Feather, 1966; Feather, 1959a, 1967c). But in other cases incentive values and expectations will be independent. Moreover, in ways not yet completely understood, the quality and quantity of particular incentives influence their value for individuals. We clearly need more theoretical consideration and empirical study of the various factors that influence incentive values.

As McClelland (1971) points out, it is rather easy to identify incentives (such as food and money) within any situation, but the "pulling power" of any positive incentive *for an individual* depends in part upon the strength of the underlying motivational dispositions that the incentive satisfies. Thus, although money may be an effective incentive generally, it works better for some people than for others, depending upon the underlying motives it satisfies. The same point was made previously by Atkinson and Feather (1966, p. 360) in the context of a theory of achievement motivation. The subjective attractiveness or *positive valence* of success for an individual at a particular level of task difficulty was conceived in terms of the positive incentive value of success for that level weighted by the strength of his motive to achieve success, positive valence being higher the stronger the motive. And the subjective repulsiveness or *negative valence* of failure was similarly conceived in terms of a particular negative incentive value of failure weighted by the strength of the motive to avoid failure.

Thus, motives may be viewed as affecting the valences of outcomes in specific situations so that these outcomes become more or less attractive or repulsive (with stronger or weaker "fields of force"—to use Lewin's [1935] term), subject in part to the motive structure of the person. In the same way one can assume (as French & Kahn [1962] do) that the valences of particular incentives are related to a person's dominant values. Like motives, values can influence valences. Money, for example, may be a potent incentive for people who assign a very high priority to *a comfortable life* in their value systems. Its incentive properties may also be bound up with the relative importance assigned to *a sense of accomplishment* and to other general values on Rokeach's lists. This type of analysis is clearly consistent with the view that values may be treated as a particular subclass of motives.

We should also note that incentives may be negative as well as positive. Actions can lead to punishments and costs as well as to goals and rewards. The valence of these negative incentives may also be weighted by the strength of underlying motives and values (as in the example above on the negative valence of failure).

Are there distinct roles for terminal and instrumental values as sources of valence? One can speculate that terminal values may influence the valence of specific outcomes or "end-states"—some outcomes being seen as more attractive (or repulsive) than others, whereas instrumental values may influence the valence of specific instrumental behaviors or means to ends—some courses of action being seen as more attractive (or repulsive) than others. For instance, money may be a more potent incentive for the person who assigns high importance to the terminal value *a comfortable life,* but the alternative means of obtaining it may vary in their valence, depending upon the rank order of relevant instrumental values. Honest courses of action may be more attractive to those who rank being *honest* high in their instrumental value systems than to those who rank it low, and so on. In a specific situation, therefore, different means to the same end may vary in their valence, contingent in part upon a person's dominant instrumental values, and different ends or goals that might be pursued may differ in their valence, contingent in part upon a person's dominant terminal values. The behavior that emerges in any given situation, then, depends not only upon the relative valence of different possible outcomes, but also upon the relative valence of alternative courses of action relating to the same possible outcome. And, in each case relevant values may be assumed to be important sources of these valences.

Finally, both expectancies and incentive values have a closer connection to the immediate situation than general motives and values that are assumed to transcend situations and to be person variables rather than situational variables.

EXPECTANCY-VALUE THEORY: COMBINING THE VARIABLES

Let us assume that we have a detailed specification in which each person is described in terms of his relevant motives and values and in which the situation is mapped according to the different possible outcomes that might occur and the alternative means of achieving each outcome. Let us also assume that we are able to specify the conditions under which particular motives or values are aroused and become salient. Then one should be able to take account of the situationally elicited expectancies and the subjective values (or valences) of different possible outcomes and courses of action in order to determine for each individual the strength of tendencies to perform particular responses that might be expected to lead to *positive* incentives and the strength of tendencies not to perform particular responses that might be expected to lead to *negative* incentives—or (in the more recent terminology) the strength of *instigating* and *inhibitory forces* (Atkinson & Birch, 1970, 1974). There would be other variables to consider as well, such as whether the necessary actions are available within the response repertoires of individuals, whether present actions can be related to future goals, whether there are unresolved tendencies carrying over from past situations, and so on. Furthermore, it should be remembered that actions are typically *overdetermined*. The sets of tendencies are typically related to more than one motive or general value. All of these considerations have been discussed in considerable detail in the applications of expectancy-value theory to the achievement domain that we noted earlier (for example, Atkinson & Feather, 1966; Atkinson & Raynor, 1974) and to other domains as well (such as information-seeking behavior, Feather, 1967*a*).

This kind of approach, which relates values to action in terms of expectancy-value theory, would call for far more sophisticated studies of values and action than have been conducted previously. These studies would require the manipulation of general values and their conditions of arousal by procedures involving selective and experimental control. They would also require the manipulation of the different possible ends or outcomes (positive and negative) that the situation may provide and the alternative means or possible courses of action that are related to each potential outcome. In this way one could systematically vary both means-end expectancies and valences.

Such an approach to values and action could turn out to be theoretically integrative and heuristic. If one were using the Value Survey only, the approach would be limited by the fact that Rokeach's list contains only positive terminal and instrumental values and no negative values at all. Measures of the strength of "avoidance" motives would be needed as well because these motives are assumed to be major determinants of inhibitory forces within the dynamics of action (Atkinson & Birch, 1974), just as "approach" motives are assumed to be major determinants of instigating forces.

The preceding, rather abstract discussion can be made more concrete by means of three examples. First, *freedom* as a value may become especially salient when freedom of action is threatened (see the literature on psychological reactance, Brehm, 1966). When the value is aroused, certain possible outcomes relating to the restoration of freedom may become more or less valent, depending in part upon the strength of *freedom* within each person's terminal value system and also upon the amount and quality of the outcome. The ensuing behavior would depend not only upon the degree of valence that these possible outcomes possess, but also upon the strength of the expectancies associated with those available courses of action that are seen as relevant to the desired consequences. Subject to present situational constraints and the past experience of the person, some alternative courses of action may be viewed as more likely to lead to successful restoration of freedom than others. And some of these instrumental behaviors may be more positively valent than others, depending upon the relative importance assigned to particular instrumental values (in line with our speculation in the preceding section). For example, novel and unusual solutions to the problem may be more attractive to individuals who assigned being *imaginative* a key place in their instrumental value systems; courses of action that include standing up for one's beliefs may have stronger positive valence (or attractiveness) to individuals who assigned a high priority to being *courageous,* and so on.

So far we have considered only factors that would affect instigating forces to action. But it should be clear that there may also be inhibitory forces that block action within situations. In the present example, some courses of action viewed as possible means to restoring freedom may also be seen to have high costs to the individual in the form of punishments and sanctions. These actions would, therefore, be resisted to some degree.

As a second example, we saw in Chapter 7 that student activists assigned a very high priority to *equality* in their terminal value systems. Assuming that values are sources of valence, it follows that various outcomes involving the preservation of existing equalities and the removal of inequalities on the college campus would have higher subjective value (or positive valence) for these activists than for nonactivists, who ranked *equality* lower in importance. Similarly, some ways of achieving these outcomes would have higher valence than others, according to the relative importance assigned to particular instrumental values. Thus, courses of action corresponding to the instrumental values *courageous, helpful, imaginative,* and *loving* might be more attractive for activists than for nonactivists, and courses of action corresponding to the instrumental values *ambitious, capable, cheerful, clean, obedient, polite,* and *responsible* might be less attractive for activists than for nonactivists (see Table 7.2). Some courses of action would be viewed as more likely to lead to success than others (that is, they would be associated with higher expectancies of success than others), depending upon each individual's past experience and the present circumstances. And, particularly on college campuses where sanctions are not always clear or easy to enforce, the strength of inhibitory forces that block action may be low. One could add other variables to this analysis, but already it should be clear that it captures many of the factors that have been mentioned in discussions of student activism (Chapter 7).

A final example: It is possible that the relative importance assigned to being *logical* (consistent, rational) would be associated with differences in the attractiveness of consistent modes of response among individuals. If this particular value were tied into expectancy-value theory as a personality characteristic that influences the valence of specific alternative courses of action in the immediate situation, it might provide a means of dealing with some of the complex questions that relate to individual differences in how people cope with cognitive inconsistencies (Abelson et al., 1968; Feather, 1967*a*, 1971*a*).

In conceptualizing each of the three examples just provided, one could consider other variables, some of which (like availability of responses, persisting inertial tendencies, and long-term future goals) we have mentioned before (see also Atkinson & Feather, 1966; Atkinson & Raynor, 1974). Moreover, the examples given are oversimplifications because they focused upon single values only. Typically, behavior is overdetermined, embracing the effects of more than one motive or value and involving complex sets of instigating and inhibitory forces for which rules of combination have to be specified.

The important point, however, is that it should be possible to consider the relationship of values to action within the framework of expectancy-value theory. This theory gives prominence to the multiplicative combination of expectancies and valences as determinants of instigating and inhibitory forces. In this approach general values aroused within a situation would enter as sources of *valence* for each individual. But the behavior that ensues would be related not only to these valences, but also to the individual's *expectations* about the likely consequences of available means—the perceived likelihood that specific courses of action will lead to positively or negatively valent outcomes. One therefore deals with a set of forces at the individual level in which valences are weighted by subjective probabilities. These forces, along with other variables (especially the unresolved, persisting motivational tendencies that the individual brings with him to the situation), may be assumed to be the basis for the direction that his behavior takes and for the changes that occur in the stream of activity.

CONFIDENCE IN THE ENVIRONMENT AND THE VALUE MATCH

The previous discussion has been restricted mainly to particular values and their relevance for action. But one can also relate entire value systems to action. Indeed, a basic assumption made in the studies of educational choice described in Chapter 3 was that students would tend to select educational environments that in their opinion best fitted their own personality characteristics, within the limits of choice open to them. More generally, this principle was seen as specifying one important mode of resolving a mismatch between person and environment—the selection of or migration to a more congenial environment.

This mode of response can also be understood in expectancy-value terms. A close fit between individual characteristics and commensurable aspects of the environment would probably be associated with a high expectation that valued reinforcements or rewards should prove to be available within that environment, these reinforcements outweighing possible threats or costs to the person (see Chapter 3). For example, if a person saw his own value systems as closely matching the perceived value systems of a particular environment, then he should be more likely to expect that his values will tend to be satisfied by that environment in the order of importance that he assigns to them. Where there is a significant mismatch, many of the person's important values would not be satisfied—that is, the amount and spread of reinforcements would be less. Similarly, the closer the match between a person's abilities and the demands that a situation makes upon him, the higher and more frequent should be the levels of positive reinforcement in that situation and the lower and less frequent should be the negative outcomes.

A close match between personal characteristics and commensurable properties of the environment should, therefore, be associated with high confidence in that environment as a source of positive reinforcements relative to negative costs. At a cognitive level, therefore, one can relate preference for matching environments to this general expectation about the more frequent availability of positive reinforcements, an expectation that is based upon present reality and one's experience in the past. In this way one can relate the matching principle and its relevance to selection of environments to expectancy-value theory, though at a very general level.

Furthermore, as we have argued before, preference for matching environments can also be related to the individual's attempts to achieve consistent states of affairs at the cognitive level as he responds to discrepancies between abstract and perceived cognitive structures. But the principle of consistency should not be assigned sovereign status. As noted above, *what choice might be expected to lead to and the perceived likelihood of those consequences* are basic considerations in the analyses of how people attempt to resolve inconsistencies. Action occurs within a structure of means-end relationships and has regard to expected consequences.

CONCLUDING REMARKS

In this final chapter we have reviewed many of the ideas discussed in previous chapters, and we have pointed to some new directions both in research and in theoretical conceptualization. Our program of studies has answered some questions and has uncovered some new issues. But that is as it should be. Social science rarely comes up with final answers. The quest for understanding is an ongoing pursuit, shaped by the values and paradigms that influence us at the moment, stimulated on occasion by flashes of insight and by the emergence of new ways of thinking about problems. Social science is a combined effort, and it is to be hoped that it will move to higher levels of organization, understanding, and achievement.

It should be clear that we view the concept of value as playing an important integrative role in social science, enabling one to deal with the individual in society—to build a bridge between the study of the individual and the more general analysis of social process and social structure.

We have reported a program of studies that is cumulative and continuing. We firmly believe that the study of human values is one of the central tasks for social science in the future. Let us approach this task with interdisciplinary cooperation in the hope not only of clarifying questions that are important for society, but also of discovering more about the nature of man.

References

ABELSON, R. P., ARONSON, E., McGUIRE, W. J., NEWCOMB, T. M., ROSENBERG, M. J., & TANNENBAUM, P. H. (Eds.). *Theories of cognitive consistency: A sourcebook.* Chicago: Rand McNally, 1968.

ABRAHAMSON, P. R. Generational change in American electoral behavior. *American Political Science Review,* 1974, *68,* 93–105.

ABRASH, D. T., & SCHNEIDER, F. W. Relationship between masculinity and academic adjustment in coeducational and all-male schools. Paper read at Southeastern Psychological Association, New Orleans, April, 1973.

ADELSON, J. What generation gap? *New York Times Magazine,* Jan. 18, 1970.

ADORNO, T. W., FRENKEL-BRUNSWIK, E., LEVINSON, D. J., & SANFORD, R. N. *The authoritarian personality.* New York: Harper, 1950.

ALBERT, E. M. Value systems. In D. L. Sills (Ed.), *International encyclopedia of the social sciences.* New York: Crowell Collier and Macmillan, 1968.

ALKER, H. R., JR. A typology of ecological fallacies. In M. Dogan & S. Rokkan (Eds.), *Quantitative ecological analysis in the social sciences.* Cambridge: MIT Press, 1969.

ALLPORT, G. W. Attitudes. In C. Murchison (Ed.), *Handbook of social psychology.* Worcester, Mass.: Clark University Press, 1935.

ALLPORT, G. W. *The nature of prejudice.* Reading, Mass.: Addison-Wesley, 1954.

ALLPORT, G. W., & VERNON, P. E. *A study of values: Manual of directions.* Boston: Houghton Mifflin, 1931.

ALLPORT, G. W., VERNON, P. E., & LINDZEY, G. *A study of values: Manual of directions (rev. ed.).* Boston: Houghton Mifflin, 1951.

ANASTASI, A. *Psychological testing.* New York: Macmillan, 1968.

ANDERSON, N. H. Likeableness ratings of 555 personality-trait words. *Journal of Personality and Social Psychology,* 1968, *9,* 272–279.

ANDRY, R. G. *Delinquency and parental pathology.* London: Methuen, 1960.

APPLEYARD, R. T. The population. In A. F. Davies & S. Encel (Eds.), *Australian society: A sociological introduction* (1st ed.). Melbourne: Cheshire, 1965.

ARMER, M. Methodological problems and possibilities in comparative research. In M. Armer & A. D. Grimshaw (Eds.), *Comparative social research: Methodological problems and strategies.* New York: Wiley, 1973.

ARMER, M., & GRIMSHAW, A. D. (Eds.). *Comparative social research: Methodological problems and strategies.* New York: Wiley, 1973.

ARONSON, E. Dissonance theory: Progress and problems. In R. P. Abelson, E. Aronson, W. J. McGuire, T. M. Newcomb, M. J. Rosenberg, & P. H. Tannenbaum (Eds.), *Theories of cognitive consistency: A sourcebook.* Chicago: Rand McNally, 1968.

ARONSON, E. *The social animal.* San Francisco: Freeman, 1972.

ASTIN, A. W., & PANOS, R. J. *The educational and vocational development of American college students.* Washington: American Council on Education, 1969.

ATKINSON, J. W. *An introduction to motivation.* Princeton: Van Nostrand, 1964.

ATKINSON, J. W., & BIRCH, D. *The dynamics of action.* New York: Wiley, 1970.

ATKINSON, J. W., & BIRCH, D. The dynamics of achievement-oriented activity. In J. W. Atkinson & J. O. Raynor (Eds.), *Motivation and achievement.* Washington: Winston, 1974.

ATKINSON, J. W., & FEATHER, N. T. (Eds.). *A theory of achievement motivation.* New York: Wiley, 1966.

ATKINSON, J. W., & LITWIN, G. H. Achievement motive and test anxiety conceived as motive to approach success and to avoid failure. *Journal of Abnormal and Social Psychology,* 1960, *60,* 52–63.

ATKINSON, J. W., & RAYNOR, J. O. (Eds.). *Motivation and achievement.* Washington: Winston, 1974.

BALTES, P. B., & NESSELROADE, J. R. Cultural change and adolescent personality development: An application of longitudinal sequences. *Developmental Psychology,* 1972, *7,* 244–256.

BARKER, R. *Ecological psychology.* Stanford: Stanford University Press, 1968.

BARTLETT, F. C. *Remembering: A study in experimental and social psychology.* Cambridge: At the University Press, 1932.

BECKER, G., & BAKAL, D. A. Subject anonymity and motivational distortion in self-report data. *Journal of Clinical Psychology,* 1970, *26,* 207–209.

BECKER, H. S. *Outsiders: Studies in the sociology of deviance.* New York: Free Press, 1963.

BEECH, R. P. Value systems, attitudes, and interpersonal attraction. *Dissertation Abstracts,* 1967, *28A,* 1125–1126.

BEECH, R. P., & SCHOEPPE, A. Development of value systems in adolescents. *Developmental Psychology,* 1974, *10,* 644–656.

BENGTSON, V. L. The generation gap: A review and typology of social-psychological perspectives. *Youth and Society,* 1970, *2,* 7–32.

BENGTSON, V. L., & BLACK, K. D. Intergenerational relations and continuities in socialization. In P. B. Baltes & K. W. Schaie (Eds.), *Life-span developmental psychology: Personality and socialization.* New York: Academic Press, 1973.

BENGTSON, V. L., FURLONG, M. J., & LAUFER, R. S. Time, aging, and the continuity of social structure: Themes and issues in generational analysis. *Journal of Social Issues,* 1974, *30* (2), 1–30.

BERLYNE, D. E. *Conflict, arousal, and curiosity.* New York: McGraw-Hill, 1960.

BERLYNE, D. E. *Structure and direction in thinking.* New York: Wiley, 1965.

BERLYNE, D. E. Curiosity and exploration. *Science,* 1966, *153,* 25–33.

BERRY, J. W. On cross-cultural comparability. *International Journal of Psychology,* 1969, *4,* 119–128.

BESWICK, D. G. Cognitive process theory of individual differences in curiosity. In

H. I. Day, D. E. Berlyne, & D. E. Hunt (Eds.), *Intrinsic motivation: A new direction in education.* Toronto: Holt, Rinehart, & Winston, 1971.

BESWICK, D. G., & HILLS, M. D. An Australian ethnocentrism scale. *Australian Journal of Psychology,* 1969, *21,* 211–225.

BESWICK, D. G., & HILLS, M. D. A survey of ethnocentrism in Australia. *Australian Journal of Psychology,* 1972, *24,* 153–163.

BETTELHEIM, B. Obsolete youth. *Encounter,* 1969, *33,* 29–42.

BETTELHEIM, B., & JANOWITZ, M. *Social change and prejudice.* London: Collier-Macmillan, 1964.

BLALOCK, H. M., JR. *Causal inferences in nonexperimental research.* Chapel Hill: University of North Carolina Press, 1961.

BLOCK, J. H. Conception of sex role: Some cross-cultural and longitudinal perspectives. *American Psychologist,* 1973, *28,* 512–526.

BLOCK, J. H., HAAN, N., & SMITH, M. B. Socialization correlates of student activism. *Journal of Social Issues,* 1969, *25* (4), 143–177.

BORDUA, D. J. Delinquent subcultures: Sociological interpretations of gang delinquency. *Annals of the American Academy of Political and Social Science,* 1961, *338* (November), 119–136.

BORRIE, W. D. *The cultural integration of immigrants.* Paris: UNESCO, 1959.

BORRIE, W. D. Note on the series. In J. I. Martin, *Community and identity: Refugee groups in Adelaide.* Canberra: Australian National University Press, 1972.

BOSHIER, R. Conservatism within families: A study of the generation gap. In G. D. Wilson (Ed.), *The psychology of conservatism.* New York: Academic Press, 1973.

BOWERS, K. S. Situationism in psychology: An analysis and a critique. *Psychological Review,* 1973, *80,* 307–336.

BRAUNGART, R. G. The sociology of generations and student politics: A comparison of the functionalist and generational unit models. *Journal of Social Issues,* 1974, *30* (2), 31–54.

BREHM, J. W. *A theory of psychological reactance.* New York: Academic Press, 1966.

BRIGHAM, J. C. Ethnic stereotypes. *Psychological Bulletin,* 1971, *6,* 15–38.

BRIM, O. G., JR., & WHEELER, S. *Socialization after childhood: Two essays.* New York: Wiley, 1966.

BRISLIN, R. W., LONNER, W. J., & THORNDIKE, R. M. *Cross-cultural research methods.* New York: Wiley, 1973.

BRONFENBRENNER, U. Freudian theories of identification and their derivatives. *Child Development,* 1960, *31,* 15–40.

BROWN, D. Personality, college environments, and academic productivity. In N. Sanford (Ed.), *The American College.* New York: Wiley, 1962.

BROWN, R. *Social psychology.* New York: Free Press, 1965.

BRUNER, J. S. (with J. M. Anglin) *Beyond the information given: Studies in the psychology of knowing.* New York: Norton, 1973.

BRUNSWIK, E. The conceptual focus of some psychological systems. *Journal of Unified Science,* 1939, *8,* 36–49.

BRUNSWIK, E. Representative design and probabilistic theory in a functional psychology. *Psychological Review,* 1955, *62,* 193–218.

BUSS, A. R. Generational analysis: Description, explanation, and theory. *Journal of Social Issues,* 1974, *30* (2), 55–71.

BYRNE, D. *The attraction paradigm.* New York: Academic Press, 1971.

CAMPBELL, A., & CONVERSE, P. E. (Eds.). *The human meaning of social change.* New York: Russell Sage Foundation, 1972.

CAMPBELL, D. T. Methodological suggestions from a comparative psychology of knowledge processes. *Inquiry,* 1959, *2,* 152–182.

CAMPBELL, D. T. Blind variation and selective retention in creative thought as in other knowledge processes. *Psychological Review,* 1960, *67,* 380–400.

CAMPBELL, D. T. Stereotypes and the perception of group differences. *American Psychologist,* 1967, *22,* 817–829.

CAMPBELL, D. T. Reforms as experiments. *American Psychologist,* 1969, *24,* 409–429.

CAMPBELL, D. T. Evolutionary epistemology. In P. A. Schilpp (Ed.), *The philosophy of Karl R. Popper.* LaSalle, Ill.: Open Court Publishing Co., 1974.

CAMPBELL, D. T., & FISKE, D. W. Convergent and discriminant validation by the multitrait-multimethod matrix. *Psychological Bulletin,* 1959, *56,* 81–105.

CAMPBELL, D. T., & STANLEY, J. C. Experimental and quasi-experimental designs for research on teaching. In N. L. Gage (Ed.), *Handbook of research on teaching.* Chicago: Rand McNally, 1963.

CAMPBELL, E. Q. Adolescent socialization. In D. A. Goslin (Ed.), *Handbook of socialization theory and research.* Chicago: Rand McNally, 1969.

CANTRIL, H. *The pattern of human concerns.* New Brunswick, N.J.: Rutgers University Press, 1965.

CLARK, C. M. G. *A short history of Australia* (1st ed.). London: Heinemann, 1963.

CLARK, K. B., & CLARK, M. P. Racial identification and racial preference in Negro children. In T. M. Newcomb & E. L. Hartley (Eds.), *Readings in social psychology.* New York: Holt, 1947.

CLARKE, G. *Urban Australia.* In A. F. Davies & S. Encel (Eds.), *Australian society: A sociological introduction* (2nd ed.). Melbourne: Cheshire, 1970.

CLOWARD, R. A., & OHLIN, L. E. *Delinquency and opportunity.* New York: Free Press, 1960.

COCHRANE, R. Values as correlates of deviancy. *British Journal of Social and Clinical Psychology,* 1974, *13,* 257–267.

COCHRANE, R., & ROKEACH, M. Rokeach's value survey: A methodological note. *Journal of experimental research in personality,* 1970, *4,* 159–161.

COFER, C. N., & APPLEY, M. H. *Motivation: Theory and research.* New York: Wiley, 1964.

COHEN, A. K. *Delinquent boys: The culture of the gang.* New York: Free Press, 1955.

COHEN, A. K., & SHORT, J. F., JR. Crime and juvenile delinquency. In R. K. Merton & R. Nisbet (Eds.), *Contemporary social problems* (3rd ed.). New York: Harcourt Brace Jovanovich, 1971.

COLE, M., GAY, J., GLICK, J. A., & SHARP, D. W. *The cultural context of learning and thinking.* New York: Basic Books, 1971.

COLE, M., & SCRIBNER, S. *Culture and thought.* New York: Wiley, 1974.

COLEMAN, J. S. *The adolescent society.* New York: Free Press, 1961.

COMREY, A. L. *A first course in factor analysis.* New York: Academic Press, 1973.

CONGALTON, A. A. *Status and prestige in Australia.* Melbourne: Cheshire, 1969.

CONGER, J. J., & MILLER, W. C. *Personality, social class, and delinquency.* New York: Wiley, 1966.

CONNELL, R. W. Political socialization in the American family: The evidence re-examined. *Public Opinion Quarterly,* 1972, *36,* 323–333.

CONNELL, R. W. You can't tell them apart nowadays, can you? *Search,* 1974, *5,* 282–285.

CONNELL, W. F., STROOBANT, R. E., SINCLAIR, K. E., CONNELL, R. W., & ROGERS, K. W. *12 to 20: Studies of city youth.* Sydney: Hicks Smith, 1975.

CONVERSE, P. E., & SCHUMAN, H. "Silent majorities" and the Vietnam war. *Scientific American,* 1970, *222,* 17–25.

COOK, T. D., & CAMPBELL, D. T. The design and conduct of quasi-experiments and true experiments in field settings. In M. D. Dunnette (Ed.), *Handbook of industrial and organizational research.* Chicago: Rand McNally, forthcoming.

COOMBS, C. H. *A theory of data.* New York: Wiley, 1964.

COOMBS, C. H., DAWES, R. M., & TVERSKY, A. *Mathematical psychology: An elementary introduction.* Englewood Cliffs, N.J.: Prentice-Hall, 1970.

COSER, L., & ROSENBERG, B. (Eds.). *Sociological theory: A book of readings.* London: Macmillan, 1969.

CRAIK, K. H. Environmental psychology. In *New directions in psychology, 4.* New York: Holt, Rinehart, & Winston, 1970.

CRONBACH, L. J., & FURBY, L. How we should measure "change"—or should we? *Psychological Bulletin,* 1970, *74,* 68–80.

CROSS, D. G. *Values and value systems as ascribed to self and parents by delinquents and non-delinquents.* Unpublished B.A. honor's thesis, Flinders University of South Australia, 1972.

DALE, R. R. *Mixed or single-sex school?* (Vol. 1). London: Routledge & Kegan Paul, 1969.

DALE, R. R. *Mixed or single-sex school?* (Vol. 2). London: Routledge & Kegan Paul, 1971.

DAVIES, A. F., & ENCEL, S. (Eds.). *Australian society* (2nd ed.). Melbourne: Cheshire, 1970.

DAWES, R. M. *Fundamentals of attitude measurement.* New York: Wiley, 1972.

DAWSON, J. L. M. Theory and research in cross-cultural psychology. *Bulletin of the British Psychological Society,* 1971, *24,* 291–306.

DAWSON, M. (Ed.). Australian families. *Search,* 1974, *5,* 277–348.

DAY, H. I., BERLYNE, D., & HUNT, D. E. (Eds.). *Intrinsic motivation: A new direction in education.* Toronto: Holt, Rinehart, & Winston, 1971.

DEUTSCHER, I. Asking questions cross-culturally: Some problems of linguistic comparability. In D. P. Warwick & S. Osherson (Eds.), *Comparative research methods.* Englewood Cliffs, N.J.: Prentice-Hall, 1973.

DICKSON, D. J. Religion and the missions. In R. G. Ward & D. A. M. Lea (Eds.), *An atlas of Papua and New Guinea.* Glasgow: Collins, 1970.

DOGAN, M., & ROKKAN, S. (Eds.). *Quantitative ecological analysis in the social sciences.* Cambridge: MIT Press, 1969.

DOUVAN, E., & ADELSON, J. *The adolescent experience.* New York: Wiley, 1966.

DOWNS, R. M., & STEA, D. *Image and environment: Cognitive mapping and spatial behavior.* Chicago: Aldine, 1973.

DUKES, W. F. Psychological studies of values. *Psychological Bulletin,* 1955, *52,* 24–50.

DUNSDORFS, E. [Third Latvia.] *Tresa Latvija.* Melbourne: Loma Printing Service, 1968.

DWYER, M. G. *Human values in agriculture.* Unpublished M.Sc. thesis, University of Melbourne, 1974.

EISENSTADT, S. N. *The absorption of immigrants.* London: Routledge & Kegan Paul, 1954.

EISENSTADT, S. N. *From generation to generation.* Glencoe, Ill.: Free Press, 1956.

EISENSTADT, S. N. Archetypal patterns of youth. In E. H. Erikson (Ed.), *Youth: Change and challenge.* New York: Basic Books, 1963.

EKEHAMMAR, B. Interactionism in personality from a historical perspective. *Psychological Bulletin,* 1974, *81,* 1026–1048.

ELDER, G. H. *Children of the great depression.* Chicago: University of Chicago Press, 1974.

ELINSON, J., & HAINES, V. T. Role of anonymity in attitude surveys. *American Psychologist,* 1950, *5,* 315.

ELLERMAN, D. A. *Australian student activists: Some psychological characteristics.* Unpublished M.A. thesis, Flinders University of South Australia, 1975.

EMMERICH, W. Socialization and sex-role development. In P. B. Baltes & K. W. Schaie (Eds.), *Life-span developmental psychology: Personality and socialization.* New York: Academic Press, 1973.

ENCEL, S. *Equality and authority.* London: Tavistock, 1970. (a)

ENCEL, S. The family. In A. F. Davies & S. Encel (Eds.), *Australian society: A sociological introduction* (2nd ed.). Melbourne: Cheshire, 1970. (b)

EPSTEIN, Y. M., KRUPAT, E., & OBUDHO, C. Clean is beautiful: The effects of race and cleanliness on children's preferences. *Journal of Social Issues,* in press, 1975.

ERIKSON, E. H. *Childhood and society.* New York: Norton, 1950.

ERIKSON, E. H. Identity and the life cycle: Selected papers. *Psychological Issues,* 1959, *1,* Monograph 1.

ERIKSON, E. H. *Identity: Youth and crisis.* New York: Norton, 1968.

ERIKSON, E. H. Reflections on the dissent of contemporary youth. *Daedalus,* 1970, *99,* 154–176.

EYSENCK, H. J. *Crime and personality.* London: Routledge & Kegan Paul, 1964.

FEAGIN, J. R. Poverty: We still believe that God helps those who help themselves. *Psychology Today,* 1972, *6,* 101–129.

FEATHER, N. T. Subjective probability and decision under uncertainty. *Psychological Review,* 1959, *66,* 150–164. (a)

FEATHER, N. T. Success probability and choice behavior. *Journal of Experimental Psychology,* 1959, *58,* 257–266. (b)

FEATHER, N. T. The relationship of persistence at a task to expectation of success and achievement related motives. *Journal of Abnormal and Social Psychology,* 1961, *63,* 552–561.

FEATHER, N. T. The study of persistence. *Psychological Bulletin,* 1962, *59,* 94–115.

FEATHER, N. T. Mowrer's revised two-factor theory and the motive-expectancy-value model. *Psychological Review,* 1963, *70,* 500–515.

FEATHER, N. T. A structural balance model of communication effects. *Psychological Review*, 1964, *71*, 291–313.

FEATHER, N. T. The prediction of interpersonal attraction: Effects of sign and strength of relations in different structures. *Human Relations*, 1966, *19*, 213–237.

FEATHER, N. T. An expectancy-value model of information-seeking behavior. *Psychological Review*, 1967, *74*, 342–360. (a)

FEATHER, N. T. A structural balance approach to the analysis of communication effects. In L. Berkowitz (Ed.), *Advances in experimental social psychology* (Vol. 3). New York: Academic Press, 1967. (b)

FEATHER, N. T. Valence of outcome and expectation of success in relation to task difficulty and perceived locus of control. *Journal of Personality and Social Psychology*, 1967, *7*, 372–386. (c)

FEATHER, N. T. Attitude and selective recall. *Journal of Personality and Social Psychology*, 1969, *12*, 310–319. (a)

FEATHER, N. T. Attribution of responsibility and valence of success and failure in relation to initial confidence and task performance. *Journal of Personality and Social Psychology*, 1969, *13*, 129–144. (b)

FEATHER, N. T. Balancing and positivity effects in social recall. *Journal of Personality*, 1970, *38*, 602–628. (a)

FEATHER, N. T. Educational choice and student attitudes in relation to terminal and instrumental values. *Australian Journal of Psychology*, 1970, *22*, 127–144. (b)

FEATHER, N. T. Value systems in state and church schools. *Australian Journal of Psychology*, 1970, *22*, 299–313. (c)

FEATHER, N. T. Organization and discrepancy in cognitive structures. *Psychological Review*, 1971, *78*, 355–379. (a)

FEATHER, N. T. Similarity of value systems as a determinant of educational choice at university level. *Australian Journal of Psychology*, 1971, *23*, 201–211. (b)

FEATHER, N. T. Test-retest reliability of individual values and value systems. *Australian Psychologist*, 1971, *6*, 181–188. (c)

FEATHER, N. T. Value differences in relation to ethnocentrism, intolerance of ambiguity, and dogmatism. *Personality: An International Journal*, 1971, *2*, 349–366. (d)

FEATHER, N. T. Value similarity and school adjustment. *Australian Journal of Psychology*, 1972, *24*, 193–208. (a)

FEATHER, N. T. Value similarity and value systems in state and independent secondary schools. *Australian Journal of Psychology*, 1972, *24*, 305–315. (b)

FEATHER, N. T. Value systems and education: The Flinders programme of value research. *Australian Journal of Education*, 1972, *16*, 136–149. (c)

FEATHER, N. T. Cognitive differentiation, cognitive isolation, and dogmatism: Rejoinder and further analysis. *Sociometry*, 1973, *36*, 221–236. (a)

FEATHER, N. T. Effects of response anonymity on assessment of own and school value systems and satisfaction with school. *British Journal of Educational Psychology*, 1973, *43*, 140–150. (b)

FEATHER, N. T. The measurement of values: Effects of different assessment procedures. *Australian Journal of Psychology*, 1973, *25*, 221–231. (c)

FEATHER, N. T. Value change among university students. *Australian Journal of Psychology*, 1973, *25*, 57–70. (d)

FEATHER, N. T. Coeducational, values, and satisfaction with school. *Journal of Educational Psychology*, 1974, *66*, 9–15. (a)

FEATHER, N. T. Explanations of poverty in Australian and American samples: The person, society, or fate? *Australian Journal of Psychology*, 1974, *26*, 199–216. (b)

FEATHER, N. T. Factor structure of the conservatism scale: Results from an Australian survey. *Australian Psychologist*, 1975, *10*, 179–184. (a)

FEATHER, N. T. Values and income level. *Australian Journal of Psychology*, 1975, *27*, 23–30. (b)

FEATHER, N. T., & COLLINS, J. M. Differences in attitudes and values of students in relation to program of study at a college of advanced education. *Australian Journal of Education*, 1974, *18*, 16–29.

FEATHER, N. T., & CROSS, D. G. Value systems and delinquency: Parental and generational discrepancies in value systems for delinquent and non-delinquent boys. *British Journal of Social and Clinical Psychology*, 1975.

FEATHER, N. T., & HUTTON, M. A. Value systems of students in Papua New Guinea and Australia. *International Journal of Psychology*, 1974, *9*, 91–104.

FEATHER, N. T., & PEAY, E. R. The structure of terminal and instrumental values: Dimensions and clusters. *Australian Journal of Psychology*, in press.

FEATHER, N. T., & RUDZITIS, A. Subjective assimilation among Latvian adolescents: Effects of ethnic schools and perceptions of value systems. *International Migration*, 1974, *12*, 71–87.

FEATHER, N. T., & SIMON, J. G. Attribution of responsibility and valence of outcome in relation to initial confidence and success and failure of self and other. *Journal of Personality and Social Psychology*, 1971, *18*, 173–188.

FEATHER, N. T., & WASYLUK, G. Many roads lead to Rome: A reply to Witton. *Australian and New Zealand Journal of Sociology*, 1973, *9* (3), 25–26. (a)

FEATHER, N. T., & WASYLUK, G. Subjective assimilation among Ukrainian migrants: Value similarity and parent-child differences. *Australian and New Zealand Journal of Sociology*, 1973, *9* (1), 16–31. (b)

FELDMAN, K. A., & NEWCOMB, T. M. *The impact of college on students* (Vols. 1 and 2). San Francisco: Jossey-Bass, 1969.

FENDRICH, J. M. Activists ten years later: A test of generational unit continuity. *Journal of Social Issues*, 1974, *30* (3), 95–118.

FERGUSON, T. *The young delinquent and his social setting*. Oxford: Oxford University Press, 1952.

FESTINGER, L. Informal social communication. *Psychological Review*, 1950, *57*, 271–282.

FESTINGER, L. A theory of social comparison processes. *Human Relations*, 1954, *7*, 117–140.

FESTINGER, L. *A theory of cognitive dissonance*. Evanston, Ill.: Row, Peterson, 1957.

FESTINGER, L. Behavioral support for opinion change. *Public Opinion Quarterly*, 1964, *28*, 404–417.

FEUER, L. S. *The conflict of generations*. New York: Basic Books, 1969.

FIEDLER, F. E. *A theory of leadership effectiveness*. New York: McGraw-Hill, 1967.

FINNEY, R. S. Would-be entrepreneurs? A study of motivation in New Guinea. *New Guinea Research Bulletin*, No. 41, Canberra: Australia National University, 1971.

FISHBEIN, M. The prediction of behaviors from attitudinal variables. In C. D. Mortensen & K. K. Sereno (Eds.), *Advances in communication research*. New York: Harper & Row, 1973.

FISHBEIN, M., & AJZEN, I. Attitudes and opinions. *Annual Review of Psychology*, 1972, *23*, 487–544.

FISHBEIN, M., & AJZEN, I. Attitudes towards objects as predictors of single and multiple behavioral criteria. *Psychological Review*, 1974, *81*, 59–74.

FISHKIN, J., KENISTON, K., & MACKINNON, C. Moral reasoning and political ideology. *Journal of Personality and Social Psychology*, 1973, *27*, 109–119.

FLACKS, R. The liberated generation: An exploration of the roots of social protest. *Journal of Social Issues*, 1967, *23* (3), 52–75.

FOA, U. G., & FOA, E. B. *Societal structures of the mind*. Springfield, Ill.: Charles C. Thomas, 1974.

FRENCH, J. R. P., JR., & KAHN, R. L. A programmatic approach to studying the industrial environment and mental health. *Journal of Social Issues*, 1962, *18* (3), 1–47.

FREY, F. W. Cross-cultural survey research in political science. In R. T. Holt & J. E. Turner (Eds.), *The methodology of comparative research*. New York: Free Press, 1970.

FRIEDMAN, L. N., GOLD, A. R., & CHRISTIE, R. Dissecting the generation gap: Intergenerational and intrafamilial similarities and differences. *Public Opinion Quarterly*, 1972, 334–346.

FRIJDA, N. H., & JAHODA, G. On the scope and methods of cross-cultural research. *International Journal of Psychology*, 1966, *1*, 109–127.

FULLER, C. Effect of anonymity on return rate and response bias in a mail survey. *Journal of Applied Psychology*, 1974, *59*, 292–296.

GELLER, J. D., & HOWARD, G. Some sociopsychological characteristics of student political activists. *Journal of Applied Social Psychology*, 1972, *2*, 114–137.

GETZELS, J. W. A social psychology of education. In G. Lindzey & E. Aronson (Eds.), *The handbook of social psychology* (Vol. 5). Reading, Mass.: Addison-Wesley, 1969.

GIBBONS, D. C. *Delinquent behavior*. Englewood Cliffs, N.J.: Prentice-Hall, 1970.

GLENN, N. D. Class and party support in the United States: Recent and emerging trends. *Public Opinion Quarterly*, 1973, *37*, 1–20.

GLENN, N. D., & HEFNER, T. Further evidence on aging and party identification. *Public Opinion Quarterly*, 1972, *36*, 31–47.

GLUECK, S., & GLUECK, E. *Unraveling juvenile delinquency*. Cambridge: Harvard University Press, 1950.

GLUECK, S., & GLUECK, E. *Predicting delinquency and crime*. Cambridge: Harvard University Press, 1959.

GLUECK, S., & GLUECK, E. *Family environment and delinquency*. Boston: Houghton Mifflin, 1962.

GLUECK, S., & GLUECK, E. *Toward a typology of juvenile offenders: Implications for therapy and prevention*. New York: Grune & Stratton, 1970.

GOFFMAN, E. *The presentation of self in everyday life.* Garden City, N.Y.: Doubleday, 1959.

GOFFMAN, E. *Asylums.* Garden City, N.Y.: Doubleday, 1961.

GOFFMAN, E. *Stigma: Notes on the management of spoiled identity.* Englewood Cliffs, N.J.: Prentice-Hall, 1963.

GOLD, M. *Delinquent behavior in an American city.* Belmont, Calif.: Brooks-Cole, 1970.

GORDON, C., & GERGEN, K. J. (Eds.). *The self in social interaction.* (Vol. 1). New York: Wiley, 1968.

GORDON, M. M. *Assimilation in American life.* New York: Oxford University Press, 1964.

GORSUCH, R. L. Rokeach's approach to value systems and social compassion. *Review of Religious Research,* 1970, *11,* 139–143.

GOULD, R. Adult life stages: Growth toward self-tolerance. *Psychology Today,* 1975, *8,* 74–78.

GREENSTEIN, T., & BENNETT, R. R. Order effects in Rokeach's Value Survey. *Journal of Research in Personality,* 1974, *8,* 393–396.

GRYGIER, T., CHESLEY, J., & Tuters, E. W. Parental deprivation: A study of delinquent children. *British Journal of Criminology,* 1969, *9,* 209–253.

GUTTMAN, L. A general nonmetric technique for finding the smallest coordinate space for a configuration of points. *Psychometrika,* 1966, *33,* 469–506.

HAAN, N., SMITH, M. B., & BLOCK, J. Moral reasoning in young adults: Political-social behavior, family background, and personality correlates. *Journal of Personality and Social Psychology,* 1968, *10,* 183–201.

HANCOCK, W. K. *Australia.* London: Ernest Benn, 1930.

HANEY, B., & GOLD, M. The juvenile delinquent nobody knows. *Psychology Today,* 1973, *7,* 49–55.

HANNAN, M. T. Problems of aggregation. In H. M. Blalock, Jr. (Ed.), *Causal models in the social sciences.* Chicago: Aldine–Atherton, 1971.

HARARY, F., NORMAN, R. Z., & CARTWRIGHT, D. *Structural models: An introduction to the theory of directed graphs.* New York: Wiley, 1965.

HARRISON, J. D. The Kluckhohn value-orientation research instrument used in Papua New Guinea. *New Guinea Psychologist,* 1974, *6,* 3–8.

HARVEY, O. J., HUNT, D. E., SCHRODER, H. M. *Conceptual systems and personality organization.* New York: Wiley, 1961.

HAUTALUOMA, J. E., & SCOTT, W. A. Values and sociometric choices of incarcerated juveniles. *Journal of Social Psychology,* 1973, *91,* 229–237.

HAVIGHURST, R. J. *Developmental tasks and education.* New York: David McKay, 1972.

HAVIGHURST, R. J. History of developmental psychology: Socialization and personality development through the life span. In P. B. Baltes & K. W. Schaie (Eds.), *Life-span developmental psychology: Personality and socialization.* New York: Academic Press, 1973.

HAYS, W. L. *Quantification in psychology.* Belmont, Calif.: Brooks-Cole, 1967.

HEBB, D. O. *The organization of behavior.* New York: Wiley, 1949.

HEIDER, F. Attitudes and cognitive organization. *Journal of Psychology,* 1946, *21,* 107–112.

HEIDER, F. *The psychology of interpersonal relations.* New York: Wiley, 1958.

318   REFERENCES

HELSON, H. *Adaptation-level theory: An experimental and systematic approach to behavior.* New York: Harper, 1964.

HERZBERG, F., MAUSNER, B., & SNYDERMAN, B. B. *The motivation to work* (1st ed.). New York: Wiley, 1959.

HESS, R. D., & HANDEL, G. *Family worlds, a psychosocial approach to family life.* Chicago: University of Chicago Press, 1959.

HICKS, R. E. Vocational interests, values, and abilities of some Australian high school students in Papua New Guinea: Cross-cultural comparisons. *New Guinea Psychologist,* 1974, 6, 17–24.

HILL, R. *Family development in three generations.* Cambridge, Mass.: Schenkman, 1970. (a)

HILL, R. The three-generation research design: Method for studying family and social change. In R. Hill & R. Konig (Eds.), *Families in east and west: Socialization process and kinship ties.* Paris: Mouton, 1970. (b)

HILL, R., & ALDOUS, J. Socialization for marriage and parenthood. In D. A. Goslin (Ed.), *Handbook of socialization theory and research.* Chicago: Rand McNally, 1969.

HOFSTADTER, R. *Anti-intellectualism in American life.* New York: Knopf, 1963.

HOGE, D. R., & BENDER, I. E. Factors affecting value change among college graduates in adult life. *Journal of Personality and Social Psychology,* 1974, 29, 572–585.

HOLLAND, J. L. *The psychology of vocational choice: A theory of personality types and model environments.* Waltham, Mass.: Blaisdell, 1966.

HOLLAND, J. L. *Making vocational choices: A theory of careers.* Englewood Cliffs, N. J.: Prentice-Hall, 1973.

HOLLEN, C. C. *The stability of values and value systems.* Unpublished M.A. thesis, Michigan State University Library, 1967.

HOMANT, R. Semantic differential ratings and rank-ordering of values. *Educational and Psychological Measurement,* 1969, 29, 885–889.

HUBER, J., & FORM, W. H. *Income and ideology: An analysis of the American political formula.* New York: Free Press, 1973.

HUDSON, L. *Contrary imaginations: A psychological study of the young student.* New York: Schocken, 1966.

HUNT, D. E. *Matching models in education.* Toronto: Ontario Institute for Studies in Education, 1971.

HUNT, J. McV. *Intelligence and experience.* New York: Ronald, 1961.

HUNT, J. McV. Toward a history of intrinsic motivation. In H. I. Day, D. E. Berlyne, & D. E. Hunt (Eds.), *Intrinsic motivation: A new direction in education.* Toronto: Holt, Rinehart, & Winston, 1971.

HUTTON, M. A., & RUMENS, J. Long and short expatriate contact areas of Papua New Guinea. *New Guinea Psychologist,* 1974, 6, 34–35.

HYMAN, H., & SINGER, E. An introduction to reference group theory and research. In H. Hyman & E. Singer (Eds.), *Readings in reference group theory and research.* New York: Free Press, 1968.

INSEL, P. M., & MOOS, R. H. Psychological environments: Expanding the scope of human ecology. *American Psychologist,* 1974, 29, 179–188.

ITTELSON, W. H., PROSHANSKY, H. M., RIVLIN, L. G., & WINKEL, G. H. *An introduction to environmental psychology.* New York: Holt, Rinehart, & Winston, 1974.

JACOB, P. E. *Changing values in college: An exploratory study of the impact of college teaching.* New York: Harper, 1957.

JAMES, L. R., & JONES, A. P. Organizational climate: A review of theory and research. *Psychological Bulletin,* 1974, *81,* 1096–1112.

JAUNZEMS, I., & BROWN, L. B. A social-psychological study of Latvian immigrants in Canberra. *International Migration,* 1972, *10,* 53–70.

JENNINGS, M. K., & NIEMI, R. G. *The political character of adolescence.* Princeton: Princeton University Press, 1974.

JENNINGS, M. K., & NIEMI, R. G. Continuity and change in political orientations: A longitudinal study of two generations. *American Political Science Review,* in press.

JESNESS, C. F. *The Jesness inventory: Development and validation.* Research Report No. 29, Sacramento: California Youth Authority, 1962.

JOHNSTON, R. *Immigrant assimilation.* Perth, W. A.: Paterson Brokensha, 1965.

JOHNSTON, R. *Future Australians: Immigrant children in Perth, Western Australia.* Canberra: Australian National University Press, 1972.

JONES, E. E., & GERARD, H. B. *Foundations of social psychology.* New York: Wiley, 1967.

JONES, F. L. Ethnic concentration and assimilation: An Australian case study. *Social Forces,* 1967, *45,* 412–423.

JONES, J. C., SHALLCRASS, J., & DENNIS, C. C. Coeducation and adolescent values. *Journal of Educational Psychology,* 1972, *63,* 334–341.

JOYCE, J. T. C. A preliminary study of cultural differences in values influencing western education in the Enga district. Part I: Personal and clan values. *New Guinea Psychologist,* 1974, *6,* 9–16. (a)

JOYCE, J. T. C. A preliminary study of cultural differences in values influencing western education in the Enga district. Part II: Moral development and cognitive factors. *New Guinea Psychologist,* 1974, *6,* 63–77. (b)

KAGAN, J. Acquisition and significance of sex typing and sex role identity. In L. Hoffman & M. Hoffman (Eds.), *Review of child development* (Vol. 1). New York: Russell Sage, 1964.

KAPLAN, S. Cognitive maps in perception and thought. In R. M. Downs & D. Stea (Eds.), *Image and environment: Cognitive mapping and spatial behavior.* Chicago: Aldine, 1973.

KASSCHAU, P. L., RANSFORD, H. E., & BENGTSON, V. L. Generational consciousness and youth movement participation: Contrasts in blue collar and white collar youth. *Journal of Social Issues,* 1974, *30* (3), 69–94.

KATZ, C., KATZ, F. M., & OLPHERT, W. B. *What happens to students.* Unpublished manuscript, University of New England, Armidale, New South Wales, 1965.

KATZ, D. The functional approach to the study of attitudes. *Public Opinion Quarterly,* 1960, *24,* 163–204.

KATZ, D. Factors affecting social change: A social-psychological interpretation. *Journal of Social Issues,* 1974, *30* (3), 159–180.

KATZ, D., & GEORGOPOULOS, B. S. Organizations in a changing world. *Journal of Applied Behavioral Science,* 1971, *7,* 342–370.

KATZ, D., & STOTLAND, E. A preliminary statement to a theory of attitude structure and change. In S. Koch (Ed.), *Psychology: A study of a science.* New York: McGraw-Hill, 1959.

KELLY, G. A. *The psychology of personal constructs.* New York: Norton, 1955.

KELLY, K., SILVERMAN, B. I., & COCHRANE, R. Social desirability and the Rokeach value survey. *Journal of Experimental Research in Personality,* 1972, *6,* 84–87.

KELMAN, H. C. Processes of opinion change. *Public Opinion Quarterly,* 1961, *25,* 57–78.

KELMAN, H. C. Attitudes are alive and well and gainfully employed in the sphere of action. *American Psychologist,* 1974, *29,* 310–324. (a)

KELMAN, H. C. Social influence and linkages between the individual and the social system: Further thoughts on the processes of compliance, identification, and internalization. In J. Tedeschi (Ed.), *Perspectives on social power.* Chicago: Aldine, 1974. (b)

KENISTON, K. The sources of student dissent. *Journal of Social Issues,* 1967, *23* (3), 108–137.

KENISTON, K. *Young radicals: Notes on committed youth.* New York: Harcourt, Brace & World, 1968.

KENISTON, K. *Youth and dissent: The rise of a new opposition.* New York: Harcourt Brace Jovanovich, 1971.

KENISTON, K. *Radicals and militants: Empirical research on campus unrest.* Lexington, Mass.: Lexington Books, D.C. Heath, 1973.

KERPELMAN, L. C. *Activists and nonactivists: A psychological study of American college students.* New York: Behavioral Publications, 1972.

KISH, G. B., NETTERBEG, E. E., & LEAHY, L. Stimulus-seeking and conservatism. *Journal of Clinical Psychology,* 1973, *29,* 17–20.

KLAUSNER, S. Z. *On man in his environment.* San Francisco: Jossey-Bass, 1971.

KLOPFER, P. H. *Habitats and territories: A study of the use of space by animals.* New York: Basic Books, 1969.

KLUCKHOHN, C. Values and value orientations in the theory of action. In T. Parsons & E. A. Shils (Ed.), *Toward a general theory of action.* Cambridge: Harvard University Press, 1951.

KLUCKHOHN, F. R., & STRODTBECK, F. L. *Variations in value orientations.* Evanston, Ill.: Row, Peterson, 1961.

KOFFKA, K. *Principles of gestalt psychology.* New York: Harcourt, Brace, 1935.

KOHLBERG, L. A cognitive-developmental analysis of children's sex-role concepts and attitudes. In E. E. Maccoby (Ed.), *The development of sex differences.* Stanford: Stanford University Press, 1966.

KOHLBERG, L. Stage and sequence: The cognitive-developmental approach to socialization. In D. A. Goslin (Ed.), *Handbook of socialization theory and research.* Chicago: Rand McNally, 1969.

KOHLER, W. *The place of value in a world of facts.* New York: Liveright, 1938.

KOHN, M. L. *Class and conformity: A study in values.* Homewood, Ill.: Dorsey, 1969.

KRECH, D., & CRUTCHFIELD, R. S. *Theory and problems of social psychology.* New York: McGraw-Hill, 1948.

KRUSKAL, J. B. Multidimensional scaling by optimizing goodness of fit to a nonmetric hypothesis. *Psychometrika,* 1964, *29,* 1–27.

KUKURS, I. *The assimilation of Latvian immigrants in Australia.* Unpublished M.A. thesis, University of Adelaide, 1968.

KUNZ, E. F. European migrant absorption in Australia. *International Migration,* 1971, *9,* 68–79.

LANCE, G. N., & WILLIAMS, W. T. Mixed-data classificatory programs: I. Agglomerative systems. *The Australian Computer Journal,* 1967, *1,* 15–20.

LAUFER, R. S., & BENGTSON, V. L. Generations, aging, and social stratification: On the development of generational units. *Journal of Social Issues,* 1974, *30* (3), 181–205.

LEE, T. R. Psychology and living space. In R. M. Downs & D. Stea (Eds.), *Image and environment: Cognitive mapping and spatial behavior.* Chicago: Aldine, 1973.

LeVINE, R. A., & CAMPBELL, D. T. *Ethnocentrism: Theories of conflict, attitudes, and group behavior.* New York: Wiley, 1972.

LEWIN, K. *A dynamic theory of personality.* New York: McGraw-Hill, 1935.

LEWIN, K. *Field theory in social science.* New York: Harper, 1951.

LIPSET, S. M. *The first new nation.* New York: Basic Books, 1963. (a)

LIPSET, S. M. The value patterns of democracy: A case study in comparative analysis. *American Sociological Review,* 1963, *28,* 515–531. (b)

LIPSET, S. M. *Rebellion in the university.* Boston: Little, Brown & Co., 1972.

LITTLE, G. *The university experience.* Melbourne: Melbourne University Press, 1970.

MAAS, H. S., & KUYPERS, J. A. *From thirty to seventy: A forty-year longitudinal study of adult life styles and personality.* San Francisco: Jossey-Bass, 1974.

MACCOBY, E. E. (Ed.). *The development of sex differences.* Stanford: Stanford University Press, 1966.

McCLELLAND, D. C. Methods of measuring human motivation. In J. W. Atkinson (Ed.), *Motives in fantasy, action, and society.* New York: Van Nostrand, 1958.

McCLELLAND, D. C. Toward a theory of motive acquisition. *American Psychologist,* 1965, *20,* 321–333.

McCLELLAND, D. C. Longitudinal trends in the relation of thought to action. *Journal of Consulting Psychology,* 1966, *30,* 479–483.

McCLELLAND, D. C. *Assessing human motivation.* New York: General Learning Press, 1971.

McCLELLAND, D. C., ATKINSON, J. W., CLARK, R. A., & LOWELL, E. L. *The achievement motive.* New York: Appleton-Century, 1953.

McCLELLAND, D. C., & WINTER, D. G. *Motivating economic achievement.* New York: Free Press, 1969.

McDOUGALL, W. *An introduction to social psychology.* London: Methuen, 1926.

McGUIRE, W. J. The nature of attitudes and attitude change. In G. Lindzey & E. Aronson (Eds.), *The handbook of social psychology* (Vol. 3). Reading, Mass.: Addison-Wesley, 1969.

McLELLAN, D. D. *Values, value systems, and the developmental structure of moral judgment.* Unpublished M.A. thesis, Michigan State University Library, 1970.

McREYNOLDS, P. The three faces of cognitive motivation. In H. I. Day, D. E. Berlyne, & D. E. Hunt (Eds.), *Intrinsic motivation: A new direction in education.* Toronto: Holt, Rinehart, & Winston, 1971.

MANNHEIM, K. *Essays on the sociology of knowledge.* London: Routledge & Kegan Paul, 1952.

MARTIN, J. I. *Refugee settlers: A study of displaced persons in Australia.* Canberra: Australian National University Press, 1965.

MARTIN, J. I. *Community and identity: Refugee groups in Adelaide.* Canberra: Australian National University Press, 1972.

MASLOW, A. H. *Motivation and personality.* New York: Harper & Row, 1954.

MATZA, D. *Delinquency and drift.* New York: Wiley, 1964.

MATZA, D., & SYKES, G. Juvenile delinquency and subterranean values. *American Sociological Review,* 1961, *26,* 712–719.

MAYER, K. B. Social stratification in two equalitarian societies: Australia and the U.S. *Social Research,* 1964, *31,* 435–465.

MEAD, M. Cultural determinants of behavior. In A. Roe & G. C. Simpson (Eds.), *Behavior and evolution.* New Haven: Yale University Press, 1958.

MEDINNUS, G. R. Delinquents' perceptions of their parents. *Journal of Consulting Psychology,* 1965, *29,* 592–593.

MERTON, R. K. *Social theory and social structure* (Rev. ed.). New York: Free Press, 1968.

MERTON, R. K. Social problems and sociological theory. In R. K. Merton & R. Nisbet (Eds.), *Contemporary social problems* (3rd ed.). New York: Harcourt Brace Jovanovich, 1971.

MILLER, G. A., GALANTER, E., & PRIBRAM, K. H. *Plans and the structure of behavior.* New York: Holt, 1960.

MILLER, W. B. Lower class culture as a generating milieu of gang delinquency. *Journal of Social Issues,* 1958, *14,* 5–19.

MISCHEL, W. Sex-typing and socialization. In P. H. Mussen (Ed.), *Carmichael's handbook of child psychology* (Vol. 2). New York: Wiley, 1970.

MITCHELL, J. V., JR. Education's challenge to psychology: The prediction of behavior from person-environment interactions. *Review of Educational Research,* 1969, *39,* 695–721.

MITCHELL, T. R. Expectancy models of job satisfaction, occupational preference and effort: A theoretical, methodological, and empirical appraisal. *Psychological Bulletin,* 1974, *81,* 1053–1077.

MOOS, R. Conceptualizations of human environments. *American Psychologist,* 1973, *28,* 652–665.

MORRIS, C. W. *Varieties of human value.* Chicago: University of Chicago Press, 1956.

MOULIK, T. K. Income aspiration, entrepreneurship, and the social norm of egalitarianism. In C. J. S. Brammall, R. E. Hicks, & M. A. Hutton (Eds.), *Psychology in Papua New Guinea: A 1972 perspective,* forthcoming.

MULFORD, W. R., & YOUNG, R. E. Cognitive development studies in Papua New Guinea. *New Guinea Psychologist.* 1973 (Monograph Supplement No. 5).

MURRAY, H. *Explorations in personality.* New York: Oxford University Press, 1938.

NEL, E., HELMREICH, R., & ARONSON, E. Opinion change in the advocate as a function of the persuasibility of his audience: A clarification of the meaning of dissonance. *Journal of Personality and Social Psychology,* 1969, *12,* 117–124.

NELSON, H. Contact and administration control. In R. G. Ward & D. A. M. Lea (Eds.), *An atlas of Papua and New Guinea.* Glasgow: Collins, 1970.

NELSON, H. *Papua New Guinea: Black unity or black chaos.* Ringwood, Vic.: Penguin, 1972.

NEUGARTEN, B. L. *Personality in middle and late life.* New York: Atherton Press, 1964.

NEUGARTEN, B. L. Adult personality: Toward a psychology of the life-cycle. In B. L. Neugarten (Ed.), *Middle age and aging: A reader in social psychology.* Chicago: University of Chicago Press, 1968.

NEUGARTEN, B. L., & MOORE, J. W. Age norms, age constraints, and adult socialization. *American Journal of Sociology,* 1965, 70, 232–235.

NEWCOMB, T. M. *Personality and social change.* New York: Holt, Rinehart, & Winston, 1943.

NEWCOMB, T. M. *The acquaintance process.* New York: Holt, Rinehart, & Winston, 1961.

NEWCOMB, T. M. Stabilities underlying changes in interpersonal attraction. *Journal of Abnormal and Social Psychology,* 1963, 66, 376–386.

NEWCOMB, T. M. Interpersonal balance. In R. P. Abelson, E. Aronson, W. J. McGuire, T. M. Newcomb, M. J. Rosenberg, & P. H. Tannenbaum (Eds.), *Theories of cognitive consistency: A sourcebook.* Chicago: Rand McNally, 1968.

NEWCOMB, T. M., KOENIG, K. E., FLACKS, R., & WARWICK, D. P. *Persistence and change: Bennington College and its students after 25 years.* New York: Wiley, 1967.

NIE, N., BENT, D. H., & HULL, C. H. *S.P.S.S. statistical package for the social sciences.* New York: McGraw-Hill, 1970.

NUNNALLY, J. C. Research strategies and measurement methods for investigating human development. In J. R. Nesselroade & H. W. Reese (Eds.), *Life-span developmental psychology: Methodological issues.* New York: Academic Press, 1973.

OFFER, D., & OFFER, J. Three developmental routes through normal male adolescence. In S. C. Feinstein & P. Giovacchini (Eds.), *Adolescent Psychiatry.* New York: Basic Books, forthcoming.

OSGOOD, C. E. Semantic differential technique in the comparative study of cultures. *American Anthropologist,* 1964, 66, 171–200.

OSGOOD, C. E., SUCI, G. J., & TANNENBAUM, P. H. *The measurement of meaning.* Urbana, Ill.: University of Illinois Press, 1957.

PARSLER, R. Some aspects of embourgeoisment in Australia. *Sociometry,* 1971, 5, 95–112.

PARSONS, T. M. *The social system.* Glencoe, Ill.: The Free Press, 1951.

PARSONS, T. M. Pattern variables revisited. *American Sociological Review,* 1960, 25, 467–483. (a)

PARSONS, T. M. *Structure and process in modern societies.* Glencoe, Ill.: Free Press, 1960. (b)

PARSONS, T. M. Youth in the context of American society. In E. H. Erikson (Ed.), *Youth: Change and challenge.* New York: Basic Books, 1963.

PARSONS, T. M. On the concept of value-commitments. *Sociological Inquiry,* 1968, 38, 135–159.

PARSONS, T. M., & BALES, R. F. *Family socialization and interaction process.* Glencoe, Ill.: Free Press, 1955.

PAYNE, S., SUMMERS, D. A., & STEWART, T. R. Value differences across three generations. *Sociometry,* 1973, 36, 20–30.

PEAK, H. Activation theory. In R. P. Abelson, E. Aronson, W. J. McGuire, T. M. Newcomb, M. J. Rosenberg, & P. H. Tannenbaum (Eds.), *Theories of cognitive consistency: A sourcebook.* Chicago: Rand McNally, 1968.

PEAY, E. R. Hierarchical clique structures. *Sociometry,* 1974, *37,* 54–65.

PERVIN, L. A. Performance and satisfaction as a function of individual-environment fit. *Psychological Bulletin,* 1968, *69,* 56–68.

PETTIGREW, T. F. Social evaluation theory: Convergence and applications. In D. Levine (Ed.), *Nebraska symposium on motivation.* Lincoln: University of Nebraska Press, 1967.

PIAGET, J. *The psychology of intelligence.* London: Routledge & Kegan Paul, 1950.

PIAGET, J. *The origin of intelligence in the child.* London: Routledge & Kegan Paul, 1966.

PIAGET, J. *Six psychological studies.* New York: Random House, 1967.

PIAGET, J. *Structuralism.* London: Routledge & Kegan Paul, 1971.

POTTER, D. M. *People of plenty.* Chicago: University of Chicago Press, 1954.

PRICE, C. A. *Southern Europeans in Australia.* Canberra: Australian National University Press, 1963.

PRICE, C. A. (Ed.). *Australian immigration: A bibliography and digest,* No. 2, Department of Demography, Australian National University, 1970. (a)

PRICE, C. A. Immigrants. In A. F. Davies & S. Encel (Eds.), *Australian society: A sociological introduction* (2nd ed.). Melbourne: Cheshire, 1970. (b)

PROSHANSKY, H. M., ITTELSON, W. H., & RIVLIN, L. G. (Eds.). *Environmental psychology: Man and his physical setting.* New York: Holt, Rinehart, & Winston, 1970.

PRZEWORSKI, A., & TEUNE, H. Equivalence in cross-national research. In D. P. Warwick & S. Osherson (Eds.), *Comparative research methods.* Englewood-Cliffs, N.J.: Prentice-Hall, 1973.

QUAY, H. C. (Ed.). *Juvenile delinquency.* Princeton: Van Nostrand, 1965.

RAYNOR, J. O. Future orientation in the study of achievement motivation. In J. W. Atkinson & J. O. Raynor (Eds.), *Motivation and achievement.* Washington, D.C.: Winston, 1974. (a)

RAYNOR, J. O. *The engagement of achievement-related motives: Achievement arousal vs. contingent future orientation.* Paper read at APA Annual Convention, New Orleans, August, 1974. (b)

RICHARDSON, A. A theory and method for the psychological study of assimilation. *International Migration Review,* 1967, *2,* 3–30.

RIEGE, M. G. Parental affection and juvenile delinquency in girls. *British Journal of Criminology,* 1972, *12,* 55–73.

RIEGEL, K. F., RIEGEL, R. M., & MEYER, G. Sociopsychological factors of aging: A cohort-sequential analysis. *Human Development,* 1967, *10,* 27–56.

RILEY, M. W. Aging and cohort succession: Interpretations and misinterpretations. *Public Opinion Quarterly,* 1973, *37,* 35–49.

RILEY, M. W., & FONER, A. *Aging and society: An inventory of research findings* (Vol. 1). New York: Russell Sage Foundation, 1968.

RILEY, M. W., FONER, A., HESS, B., & TOBY, M. L. Socialization for the middle and later years. In D. A. Goslin (Ed.), *Handbook of socialization theory and research.* Chicago: Rand McNally, 1969.

RILEY, M. W., JOHNSON, M., & FONER, A. *Aging and society: A sociology of age stratification* (Vol. 3). New York: Russell Sage Foundation, 1972.

RIM, Y. Values and attitudes. *Personality: An International Journal,* 1970, *1,* 243–250.

ROBINSON, W. S. Ecological correlations and the behavior of individuals. *American Sociological Review*, 1950, *15*, 351–357.

ROKEACH, M. *The open and closed mind.* New York: Basic Books, 1960.

ROKEACH, M. A theory of organization and change within value-attitude systems. *Journal of Social Issues*, 1968 (1), *24*, 13–33. (a)

ROKEACH, M. Attitude change and behavioral change. In M. Rokeach (Ed.), *Beliefs, attitudes, and values.* San Francisco: Jossey-Bass, 1968. (b)

ROKEACH, M. *Beliefs, attitudes, and values.* San Francisco: Jossey-Bass, 1968. (c)

ROKEACH, M. The nature of attitudes. In D. L. Sills (Ed.), *International encyclopedia of the social sciences.* New York: Crowell Collier and Macmillan, 1968. (d)

ROKEACH, M. The organization and modification of beliefs. In M. Rokeach (Ed.), *Beliefs, attitudes, and values.* San Francisco: Jossey-Bass, 1968. (e)

ROKEACH, M. Value systems in religion. *Review of Religious Research*, 1969, *11*, 3–23. (a)

ROKEACH, M. Religious values and social compassion. *Review of Religious Research*, 1969, *11*, 24–38. (b)

ROKEACH, M. *The nature of human values.* New York: Free Press, 1973.

ROKEACH, M. Change and stability in American value systems, 1968–1971. *Public Opinion Quarterly*, 1974, *38*, 222–238.

ROKEACH, M., & BERMAN, E. *Values and needs.* Unpublished paper, 1971.

ROKEACH, M., & PARKER, S. Values as social indicators of poverty and race relations in America. *Annals of the American Academy of Political and Social Science*, 1970, *388*, 97–111.

ROSEN, N. A. Anonymity and attitude measurement. *Public Opinion Quarterly*, 1961, *24*, 675–679.

ROSENBERG, M. *Occupations and values.* Glencoe, Ill.: Free Press, 1957.

ROSENBERG, M. *Society and the adolescent self-image.* Princeton, N.J.: Princeton University Press, 1965.

ROSENBERG, M. J., VERBA, S., & CONVERSE, P. E. *Vietnam and the silent majority.* New York: Harper & Row, 1970.

ROWLEY, C. D. *The New Guinea villager: The impact of colonial rule on primitive society and economy.* New York: Praeger, 1966.

RUDZITIS, A. *Subjective assimilation of a group of Latvian adolescents.* Unpublished B.A. honors thesis, Flinders University of South Australia, 1972.

RUMENS, J. Schools. In R. G. Ward & D. A. M. Lea (Eds.), *An atlas of Papua and New Guinea.* Glasgow: Collins, 1970.

RYAN, P. (Ed.). *Encyclopaedia of Papua and New Guinea* (Vols. 1–3). Melbourne: Melbourne University Press (in association with the University of Papua New Guinea), 1972.

SAMPSON, E. E. Student activism and the decade of protest. *Journal of Social Issues*, 1967, *23* (3), 1–33.

SCHAIE, K. W. A reinterpretation of age related changes in cognitive structure and functioning. In L. R. Goulet & P. B. Baltes (Eds.), *Life-span developmental psychology: Research and theory.* New York: Academic Press, 1970.

SCHAIE, K. W. Methodological problems in descriptive developmental research on adulthood and aging. In J. R. Nesselroade & H. W. Reese (Eds.), *Life-span developmental psychology: Methodological issues.* New York: Academic Press, 1973.

326   REFERENCES

SCHAIE, K. W., & GRIBBIN, K. Adult development and aging. *Annual Review of Psychology,* 1975, *26,* 65–96.

SCHAIE, K. W., & LABOUVIE-VIEF, G. Generational versus ontogenetic components of change in adult cognitive behavior: A fourteen-year cross-sequential study. *Developmental Psychology,* 1974, *10,* 305–320.

SCHAIE, K. W., LABOUVIE, G. V., & BUECH, B. V. Generational and cohort-specific differences in adult cognitive functioning: A fourteen-year study of independent samples. *Developmental Psychology,* 1973, *9,* 151–166.

SCHAIE, K. W., & PARHAM, I. A. Social responsibility in adulthood: Ontogenetic and sociocultural change. *Journal of Personality and Social Psychology,* 1974, *30,* 483–492.

SCHEIBE, K. E. *Beliefs and values.* New York: Holt, Rinehart, & Winston, 1970.

SCHEFFÉ, H. *The analysis of variance.* New York: Wiley, 1959.

SCHUESSLER, K. F., & CRESSEY, D. R. Personality characteristics of criminals. *American Journal of Sociology,* 1950, *55,* 476–484.

SCHUMAN, H. The random probe: A technique for evaluating the validity of closed questions. In D. P. Warwick & S. Osherson (Eds.), *Comparative research methods.* Englewood-Cliffs, N.J.: Prentice-Hall, 1973.

SCHUR, E. *Labeling deviant behavior: Its sociological implications.* New York: Harper & Row, 1971.

SCHUTZ, W. C. *The interpersonal underworld.* Palo Alto, Calif.: Science and Behavior Books, 1966.

SCOTT, W. A. *Values and organizations.* Chicago: Rand McNally, 1965.

SCOTT, W. A. Attitude measurement. In G. Lindzey & E. Aronson (Eds.), *The handbook of social psychology* (Vol. 2). Reading, Mass.: Addison-Wesley, 1968.

SEARS, D. O. Political behavior. In G. Lindzey & E. Aronson (Eds.), *The handbook of social psychology* (Vol. 5). Reading, Mass.: Addison-Wesley, 1969.

SECORD, P. F., & BERSCHEID, E. S. Stereotyping and the generality of implicit personality theory. *Journal of Personality,* 1963, *31,* 65–78.

SELIGMAN, M. E., & HAGER, J. L. (Eds.). *Biological boundaries of learning.* New York: Appleton-Century-Crofts, 1972.

SIEGEL, S. *Nonparametric statistics for the behavioral sciences.* New York: McGraw-Hill, 1956.

SIMON, J. G. & FEATHER, N. T. Causal attributions for success and failure at university examinations. *Journal of Educational Psychology,* 1973, *64,* 46–56.

SIMPSON, G. G. Behavior and evolution. In A. Roe & G. G. Simpson (Eds.), *Behavior and evolution.* New Haven: Yale University Press, 1958.

SKINNER, B. F. *Contingencies of reinforcement.* New York: Appleton-Century-Crofts, 1969.

SKINNER, B. F. *About behaviorism.* New York: Knopf, 1974.

SMITH, M. B. *Social psychology and human values.* Chicago: Aldine, 1969.

SMITH, M. B., BRUNER, J. S., & WHITE, R. W. *Opinions and personality.* New York: Wiley, 1956.

SMITH, P. C. The development of a method of measuring job satisfaction: The Cornell studies. In E. A. Fleishman (Ed.), *Studies in personnel and industrial psychology.* Homewood, Ill.: Dorsey Press, 1967.

SMITH, P. C., KENDALL, L. M., & HULIN, C. I. *The measurement of satisfaction in work and retirement.* Chicago: Rand McNally, 1969.

SPRANGER, E. *Types of men.* Halle: Niemeyer, 1928.

STERN, G. C. *People in context: Measuring person-environment congruence in education and industry.* New York: Wiley, 1970.

STOTLAND, E., & CANON, L. K. *Social psychology: A cognitive approach.* Philadelphia: Saunders, 1972.

TAFT, R. Opinion convergence in the assimilation of immigrants. *Australian Journal of Psychology,* 1962, *14,* 41–54.

TAFT, R. *From stranger to citizen.* Nedlands, W. A.: University of Western Australia Press, 1965.

TAFT, R., & WALKER, K. F. Australia. In A. M. Rose (Ed.), *The institutions of advanced societies.* Minneapolis: University of Minnesota Press, 1958.

TAGIURI, R., & PETRULLO, L. (Eds.). *Person perception and interpersonal behavior.* Stanford: Stanford University Press, 1958.

TAJFEL, H. Cognitive aspects of prejudice. *Journal of Social Issues,* 1969, *25,* 79–97.

THISTLETHWAITE, D. L. Some ecological effects of entering a field of study. *Journal of Educational Psychology,* 1969, *60,* 284–293.

THISTLETHWAITE, D. L. Accentuation of differences in values and exposures to major fields of study. *Journal of Educational Psychology,* 1973, *65,* 279–293.

THOMPSON, G. C., & GARDNER, E. F. Adolescents' perceptions of happy-successful living. *Journal of Genetic Psychology,* 1969, *115,* 107–120.

THRASHER, F. M. *The gang.* Chicago: University of Chicago Press, 1927.

TOLMAN, E. C. *Purposive behavior in animals and men.* New York: Century, 1932.

TOLMAN, E. C. *Behavior and psychological man.* Berkeley and Los Angeles: University of California Press, 1958.

TRIANDIS, H. C. *Attitude and attitude change.* New York: Wiley, 1971.

TRIANDIS, H. C. *The analysis of subjective culture.* New York: Wiley, 1972.

TROLL, L. E., NEUGARTEN, B. L., & KRAINES, R. J. Similarities in values and other personality characteristics in college students and their parents. *Merrill-Palmer Quarterly,* 1969, *15,* 323–336.

TURNER, F. J. *The frontier in American history.* New York: Holt, 1920.

VEIDEMANIS, J. [Immigrant life in the United States: A sociological view.] *Imigrantu dzives procesi Savienotajas Valstis sociologiska skatijuma.* In Biezais, H. (Ed.), [Research and findings.] *Ieskatitais un Atzitais.* Stockholm: Daugava, 1963.

VERINIS, J. S., BRANDSMA, J. M., & COFER, C. N. Discrepancy from expectation in relation to affect and motivation: Tests of McClelland's hypothesis. *Journal of Personality and Social Psychology,* 1968, *9,* 47–58.

WALDO, C. P., & DINITZ, S. Personality attributes of the criminal: An analysis of research studies, 1950–1965. *Journal of Research in Crime and Delinquency,* 1967, *4,* 185–202.

WARD, R. *The Australian legend.* Melbourne: Oxford University Press, 1958.

WARD, R. G. Distribution and density of population. In R. G. Ward & D. A. M. Lea (Eds.), *An atlas of Papua and New Guinea.* Glasgow: Collins, 1970.

WARR, P. B., & KNAPPER, C. *The perception of people and events.* London: Wiley, 1968.

WARWICK, D. P., & OSHERSON, S. Comparative analysis in the social sciences. In D. P. Warwick & S. Osherson (Eds.), *Comparative research methods.* Englewood Cliffs, N.J.: Prentice-Hall, 1973. (a)

WARWICK, D. P., & OSHERSON, S. (Eds.). *Comparative research methods.* Englewood Cliffs, N.J.: Prentice-Hall, 1973. (b)

WASBURN, P. C. Student protesters and gang delinquents: Toward a theory of collective deviance. Working paper No. 62, Department of Sociology and Anthropology, Purdue University, 1973.

WASYLUK, G. *The subjective assimilation of a migrant group.* Unpublished B.A. honors thesis, Flinders University of South Australia, 1971.

WEBB, E. J., CAMPBELL, D. T., SCHWARTZ, R. D., & SECHREST, L. *Unobtrusive measures: Nonreactive research in the social sciences.* Chicago: Rand McNally, 1966.

WEINER, B. *Theories of motivation: From mechanism to cognition.* Chicago: Markham, 1972.

WEST, D. J. *The young offender.* London: Duckworth, 1967.

WEST, D. J. *Present conduct and future delinquency.* Cambridge: Cambridge University Press, 1970.

WHITING, J. W. M. Methods and problems in cross-cultural research. In G. Lindzey & E. Aronson (Eds.), *Handbook of social psychology* (Vol. 2). Reading, Mass.: Addison-Wesley, 1968.

WICKER, A. W. Attitudes vs. actions: The relationship of verbal and overt behavioral responses to attitude objects. *Journal of Social Issues,* 1969, *25* (4), 41–78.

WILLIAMS, R. M. Values. In D. L. Sills (Ed.), *International encyclopedia of the social sciences.* New York: Crowell Collier and Macmillan, 1968.

WILLIAMS, R. M. Change and stability in values and value systems. In B. Barber & A. Inkeles (Eds.), *Stability and social change.* Boston: Little, Brown, 1971.

WILSON, G. D. A dynamic theory of conservatism. In G. D. Wilson (Ed.), *The psychology of conservatism.* New York: Academic Press, 1973. (a)

WILSON, G. D. The concept of conservatism. In G. D. Wilson (Ed.), *The psychology of conservatism.* New York: Academic Press, 1973. (b)

WILSON, G. D. The factor structure of the C-Scale. In G. D. Wilson (Ed.), *The psychology of conservatism.* New York: Academic Press, 1973. (c)

WILSON, G. D. (Ed). *The psychology of conservatism.* New York: Academic Press, 1973. (d)

WILSON, G. D., & PATTERSON, J. R. A new measure of conservatism. *British Journal of Social and Clinical Psychology,* 1968, *7,* 264–269.

WINCH, R. F., & CAMPBELL, D. T. Proof? No! Evidence? Yes! The significance of tests of significance. *American Sociologist,* 1969, *4,* 140–143.

WINER, B. J. *Statistical principles in experimental design.* New York: McGraw-Hill, 1962.

WITTON, R. A. How should social scientists study values? *Australian and New Zealand Journal of Sociology,* 1973, *9* (3), 24–25.

WOHLWILL, J. F. Methodology and research strategy in the study of developmental change. In L. R. Goulet & P. B. Baltes (Eds.), *Life-span developmental psychology: Research and theory.* New York: Academic Press, 1970.

WOOD, J. L. *The sources of American student activism.* Toronto: Lexington Books/ Heath & Co., 1974.

WOODRUFF, D. S., & BIRREN, J. E. Age changes and cohort differences in personality. *Developmental Psychology,* 1972, *6,* 252–259.

WURM, S. A. Indigenous languages. In R. G. Ward & D. A. M. Lea (Eds.), *An atlas of Papua and New Guinea.* Glasgow: Collins, 1970.

WYLIE, R. C. The present status of self theory. In E. F. Borgatta & W. W. Lambert (Eds.), *Handbook of personality theory and research.* Chicago: Rand McNally, 1968.

WYLIE, R. C. *The self-concept* (Rev. ed., Vol. 1). Lincoln: University of Nebraska Press, 1974.

YANKELOVICH, D. *The new morality: A profile of American youth in the 70's.* New York: McGraw-Hill, 1974.

YINGER, J. M. *Toward a field theory of behavior.* New York: McGraw-Hill, 1965.

YOUNG, F. W. TORSCA-9: A FORTRAN IV program for nonmetric multidimensional scaling. *Behavioral Science,* 1968, *13,* 343–344.

YOUNG, R. E., SCHUBERT, E., & JACKA, M. Hopes and fears in Papua New Guinea 1972–73: A pilot study. *New Guinea Psychologist,* 1974, *6,* 56–62.

ZAJONC, R. B. Cognitive theories in social psychology. In G. Lindzey & E. Aronson (Eds.), *The handbook of social psychology* (Vol. 1). Reading, Mass.: Addison-Wesley, 1968.

ZUBRZYCKI, J. Some aspects of structural assimilation of immigrants in Australia. *International Migration,* 1968, *6,* 102–111.

Name Index

Subject Index

Aberrant, as type of deviant behavior, 192–93

Abilities/value, discussion of, 68–69

"Ability" factor, as influence on ranking, 293–94

Aborigines, responses to Ethnocentrism Scale, 248

Abstract structures, 273–75
as dynamic of person-environment fit, 60–61
functions of, 13–14, 15

Abstractions, and value, 3

A-B-X model, of systems of orientations, 266–67

Academic performance, activists vs. non-activists, 163–64

Academy of the Social Sciences (Australia), 238

Acculturation, as criterion of migrant assimilation, 234

Accuracy of judgment, as index of assimilation, 264–67

Accuracy of perception of other's values, as index of assimilation, 258

Achievement:
America and Australia compared, 201–203
as American goal, 211–212

Achievement-ascription, as pattern variable, 206–207

Achievement motivation, and behavior, 296, 297

Achievement situations, and expectancy-value theory, 13

Action: see Behavior

Activists: see Student Activists

Adaptive choice, 68–69

Adelaide surveys, 39–41, 71–81, 82, 83, 88, 107, 208, 222, 261, 280
schools survey, 231
social attitudes survey, 136, 142, 150
social surveys, 121–25

Adelaide University Science Association, 240

Adjustment, investigating level of, 70–71

Adjustment scores, coeducational and single-sex schools, 84–86

Administrative College, Port Moresby, 221

Adolescence:
key terms in development, 129
value discrepancies projected, 106–12
way of viewing key values, 120–21

Affective component, of belief, 5

Age differences: see also Generational comparisons
Australia compared to United States, 216
and generational effects, 142

Alienation, as factor in student activism, 155–56

Allport-Vernon-Lindzey "Study of Values," 48, 106, 186, 198, 230, 270, 271

Alpha press, as term, 267

Ambitious, as value, 31, 40, 42, 45, 46, 52, 53, 64, 67, 96, 102, 146, 160, 161, 184, 189, 191, 208, 216, 259, 304

American society: see also United States
superordinate goals in, 190–91

"Anglo-conformity" goal, in assimilation process, 235

Anomie, Merton's analysis of, 282

"Approach" motives, 303

337

DATE DUE